LOAF, CRUST AND CRUMB

· LOAF, CRUST · AND CRUMB

Silvija Davidson

MICHAEL JOSEPH

LONDON

For Ramša and Venī

MICHAEL JOSEPH LTD

Published by the Penguin Group
27 Wrights Lane, London w8 5tz
Viking Penguin Inc., 375 Hudson Street, New York, New York 10014, USA
Penguin Books Australia Ltd, Ringwood, Victoria, Australia
Penguin Books Canada Ltd, 10 Alcorn Avenue, Toronto, Ontario, Canada m4v 3b2
Penguin Books (NZ) Ltd, 182–190 Wairau Road, Auckland 10, New Zealand

Penguin Books Ltd, Registered Offices: Harmondsworth, Middlesex, England

First published 1995
Copyright © Silvija Davidson 1995

Typeset by Datix International Limited, Bungay, Suffolk
Printed in England by Clays Ltd, St Ives plc

Set in 11.5/13.5 pt Monophoto Garamond and Gill Sans

A CIP catalogue record for this book is available from the British Library

ISBN 0 7181 3825 2

The moral right of the author has been asserted

· CONTENTS ·

· ACKNOWLEDGEMENTS ·

My abiding thanks to everyone who instilled in me a passion for good bread; I suspect my parents, recalling the bread of their homeland, had much to do with it. An equal thanks to those who saw a book in the making: my agent Caroline Davidson, my editor Louise Haines, and my friend Sri Owen. A large and lumbering manuscript was deftly reduced to size by Jane Middleton. Friends and colleagues who shared much knowledge include Clarissa Dickson-Wright, Hugo Dunn-Meynell, Jaakko Rahola, Merete Bergmann.

Recipes come from many sources; even the most traditional are not writ in stone but skilfully interpreted by cooks and writers down the ages. All too often it is not possible to discern, let alone credit the original source. Throughout the text I have listed books and authors where I could locate the germ of an idea – the Bibliography undoubtedly holds clues to others. My inadequate thanks and apologies to anyone inadvertently omitted. For permission to quote a recipe almost verbatim I must thank Arabella Boxer and the publishers of her *Book of English Food*.

Many bakers have readily shared their knowledge and fiercely expressed their opinions. I must thank in particular Andrew Whitley of the Village Bakery, Hugh Lillingston of Innes, Martin Port of Kroustie, Marcus Hampton of Bakoven, Stefan Najduc of Barbakan, Margaret Joyce of Loaves and Fishes; also the bread department managers of Harrods, Harvey Nichols and Selfridges and the ever helpful PR staff of Sainsbury and Safeway. Much valued information and interest were supplied by Patricia Michelson of La Fromagerie.

Thanks too, to friends who took care to encourage more than criticise. The greatest burden, diplomatic and gustatory, undoubtedly fell on my husband, David; it is fortunate that we share a love of good bread.

· PREFACE ·

'Bread is . . . a food that can be replaced by no other . . . suitable to every time of day, every age of life, and every temperament . . . we turn our hearts to it almost as soon as we are born and never tire of it to the hour of our death.' It comes as no surprise that this resonant claim was penned by a Frenchman, the eighteenth-century agronomist and author Antoine Augustin Parmentier. In present-day Britain we need not look to France before adding, with some certainty, that good bread is one of the least expensive and most enjoyable of gourmet foods available.

That at least is my conviction, and one based on shop-bought rather than home-made bread. It is a claim I would have hesitated to make a mere ten years ago, simply because good bread then was a challenge to track down. Now, however, it tumbles off almost every supermarket shelf, claims a corner in any self-respecting deli and has inveigled itself into city sandwich bars.

More dramatically still, the humble loaf has suddenly assumed ideas above its station: powdered and prinked, done up in designer gear, it presents itself as the ultimate table accessory. Breads in a kaleidoscope of colours promise wild, novel experiences; some even offer a route to nirvana.

There is no denying the dull show of defiance put up by factory-baked breads – a task force representing some 80 per cent of British production. Stolidly squared, wrapped and sliced, this fast-processed, high-volume achievement of modern technology would inspire neither Parmentier's affection nor many notions of gourmandise.

At times there is no straight choice between the good, the bad and the pretty: both designer creations and factory foodstuff can adopt canny disguises, or even join forces to masquerade as good bread. At the same time, the most unexpected of alliances turn out to be happy ones: fine ciabatta is produced at mass-market level, and sound organic loaves can be found among the ranks of sliced whites.

I had tasted every shop-sold bread within reasonable reach before deciding to write this book, and subsequently sampled many more. I found breads I could happily live off (and do), others that seemed perfect in the right place at the right time, and a whole lot more that left me indifferent or dismayed. I bought a freezer to accommodate the hundreds of worthy loaves I could not use at once, and when that overflowed I set about exploring recipes that did justice to good leftovers.

This resultant guide to breads sold in the UK is, inevitably, a subjective one, though written with the conviction that all of us can recognise a really well-made and delicious bread in any category. I have taken care to indicate in the text where I recognise a preference or a dislike to be arbitrary. I apologise in advance to readers who may find this book overly opinionated, but I hesitate to extend any apology to producers of poor or, worse, pretentious and overpriced bread.

So many breads come into their own only when eaten with particular foods that this consideration – more, even, than the vast variety on offer – prompted me to write the directory of breads. I enjoyed my first taste of East European dark rye bread alongside smoked meats, pickled herrings and caraway cheeses as soon as I cut my milk teeth, and still prefer these breads in specific contexts rather than as a daily staple.

I also inherited a Continental – and post-War refugee – regard for stale crusts and learned that feeding the ducks had its merits, if the bread was white and sliced, but stale ryebread made fine soups and puddings. I hope some of the recipes in the second half of this book will convince you that it can be worth buying bread purely as an ingredient for another dish; certainly, if you are unsure whether you will like a particular bread, there will probably be a suitable recipe in this book for using it up.

In the directory I have tried to include all categories of bread available at the time of writing, but invention in the field bubbles like a runaway dough and more varieties may have appeared by the time of publication. I have reluctantly omitted baked goods such as sweet scones and soda-raised sweet breads or cakes; yeast-raised buns that are more cake than bread, such as doughnuts, rum babas and 'fantasy' filled panettone; and the whole realm of crispbreads and rusk-like toasts. Furthermore I have not attempted to evaluate the vast range of mass-produced, pre-sliced sandwich loaves, although they are touched on in the Introduction and in directory entries for white, brown, multigrain breads, and so on. There are undoubtedly varia-tions in quality in this category – how could there not be, with some loaves costing the few pence it takes to paste together air and water with a modicum of flour and a clutch of chemicals, while others jostle for position in the newly formed 'Premium' range, where considerations such as unbleached flour, long fermentation and even flavour, come into play.

I want to find, and to enjoy on a daily basis, well-made, delicious and nutritious breads, and I should like everyone else to be able to do the same. I don't buy the cliché that without chemical-boosted, fast-process loaves there would not be enough bread to go round. The more we appreciate and demand good bread and pay a fair price for it the better served we will be. This may or may not mean supporting your local baker before looking to the superstores; what it does mean is seeking out the best wherever you find it and refusing to accept anything less.

The re-emergence of skilled bakers, combined with improved distribution, is placing good bread within everyone's reach. If we respond with enthusiasm the reach will become an easy one and the choice delightfully varied. I hope this book will serve as a pointer to the styles of bread you might enjoy and will encourage you to request the best. The prospect of enjoying the finest of all foods on a daily basis and in life-sustaining quantity is immensely cheering.

· INTRODUCTION ·

'Bread is older than man' runs a reverential Hungarian saying. More accurately (if less poetically), bread was perhaps the first food man processed. Strange to contemplate, this ancient staple is not at all necessary to survival, yet it can be life-sustaining and is often used as a symbol of all food and of life itself. Bread can be the crudest or the most refined of foodstuffs, uniquely wholesome or thoroughly de-natured, distressingly flavourless or incontestably delicious, and end-less in its variety. Before turning to the directory and recipes, it might be useful to glance at the history and make-up of this basic commodity that embodies such extremes.

A BRIEF HISTORY OF BREADMAKING

The first seed plants – wild wheat and barley – were cultivated in the fertile crescent of Mesopotamia some 8000 years BC; the first 'breads' were undoubtedly dried-out or stone-baked porridge-pastes of pounded grain and water. At some unknown time the porridge was seen to bubble spontaneously and aerate and the baked result found to be lighter, more palatable. Perhaps an observant cook made a link with the brewing process; at any rate, the phenomenon was harnessed and by 3000 BC sourdough fermentation was in regular use in Egypt. Hieroglyphs record a sophisticated baking industry: at least 50 varie-ties of variously shaped breads, some flavoured with seeds, some scented with honey, others enriched with eggs and milk, were baked in the first closed-chamber clay ovens.

While the ancient Greeks enjoyed fine breads (though less sophisti-cated than those of Egypt) it was Rome that developed the industry, inventing the rotary stone quern for the grinding of grain as well as the first mechanical (slave and donkey driven) dough mixer, and creating craft guilds of bakers. The Roman invasion of 55 BC revolutionised bread baking in Britain, not least through the introduc-tion of reserved dough 'leaven' as a raising agent.

The first millennium AD saw the advent of heavyweight ploughs, efficient windmills and hair sieves for sifting out bran. In Britain the four main bread-making grains – hardy varieties of wheat, oats, barley and rye – all flourished, but reliable rye was the staple. Ale 'barm' was the most common form of yeast leavening. The words lord (from *hlaefward*, guardian of the loaf) and lady (*hlaefdige*, kneader of the loaf) crept into the English language.

The Middle Ages brought the creation of bakers' guilds in Britain and the first external regulatory bodies; in 1266 the Assize of Bread set out to control the weight and price of loaves. The battle between cheating, bread-adulterating bakers and law-enforcing bodies was to carry on for centuries.

Major changes occurred in the Georgian era: agricultural systems were rendered more efficient; silk sieves were introduced for sifting fine white wheaten flour; brewer's and distiller's yeast were added directly to flour in place of a pre-fermented barm or leaven; Cornish tin mining yielded baking tins suitable for sandwich and toasting loaves. In 1783 the first chain of bakery shops was set up in Britain.

The Industrial Revolution brought a drift of workers from rural to urban areas with starvation and famine hard on its heels. Protectionist Corn Laws were repealed to allow life-saving imports of strong Canadian flours. The introduction of baking powder in 1856 enabled easy production of scones, soda breads and the like. In 1857 Louis Pasteur discovered that yeast was a unicellular organism propagated by cell division, leading to the development of baker's yeast. Revolutionary steel roller mills arrived in the 1870s with the ability to produce bran- and wheatgerm-free white flour at speed and in quantities that could feed the expanding population. Efficient gas ovens replaced the wood- and coal-fired brick structures.

The twentieth century has seen many 'refinements', from chemical bleaching and ageing of flour to the enrichment of white flour with calcium, iron and vitamins. Undoubtedly the most significant feature, however, was the introduction, some thirty years ago, of the Chorleywood Bread Process (CBP), replacing slow fermentation with rapid mechanical agitation of dough, and ensuring consistent high-volume, soft-texture results. The effects of the CBP have been dramatic, ranging from the creation of hot bread shops and instore bakeries to the concentration of milling and bread-making in the hands – or rather, machines – of a very few large companies. Independent bakeries and skilled bakers have been largely replaced by automated processes and semi-skilled labour. Never have we had cheaper white bread on the shelves, and on every day of the week.

THE MILLED GRAIN

Here wheat is used as a model; similar properties and considerations apply to other forms of cultivated grain.

A wheat grain consists of three principal parts: the germ, which contains the embryo plant and the scutellum – a means of mobilising food reserves when the grain germinates – rich in oils, minerals and B vitamins; bran, which protects the inner seed from attack by predators and from desiccation; and the endosperm, storage tissue containing food reserves which consist mainly of starch, with some protein and a trace of fat. The germ comprises around 3 per cent of the whole grain, the bran some 15 per cent and the endosperm 82 per cent.

Wheat grain can be vitreous (firm and brittle) or mealy (starchy) in texture, reflecting the texture of the endosperm. It can also be described as hard or soft, depending on the way the endosperm fractures in milling, and strong or weak, depending on protein content and quality. The strength of the flour affects the rise of the loaf and the structure of its crumb. Hardness describes a milling character and strength a baking character, but hard wheats tend to be strong and soft wheat weak, and flours (milled wheat) are often described as either 'strong' or 'soft'.

Harvested wheat is cleaned and conditioned (its moisture content adjusted to ideal milling levels), graded and selected to form a grist. A grist is the miller's choice of wheats (hard, soft, strong, weak) blended to suit a particular purpose. Small differences in protein content, for instance, will yield loaves of wholly different character, and different baking processes demand flours of different strengths. Commercial considerations come into play, too – the ideal mix is often compromised by concerns of cost (soft European wheats are, generally speaking, cheaper than hard imported grain, due partly to restrictive or protectionist legislation).

From a millennium BC until 130 years ago wheat was milled by the same basic process – grinding between two large, flat, circular stones, one stationary and the other rotating. The power was variously supplied by slaves, animals, water, wind and, latterly, electricity. The invention of the roller mill in the 1860s brought about a dramatic revolution. The circular rollers were initially made of porcelain and powered by steam but steel and electricity soon ensured unmatchable efficiency. Rotating at different speeds in opposite directions, the rollers tear open the grain and remove as much as possible of the bran and germ from the white endosperm. Flour particles are then sieved, graded and remilled as necessary in a gradual reduction process.

Roller milling ensures a fine grind and near-total separation of bran and germ from the endosperm, resulting in white flour. To obtain wholemeal flour, or produce a flour of a particular percentage of extraction, an appropriate proportion of 'wheatfeed' (bran plus germ) is mixed back into the milled endosperm. To obtain white flour from stoneground grain (effectively whole meal), the flour is sifted or 'bolted' as finely as possible, but a proportion of bran and germ remains inseparable from the endosperm and the resultant flour is off-white and flecked with brown. Although stone grinding is still practised by a few small millers, very little bolted white flour is used commercially.

FLOUR INTO BREAD

At one level, converting flour into bread is so simple as to seem natural and inevitable – the earliest leavened breads relied on airborne yeasts to leaven a simple mixture of crushed grain and water, and a hot stone to dry out the dough. Contemporary sourdough baking at a controlled level, perhaps in a woodfired brick oven, also appears simple, but in fact requires highly developed skills and judgement, ranging from flour selection, through constant adjustment of fermentation conditions, to positioning loaves in the oven in the right place at the right time.

Breadmaking at home demands less skill but is already more complex in terms of manufactured yeast, the self-regulating oven. A local baker using commercial yeast and some level of mechanical assistance has many more aspects to consider, not least the production of a variety of breads by a particular time of day; here traditional skills and technology may work in tandem. In huge plants supplying bread by the ton, complex systems are vast, operators' skills largely minimal. At the ultimate extreme of this type of baking, a bag of flour and a packet of magic powder go in at one end and ready loaves emerge at the other, with a little button pushing in between.

To describe the various processes fully would require a book or several, but it is perhaps useful to glance at the range of fermentation and baking methods that are used to produce the bread we buy.

The Basic Requirements for Bread

Flat-breads such as chapati can be made perfectly well without any leavening at all, as can compacted cakes of sprouted grain. Soda breads rely on a simple chemical aeration of dough to create a light crumb structure. All other forms of bread require active yeast in some form, together with food for the yeast. This food takes the form of sugars, which are largely derived from the starches in the flour and converted into glucose and fructose by enzymes in both flour and yeast. As the yeast feeds, other enzymes convert the sugar into carbon dioxide and ethyl alcohol. The alcohol evaporates during baking but the carbon dioxide is trapped within the dough.

The yeast cannot create actual gas cells – in order for bubbles to be created, dough must be kneaded or processed in the presence of air. The carbon dioxide can then swell those bubbles. Next, the bubbles must be trapped in the dough. This is achieved via a stretchy network of protein cells which is formed by agitating the wetted flour, i.e. kneading the dough. This substance is known as gluten, and the strength of flours is measured by their gluten-forming potential.

The effectiveness of the yeast and the rate of fermentation are affected by temperature, the nature of the available sugars and of the enzymes present, and any other dough ingredients that might slow or speed the process.

Finally, the action of the yeast must be stopped, the gas bubbles permanently trapped, and the flour starches 'set' and rendered digestible – which is where baking comes in. Heat creates an inner layer of soft crumb and an outer layer of harder, dryer crust. It also, in common with all the other processes, develops a range of flavours in the finished loaf.

Basic Fermentation Methods

The natural-yeast method relies on yeasts present in the environment to leaven the dough. The bacteria of these yeasts, known as *lactobacilli*, produce lactic and acetic acid as they consume maltose in the flour. Fermentation that relies on airborne bacteria may be slow to start and so sourdough cultures have been developed containing particular strains of wild yeasts and *lactobacilli*. Often, these simply take the form of old dough, i.e. a piece from the previous batch. Starter 'sours' are now available as powdered concentrates and pre-mixes (ready mixes of sour and flour).

Considerable time, patience and skill may be required for a naturally yeasted fermentation – some sourdough loaves take up to five days to make from scratch – and understanding the variable rhythms of the process is essential. Compressed baker's yeast, on the other hand, ensures a speedier and more easily controlled process, whatever method of mixing and proving is chosen.

The simplest method is bulk fermentation. This is sometimes known as a 'straight dough' or 'direct' method as everything is mixed together in one step. Kneading or mixing tends to be slow and gentle, fermentation takes several hours and the handled or shaped dough is allowed resting periods before baking.

A traditional alternative is the 'sponge and dough' method. Still used by some small bakeries, this involves initial (often overnight) fermentation of a small part of the dough, which is then mixed with the remaining ingredients and fermented for a very brief period before being shaped and baked. This is often regarded as a half-way house between natural and bulk fermentation.

Mechanical dough development, as characterised by the Chorley-wood Bread Process (see page 6), is by far the most widely used method of dough development in Britain and, indeed, elsewhere. The vast majority of mass-produced breads are made in this way, which is not, properly speaking, fermentation at all. The physical changes in the dough normally brought about by fermentation are replaced by intense agitation – fast and fierce mixing of the dough for less than five minutes. All the ingredients are mixed together at once, including oxidisers, emulsifiers and/or fats, extra water and higher levels of yeast than is the case with bulk fermented dough.

Even small bakeries are making use of the CBP method, though a few use other quick processes such as activated dough development, which uses chemical reducing agents, and 'no-time dough', which relies on high levels of yeast and extended mixing to produce bread in emergencies – a late order for instance. Bakers who have used this method to stand in for bulk fermentation all concur that 'no-time dough' makes poor bread. Bread needs time to develop flavour: the processes that yield this flavour are complex but the evidence is indisputable. Breads fermented by adding a lump of reserved dough from the previous batch have interesting nuances of flavour absent in 'straight dough' examples. Those made by an overnight 'sponge and dough' have more aroma, a crisper crust, finer texture and a nutty flavour. Loaves made via natural sourdough fermentation have a host of powerful, complex and varied flavours and a satisfying contrast between crust and crumb.

Where does that leave mechanically (or chemically) activated dough bread? You should judge for yourself, but it is worth bearing in mind a comment made by Andrew Whitley, baking by the most traditional of methods at the Village Bakery in Cumbria: 'Time is the single most important factor in distinguishing bread made with care and affection from bread made purely for profit.'

The Bake-off

The oven, naturally, plays its part in determining the character of the finished loaf. If you have ever eaten bread baked in a woodfired brick or stone oven, the crunchy, smoky crust alone will have demonstrated the fact ably. Proponents of brick ovens would claim that even gas- or oil-fired models guarantee a better 'bloom' on a loaf baked in direct contact with the heat-conducting base than could any other baking medium.

Not all 'oven-bottom' breads are baked in this way, of course, as there are rather few brick ovens in use nowadays. Other styles of oven can emulate the effect via floors or even shelves (in multi-deck ovens) constructed of brick or stone. The majority, however, are designed to heat up quickly and cheaply and to contain as many breads as possible – they include ovens with independently heating elements, rotating reels and tray-holding racks with efficient airflow systems. There are even ovens with swing trays, or conveyor belts passing down a tunnel. But the only label claim you are likely to see is that a brick oven, and/or wood fire have been used.

WHITE OR BROWN?

A Historical Perspective

From Roman times, perhaps even earlier, those who could afford to ate refined white bread. Small matter that strange substances such as chalk, alum, even ground bones might have been added to render it whiter; brown bread was *panis secundarius*: it mattered 'to know the colour of one's bread'.

From the Middle Ages the best soil in Britain was given over to wheat, the only grain to produce whitish bread when sifted. Bakers separated into two guilds, one for white wheat bread, the other for brown maslin (this generally contained rye or other grains and even pulses mixed with unsieved wheat). The aristocracy preferred not only white bread but white food, suggestive, as ever, of purity and refinement.

While it seems unlikely that any medieval bread could have sat easy on the stomach, 'mayne' or 'manchet' bread, the whitest available, proved a deal more digestible than branny 'tourte' or 'trete' or even the semi-refined 'chete'. The truly rich would eat the upper crust only (baked furthest from the grimy oven floor) of a manchet and perhaps a little of the soft centre with the crust chipped away. Their eating bread would be presented on a trencher, a thick slice of rough bread, cut, squared and smoothed by an expert carver for use as a plate. A besmirched trencher would be removed and passed on to servants for their supper. The less well off might well eat their trencher along with the food piled on it; but everyone aspired to manchet.

Already in the seventeenth century voices were raised in defence of roughage and nutritious wholewheat bread and the first branny, government-endorsed 'standard' loaf appeared in the eighteenth century. Nothing could deflect a mass demand for white bread, however – least of all the 1942 'national loaf', halfway between white and wholewheat and effectively grey and rather dismal. By 1956 the British government ruled that all flour of less than 100 per cent extraction must be enriched as necessary to meet minimum levels of calcium, iron and B vitamins, and ceased to endorse one colour of bread over another.

Modern Attitudes

The Flour Advisory Bureau, the UK's central source of information and advice on bread and flour, claims that all bread is equally good for you and speaks of 'honest-to-goodness sliced white'. A number of independent bakers, too, are convinced of the equal merits of white and wholewheat flour. A Surrey-based baker told me with considerable amusement how 80 per cent of his male customers buy white, yet their wives persist in buying wholewheat for the family without realising that in terms of all but roughage this might well be nutritionally inferior. As wholewheat flour is not enriched with vitamins and minerals, any that was milled from denatured or inferior grain would, he pointed out, not meet the minimum levels assured in breads of lower extraction.

Some nutrition experts present a different argument: stoneground wholewheat with 'nowt taken out' or put back in, carries a natural proportion of bran and wheatgerm, and hence vitamins and minerals. It is reasonable to suppose that these are better digested and assimilated than artificially added nutrients. A different concern is based on the fact that white bread is in effect a refined carbohydrate, releasing glucose into the blood stream faster than might be desirable. This is a point made forcefully by the controversial French diet guru Michel Montignac, who places white bread at a 'dangerously' high position on the glycaemic scale and wholewheat at a much more acceptably low level. The suggestion is that white bread will cause a rapid dip in blood sugar levels, leading to cravings and overeating; eventually the body's glucose tolerance levels will be knocked out of a desirable balance.

While all these arguments are forceful and more or less credible, each continues to be fiercely contested by those of opposing viewpoints. In any case, individual metabolisms differ enormously. The only certain advice, to my mind, is that we should listen intelligently to all the arguments and try to tune in to the reactions of our bodies. Even this may not be a final arbiter: the pleasure I gain from eating a well-made, crusty, creamy baguette seems to outweigh all other considerations.

SWEET OR SOUR?

Proponents of sourdough bread made from yeasts naturally present in the air and on the grain tend to be as zealous as supporters of wholewheat. An obvious argument in favour of sourdough bread suggests that our bodies are better adapted to bread made by this process, so it is more readily digested and does not disturb natural blood sugar levels. The pH level of these breads makes them remarkably resistant to mould and bacterial contamination, and it may be that harmful bacteria are knocked out by the action of *lactobacilli*. Claims are made that sourdough bread is kinder to teeth by dint of discouraging plaque build-up. Calcium, normally bound up by bran, is made available to the human body by sourdough enzymes. Finally, naturally leavened breads can be regarded as a living food in the manner of unpasteurised cheese and wine; this, too, must have certain nutritional implications.

Apologists for sourdough bread tend to have a passion for its characteristic acidity and complex of flavours; non-initiates are likely to regard it as something of a bitter pill. If the flavour does not convince you, no health-based argument is likely to convert you.

ORGANIC BREADS AND THE QUESTION OF ADDITIVES

Organically grown grain is produced without artificial fertilisers or pesticides. The resulting flour is likely to be more flavourful and nutritious; wheat readily asborbs natural levels of nitrogen from the soil and converts these into utilisable (good milling and baking quality) protein and gluten.

Few of us are prepared to pay the premium price commanded by an organic flour loaf – at least by a well-crafted one. That a loaf is made of organic flour does not guarantee the organic status of other ingredients, nor the absence of improvers, emulsifiers or hydrogenated fats. A fair number of such loaves are now factory-baked using the Chorleywood Bread Process which requires certain additives and well-dispersed fats. This makes 'organic' bread cheaper and more widely available but in a somewhat compromised form.

It is difficult to know whether, or to what degree, additives in bread might have a harmful effect on the human body. Generally they are included in minute quantities and a number are natural substances (malted flour, for instance). A negligible quantity is not, however, the same as absence. A more serious question mark has been raised recently about the health implications of hydrogenated (chemically hardened) fats but they continue to be widely used, in organic breads as others.

You will need to pay extra for the absence of additives and hydrogenated oils but you should be amply compensated by the flavour and texture of the bread as well as its nutritional qualities.

STALING, MOULDING AND PREVENTION

What is Stale Bread?

We know what stale bread is like: the crust becomes leathery, the crumb hard, and much of the flavour vanishes. It seems the bread is drying out. This is of course partly true – but only partly. The other part holds the crucial key to storing and 'refreshing' bread.

During baking the starch in flour absorbs water and swells to form a kind of jellified paste; this gelatinisation takes place at a temperature of 55°C/151°F. As soon as the baked bread cools to a temperature lower than 55°C/151°F (which is much higher than room temperature), the starches begin to recrystallise and solidify, squeezing out moisture, which diffuses outwards. If this did not happen the loaf would not be sliceable. Unfortunately, the process not only continues but accelerates as the temperature drops: the rate of staling is at its greatest just above 0°C/32°F, the freezing point of water. At minus 10°C/14°F the water is immobilised.

How to Slow Down or Reverse Staling

The obvious practical conclusion is that bread stales faster in the fridge than at room temperature. The best solution for long-term storage is to freeze it as rapidly as possible then defrost quickly. For short-term keeping the bread should be stored at room temperature. Nothing will prevent the crust from absorbing moisture, but you can stop it evaporating by wrapping the loaf in plastic or foil. This leaves the crust soft and rather sodden – if you prefer it to remain firm, leave the loaf unwrapped and accept some drying out.

In bread that is a few days old not much water will have been lost through evaporation, and it is possible to reverse most of the crystallisation process and re-gelatinise the starches. The bread must reach an internal temperature higher than the magic level of 55°C/151°F, and as quickly as possible. To achieve this, the loaf must be placed in a hot oven and heated for around 7–10 minutes (less for rolls). If you wrap the bread in foil to keep in the moisture the crust will grow even more leathery. To revive crust as well as crumb, a compromise is required: leave the bread unwrapped and sacrifice a little internal moisture for the sake of a crunchy crust – and make sure to eat the refreshed bread fairly quickly.

How to Prevent Moulding and Spoilage

The prime means of preventing spoilage (moulding, yeast refermentation, growth of bacteria) are out of the consumer's hands: hygiene at the bakery and the shop and the addition of preservatives to dough have the greatest impact. Refermentation of bread (characterised by an alcoholic or acid-drop smell) is largely associated with underbaking and is entirely out of our hands (take the loaf back and complain!). Moulding and the most common form of bacterial contamination can be delayed by two means: lowering the temperature of the bread (refrigeration) and keeping the plastic wrapping loose to prevent excessively moist, damp conditions. Both these measures seem to contradict the advice on prevention of staling. It is all a matter of compromise and common sense. A pre-wrapped sliced loaf is expected to keep well for at least three days at room temperature; refrigerate it and you should retard spoilage for at least a week. If you buy a toasting loaf to last a week and don't have a freezer, refrigeration makes sense (toasting will re-soften the starches); if you buy a sandwich loaf to eat untoasted, keep it at room temperature, enjoy what you can for three or four days, then dry, crumb or ditch the rest.

Very moist goods such as crumpets, pikelets, or Staffordshire oatcakes are liable to develop 'rope' fairly quickly – I have observed it on many occasions before knowing what it was. It is in fact colonisation by a very common bacterium known as *Bacillus subtilis*, present in soil and, inevitably, grain. It rather lives up to its name, as spores survive the baking process but remain, of course, invisible and ready to carry on reproducing when the conditions are right. If you fail to eat up your crumpets or pancakes within a couple of days you may be aware of a sickly-sweet smell, like overripe melons, and a sticky surface feel; pull them apart and you will notice cobweb-like, shiny strands – hence 'rope'. Again, growth is slowed down by refrigeration and almost arrested by freezing.

Rope is vastly more common but rather less dangerous than *Salmonella* or another possible contaminant, *Staphylococcus aureus*. However, mould growth in bread is likely to occur before bacterial growth and you would probably throw the bread away before either of these two bacteria can take hold. Bread is generally too dry to support the rapid growth of bacteria and the crust is particularly resistant. In other words, if you handle a crusted loaf with unwashed hands after trussing chicken or breaking eggs, the danger from eating the bread is small; if the same thing happens with a cut surface (the moist crumb) the danger of contracting food poisoning is rather higher. But this is all common sense.

To sum up, the best advice is:

Eat light, crusty bread the day it is baked.

Unless instructed to refrigerate on opening, keep bread in a dry, well-ventilated and clean container (a bread bin) or loosely wrapped. (You might prefer to keep crusty bread lightly covered or paper-wrapped despite moisture loss.)

Soft – crusted slices can be kept tightly wrapped for a day or so.

Keep moist crumpets and pancakes well wrapped to prevent moisture loss – but only for a day or so at room temperature, or a few days longer in the fridge. Toast to re-soften the starches.

Freeze all bread tightly wrapped to exclude air. Six months is fine for most loaves, three to four months for enriched or fruited breads or buns. The crust of light and crisp-crusted bread will shear off after a week or so in the freezer. Freeze and defrost all bread as quickly as possible.

Refresh breads in a hot oven. Keep soft-crusted bread foil-wrapped, crunchy-crusted loaves unwrapped. Place the latter directly on shelves, or cut-side down on a tray.

Fast-fermented breads have the shortest shelf life (unless preservatives are added). Bulk-fermented breads have a longer life due partly to the alcohol developed in fermentation. Naturally leavened sourdough breads are the longest-lived (up to two weeks), due largely to their acidity.

BREAD IN COOKERY

Our ancestors were considerably more adept than we at using stale bread. Apicius noted a recipe for something very like *pain perdu*, in which crustless white wheat bread was steeped in milk, fried in oil, and coated with honey. An English medieval version consisted of white bread toasted on a gridiron, soaked in wine, reheated and crisped and served with almond milk. Whole loaves (not always stale) were frequently enriched to make sweetmeats: 'Wastels yfarced' were early forms of white loaf from which the crumb was removed and mixed with eggs, mutton fat, currants, powdered spice, saffron and salt and packed back into the shell. Fifteenth-century 'rastons' were a touch simpler, but no less luxurious – the crumb of an already enriched bread was mixed with butter before repacking and the assembly was served steaming hot.

Crumbs were highly valued in Britain until a generation or two ago. In the Middle Ages finely grated dry crumbs were locked away with the spices, while fresher bread was 'brayed' in mortars to take up 'that which remaineth from the spices'. These crumbs found their way into all forms of dishes from sauces and pottages to coatings, stuffings and savoury-sweet puddings. Recipes were not reserved for salvaging stale crusts and crumbs: the bread and butter puddings of the 1720s were invariably made from fresh bread.

If contemporary use of bread in British cookery is pitifully meagre, it no doubt has as much to do with the cheap ubiquitousness of the fast-fermented factory loaf as with a general unwillingness to cook economically (or at all), or with the ready availability of more sophisticated options. It is difficult even to imagine venerating bread, fresh or stale, in the manner of peasant communities, where its production remains a labour of love, its flavour uncompromised and its cost relatively high.

Look outside Britain, or indeed back into its history, and you will quickly encounter enough recipes to fill several books. A good number are simple, fast and obvious; others designed to appeal to the gourmet or sophisticate. And with the resurgence of the carefully crafted loaf, and of boutique breads of cosmopolitan flavours, bread-based recipes are undergoing a revival, even a re-creation.

WHERE TO NOW?

With bread, as with many other fundamentals, we seem stuck with the legacy of the Sixties: the advent of the Chorleywood Process, supermarkets proper and mass market advertising. The battle rages for the cheapest, most convenient, ready-sliced, slow-staling loaf. Bread remains a 'known-value item', a supermarket loss-leader – sell the cheapest loaf and the consumer will assume you stock the cheapest food.

However, even within the vast market share taken up by factory baked sliced white there is a newly vigorous push for perceptible quality, and every supermarket now carries a token 'premium' loaf with a touch more flavour than the norm. Most of them also devote some shelf-space to specialist breads, be they basic ciabattas, florid focaccias or hand-crafted, organic wholewheat loaves.

The fortunes of independent bakeries have fallen as low as lower-end prices. Speak to any struggling baker and you will hear the same sorry assertion: most 'bakers' in Britain are merely machine minders; skills are vanishing irretrievably; the aim is surely to do without bakers entirely. Yet bakeries producing well-crafted, full-flavoured breads *are* somehow surviving, even rising unbidden from the ashes. If we want the quality of bread they provide and are willing to pay fairly for it they will flourish.

National Food Surveys tell us that bread consumption in the UK keeps falling; government advisory committees would spoonfeed us with six slices a day. I don't think either is helpful, however well meant. NFS statistics don't take into account the prodigious sandwich market, while instructions from on high often merely incite rebellion (quality-based subsidies might, of course, be another matter). Six bland slices would put me on hunger strike, but a few hunks of the finest bread would reinstate almost anyone's faith in good food and the joys of living.

It is tempting to conclude with an array of popular pronouncements. But I am not sure that 'good bread is a basic right for all' – perhaps we have no right to what we don't properly value. So do we get the bread we deserve? It may be that many of us have not tasted bread worthy of our support. The situation in the UK is anyway far from static – in fact it is seething with excitement, diversity and unprecedented quality. The following pages give a brief glimpse of what you may find.

· DIRECTORY · OF BREADS

· ABERDEEN BUTTERY ROWIES ·
(*butter rolls*)

These are very rich but surprisingly light and flaky little buns, traditionally layered with as much lard as butter. They are rather like plain Danish pastries or perhaps croissants (the production technique is almost identical) but the shape is a simple round or oval and the crust crisp. The salt level tends to be noticeably high.

'Butteries' rarely make their way south of the Border but it may not be long before the major supermarkets adopt them to swell the ranks of their burgeoning speciality breads. That could be a good thing, as buttery rowies are not only excellent with chunky bitter marmalade but also complement a simple broth rather well.

· AFRO-CARIBBEAN BREAD ·

Sweetish, dense-textured and often abundantly spiced, the breads produced by Britain's Afro-Caribbean bakeries reflect a unique amalgam of European, African and Carib Indian influence.

HARD DOUGH BREAD

If you go into the bakery shop and simply ask for a loaf you will almost certainly be handed a sizeable, heavy, plaited white bread. This is prepared by a highly unusual process which involves 'milling' or mechanically knocking back the yeast-leavened dough to give a close texture. In this respect, it is rather like *pain brié*, the hammered-dough sailors' bread of Normandy. The texture is dense and chewy and the flavour is markedly sweet. Where there is a cluster of Afro-Caribbean bakeries it is worth shopping around for the softest-textured loaf (levels of sweetness are pretty well constant). Appearance gives little away – you will need to sample each bakery's offering to find the style you prefer.

While the bread's density makes it an excellent sopper-up of stews and casseroles, that persistent sweetness is likely to jar on British palates in the context of European savoury foods; better, perhaps, to treat it as a teabread and enjoy it toasted and buttered.

CARIBBEAN BUN

This round, dark, fruit-riddled, spicy teabread is much less deceptive. It has a lighter texture than hard dough bread and is sweeter, with a touch of bitterness from molasses. Allspice is used abundantly, and sometimes almond extract too – to rather startling effect. Caribbean buns can be bought tea-loaf or bun size, and the products of different bakeries can vary quite considerably – the finest buns are soft textured, and warmly rather than aggressively spiced. Again, you need to shop around.

Particularly good with salted butter, the buns also toast well, with the spice growing even more aromatic. Stale, they make an interesting bread pudding with no need to add further spice or flavourings, although fresh banana and rum would not go amiss.

BULLA CAKES

Bake a Caribbean bun along the lines of an English muffin and you have a bulla cake. It resembles nothing so much as a raisin-bran-molasses muffin, but tastes quite different: the wholly or partly soda-raised bulla cake is finer-textured and considerably spicier. Serve bulla cakes split, toasted and buttered, maybe even spread with marmalade or lime curd. They are too dense for pudding use but they do keep well.

· BAGELS ·

The 'roll with a hole', with its uniquely dense crumb and glossy, chewy crust is finally invading British supermarkets and convenience stores, some half a century after its equivalent growth in popularity in the United States. However, if your only experience of a bagel is of a mass-produced, plastic-bagged specimen, you may well wonder what all the fuss is about.

WHAT MAKES A GOOD BAGEL?

A good bagel looks glossy-crusted and firm. It should *not* appear

soft, squishy and dully indistinguishable from a bap. It should feel heavy for its size compared to a simple roll, and should have a compact, yet moist and reasonably light-textured crumb. The unique texture is a result of a brief boiling before baking: much of the joy of a true bagel lies in the contrast between that moist crumb and the resilient, chewy crust, which has a slight crispness when really fresh. A plain bagel should taste slightly richer and sweeter than plain white bread, but never cloyingly so. All in all, it will be difficult to resist reaching out for a second. This is the ideal. What happened to the rest?

A HISTORY OF BAGEL BAKING

The very first bagel, it seems, was designed in 1683 by a Jewish baker living in Vienna, to resemble the shape of a riding stirrup or *Bugel*. Riding was the king of Poland's favourite pastime and the bread was created to commemorate Poland's protection of Austria from Turkish invaders. Perhaps this is simply the Jewish version of the croissant legend. Certainly the bagel has been popular throughout Eastern Europe for several centuries.

New York and London first experienced the bagel at the turn of the century as a result of the enterprise of East European Jewish immigrants. In New York a union of craftsmen was created to control apprenticeship in the unique and exacting skills required for bagel shaping, boiling and baking. Widespread distribution arrived with mechanisation. Nowadays most bagels are produced by machines that mix and extrude shaped dough at the rate of 500 bagels an hour, while steam-injected rack ovens have replaced the traditional boil-and-bake technique. However, the best bagels demand a 'taste of the hand', a quality you can still experience in Britain by seeking out bakeries that serve the Jewish community – in the Prestwich area of Manchester, or in East London, for example.

FLAVOURS AND FILLINGS

The British taste in bagels is fairly conservative: we like them plain, sometimes sprinkled with sesame or poppy seeds (or *mon*), or more popularly with kibbled onion. The sweet-toothed must content themselves with cinnamon- and raisin-flavoured bagels. If you do chance on a bagel bakery worthy of the name, however, the inevitable queueing will most likely be rewarded with a greater choice of flavours. I have found wholemeal and granary versions rather dense and dull but black pumpernickel, a soft part-rye dough flavoured with molasses, and rye with caraway are perfect partners for cream cheese or kosher chopped herring. These sweet-sour bagels also add interest to that modern classic, a bagel sandwiched with cream cheese and smoked salmon.

Bagels don't have to be filled, of course: still warm from the bakery, they are a perfect delight eaten plain. Plenty of devotees enjoy bagels of any flavour split, toasted and buttered. They are as good with soup, salad, smoked and cured fish and meat and soft cheeses as any bread roll; simply bear in mind that all bagels have at least a hint of sweetness from malted flour, honey or even sugar and are somewhat dense and chewy. This means that you would probably not serve bagels with a delicate seafood mousse, but little else seems out of bounds.

Filled-bagel enthusiasts make a case for toppings as diverse as peanut butter or caviar and as abstruse as tinned spaghetti or banana splits, while sandwich bar proprietors slap in the same fillings they use for baps, ciabatta rolls and croissants. The classic combo, and some personal favourites, are listed on pages 210–12.

REFRESHING STALE BAGELS

The recommended way is to place your bagels in a lidded casserole with a teaspoonful of water and place in the oven at 180°C/350°F/ Gas Mark 4 for about 10 minutes. This softens the crumb while retaining a chewy crust and only works for a genuine hand-made bagel. As I have a sneaking affection for very crusty bagels, I tend to refresh them, uncovered, in a hotter oven (200°C/400°F/Gas Mark 6) for about 5 minutes, but I do place a shallow tray of hot water in the oven. This works wonders for prepacked bagels, too. Steaming or microwaving leaves them floppy and somewhat rubbery.

· BAGUETTE ·

Light, crusty, creamy, waiflike and chic – these are the elusive qualities that sparked Britain's rather hopeless love affair with the Parisian baguette. For well over a decade British bakers have pursued this ideal of perfection. Mostly they have come up with somewhat stolid 'French sticks' made from an English dough mix using hard wheat flour, or imported part-baked baguettes from France. Even the imported examples fail to convince fans of the real thing. 'Expert' explanations for the poor quality of baguettes in the UK abound, citing the style of oven, a shortage of artisanal skills or, in the case of British-originated baguettes, the composition of British water. Scope for variables is rather limited: the true baguette contains just flour, water, yeast and salt, and two improvers – fava or broad bean flour and ascorbic acid – Vitamin C – added in minute amounts. Any baguette baked in France must conform to this restrictive formula by law.

THE PURSUIT OF THE IDEAL

Some seven centuries ago, in the reign of Edward I, London bakers were attempting to make 'light bread known as French bread', called 'puffe' or 'pouf'. The bread that inspired those experiments, the *pain de Gonesse* sold in Paris, frustratingly evaded imitation. This was a large, round loaf, raised with brewer's yeast, made of the finest white flour and described (by Furetière in 1690) as having 'many eyes, the marks of its quality'.

It was, of course, these eyes, or air holes, that were responsible for its lightness. No doubt one reason for the problems of imitating this type of bread in the UK has been the age-old contrast in attitude between French and British bakers: to an English baker 'eyes' have always denoted faulty technique. Maybe the universally popular ciabatta will finally change all that, establishing beyond dispute the desirability of large holes, and disabusing the British of our urge to butter every crumb (buttering holes, as Elizabeth David famously noted, is something of a problem).

What of that other elusive attribute, the crisp, flaky crust? Historically, this was a secondary consideration, and slow to gain acceptance. The *pain long*, the first real alternative to the cartwheel-shaped *boule* or *miche*, arrived on the scene in the eighteenth century, an experiment to increase the proportion of crust to crumb. This was still a hefty loaf, designed to sustain a rural French family for a number of days. Only with the growth of urbanisation and the demands of city life (no time for baking but every opportunity to buy a fresh loaf daily, or twice a day) did the ephemeral baguette – a mere 250g/8½oz in weight but 90cm/36inches long – come into being.

To the British, meanwhile, a soft expanse of butter-spreadable crumb remained of primary importance. Although fancy 'French' bread continued to be aspired to throughout the centuries, this was mainly on account of its lightness; the accompanying crust was regarded as something of a nuisance and was regularly grated away.

MACHINERY OR ANCIENT SKILLS?

Arguably, no baguette worthy of the name is suited to mechanical mixing and extrusion, which tend to be the culprits behind the dull, dry crumb and uniformly smooth crust, leathery rather than flaky, with which most of us are all too familiar. The march of mechanisation since the Second World War has been such that a movement to protect the true baguette was formed by French master bakers some ten years ago. Two brand names emerged, the Belle Epoque and the Banette, and both enjoyed popularity for a while, but the Banette has taken the crown of the new-wave baguette. It is characterised by very pointed ends, ensuring even more crust, and a distinctly creamy crumb, in colour as well as texture. This is partly due to the avoidance of even the two permitted additives, partly to the quality of the flour, and also to slower fermentation than is now the norm. The Banette may well arrive on British shores before long – thanks to the wonders of modern technology, the flour mixes, ovens, equipment and technical assistance form a compact and transportable package.

Perhaps the finest baguette-style loaf I have sampled is also a 'new-old' formula – a surprise development from that most respected and established of Parisian bakers, Bernard Ganachaud. Like the Banette, only better, the *Flûte Gana* seems to hold in perfect balance a sweet wheat aroma, cream and crunch on the palate, golden honeycomb crumb to please the eye – and a predominant feeling of lightness, despite the sense of great satisfaction, when the whole thing has been rather rapidly demolished.

This relies on a good number of 'artisanal' skills: slow fermentation using a minimum of yeast to allow the sweet wheat aroma to dominate; restrained kneading – the antithesis of fast mass-production method; hand shaping and finishing; a modern oven with a clay sole to facilitate a crisp crust – and production throughout the day.

Ganachaud is convinced that this combination of innovation and age-old skills is the right way forward. At all levels of society, even the least well off, claims the master baker, drawing on long experience, people are prepared to pay a fair price for good bread that represents fine value for money. Is he right? '*C'est le consommateur qui donnera son verdict*' (the consumer will decide) he admits. I hope it is a positive verdict, in Britain as in France.

BUYING BAGUETTES

Make sure you buy a baguette rather than a French stick; although this carries few guarantees it is at least likely to be closer to a French than a British bread. Loaves that are labelled as made with French flour will have the essential soft wheat texture and are likely to have been imported part-baked, particularly the ones sold by a deli or supermarket. A number of French-owned bakeries, clustered mainly around central London, produce baguettes to rival the best that France can offer but this by no means applies to all such bakeries, any more than it would in France; you need to shop around.

A practised eye can apparently distinguish between a machine-shaped baguette and a hand-made one at twenty paces, but I am not sure such a guessing game is worth playing. It *is* worth looking out for a slim loaf with a crust that seems friable rather than glossily smooth. Pick up the baguette if you can: those that feel solid and heavy are almost certain to be leaden and poor. After that you will simply have to buy, and taste, and decide whether to buy again.

As well as the standard baguette, a good number of outlets offer a half-length demi-baguette, perfect for a single sandwich; occasionally a mini-baguette or *baguettine*; or simply a roll, or *petit pain*. A *pain Parisien* or *Bâtard* is technically two-thirds the length of a baguette and over one and a half times the weight, but essentially made from the same dough. A number of supermarket-sold *Parisiens* are fatter, resembling a British bloomer. A *ficelle* should be slimmer and lighter still than a baguette – just over half the weight for the same length – and really is the ultimate in terms of maximum crust, minimum crumb. Cut into thin rounds, the *ficelle* provides perfect canapé bases, but it dries out even faster than the baguette.

A number of French-style bakeries offer a *baguette paysanne, baguette rustique, baguette à l'ancienne* or *baguette campagne*. These may well be sourdough loaves with a proportion of rye flour or they may simply contain a proportion of coarse-milled wheat flour or even bran. It's best to ask what the term denotes for that particular baker.

While it is well worth looking out for an 'artisanal' baguette in French-owned bakeries influenced by the French revivalist movement, the best of the imported, part-baked baguettes are really not that bad – a great improvement on French sticks and finer than much of the bread served up at Parisian tourist hotels. Once you have found a decent baguette don't settle for less, and don't give up the pursuit of the ideal. As ever, the more demand there is for quality, the more widespread will be its availability.

REVIVING STALE BAGUETTES

Baguettes, as everyone knows only too well, stale at breathtaking speed. When only a few hours old (or defrosted) a limp baguette can be crisped for 3–5 minutes in a very hot oven – for a really crisp crust, don't bother wrapping it in foil. Slightly stale baguettes can be split, toasted and used as a pizza base, or with some other soft or molten topping, hot or cold. Or you might remove some of the stale interior (process this into crumbs), brush the cut sides with plain or flavoured butter or olive oil, and bake until golden and crunchy. Fill with hot, creamy sauce-based savouries, or roasted vegetables, or an interesting salad that will not harm for warming.

I have jars full of dried-out baguette slices, and bags in the freezer full of stale or toasted chunks to use as croutons. All are useful standbys, but this is one category of bread where I probably have more leftovers than I can happily use.

· BANNOCK ·

See **Selkirk Bannock** and **Barley Bread**.

· BARA BRITH ·

The 'speckled' fruit bread of Wales exists in many versions, mainly soda-raised and undistinguished nowadays. The best are yeasted, moist with currants plumped in cold tea, and gently spiced. Bara brith certainly began life as a luxury loaf and probably contained fresh blackcurrants rather than dried vine fruit. Once dried currants became the norm the tradition of plumping the dried fruit in cold tea was established, no doubt in an attempt to replicate the juiciness of those blackcurrants.

The finest bara brith I have tasted was made in a turn-of-the-century wood-fired brick bakehouse, reconstructed in the grounds of the Welsh Folk Museum at St Fagans, near Cardiff. It was richly fruited, dense and chewy, made with organic stoneground whole-wheat flour and imbued with the tang of woodsmoke (beech and ash are favoured by the baker, Chris Aston, who claims that each type of wood makes a different contribution to the finished bread). The century-old black patina tins add a further dimension to the smoky crust. Bara brith made from white flour is just as 'traditional', however, and potentially as good.

BUYING

In most areas of Britain you will have little choice; if you live in Wales you have probably already established your favourite style. There is no one standard, although purists would probably prefer their bara brith made of white flour, yeasted, and lightly fruited with currants only – perhaps not even spiced. A good loaf is unlikely to be light as air.

In common with most teabreads, bara brith is traditionally enjoyed sliced and buttered, toasted if a little stale. Lighter styles stale fairly quickly but Chris Aston's dense loaf keeps admirably for a month if foil-wrapped and stored in a cool place. Most styles make a splendid bread pudding, a fine Welsh tradition, and need little addition apart from an egg or two.

· BARLEY BREAD ·

Once widely used in pancakes, bannocks or other bakestone or griddle breads, barley rarely lends its name to a loaf. If you shop in wholefood or specialist bread stores you may chance across an organic, sourdough fermented barley bread. The most widely distributed example is made by Natural Rise Foods and, as with their rice bread (see entry), I find that the overwhelmingly sour flavour of what is basically a wholemeal loaf with a small proportion of barley meal rather overpowers the flavour of the added grain.

If you want to try a loaf with a discernible taste of barley you will need to hunt down a bannock (the Scottish soda-raised griddle bread which rarely crosses the Border) or a Germanic or Scandinavian mixed grain bread. Barley is distinguished by a noticeable sweetness allied to a mealy earthiness; most of us are likely to have encountered it in a somewhat altered state via the malted grain added to granary or malted grain breads (see entries).

· BATH BUNS ·

Bath buns come and go on supermarket shelves but change little from one year to the next. Perhaps a little richer than plain fruited buns, they are distinguished mainly by their shape – like soft, squashed, rock cakes – and by the sprinkle of crunchy nibbed sugar on top.

Ever since I enjoyed a basketful in Bath many years ago (at a bun house which, sadly, no longer exists) I associate them with a lemony flavour that is often absent in commercial versions. However, the original Bath buns may well have been similar to a French brioche or to the local Sally Lunn (see entry), and contained no fruit or lemon at all. Those sugar nibs would have been caraway comfits (candied caraway seeds) in the eighteenth century. In her book *Food in England* Dorothy Hartley suggested that lard might be substituted for butter, her only other proviso being 'do not put currants in Bath buns'.

Recent examples I have sampled outside Bath have been replete with currants and with luridly candied peel, innocent of butter or lard, fluffed by emulsifiers, yet somehow heavy and oversweet – recognisable as Bath buns only by their shape and their sugar-strewn top. Finer examples – pale gold-crusted buns that have been enriched, fruited and sweetened with a light hand – are produced by some small bakeries both outside and within Bath (by Mount Stevens bakeries, for instance), but at present you will need luck or determination to find them. A shame – both historical recipes and those occasional excellent examples suggest this could be a uniquely rich, light, typically English bun to be baked with pride.

· BEE STINGS ·

These eccentrically named, round, flat buns originate from Germany, where they are known as *Bienenstich*. With their sticky-crisp coating of flaked almonds and a rich filling of sweet pastry cream, they won over British affections well in advance of the rather more famous stollen (see entry). At least, that was the case in my home town of Bolton, Lancashire where bee stings proved more popular than Cornish splits, and are still going strong many years later, much to the original formulation. Many small bakery chains sell them in the North but it seems they are little known in most other areas of the UK. I have come across *Bienenstich* in Oxford, while the Tarte Tropézienne (see entry), a cake-sized French version of the same idea, has its fans in the South of England.

· BLACKPOOL MILK ROLL ·

This popular, white Lancashire loaf was almost unheard of in the South of England until a few years ago, yet I recall it as the mainstay of many a family's tea during my childhood in Bolton. Hardly surprising, as Warburtons, the plant bakery that produces the loaf, is Bolton based. Its mention here is not, however, nostalgia-induced:

when a nationwide supermarket chain recently delisted the loaf (in favour of an own-label version) it was snowed under by an avalanche of letters demanding the Blackpool loaf's reinstatement in the Home Counties.

The Blackpool milk roll is hardly a purist product – like many a factory-baked loaf it relies on preservatives to boost keeping qualities and contains hydrogenated oils alongside the milk and butter that form its character. It is, however, a rich, soft, 'easy eat', popular with children for making 'funny-face' sandwiches, and it boasts an unusual shape – a ridged cylinder not unlike an American nut loaf. The ridges were apparently a useful means for Blackpool landladies to check that lodgers were not sneaking a midnight slice. Lodgers must have lost the skill, as the Blackpool milk roll is now sold pre-sliced.

· BREAD STICKS ·

Bread sticks are long, finger-thin, dried-out biscuits made of savoury, yeasted bread dough, all crust and no crumb. Most Britons' first introduction to the genre will have been a rather bland one: the cellophane-wrapped little sticks everyone used to nibble in desultory fashion while waiting for their drinks to arrive in Italian restaurants. These machine-extruded, smooth and unexciting *grissini* can still be picked up in Italian delis; undemandingly light and crumbly they are a pleasant enough nibble. However, if you search a little longer and harder – in good delis or specialist food departments – you should find *grissini* that are closer to the Piedmontese ideal: friable, crunchy, with a recognisable bread flavour and an unmistakable note of good olive oil (more often than not, lard too – check the ingredients list if you are vegetarian). The best clue to quality is their appearance – the less uniform the colour, length and thickness of each stick (good bread sticks tend to be sold clearly visible through plastic packaging), the more likely they are to be hand-made and interesting. The thinner and darker the *grissini*, the crisper they are likely to be, although some of the best examples I have enjoyed have actually been quite thick and almost soft-centred. Length varies dramatically from brand to brand, up to about 60cm/2 feet, and is not in itself a guide to quality.

Absolutely the best *grissini* will be freshly made, with a short shelf life. These have something of the taste of fresh bread and are satisfyingly crunchy. They tend to be made by small specialist bakers and have very limited distribution (try good Italian delis), partly because of their fragility, which accounts for much of their attraction.

Most *grissini* are made with hard, white wheat flour, but wholemeal or wheatmeal flours are occasionally used. They may be flavoured with coarsely-ground pepper or fennel seed, or lent additional crunch by poppy or sesame seeds. British-baked *grissini* sometimes incorporate fresh garlic.

Greek and Turkish sesame-seeded bread sticks – generally chunkier, stubbier and lighter than *grissini* – are probably best bought direct from the bakery, although Middle Eastern delis are a good source. There is little variation between brands, which are usually made in small bakeries and sold in plastic bags. A little richer than the norm are commercially produced kabira sticks, twice-baked miniature fingers of daktyla (see entry). Slightly salt and sweet, and scented with sesame, aniseed and nigella seeds, kabira sticks are rich enough to be enjoyed as biscuits, perhaps with a pre-dinner aperitif.

Supermarkets have succeeded in creating a British-made bread stick that somehow melds Italian, Greek and even German (pretzel-inspired) tradition with a distinctly British overlay. These stubby sticks flavoured with garlic or cheese and coated with salt, sesame or poppy seeds are designed as the perfect pick-up for an ever-growing array of cosmopolitan party dips. However, a glance at the ingredients lists of altogether too many examples might give pause for thought: if you prefer your oil to be olive rather than hydrogenated, stay with authentic Greek, Turkish or Italian bread sticks.

USES OF BREAD STICKS

Napoleon, who was in the happy position of having '*les petits bâtons de Turin*' mailed to him daily, probably just chewed on them while constructing his battle plans. The majority of *grissini* are still nibbled neat at parties or with a pre-prandial glass of wine, but the Piedmontese seem to have devised them to dip into *bagna cauda*, a 'warm bath' of puréed anchovy, garlic and olive oil. If you do find hand-made *grissini* it is a combination worth trying. Jars of artichoke, radicchio or walnut purées work well as dips, too. Greek and Turkish sticks (and those supermarket hybrids) are good with vegetable purées as well as hummous and taramasalata, and indeed with a wide range of *mezze* (olives, stuffed vine leaves, and so on).

Perhaps it is the lard content of a good many *grissini* that has led to the Italian habit of winding prosciutto round the tips – a not unreasonable combination, though I am less enamoured with the British idea of using smoked salmon in similar fashion. More pleasing, to my mind, is a trayful of bread sticks sitting unadorned beside a platter of *antipasti* – the crispness is a particularly welcome contrast to soft, oil-cured or grilled vegetables. If you open your packet of bread sticks to discover a batch of rod-like tooth challengers, it is best to soak them in soup, either by dipping, or breaking them into short lengths and placing them in the bowl before pouring in the soup.

I have, in an emergency, ground down bread sticks to serve as dry breadcrumbs – as long as the colour of the crumbs is unimportant this works very well.

· BRIDGE ROLLS, VIENNA ROLLS, · PAINS AU LAIT
(*enriched rolls*)

I wish these soft-crusted, rich little finger rolls were more widely available, if only because they make a perfect snack 'on the move'. Lighter than brioche, but sufficiently enriched with milk, butter and egg to need no further buttering, well-made bridge (or Vienna or milk) rolls are as easy to digest as to nibble.

Bridge rolls are a very British concept, while Vienna rolls and *pains au lait* (milk rolls) form part of the repertoire of a French bakery. (Somewhat confusingly, a Vienna roll produced by a British bakery can also mean a plain, very light-textured, crusty bun – best to check if buying by name alone.) Bridge rolls are generally finger length, while Vienna rolls are half- or quarter-baguette length, slightly narrower and characterised by horizontal slashes at frequent intervals. *Pains au lait* are the size of brioche buns, but flatter and elongated, and may be characterised by ridged cuts in the crust and a scattering of nibbed sugar. All three have a noticeable sweetness, although Vienna rolls are usually the most salty/savoury, and *pains au lait* the least so. Degrees of richness vary from baker to baker.

WHENCE THE NAMES?

Diminutive bridge rolls have an unshakable image of dainty finger-food sustenance for the leisured classes, reaching their apotheosis at bridge parties in the Twenties and Thirties. The Vienna roll was indeed created in Vienna, in 1488. In a neat reversal of sociological context, it was commissioned by Emperor Frederick V as a nourishing treat for the poor. The Emperor's likeness was stamped on the rolls, giving rise to their Austrian name of *Kaisersemmeln*. French bakers were never slow to copy a good thing – croissants are another case in point – and today *Viennoiserie* still signifies enriched 'fancy' breads, indulgences set apart from the daily staple.

The main purpose of *pains au lait* is as breakfast nourishment or, more importantly, as children's *goûter*, the elevenses snack that marks an important break in the long French school morning. Thus they tend to be particularly rich in milk and a touch blander (less sweet and less salty) than other enriched breads.

BUYING ENRICHED ROLLS

Good bakers take pride in their luxury breads; mass-produced examples generally use the cheapest ingredients and have little truck with their original virtues. Thus factory-baked, pre-packed bridge rolls tend to be pale and wan, batch-baked and dull in appearance, and puffed up to at least twice the size of a true bridge roll; the real article should be dainty, golden, glossy-crusted and firm. Both Vienna rolls and *pains au lait* should have a similar golden tone and unpuffy firmness, though the latter are essentially softer in crust and crumb; unfortunately, the most widespread, mass-produced *Viennoiserie* available in Britain (and, increasingly in France) are lumpen and dull in appearance, cloyingly sweet, and marred by vegetable fats. For these breads, more than almost any other, it is essential to find a reputable baker.

USES

In her 1974 book, *English Food*, Jane Grigson recalls with fondness her mother's bridge rolls filled with cheese and tomato paste, usually eaten as picnic fare. My own memories are of similarly basic spreads: bloater, sardine and beef pastes spread thickly on the split rolls, piled in a tottering heap on children's party platters. Bridge rolls are no longer standard fare at informal parties and picnics but I was pleased to read about an aptly luxurious use in Linda Collister's *Bread Book*: she filled them generously with Maine lobster and mayonnaise for a thoroughly adult party. Very tiny rolls can be hollowed and filled with soft cream cheese mixtures or mousses.

Vienna rolls or sticks could almost have been designed for canapé use; being rich, compact and firm, they are easy to slice thinly and can be spread quite firmly with all manner of toppings from flavoured butters to pâtés.

French pâtissiers who double as *traiteurs* often sell their *pains au lait* split and filled with all manner of delicacies, from foie gras mousse and smoked salmon to simpler lunch fare such as ham or fromage frais. If you do come across fine *pains au lait* from a small bakery, you might also try an adult version of the *goûter* – split the rolls, spoon on cool fromage frais, then top it with squares of very thin, very dark chocolate. Coffee breaks will never be the same again.

· BRIOCHE ·

Compared to the huge popularity of croissants and baguettes in the UK, the brioche, richest and most luxurious of all unfruited breads, is still a bystander on the *boulangerie* scene. Yet it is much easier to produce a sound brioche than a successful croissant or crusty baguette – which no doubt accounts for its longstanding popularity in France, centuries before the croissant or baguette ruled the bread shop.

Perhaps it is simply that in the UK we have such a wealth of scones, sponges and teacakes that we are hard put to find a space for this rich bread that is almost a cake. Significantly, most of us grew up with the mistranslated notion that Marie Antoinette lost her head for imperiously suggesting that starving Parisians rioting for bread eat cake instead. In fact, she was naively suggesting that they turn to another form of bread, the brioche (almost certainly a rather less extravagant creation in those days).

THE BUTTER BEHIND THE BRIOCHE

Disputes abound whether butter-producing Normandy or luxury-loving Paris gave birth to the first brioche (most likely the Normans produced and the Parisians purchased), but in France the quality of the butter and the minimum amount employed brook no argument. The ideal quantity is considered to be 50 to 80 per cent of the weight of the flour, with the minimum between 20 and 25 per cent (the maximum is a hefty equal quantity of butter to flour). Fresh eggs are used in a similar ratio, and sugar with restraint. Unlike the croissant, there is no *brioche ordinaire* in France, no sanctioned use of margarine or vegetable fat; those with a minimal butter content are termed *brioche commune* or simply *pain brioché*. In Britain (and, it must be said, in certain Parisian tourist hotels) bastardised, non-butter brioches are sold as a matter of course, and appear as popular as the true version with both bakers and consumers. Moreover, no distinction is made between the various styles. Another reason for its relative lack of popularity?

SHAPES AND STYLES

Brioches are available in a variety of shapes – from the tiny bun and the torpedo shapes coated in loaf sugar to the kilo-loaf *brioche à tête* or *brioche Parisienne* with its characteristic topknot and the tin-loaf version known to French bakers as *brioche Nanterre*, whose ridged top crust acts as a division mark that allows small chunks to be broken off. A less traditional shape, popular in the UK, is the crown, which pulls apart into individual buns. Occasionally you may come across a *brioche mousseline* baked as a tall tower rather like the Russian *kulich* Easter bread. This slices neatly across into attractive rounds and is used for making pâtisserie constructions. The vast majority of brioches are plain, but a loaf or *mousseline* sometimes contains dried or glacé fruit.

BUYING BRIOCHE

A really fine brioche has a deep brown, glossy crust reminiscent of varnished walnut and will feel light for its size compared to a traditional British tea loaf. The crumb inside should be the gold of farm-made butter (its glorious colour is the result of generous quantities of egg yolk as well as butter) and less compact than pain de mie or chollah (see entries). The aroma should be unmistakably buttery and fresh with a sweetness that is far from sugary, while the flavour will be rich yet light and clean. It should inspire you to carry on eating without any need for butter or jam or a wash of coffee, welcome though these are.

A handful of British bakers, and even one or two supermarkets, are achieving a loaf of this quality. Sadly, many of the brand-name and supermarket own-label versions are travesties composed of hydrogenated vegetable oils or concentrated butter (which simply does not have the fresh, clean aroma of fine Normandy butter), as well as cloyingly high quantities of sugar (or invert sugar syrup). Although these loaves are relatively cheap, a properly made brioche inevitably commands a premium price, its taste worth every penny.

USING STALE BRIOCHE

A classic brioche keeps reasonably well – it may not be quite as aromatic and soft the day after baking but a slice can be quickly warmed in the oven (no need to toast at this stage unless you wish to), which softens the crumb and releases the buttery-yeasty aromas. Staler brioche toasts very successfully and its richness makes a good foil for fruit purées or low-sugar preserves, with no additional butter required. To produce an attractive glaze, dust each side of the brioche lightly with icing sugar before toasting.

Thickly cut slices of brioche can be topped with chunks of ripe summer fruit and then baked or grilled, and they are ideal for use in apple charlottes (see page 316) or summer pudding (see page 298).

Fingers of brioche make the richest of *pain perdu* (see page 295) and are perfectly matched by those bottled tart French fruit purées that have successfully invaded British supermarkets. Serve the purées chilled or warmed as a dip, or layer fingers of fried brioche with warmed purée and top with whipped cream or a spoonful of softened vanilla ice cream. Toasted brioche cubes or croutons (possibly glazed with a dusting of icing sugar) can be scattered on fruit soups, purées or fools. Brioche crumbs, golden even before frying, have a hundred and one uses, from sophisticated fruit fritters to a coating for escalopes of foie gras (as well as rather humbler fare).

THE ULTIMATE SANDWICH?

Toasted brioche is the base for one of the world's great classic sandwiches: Anne Rosenzweig's Lobster Club. This sybaritic sandwich was created for ladies who lunch at New York's Arcadia restaurant. Evidently these ladies had no need to watch their waistlines, as the sandwich starts with toasted slices of the richest brioche known to man (or woman); three slices are slathered with lemon mayonnaise, then covered with crisp lettuce and ripe tomato followed by applewood-smoked bacon. The crowning glory is a pile of lobster tail meat. Finally a fourth slice of brioche is pressed on top and the sandwich enjoyed with the chef's instruction in mind: 'mayonnaise and tomato juice must dribble down your arms as you eat this'.

THE STUFFED BRIOCHE

One feature that may ensure the survival of the brioche in Britain is its eminent stuffability. Small buns can be filled with creamy sauce-based savouries and served warm as a dinner-party first course, while miniature buns make ideal containers for delicate pâtés and mousses. If your first inclination (like my own) is to dismiss the stuffed brioche as twee, fiddly, or somehow a cheat, try and quell the thought, as the way in which the saltily sweet bread highlights the natural sweetness of scallops, crabs, or some types of wild mushroom can hardly be bettered. Because the crumb is fairly compact, a brioche case can hold a sauce without springing a leak, and that density is also usefully heat-retaining. The ideal sauces are béchamel based, perhaps enriched with medium sherry, or a touch of saffron; suitable 'solid' elements are shellfish, ceps and chanterelles, and lightly sautéed chicken livers.

For cold mixtures to fill miniature buns, try crab and salmon mousses, the classic foie gras or, less grandly, a sherried chicken liver pâté; finely diced, grilled and marinated red peppers and Italian puréed sauce bases, particularly the artichoke- and walnut-based ones, are also good.

· BRITISH BREAD SHAPES ·

The rows and rows of British breads beckoning from bakery shelves are formed from a mere handful of doughs: white, wholemeal, brown, perhaps a milk-enriched dough, mixed grain, and malted grain. The difference lies mainly in the shape of each loaf.

Shape contributes subtly but significantly to the character of a loaf. A cob may look similar to a coburg, but the cuts in the crust of the latter increase the ratio of crust to crumb. A cottage loaf gives an even greater proportion of ridged and crunchy crust. Tin loaves, which have been largely contained in their tin during baking, have softer, thinner crusts on three sides than 'oven-bottom' loaves, which are baked directly on the floor of the oven or on a giant baking sheet known as a drawplate.

BARREL OR CRINKLED LOAF

The dough is baked in a ridged, cylindrical mould, producing a soft crust all round the finished loaf. This style is generally reserved for naturally soft-crusted, milk-enriched breads and certain 'light', low-starch loaves.

BATCH BREAD

Batch bread is both proved and baked without tins. The pieces of dough are 'batched' or pressed together so that they are all touching each other. Shapes are very varied, from finger rolls to something approaching a chimney stack; the common feature is the absence of crust where the loaves have been touching. The method is used with all manner of flours and doughs to produce a softer loaf.

There are some interesting variations of the definition. In Wales a batch loaf may in fact denote a bread in the shape of a crusty cob. Irish batch bread is fairly squat, while Scottish batch bread is markedly taller than it is wide.

BLOOMER, LONDON BLOOMER

A very popular shape, this is a plump, oval loaf that has been oven-bottom baked and has a large number of diagonal slashes scored deep in the upper crust. Elizabeth David comments in her classic work on bread that the name used to denote a high-grade, enriched dough loaf. Nowadays even large industrial bakeries produce a bloomer, but ready-sliced and overwrapped which means the crust is no longer crunchy and half the point of the shape is lost. Virtually any type of flour can be baked into a bloomer shape, including British-made light rye breads, but white bloomers are undoubtedly the most popular.

BRICK, SISTER BRICK

Two rectangular (brick-shaped) loaves are baked in a very long or wide tin and joined to each other on one side to produce a modified 'batch' effect – one crustless side where the loaves have been joined and broken apart. These are more often produced by small craft bakeries than large factories, which are better equipped to make fully batched bread.

CHEQUERBOARD, COLLEGE OR PORCUPINE

Using a basic cob shape, the chequerboard loaf has an upper crust slashed with parallel lines in a chequerboard pattern. The deeper the cuts, the more the squares open out; particularly deep cuts produce a 'porcupine' effect and create a very crusty loaf.

COB

This is perhaps the most ancient and certainly the most basic of British bread shapes. The cob is a smooth-crusted, round oven-bottom loaf and can be made from any kind of flour, though the majority are wholewheat, granary or some form of brown. The crust may be crunchy or reasonably soft. A Welsh cob resembles an English farmhouse loaf (see page 41) but is baked oven-bottom crusty.

COBURG AND PAN COBURG

The source of the name is uncertain but it can be traced to the nineteenth century, perhaps to a German baker. The coburg is basically a cob with a cross slash. Sometimes this is designed to open out and produce a shape that is almost square; others maintain their round shape and a recognisable cross on the upper crust. Most are made of white flour.

The pan coburg is part tin-baked, part-crusty, with the effect that the base is soft-crusted while the billowing, rounded upper crust (still cross-cut) is crunchy. Once known as a cauliflower loaf, this is now rarely found commercially.

COTTAGE

The most quintessentially English of all loaf shapes, this consists of a small round of dough placed atop a larger one. A hole is pushed through the centre with a spoon handle, rolling pin or skilled fingers. To maximise the crust, the sides are sometimes notched with vertical cuts and even scissor-cut to open out to a hedgehog effect. This exercises the baker's skill considerably, and is ill suited to mass production – with the effect that the genuine cottage loaf makes all too rare an appearance. Most are made from white flour.

DANISH

This loaf has a cylindrical shape with a deep central slash, baked oven-bottom style and crusty. Like the bloomer, this shape has been adapted by large factories to produce a wrapped, soft-crusted loaf often described as 'light' – in other words with a high water and low starch content. This 'lightness' then becomes the loaf's only distinguishing feature – it might as well be tin-baked. It is usually made from white flour.

FARMHOUSE LOAF

This is quite simply a tin loaf baked in a wide, squat tin with the word farmhouse impressed on the sides. These tins date back to the era of Hovis loaves (see entry), when there was a reaction against flavourless roller-milled flour and the quest began for a wholesome loaf. The name gives no indication of the type of flour or style of dough employed – a wide variety of both is used.

PLAIT

These may be made up of any number of strands from one to eight, with three strands as the simplest and most popular option. Plaited wholemeal loaves are produced by small, specialised bakeries but the majority are made from white flour and are either plain and crisp crusted or enriched and soft crusted.

SPIRAL OR SNAIL

Just as it sounds – dough twisted into a fat spiral. This shape may occasionally be crusty and white but it is usually reserved for enriched dough loaves, when it is glazed with egg and has a soft crust.

STICK

The stick is an adaptation of the baguette (see entry), but fatter and more solid. The same bakery might offer a French stick and a baguette with the former making no attempt to emulate the light, holey crumb and flaky crust of the French bread; rather it will be an English bread made from largely high-protein wheat, baked in a stick shape. Sticks are baked from all varieties of flour.

TIN LOAF, SANDWICH TIN, SPLIT TIN

As the names suggest, these loaves are baked in rectangular tins, with the result that all the sides except the top have a relatively soft crust. A split tin is the equivalent of a Danish loaf (see page 41), with a single deep slash running the length of the loaf. A sandwich tin is usually baked completely enclosed like the French *pain de mie* (see entry). This loaf is designed for slicing to any thickness and is the most popular shape for mass-produced bread.

VIENNA, VIENNA BATON, LEMON LOAF

A shape adopted from crusty continental loaves. The Vienna is a torpedo-shaped baton with pointed ends and one or more diagonal slashes – perhaps the crustiest of all the loaf shapes. The dough is usually a particularly light one made of white flour, an approximation of the baguette.

BUN SHAPES

These can echo any of the larger loaves, from cottage to farmhouse. They may also be knotted and sprinkled with poppy seeds – these buns are usually soft, and made of white flour; or sometimes batched in a clover leaf of three round buns or as a cluster, a ring of several round buns – these are part crusty and designed to pull apart easily. Long rolls are usually batch baked, and are known as Scotch rolls when dusted with flour and soft on top. Scottish morning rolls, or simply morning rolls or softies, are made of the same dough as Scots baps (see entry) but shaped as plump rounds and glazed with cream rather than flour-dusted. Finger rolls are thin and long but twice the size of bridge rolls (see entry).

· BROWN BREAD ·

'White or brown?' is still a routine question in sandwich bars that have no truck with fashion, while assistants in bread shops are prone to answering queries about a particular loaf with the catch-all, 'It's a brown loaf, madam', if a bread is anything other than white. Strictly speaking, both are bending the law if the bread is actually wheatgerm or wholewheat or, at the other end of the scale, a brownish shade but short of a legally fixed minimum fibre content – government regulations declare that brown bread must have a wheat fibre content of at least 0.6 per cent weight of dry matter. Wheatgerm and wholewheat breads have separate definitions, with the latter particularly strict. By contrast, the legal definition of brown bread is somewhat lax and, by allowing caramel colouring as an additive, leads to much consumer confusion. It is easy to assume that a loaf with an attractive deep brown colour contains a good proportion of wholewheat flour (milled from all parts of the grain including bran and germ) but in fact it may contain almost none; it could well be caramel-coloured white bread with a touch of added bran.

It pays to read the label carefully and to make few assumptions. If the loaf you have purchased has a proprietary name, you may find it listed in this directory. If you have bought your brown loaf loose, ask the shop for more precise information.

· BURGER BUNS ·

The majority of burger buns conform admirably to most consumers' criteria: they are large, soft, white, light and supremely squishy. Sesame seeds are provided as much for instant recognition as for any contribution of flavour or texture (though, God knows, the standard burger bun needs all it can get of these). A further distinguishing factor is a ridged mark around the circumference, a kind of cutting guideline.

A determined search for buns of good texture and flavour has yielded little. Here are two possible solutions for anyone fond of good burgers but averse to bouncy cottonwool buns. Try slicing one of the 7.5cm/3inch focaccia rolls arriving on the bread scene (see **focaccie and focaccette**). Herb, tomato and onion flavours are particularly good with burgers. Or you could track down one of the French bakeries complementing '*le bifburger*' with buns made out of *pain Viennois* dough enriched with milk and butter. These are easily squashed. Nor is there any problem in asking for the buns by name: in French they are known as 'Hamburger sesame'.

· CAMPAILLOU ·

See **Pain de Campagne**.

· CANAILLOU ·

See **Pain de Campagne**.

· CARTA DA MUSICA/PANE CARASAU ·

This is a spectacular-looking sheaf composed of large rounds of flat, crisp, paper-thin Sardinian bread. Traditionally straw-fire baked, it may be leavened or not, but it is always crisp, dry and fragile.

Transporting the sizeable boxed sheaf home in a shopping bag is no mean achievement, though finding it in the first place may be an even greater one – at present only a few specialist delis afford shelf space to the *carta*.

Enjoying it is less of a problem. The brittle sheets are rather delicious straight from the packet, and just the thing to accompany chargrilled vegetables. They soften readily when dampened with a little water, or water and olive oil with perhaps a touch of lemon, and can then be rolled round a filling – Sardinian sheep's cheese or pungent salami would be rather appropriate – or simply eaten as an accompaniment to a wide range of *antipasti* or salads. Softened *carta da musica* can be substituted for pasta in dishes such as baked cannelloni or lasagne. At the opposite end of the scale, the dry bread can be seasoned with olive oil and a sprinkling of salt and baked briefly in a hot oven, emerging glistening, savoury and very crisp indeed, like a delicate version of corn chips. Like pitta, it can then be added to a *fattoush*-style salad (see page 220).

· CASARECCIO ·

This simply means 'of the house' and has overtones of family and homeliness. In Italy the word is applied to a style of cuisine rather than a type of bread. However, a number of British-made breads have adopted the term, which in no way tells you what to expect: the ones I have come across vary from a plain crusty white cob to a meal-in-a-slice confection of maize and wheat dough made with virgin olive oil and stuffed with cheese and salami.

· CHAPATIS ·

The chapati is the simplest, most basic and ubiquitous of Indian breads and the first to be popularised in the West. A small, round flat-bread baked on a griddle, or *tava*, the traditional chapati is composed of finely ground wholewheat flour, gram (chickpea) flour or occasionally cornflour, plus water and salt.

Commercially prepared chapatis are a little different, designed to remain reasonably soft for prolonged periods in their plastic packaging and to be 'tasty' even without accompaniment. These chapatis are more off-white than brown, prepared with a low-extraction wheat flour rather than wholemeal *atta* or gram flour. They are likely to be enriched with milk and vegetable oil, seasoned with sugar as well as salt, and chemically raised rather than unleavened. Commercial production and distribution are in the hands of a very few companies at present and their products all follow the same pattern.

USING PREPACKAGED CHAPATIS

Chapatis tend to be less popular than naan bread (see entry), which is softer, more pitta-like, and can even double as a pizza base. Outside Punjab and the north, however, it is the chapati that is most widely used in India, both as an accompaniment to and as a means of picking up all manner of foods; personally I find the taste of even the commercial versions cleaner and less intrusive than that of commercial Naan. As it is a drier bread, however, you might prefer to use it with moist curries and vegetable dishes or with soups and dips. Unless the chapatis are destined to be soaked in sauce they really do need to be eaten warm and soft in order to be pleasant. The packaging on commercially made ones generally suggests grilling, but warming in an ungreased pan works just as well. Wrap them in a cloth once softened; buttering them will also help keep them moist. Chapatis have quite a long shelf life and they keep well in the fridge once opened. Dried-out chapatis can be crisped in the oven and used rather like toasted pitta (see entry), though they are somewhat thicker in texture.

· CHEESE BREAD ·

See **Flavoured Breads**.

· CHELSEA BUNS ·

Chelsea buns have been eulogised like no other. Eighteenth-century songs speak of 'smoking hot, piping hot Chelsea buns', 'fragrant as honey and sweeter in taste! As flaky and white as if baked by the light'. In *A Morning's Walk to Kew* (1817) Sir Richard Phillips wondered why 'their delicate flavour, lightness and richness, have never been successfully imitated'.

Modern buns have failed to inspire such praise: presumably those of Sir Richard's day were not only inimitable but unrepeatable a generation later. The famous Chelsea Bun House in Pimlico, set up in the reign of King George II, and where for thirty years Sir Richard bought the buns created by a flamboyant baker nicknamed Captain Bun, closed in 1839, and its re-creation for the Festival of Britain in 1951 proved temporary.

On the basis of past definition, the spiral-rolled Chelsea bun should be enriched with butter and egg, filled with currants, spice and muscovado sugar and glazed with milk and sugar, or with butter and honey for a particularly sticky top. One bun that answers to the description of luscious, spicy stickiness is that sold by Fitzbillies bakery to generations of Cambridge students. Soaked with tooth-challenging caramel, nicely balanced by the acidity of the currants and a subtle dose of cinnamon, these are glorious buns. Flaky, white and light they are not, but then no one really considers these sticky brown sweetmeats as even close cousins of the mass-produced Chelsea bun, or indeed of those produced by any other bakery or tea shop.

Modern Chelsea buns are a standardised product – wherever you buy them you will take away a squat, square bun looking like a cross-section of Swiss roll. You can still have a good deal of fun unwinding it strip by strip, but the dough is barely enriched and certainly not flaky. The filling is likely to contain currants and perhaps sultanas and even candied peel, but only the merest hint of spice, and your teeth will most likely be gritted by white caster sugar, both in the filling and on the barely glazed top. A very few well-crafted examples apart, the main interest of the modern bun is simply that of its structure.

· CHOLLAH ·

This widely enjoyed Jewish festival and Sabbath bread is instantly recognisable by its plaited shape; the skill involved in plaiting the six strands is a source of great pride (and competition) among Jewish bakers.

The basic white yeast dough is enriched with oil, usually with egg, too, and lightly sweetened – traditionally with honey but more often than not with sugar. Other traditional shapes do exist: round or spiral chollahs eaten at Jewish New Year celebrations are available year-round at a number of the larger bakeries. These are sometimes sold as *boulka*, though that name should really be reserved for the similarly shaped rolls traditionally made for wedding festivities, but once again sold daily at stores such as Harrods and Selfridges.

Quality and style vary, and while supermarket instore bakeries are now producing passable versions, the best come from craft bakeries. The finest examples I have come across have been from Manchester-based bakers and have combined richness with lightness and uncloy-ing sweetness. Most major cities boast a Jewish bakery or two which will often supply large stores or delis.

A number of non-Jewish British bakers produce a non-kosher, all-butter version – basically a plaited brioche. These are just as delicious as the vegetable-fat versions, if not more so. All are excellent eaten plain or with preserves or honey. Stale, they can be used in much the same way as brioche (see entry) as well as in numerous dessert recipes; to my mind all these breads make the finest of bread puddings.

· CIABATTA ·

This bread more than any other has been responsible for the creation of specialist bread departments in supermarkets, where previously a few rye loaves and the odd brick of Vollkornbrot languished forlornly. Now it seems the majority of Britons can no more contemplate life without the Italian newcomer than imagine the absence of sliced white.

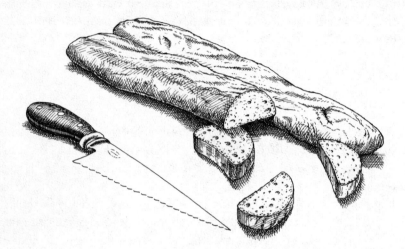

While it seems incredible that a simple foreign bread should conquer the conservative British palate with a verve parallel to that of the pizza, the ciabatta has undeniable all-round appeal. It is gently, invitingly aromatic, a white bread sufficiently flavourful to enjoy on its own yet incapable of overwhelming any accompaniment, jam included. The crumb is light and soft as down but far from woolly, while the thin crust is satisfyingly chewy or crunchy or both, but never tooth-challenging. Moreover, it cuts easily into slices thick or thin, tears into chunks, and holds juicy toppings or fillings without springing a leak. The only thing you can't do with ease is butter the large holes – somehow we have forgiven this lapse, perhaps in the startling realisation that such an oil-rich bread does not need it.

A SHORT HISTORY OF THE REVOLUTION

Unlike its Pugliese cousin, the ciabatta is a modern shape of bread, rather like the French baguette and ficelle. Its name, however, could hardly be less suggestive of the ethereal magic of a wand (the original meaning of baguette) – it simply reflects the shape of a homely, well-worn slipper, flat, oval, irregular. Perhaps a comfortable slipper makes the wearer feel they are walking on air.

The ciabatta's arrival in Britain was largely achieved by Peggy Czyzak-Dannenbaum, whose La Fornaia bakery opened in London a mere ten years ago as a sister venture to the Il Fornaio chain, established in Europe and on America's West Coast by the Veggetti family, Lombardian bakery designers intent on rescuing traditional Italian breads and baking processes. One or two of the capital's Italian bakers had previously been experimenting with a similar bread produced on a small scale but from the moment this star of La Fornaia's repertoire hit a supermarket shelf, the ciabatta became an instant success.

BUYING CIABATTA

La Fornaia's ciabatta is widely available at Marks & Spencer and also in some delis under the La Fornaia label. It has spawned many imitators, few, if any, quite as good so far. A number look greyish and taste unpleasantly sour. This suggests that, while commendably made with a sourdough starter, they have been overfermented in some way. Best avoided. Others simply don't have a sweet, fresh aroma – generally because an inferior oil has been used, and in insufficient quantities: fine extra virgin olive oil is the lifeblood of ciabatta. Flour, too, has its part to play; curiously, those supermarket own-label examples that have been part-baked in Italy – presumably using traditional flours – remain inferior to the Fornaia model, which employs Marriage's flour. The quantity of water is crucial, as is the skill in handling the sticky dough. One guideline when buying is that the crust should be squashable, even if crisp and crumbly in parts, and the shape slightly free-form and fluid rather than a uniform rectangle. The loaf should smell and taste fresh, sweet and gentle.

Ciabatta breads flavoured with olive, sun-dried tomato and walnut have all proved enduringly popular (see **Flavoured Breads**). The quality and intensity of flavour vary from baker to baker, with La Fornaia almost certainly taking the laurels again.

REFRESHING STALED CIABATTA

Many a writer has claimed that ciabatta does not keep. It may well be designed, in baguette fashion, to be a single-meal loaf (and probably the first that has inspired so Continental a habit in the two-slices-maximum British), but to suggest that a plump bread so rich in oil stales as quickly as a thin, oil-free loaf is plainly nonsensical. The crust does alter on keeping – wrapped, it softens to a slight chewiness; uncovered, it hardens – but the crumb remains moist for two or three days at least. I find that it responds particularly well to being refreshed in a hot oven, particularly if a tin of hot water is placed under the loaf. The crust emerges somewhat crunchier than on purchase, which no doubt alters the original character of the loaf but is quite glorious in its own right.

Stale ciabatta has inspired bars, bistros and pricier establishments to produce countless crostini (canapé-sized Tuscan toasts topped with pungent spreads, relishes and purées) and over-slim bruschetta (chargrilled, chunky slices of country bread anointed with oil and, in recent years, tomato). These are simple to construct at home, with the exception of the truly chargrilled examples, but you will probably find your ciabatta better employed in mopping up sauces and dressings than as a base for them. There again, a bruschetta constructed on a piece of ciabatta split in half rather than a holey slice is undeniably delicious (see pages 187–90).

I find both stale chunks and fresh crumbs of ciabatta ideal for just about any of the recipes in the book – once soaked, the bread reconstitutes well without going pappy and the crumbs, which grind down fine, are as suited to sweet dishes as to savoury.

USES OF CIABATTA

The commercial possibilities for ciabatta-based garlic or pesto-packed bread and for mock pizza – both previously confined to French sticks – appear endless. The good news is that both are very easily produced at home and are likely to be more generously filled or covered if you are the chef; moreover, you can make your own fresh pesto (perhaps some variant of the increasingly chic red pesto), and select the finest tomatoes, anchovies and so on for the pizza. Neither really requires much instruction – simply use as much pesto per loaf or roll, as you feel inclined; the same applies to the pizza-style toppings piled on to halved loaves or rolls. Both need about 10 minutes in a fairly hot oven – 200°C/400°F/Gas Mark 6 – by which time the pesto loaf will be crisp crusted and hot throughout, and the pizza topping bubbling.

For ideas for ciabatta sandwiches see pages 214–15.

· CILICIAN BREAD ·

Uniquely produced in Britain by Abel Bakeries – one of the major suppliers of naan and pitta to the supermarkets – these small, flat rounds resemble nothing so much as miniature pizzas speckled with cheese, seeds and spices.

It is difficult to test the manufacturer's claim that their latest flat-bread is in fact made 'to an ancient Turkish recipe'. I rather suspect that Turks, ancient or otherwise, would have little truck with vegetarian Cheddar, but the seed and spice mixture – sesame and poppy seeds, cumin and ginger – sounds authentic. Indeed, the bread is strikingly reminiscent of a recipe for *hasd hats*, or 'fat bread', given by Arto der Haroutunian in his book *Vegetarian Dishes from the Middle East*. He linked it to a medieval recipe unearthed by Claudia Roden for the bread of 'Franks and Armenians', and suggested that some village in erstwhile Cilicia (now the Hattay region of Southern Turkey) is no doubt still baking a bread very like it.

The flavour is as intriguing as the bread's pedigree – somehow the cheese melds well with the smoky, pungent spice, lending a rich roundness to the whole. That cheese content ensures that a round of Cilician bread would make a meal in itself, perhaps accompanied by an assertively dressed salad. However, I can see it becoming rather popular at barbecues, if only because when grilled, its assertive, smoky spiciness evokes a barbecue – it would be rather good with a herbed, marinated joint of lamb.

With Turkish dishes in mind, I would pair Cilician bread with spinach and carrot soups, any number of aubergine dishes, and simple herb and lettuce salads dressed with olive oil.

· CORNISH SPLITS ·

Also known as Devonshire Splits, in the West Country these are simply light, soft, sweet, yeasted buns enriched with milk and butter (sometimes lard). Although they are traditionally made with the finest white flour, shades of brown and the inevitable granary are currently in demand. Their only occasional embellishment is a light dusting of icing sugar. In the West Country shoppers rush home, split open the buns and pile in raspberry conserve and wonderfully fresh, locally produced clotted cream. If they pause to warm them first the resulting combination is finer than can be achieved with any but the lightest of soda-raised scones.

However, what most of Britain recognises as Cornish splits are somewhat different: generally made to a standard bun recipe that does service for Bath buns, Chelsea buns or iced fingers, they are sold ready split, jammed and creamed – recognisable, but hardly distinguished, by those slicks of red and white. There is no reason why they should not be good, but tacitly accepted 'reasonable' (i.e. cheapskate) pricing ensures they rarely are.

It would be better if bakers countrywide were to forget about the embellishments and simply bake a great bun – which should still work out cheaper than a brioche. Should you chance upon such an enlightened product you might like to experience an alternative filling, equally traditional and as dramatic as its name suggests: Thunder and Lightning aptly describes a split bun filled with clotted cream and drizzled with dark, bitter treacle.

· CORNMEAL BREAD ·

Quite distinct from the soda-raised quickbreads of American tradition, British-baked cornmeal (or maize) breads are rather diverse in character. A number of enterprising small bakeries simply add a small proportion of coarse yellow cornmeal to a basic white loaf or roll for a touch of colour and crunch. Some are prettily shaped to resemble an ear of corn.

More interesting and distinctive in flavour is the Italian *pane di mais*, a loaf containing a fair proportion (perhaps a third to a half total weight of flour) of polenta flour, and a dash of olive oil. Attractively gritty when very fresh, this goes well with soups of all kinds, rich, creamy cheeses such as Gorgonzola, and soft, oil-grilled vegetables.

A recent and attractive addition to the range is La Fornaia's torpedo-shaped loaf which is crusty, very light in texture, but punctuated by chewy nuggets of sweetcorn as well as sunflower seeds. An excellent soup and salad accompaniment.

All cornmeal breads seem to stale rather rapidly, even those with olive oil in the dough, and become rather unpleasant to eat plain. Toasting the bread more than revives it, however, releasing a sweet, fresh corn aroma which is curiously absent from even the freshest of cold loaves. The *pane di mais* makes excellent crostini bases when thickly sliced, cut into small squares and toasted – good with creamy-textured, savoury toppings. Stale cornmeal bread is a reasonable substitute for Portuguese *broa* in *açorda* (see page 228) and *migas* (see page 253), and fine for stuffings, where the crumbs will usefully absorb and retain cooking juices, oil or other moistening agents, and contribute an unpappy texture.

· CRAMIQUE ·

Cramique is the fruited teabread of Belgium, with a butter- and egg-enriched dough halfway between *pain de mie*, or milk bread, and brioche. A splendid example, packed full of fruit and with the characteristic dark, glossy, almost burnt upper crust is baked by the Surrey-based Belgian Patisserie – sadly, distribution is not very wide. Use just like any other teabread.

· CROISSANTS ·

I have yet to meet anyone who does not have a decided opinion on what constitutes the ideal croissant and where to buy it – and few suggest a trip across the Channel. Indeed, a recent national newspaper debate on the joys and trials of holidaying in France provoked a number of letters claiming that even the croissants are better in Britain. To which I must add that even certain supermarkets are now producing croissants of great finesse, difficult to fault.

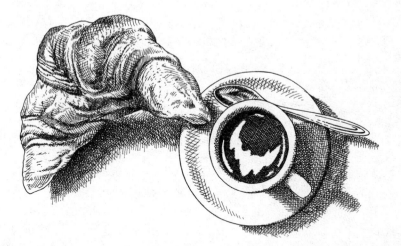

THE IDEAL

I think most people would agree on the following desirable features: the crescent-shaped pastry can be near-straight or curved but should be light, crisp and flaky. It should have a good, yeasty aroma, more pronounced when the croissant is warm. Its soft, moist centre should pull apart in layers (but can of course be cut neatly), a result of the proper baking method which involves interleaving butter between layers of yeasted dough. Most important of all, it should be distinctly, sweetly buttery with a clean aftertaste – vegetable fats and margarine tend to leave a film of fat on the palate. Levels of salt and the possibly iniquitous addition of sugar remain matters of heated debate.

TRACKING DOWN THE IDEAL

French bakers distinguish between butter-based croissants and those made with vegetable fat in two essential ways: by name and shape. The *croissant au beurre* is more or less straight while the vegetable-fat *croissant ordinaire* is curved into a half-moon – though bakers who produce only butter croissants tend to use the more attractive curved shape. British bakers are not bound by these conventions: you will need to ask, and taste – or read the packet. Use of Normandy butter is a fair recommendation, an absence of unnecessary 'improvers' another. If you don't want the bother of crisping your croissants at home you will simply have to buy them loose and as fresh from the oven as possible. Then it is merely a matter of establishing a favoured style from a local bakery. It may well be worth comparing your bakery's croissant with one of the finer supermarket-sold examples (duly crisped).

NOT FRENCH AFTER ALL?

Recent research into the history of this uniquely shaped yeasted pastry has begun to scotch the pretty story about nightworking bakers in seventeenth-century Budapest or Vienna (depending on which version of the story you favour) saving the citizens of the besieged city from Turkish invasion and being rewarded with permission to produce an exclusive pastry in the shape of the Ottoman crescent moon. The French wish it to be known that the croissant has a thoroughly French, indeed Parisian pedigree. Although the first recipe for croissants as we know them was not published until 1906, pastries in the shape of '*croissans*' are mentioned in the records of a sixteenth-century banquet given in honour of the queen by the pontiff of Paris – well before the Austro-Hungarian initiative. The French can also take the dubious honour of proliferating recipes for the *croissant ordinaire*.

THE CROISSANT SANDWICH

In the UK the majority of croissants are no longer eaten at breakfast, with marmalade, jam or yet more butter, or dunked neat into milky coffee. Instead they have become denizens of sandwich bars and chilled takeaway cabinets, where they can be spied spilling very British fillings, from coleslaw to grated Cheddar. It must be said that even respectable Parisian patisseries doubling as *traiteurs* boast a range of filled croissants, though here the contents display some Gallic chic and are generally elegant concoctions with foie gras mousse or *crudités* (usually a little crunchy salad), or a cool interpretation of the classic *croque monsieur* – thin slithers of cooked, smoked ham and Gruyère.

However, chilled croissants of any pedigree are all too often an unhappy marriage of opposites – in keeping the filling cool and fresh, the fat in the croissant is chilled to solidity. By all means fill a freshly baked croissant with liver mousse, but make sure you eat it at once.

THE HOT FILLED CROISSANT

Hot filled croissants are another matter – a *croissant croque*, inspired by the *croque monsieur*, is cruelly calorific but presents a tremendous marriage of flavours and textures: flaky pastry, oozing cheese and salty ham. To produce one for yourself, fill a croissant with grated or very thinly sliced Gruyère and a thin slice of good-quality ham, folded to fit. Bake at 190°C/375°F/Gas Mark 5 for about 5 minutes, then eat while the cheese flows.

I am not sure any other combination of cheese and croissant is quite as good, but molten Camembert and sautéed apple or a spoonful of fruit chutney; Roquefort and a couple of broken toasted walnuts; buffalo mozzarella and a diced anchovy or sliced sun-dried tomato; and fresh goat's cheese all on its own are all fine assemblies. An excellent British breakfast filling is a generous helping of creamy scrambled eggs and a crisply cooked, crumbled rasher of smoked streaky bacon. Another surprisingly good filling is a hot, unsloppy ratatouille of roasted vegetables.

A third style of filling plays with the eternally attractive hot-and-chilled combinations: steaming-hot croissant with fridge-cold fromage frais, perhaps seasoned, herbed, or mixed with finely diced pungent olives; Greek yoghurt, mint and cucumber, or honey; crème fraîche and sautéed cinnamon apples. My own favourite is soft-set, low-sugar French fruit preserves with either cream, yoghurt or soft cheese.

REVIVING STALE CROISSANTS

If kept cool and sealed, croissants can be revived successfully in a hot oven – certainly well enough to frame a filling – up to three days after purchase. Pre-packed croissants will anyway need to be heated through in a moderately hot oven whichever way you plan to enjoy them. As with most breads, however, freezing while fresh is the best way of keeping a batch you cannot use up at once.

· CRUMPETS AND PIKELETS ·

Writers tend to speak of commercial crumpets and rubber in the same condemnatory breath. Elizabeth David ventured a stage further: 'Perhaps indeed they are delivered direct from a plastics recycling plant, and have never been near a bakery' (*English Bread and Yeast Cookery*). Consumers by the thousand seem not to share that suspicion: crumpets and their flatter cousins, pikelets, continue to leap off bakery shelves. But perhaps this merely testifies to our love of melted butter, for which the uniquely holey and austere crumpet (made of plain white flour, water, salt, yeast and soda) is the supreme vehicle.

HOW TO FIND A FINE CRUMPET

Home bakers maintain that commercially produced crumpets are not worth eating. Hot-off-the-griddle crumpets are certainly cheese to pre-packaged chalk – but once they are cooled and a few hours old the difference is no longer dramatic. The same applies to crumpets or pikelets produced by craft bakeries. These tend to experiment with brown flours or oatmeal for a touch of flavour but by the time their crumpets have crossed the counter they are generally as rubbery as the more commercial product.

Although there are minor variations between different brands of crumpet they all come in a standard size and all tend to be leavened by both yeast and bicarbonate of soda. All crumpets are best toasted – if the grill or fire is hot enough the surfaces will crisp and the centre soften. And the final flavour will depend more on the quality of the butter you spread on them than on the basic dough.

BUTTERED CRUMPETS AND MORE

On the subject of buttering, it is widely accepted that the smooth side is toasted first and then the holey top, which comes into contact with the butter. In *Food in England* Dorothy Hartley suggests that stale crumpets can be revived by dipping them in milk and warming them through in a hot oven before toasting. I daresay most of us won't bother switching on our ovens for this, any more than we would complicate our crumpets with toppings other than honey, syrup, or soft-set jam. They are, however, useful bases for simple savoury toppings such as scrambled egg or melted cheese.

A NOTE ON PIKELETS

Pikelets toast up a little crisper than crumpets but serve much the same purpose. Fairly flat, free-form versions of the ring-baked crumpet (the basic dough is identical), they have retained regional associations, particularly with the Pennines and Staffordshire. The name is almost certainly an anglicisation of the Welsh griddle cake known as *pyglyd* – though something very like a pikelet is confusingly known as *crempog* in Wales. Supermarket pikelets are invariably regularly ring-shaped instead of free-form.

· DAKTYLA ·

The daktyla is the armadillo of the bread world; with its ridged and speckled crust it cuts a distinctive figure on the supermarket shelf. A few years ago this Greek bread made only an occasional appearance in British shops but with the abiding popularity of Greek-style dips and our growing interest in *mezze* (Greek, Lebanese and generally Middle Eastern appetisers and snacks), the daktyla is here to stay.

As produced by Greek, Cypriot and Turkish bakers, the daktyla is a simple white or wholewheat bread with two distinctive features: the flavour and texture are enlivened by a generous sprinkling of white sesame and black nigella seeds, and the long, narrow loaves have been divided to indicate convenient sections which can be broken off easily into individual portions. Large industrialised bakeries have adapted the loaves to suit their fast-rise machinery – which means added emulsifiers, oxidators, fats, dextrose, *et al* – and are producing a much puffier, less clean-flavoured loaf. The seeds are still there, with nigella adding its distinctive, slightly peppery, somewhat medicinal-herbal note, but the bread is somehow wan and bloated. Perhaps British conservatism is partly to blame: one supermarket bakery manager told me that the best-selling daktylas were those that tried to pass themselves off as bloomers.

In the absence of the real thing, the mass-produced daktyla does at least present a contrast to pittas and flat-breads. It's worth investigating, particularly if you are having a *mezze*-style picnic or party – look out for loaves without hydrogenated oils and generally as few additives as possible. Best of all, check whether an artisan-baked loaf is available locally.

· DANISH BREAD ·

If you ask for a 'Danish' loaf in an English bakery, you will almost certainly be handed an English white flour loaf in a distinctive shape (see page 41). This has little or no connection with breads originating in Denmark or baked to Danish recipes. If you do chance upon a Danish bakery – in London or other major cities – you may find, in addition to light, white, crusty loaves sprinkled with poppy seeds, numerous light rye breads. These are free-form rather than tin baked, and fairly crusty. The rye content varies, but they all have an element of sweetness, perhaps from malt, and a rich, sweet-sour flavour; some may be scented with caraway.

The bread that most of us recognise as Danish comes in a cellophane-wrapped packet containing slices of rich, dark, compact rye. This long-life style of bread is widely distributed and you will probably find it sitting next to rather similar-looking packets of Westphalian-style German bread. The Danish version is more open textured (and thus lighter), a little paler in colour, and sweeter than its German counterpart. Like the German breads it is predominantly rye flavoured and noticeably sour, and the texture demands similar treatment: the thin slices need careful separation with a knife and once opened the bread should be stored in a cool place, if not chilled. There is usually a choice of styles available, generally based on the amount and distribution of whole grains in the dough. Whole-grain, medium-grain and seeded breads may be named as such or may bear the name of a town or area of Denmark (for example, Elsinore, Jutland, Zeeland). The names really only signify something once you come to know the range of a particular producer. Fortunately the texture is quite visible through the cellophane.

Occasionally you may come across Danish-style breads that have been produced in Holland or Germany; these are generally very similar to the genuine Danish product, with a noticeably sweet character. A number of British bakeries also make a very similar bread from an imported mix, known as Kernebrød. This is a seeded loaf (sunflower seeds and linseeds) with sweetness coming only from malted grain flour. The final result depends on the baker's input as much as on the basic mix – the Innes bakery, for instance, adds its own sourdough starter. It is an attractive bread, with a high proportion of whole or kibbled grain.

USES OF DANISH BREAD

Whether used as an open-sandwich base or simply as an accompaniment, ready-sliced dark, grainy rye bread should be generously spread with creamy butter to offset its intense flavour. Open sandwich toppings should be piled high to ensure the bread base does not overwhelm the rest. If you are sampling dark rye bread for the first time and are unwilling to commit yourself to a blanket of butter, try teaming the bread with a simple egg mayonnaise, or perhaps smoked ham and gherkin, as a starting point. The combination of sweet-sour rye with cured fish and meat, certain cheeses, or salads and pickles can be magical, and that blowsy flavour transforms bland staples such as hard-boiled egg and cold roast chicken. On the other hand it will overwhelm delicate flavours, and the Danes themselves tend to use wholemeal or white breads, or a light rye, to combine with cooked prawns or poached or smoked salmon. For more on open sandwiches, see pages 215–16.

· DEVONSHIRE SPLITS ·

See **Cornish Splits.**

· EDINBORO LOAF ·

Most customers of London's 'top people's stores' who buy this wholewheat loaf to accompany their smoked salmon no doubt do so in the conviction that both share a noble Scottish pedigree. Certainly the two products seem made for each other – the bread, like the salmon, has a distinct sweetness as well as a noticeable saltiness. It has a dense, moist crumb that enables it to be sliced thinly and the simple wholewheat flavour is not too assertive for the fish.

The Edinboro loaf is not a whit Scottish, however, but London conceived and baked. Devised by Harrods some twenty-five years ago to accompany their smoked salmon, it has since spread to other stores. I daresay its devotees remain faithful to their sloping-sided loaf (baked in a custom-designed tin) even when aware of its pedigree.

· FICELLE ·

See **Baguette.**

· FINNISH BREAD ·

Finnish crispbreads have been with us for some time, but the breads proper are only just set to make an entry into the UK, and indeed the rest of the world. It seems strange that the bread famously acknowledged as 'the most nutritious in the world' should be so little known outside its country of origin; the reason is simply that until recently Finland's small-scale producers have had little interest in increasing production outside the immediate needs of the local community.

You should soon be able to find three basic styles in specialised outlets. The first of these resembles a softened crispbread; dark, chewy, rye-based, it has a distinctive, circular shape with a central hole, which was a means of hanging the bread on rafters to dry. This is a legacy of the extraordinarily restrictive baking practices that persisted for centuries in western Finland, where baking took place just three times a year at harvest, Christmas, and in the spring, before the snows that protected the straw-thatched central bakehouse roof from going up in smoke melted in the thaw. This bread is good thickly buttered and served as an accompaniment to smoked meats, cured and smoked herring, and cheeses of all kinds, and is eaten this way at breakfast as well as at lunch or supper. Numerous 'healthy' formulae have been created, based on ancient practice: nettle bread is one of the more interesting variants.

In more modern idiom is a much softer-eating, slightly sweet and sometimes spicy, sourdough-raised rye or rye and wheat loaf. Among the most famous of these is the Swedish-named *malaxlimpa*, dating from 1906. Not unlike a malt loaf, it is sticky, slightly sour, slightly sweet, and almost spicy. A fine accompaniment to salty or smoky fish, meat and cheeses and salads of all kinds, it is also rather good on its own.

A third category of bread is based on the simple, semi-soft rye breads of southeastern Finnish or Karelian tradition, to which the closest British-baked approximation is the Russian loaf produced by the Village Bakery. Some of these are flavoured with vegetables, wild berries, even mushrooms, and can be unexpectedly delicious.

We will probably have to wait for a Finnish-style bakery to be set up in Britain before we can enjoy anything approaching the full range of barley, wheat and potato breads native to Finland; the imported rye breads, meanwhile, are well worth exploring.

· FLAVOURED BREADS ·

'Why don't we take a leaf or two out of the cookery books of [the Mediterranean countries] and turn some of our over-sweetened and too-rich dough cakes into the cheese and other savoury morsels more acceptable today?' This might be a motto pinned on the product development office wall of a hundred British bakeries. In fact the words are Elizabeth David's, issued as a challenge in her book *English Bread and Yeast Cookery* in 1977. Remarking on the monotony and sweetness of English yeast dough specialities, Mrs David asked what might happen if olive oil were substituted for the lard then in common use and savoury toppings for fruit and sugar. It has taken nigh on twenty years to come up with an answer, and it is perhaps surprising that the generally prescient Mrs David did not at once anticipate the consequence: a handful of interesting loaves that may have some future, plus a vast array of unfortunate dog's dinners.

Add olive oil to a dough suited to making teacakes and you still end up with a teacake, not a bread fit to serve with soup, cheese or salad. Add a medley of 'likely' colours and flavours – tomato purée, chilli, spinach and nutmeg, Cheddar cheese with pesto, barely cooked onions – and you end up with a battleground of flavours and textures. The number of such breads is legion, their attraction that of novelty combined with the current pervasive notion that all things Mediterranean are by definition life-enhancing. Examine the labels more closely and you will find that a good many contain a bevy of emulsifiers and improvers, those adjuncts of the fast-bake system, and a dose of hydrogenated vegetable oils in place of the considerably more expensive olive oil. While posing as wholesome, health-boosting products these breads are a con.

How many loaves in the BritMed genre, I wonder, are baked and bought on the basis of flavour rather than fashion? Not all flavours last the month, though the genre persists, and it will be interesting to see how long it takes for the poor breads to be sifted out from the sound. Meanwhile, the flavours are too myriad to chart in full – and there's one born every day. Here is a run through the major contenders.

FRUIT OR FRUIT AND NUT BREADS

For breads that maintain a link or two with traditional British teatime fare, see **Fruited Loaves**. Others are mentioned in separate categories, such as **Walnut Bread**. This still leaves a new range of fruited breads in French or American styles, and those that meld olive oil with a distinctly English style.

French-style fruit and nut breads range from wholemeal loaves with pecans and raisins, through wheat and rye loaves with fresh citrus zests to the inevitable *pain exotique* with tropical fruits and coconut. Tropical and citrus breads do not really belong in a savoury context, though citrus bread is an interesting complement to smoked and slightly oily fish. Pecan-raisin bread is an obvious partner for the cheese board (it was in fact created by Jacky Lesellier of the Bagatelle bakery specifically for Stilton). A more powerful version made with pecans and molasses is sold by cheese specialist Patricia Michelson of La Fromagerie in North London to accompany her range of Roquefort cheeses. Another loaf along similar lines – molasses, nuts and raisins – claims American pedigree (specifically Arizona) and is an excellent coffee bread.

One or two British bakeries have taken to incorporating olive oil in a basic white bread dough and adding dried apricots. These work very well as teabreads, or perhaps breakfast breads, but their cakey texture does not lend itself to savoury use – except perhaps with simple cream or curd cheeses. If you chance upon an apricot bread with a drier crumb, it should work well with chicken or pork, walnut and bacon salads, or even crumbly, salty farmhouse cheeses such as Cheshire.

HERB AND SPICE BREADS

The herb you can barely escape in any bread with Mediterranean pretensions is basil, which is allowed a star turn in its own right, both in the famously pricey Manoucher basil loaf (in which the basil tastes remarkably fresh and true) and in English breads incorporating dried basil or some form of pesto: one execrable dried basil loaf reminded me of spearmint toothpaste. Pesto rolled into a tight daktyla-style loaf, as produced by Innes, may be a tad incongruous but makes for an acceptably balanced, if undeniably rich, loaf, fine with sheep's cheese or a simple salad. Packed into a soft-textured, fluffy tin loaf, pesto is simply an unwanted intruder, the bread too flabby to act as a foil to its pungency.

Thyme, sage and rosemary also make their presence felt, but mainly in focaccia-style breads (see **Focaccie and Focaccette**) and often in combination with Cheddar or goat's and sheep's cheeses. The greatest potential problem is that of a palate-drying mustiness. Reasonably successful are French approaches to the genre: the combination of carrot and thyme has proved popular for a number of bakeries. Here the light dryness of the roll or loaf is moistened by the addition of carrot, while the sweetness of the carrot tempers the austerity and power of dried thyme. A good soup bread.

French bakeries have also come up with variations on a Provençal theme, adding garlic and/or onion along with *fines herbes* to a basic French wheaten dough; presented as soft-crusted, light-textured round rolls these are perfect for *pan bagnat*, the famous Niçois sandwich (see page 198), since they demand powerfully flavoured fillings such as anchovy, tuna, olives and oil-dressed salad.

Spices commonly in use range from sweet-scented cinnamon to lip-searing black pepper and chilli. The former tends to be an innocuous teabread, better, I feel, in puddings or simply toasted and buttered, than eaten plain. The latter style can be interesting – Innes, for instance, uses mustard seeds to add textural interest without overmuch heat – but is more likely to prove overwhelming. Best confined to a stuffing.

OLIVE BREAD

Here we have a vast array, mainly confined to ciabatta or focaccia breads, which is fine, but also found in English-style loaves, which is not. Olive-and-pesto tin loaves may be the right shape for sandwiches but they are too soft to support a cream or curd cheese and too pungent to complement most other ingredients. More successful is the Village Bakery's well-made Greek olive loaf, a light-textured but decidedly unfluffy bread flavoured with green and black olives, onions, olive oil and pumpkin seeds. This has a good flavour and texture balance and is rightly winning widespread popularity.

The French are, naturally, keeping up with the competition and using French-grown olives in crisp-crusted light-textured loaves, correctly deeming this style more acceptable to the British than the dense campagne-style olive breads popular in France.

SUN-DRIED TOMATO BREAD

Who dares *not* offer at least one token loaf flavoured with sun-dried tomatoes? Whether you are inspired by French, Swiss, German or Italian styles, or dyed-in-the-wool British, a tomato bread you must bake.

In Italy sun-dried tomatoes are essentially an *antipasto*, not a bread ingredient; yet Britain alone must have stripped Calabria bare in its efforts to feed what appears to be insatiable demand. There is no doubt that sun-dried tomatoes are massively flavourful, and partnered with bread they seem to appeal to everyone. Truth to tell, traditional or no, these breads can be very attractive.

Italian-style breads such as ciabatta, focaccia, and schiacciata carry off the tomato element to perfection. A light, simple, oil-soaked dough seems to be just what is needed to counterbalance the concentrated acidic richness of the dried tomato. Close your eyes as you bite into the majority of British tomato breads, however, and you might think you were eating a teabread – until you are delivered a saline shock. That natural inclination to soft, rich cakeiness observed by Elizabeth David simply envelops this strange new ingredient and somehow subsumes it. Cheapskate use of tomato paste does nothing to help: one supermarket example I tried might as well have been streaked with jam. An occasional example suggests that it *is* possible to make a decent, British-style loaf flavoured in an unconventional manner. Yet again, the Village Bakery scores highly with its Italian tomato loaf, well-risen, light-textured and uncakey, the sun-dried tomatoes balanced with onion and herbs (and no purée). Other bakeries have succeeded in adding a judicious amount of tomato to their cheese breads (see below). Too many, however, are baked in cynical disregard for quality and flavour.

CHEESE BREAD

Baking cheese in bread seems such a natural development of eating cheese with bread; all cultures that produce both have developed some ingenious combination. The Caucasus boasts the Georgian *khachapuri*, the Balkans *tutmanik*, the Middle East Cilician bread (see entry); North Americans add cheese to their popovers, El Salvadorians to *pupusas*. Closer to home, France and Italy offer *brioche de gannat* and *crescia di pasqua*.

What of Britain? Barley bannocks, soda breads, wholemeal baps and white bloomers all seem fair candidates for taking on farmhouse cheeses. Surprisingly, though, the proliferation of cheese breads seems to be a modern phenomenon. The crop ranges from simple white buns with a sprinkling of Cheddar on the upper crust to wholemeal loaves replete with cheese, onions and a clutch of herbs; from English-style cobs with Parmesan, oil and Provençal herbs to focaccia and schiacciata with English Cheddar. Naturally, the larger industrial bakeries are also in on the act, producing loaves in the modish BritMed genre – usually a pappy, fast-rise white loaf dosed with olive oil and marbled with English cheese and onions; maybe also Parmesan for added Italian credibility.

I must come clean and confess that the majority of these breads (even the most basic) do not appeal to me, despite their obvious popularity. The main problem is the inescapably musty aroma that hits you once the majority of cheese breads are cold – which of course is how you buy them unless you live next door to a bakery. Overwrapping exacerbates the problem and dried herbs magnify the effect dramatically. Parmesan breads I generally find both too strongly flavoured and rather too astringent.

I can, however, discern more attractive qualities, too. Hot from the oven or sliced and toasted, the wholemeal-based loaves are highly aromatic, with something of the appeal of bubbling-hot cheese. Add a simple soup and you have the impression of a rounded meal. Plain white loaves with a modest sprinkling of cheese round off a salad sandwich in terms of both flavour and nutrition. A Parmesan bread can provide a parallel balancing act to a plate of chargrilled, oil-based vegetables. Even the mass-produced rolls and loaves have an appealing aroma when heated or toasted, and that pappy texture evidently appeals to many a British palate. Interestingly enough, the problem of mustiness virtually disappears if the bread is made with a sharp sheep's cheese, such as feta or pecorino, or goat's cheese, neither of which smells stale once cooked and cooled. Two loaves merit specific mention: the Cranks' cheese bap, which prompted a spate of Cheddar loaves, and the more recent Innes cheese schiacciata. Cranks claims that it all comes down to good cheese and plenty of it. I have an idea that there is something about the moist density of their bread, which is made from a barely kneaded wholewheat dough, combined with a cheese on the mild side of powerful that tips the balance in favour of freshness. The Innes loaf, whose recipe is Canadian-Italian in inspiration, is based on sourdough, and the resulting lactic and acetic acid in the bread is high enough to combat any stale aroma that Cheddar or dried herbs might produce. A modicum of olive oil helps to maintain that impression of freshness for several days.

. . . AND THE REST

When I admitted to Andrew Whitley of the Village Bakery that I felt ambivalent about his palate-smacking wild mushroom and garlic bread he confessed that he too had mixed feelings about the drive to ever-more intriguing or exotic inventions. Which does not mean, I hasten to say, that he is not proud of the bread in question. It has a powerful wild mushroom flavour and would be a fine accompaniment to an omelette, creamy cheese, or chicken consommé.

Doubtless there will be imitators of this loaf as there have been of the same bakery's Greek olive and Italian tomato breads – and a good many will make a considerable hash of it. Third-rate imitation is annoying enough, but the real disservice done to the cause of good bread is the deflection of effort and interest away from a sound, basic loaf to unnecessary exotica. It is a waste of an expert baker's time and skill; it turns the consumer's interest away from understanding what really good bread is about; and it encourages inflated pricing of poorly conceived but flashily fashionable loaves.

A number of good bakers will probably succeed in turning the tide by acting on their convictions of what is really needed. Andrew Whitley, for instance, told me that he is working on what has yet to be achieved: a pure English Maris Widgeon loaf 'in order to bring out that wheat's celebrated flavour'. He added that 'rather than find ever-more exotic things to put in dough I would like to concentrate on creating really good *basic* breads.' Perhaps the flavours of those basic breads will really surprise us.

· FOCACCIE AND FOCACCETTE ·

At its most basic a flat, soft, dimpled, oil-rich and salt-crunchy bread, focaccia has become a great toy for bread designers, the obvious successor to flavoured ciabatta and with all the adaptability of a pizza.

THE FOCACCIA IN ITALY

As Italian cookery authority Marcella Hazan explains, focaccia is a hearth bread or *panis focacius* (Latin *focus* meaning hearth). It predates the bread oven: originally the risen dough would have been slapped on to a stone slab, flattened and covered with hot ashes. Later, the dough was shaped to fit large, round, copper baking tins, which were then placed in a wood-burning brick oven. The focaccia that spawned our current range is from Liguria, and known rather significantly elsewhere in Italy as *pizza genovese*. It is most often produced in Genoa as a simple flat sheet, its surface dimpled by finger to contain rivulets of oil. This is how many Italian delis in Britain have always presented it – a square chunk cut from the sheet and sold by weight.

Shape, thickness and baking methods engender much argument in Italy, with gastronomic congresses devoted to defining the authentic focaccia. There seems to be some consensus at least on the essential flavourings: Ligurian olive oil, coarse salt and herbs.

RECENT DEVELOPMENTS

Franco Galli, of the American Il Fornaio chain, claims Italian authenticity for the rolls known as focaccette, sprinkled with sea salt and scattered with paper-thin onion slices. These have crossed the Atlantic with varied degrees of deliciousness. A fairly plain roll with a scattering of cracked pepper and coarse salt can be pleasing and versatile. Ones enriched with olive, sun-dried tomato, and herbs tend to reflect the quality of the added ingredient – all too often unworthy of the bread dough, with a tendency to harsh astringency, or mustiness in the case of dried herbs.

Large focaccie have many incarnations. Italian delis still sell chunks of the finger-coating, tongue-curing, oil-and-salt only variety, and one or two modern bakeries are following suit, or embellishing simply (and traditionally) with a scattering of rosemary or of thinly sliced onion or garlic. Bakers with colourfully inventive tendencies are either imitating, with limited success, another transatlantic émigré, the Mediterranean sunset loaf (see entry), drenched in oil and packed with sun-dried tomatoes, olives and herbs, or, spurred on by supermarket buyers, they are dressing up the focaccia as a pizza in every conceivable incarnation, from a simple, smooth-surfaced round to an all-singing, all-dancing assembly with roasted vegetables, mushrooms, peperoni, cheese and herbs. Not entirely without Italian precedent (remember the *pizza genovese*), these should, however, be more honestly labelled as pizza.

Finally, a few British bakeries are making what can only be termed a British focaccia (though even this, I am told, has a Canadian precedent) composed of English flour leavened by a traditional British sourdough, oiled and herbed with subtlety – and resembling nothing so much as a herbed ciabatta.

BUYING FOCACCIA

With such a variety of styles and fast-food availability (more focaccie sit shoulder-rubbing pizzas in cold cabinets and freezers nowadays than are sold on fresh bread shelves) it all comes down to a matter of personal preference. For my money, the finest are the most versatile, the oil-dimpled chunks or rounds sprinkled with salt and maybe pepper that you can nibble while shopping, or while relaxing with a glass of *aperitivo* wine, or alongside a platter of *antipasti*. Herb-sprinkling may be just as traditional but it is all too often unthinkingly executed in Britain, with a palate-assaulting quantity of dry and dusty herb destroying any fresh bread flavour. One or two well-constructed examples do exist, but you will need to search hard and trust your palate rather than fashion. A number of the pizza look-alikes are undoubtedly delicious – my own favourites make much use of grilled vegetables and are most likely to be found in supermarkets. Here you have a wide and reasonably happy hunting ground.

USES OF FOCACCIE

The plain focaccia is undoubtedly versatile but it is wise to choose accompaniments with a lowish salt content. Accompaniments can, of course, equally well be fillings. Flavoured focaccette make perfect sandwich rolls when filled with simple, fresh, low-salt ingredients such as buffalo mozzarella and ripe tomato, roasted or bottled chargrilled vegetables, or just fresh, crunchy salad leaves dressed with good olive oil and lemon juice. The same goes for split chunks or wedges of plainer focaccia, though here you might add judicious amounts of more assertive ingredients – fennel, salami, grilled tuna, Gorgonzola, and so on. Focaccia also adds interest to simple sandwich fillings from egg and salad to roast chicken.

Plain, salt-sprinkled focaccie are rather delicious crisped up in a hot oven, though this alters their original character somewhat; filled with warm or even room-temperature grilled vegetables they make the most delicious of Mediterranean-style sandwiches. Truth to tell, Italian methods of reheating the bread alter its character even more dramatically: the focaccia is split, filled, and sandwiched between cast-iron griddles or pans while reheating – a heavy-handed, but effective equivalent of the sandwich toaster.

· FRENCH STICK ·

See **Baguette**.

· FRUIT AND NUT BREADS ·

See **Flavoured Breads**.

· FRUITED LOAVES ·

A fruit, or tea, loaf can be as delightful or dull as any basic white or brown bread. A good number taste so undistinguished that their bread-based origins are far from obvious, and a historical reminder might be in order. Dorothy Hartley noted that 'the farmhouse cook usually keeps one small piece of dough separate, and adds eggs, sugar, spice and fruit and makes a bunloaf – or currant loaf – for tea. The Barra Brieth [sic] of Wales is this type of loaf, so is the Yorkshire tea bread, also the saffron cake of Devon, and the London currant loaf. In all its forms (and it can become an elaborate yeast cake) it is the family dough which the cook has glorified.'

MODERN VARIETIES OF FRUITED BREAD

The baking tradition described by Dorothy Hartley is pretty well lost, and with it a magnificent variety of fruited loaves and buns. Those that have survived commercially as classics of their kind, from bara brith to saffron cake, have separate entries in this book. Forays along supermarket shelves will reveal a collection of both lightly and richly fruited British loaves but unfortunately these tend to contain the usual battery of emulsifiers, improvers, and hydrogenated oils in place of butter.

Good fruited loaves made in the tradition of adding embellishments to the basic bread dough can still be found, however, produced by those small specialist bakeries that concern themselves with organic or additive-free bread, and by others that pride themselves on their intrinsic baking skills. The most purist of these (generally wholegrain organic) can seem rather austere, particularly when spice is added in the absence of sugar. Wholemeal loaves that avoid spicing are generally more successful, with an attractive balance of nuttiness and slightly sweet fruit. Lighter fruit breads can be just as delicious, and arguably sit more easily with a cup of China tea: the tea loaf from Yorkshire or elsewhere is a prime example. Basically a soft-crusted, white flour loaf with currants added, not necessarily enriched or sweetened, this really is as good or as bad as the bakery and the basic dough.

A number of craft bakeries go beyond a white-loaf-with-vine fruits basic to produce interesting variations with crushed nuts and raisins, sesame and sultana, cinnamon-raisin, apricot and walnut, to name just a few. These can be as good with fresh, crumbly, salty cheeses as toasted and buttered, or spread with jam for tea. Others begin to straddle the French tradition, producing something akin to a *pain aux noix et raisins*, wonderful with cheeses or simply with butter but less suited to strawberry jam.

French bakeries proper and some English bakeries produce fruited brioche, and in their espousal of butter-enriched dough these are actually quite close to the English currant loaves of old. Other

Continental traditions that have woven their way into the British repertoire are less close to English tradition but unarguably good to eat. German-influenced bakeries produce fruited multigrain loaves, or muesli breads, which can be rich, moist and delicious. The Anglo-Italian fruit and nut ciabatta has much to recommend it – though probably more as a complement to cheese than as a teabread. A number of American-influenced breads are claiming shelf-space in supermarkets; these range from stollen-style richly fruited confections to pre-sliced cinnamon-raisin breakfast loaves.

Despite all these examples of excellence from directions old and new, good fruited loaves in the English tradition are considerably more scarce than either fashionably exotic breads or the indifferent, poorly constructed and uniformly flavoured travesties that hide under the blanket term of fruit loaf. But they do exist, and deserve as much attention as a baguette or focaccia – once again it is a matter of seeking out and supporting the skilled bakers who maintain a tradition of excellence.

· GERMAN BREAD ·

With 200 basic styles of bread and some 1,200 rolls and *Kleingebäck* (what British bakers term morning goods), Germany probably outstrips all its European neighbours when it comes to variety, and is certainly equal to the best in terms of quality. Yet most British consumers' experience of German breads begins and ends with square packets of compact, palate-challenging dark rye.

Perhaps the trouble lies with the uninspiring nature of too many German food imports; unfairly or no, our perception of German cuisine is one of unsubtle stolidity. Fortunately the last year or two has seen considerably wider distribution of British-baked German-style loaves of remarkable diversity, even though, by and large, they are not labelled as German bread.

Basically, there are three categories of German bread available in the UK: imported loaves (the plastic-wrapped 'box' breads); loaves made from an imported flour mix and perhaps a sourdough starter, too; and ones baked from scratch by British bakeries, whether under German or British ownership.

KASTENBROT (BOX BREAD)

This unique style of bread is steam-baked in an enclosed tin for about twenty hours and emerges dark, moist and chewy, with a texture that is at once compact and resilient yet crumbly. Flour mixes vary, but all are produced by sourdough fermentation and contain a proportion of rye, usually in the form of whole, soft grains. The basic flavour is sour and savoury but with a sweet, if unsugary, edge. Kastenbrot is invariably sold thinly sliced in compact, plastic-wrapped packages. Where a supermarket sells a single style of compact German bread it is likely to be of a medium weight, but still predominantly rye based, and heavier than Danish or Swedish styles in the same range.

Numerous brands of kastenbrot are available; here is a brief guide to the more popular names, in order of rye content and weightiness.

Pumpernickel is undoubtedly the darkest and coarsest (though by no means dry or husky) of the lot, with a high whole grain content. It is almost always made entirely from rye grain and thus is suitable for anyone with a wheat allergy (always check the label, however). Also available as miniature pumpernickel rounds, sold in slim rolls for canapé use.

Schwarzbrot and **Vollkornbrot** are similarly assertive. Schwarz-brot simply means black bread and vollkornbrot wholemeal bread. When sold as box bread, both are likely to be composed entirely of rye grains and coarsely milled rye flour. Schwarzbrot will be darker, usually due to the use of molasses, which also gives it a richer flavour than the Vollkornbrot.

Roggenbrot simply means rye bread, but paradoxically the box bread style of Roggenbrot may also contain some wheat. Some loaves contain linseeds but should then be termed Leinsamenbrot.

Sonnenblumenbrot is still predominantly rye based, but contains sunflower seeds too, which give it some crunch; **Katenbrot**, another sunflower-seeded bread, may have a higher wheat content and a slightly lighter texture.

Fünfkornbrot, as the name suggests, is composed of five different grains, and may also contain seeds. **Kraftbrot** or **Weisenkeimbrot** contains wheatgerm (as well as rye); **Grahamsbrot**, made from an American flour mix, is mainly wheat with some rye. Recent developments for a health-conscious market include **Mueslibrot**, particularly good toasted, and **Fitnessbrot** with a high wheatgerm and oat content.

Landbrot stands slightly apart from the rest and is a good introduction to the range if you want to start at the lighter end of things. You will often find it sold as pain de campagne or Westphalian farm bread. As well as being much lighter than its companions, this bread is smoother textured and usually has a high wheat content. I would happily match it with frankfurters or bockwurst as well as more powerful sausages, or serve it at dinner.

All these sturdy, sour breads seem designed to accompany smoked and cured meat – from simple hams to composite sausages or aspic moulds – smoked or pickled fish, Swiss-style cheeses with their assertive sweetness, or buttery Danish and Dutch cheese scented with caraway. They are also perhaps the only breads truly happy in the company of low-fat, chalkily acidic Quark (or very-low fat fromage frais). In common with all rye breads, they are fit for almost anything once spread with a good layer of cream cheese or unsalted butter.

Most box breads have a long shelf life but need to be eaten within a few days once the packet is opened. Dry breads can be used in a number of soups and some of the Scandinavian-style dishes – even desserts, such as layered apple puddings. It is better for the balance of the dish to use breads at the lighter end of the spectrum.

KRUSTENBROT (CRUSTY BREAD)

A good number of the kastenbrot names also appear in krustenbrot guise. These are more conventional loaves, baked free-form on an oven shelf or floor. They might be available in the UK under the original German name or a translation; I have tried to use the most usual name in the following list of the major players.

Landbrot is perhaps the lightest of these loaves, with a high proportion of white wheat flour, and may have buttermilk added for an even lighter, richer texture. Its slight sourness and soft, smooth crumb make for an easy-eating, versatile loaf that will complement just about any food, with the slight acidity adding interest to bland or creamy soups and cheeses.

Bauernbrot is also sold as country or farmhouse bread but the examples you are most likely to come across are heavier than the Landbrot, with the rye more dominant.

Roggenbrot, perhaps the most established of these part-wheat, part-rye breads, is lighter than the Bauernbrot and less moist than the Landbrot – another good all-rounder.

Most German multigrain or seeded breads are also based on a fairly light mix of flours; you might come across **German sunflower**, **Mehrkorn** (literally, 'more grain') or **Goldgrain** which also comes in a walnut-added version. These multigrain breads are likely to be pre-mixes imported from Germany, but are none the worse for that. In some instances bakers add their own sourdough starter to give the bread extra character. In common with other multigrain breads (see entry), they are best with soups, salads and fairly mild cheese.

In the ultra health-conscious pre-mix league are **Marathon bread**, a power-packed but light muesli bread, and a herb bread (sold as herb and mint or herb with rye) containing club moss, nettle leaves, coriander, camomile flowers, parsley, balm leaves, hawthorn leaves, horsetail, basil, bean pods, dill tips and peppermint leaves. This may sound like the fantasy of a mad baker drunk on a cocktail of tisanes, but tastes surprisingly good, particularly with vegetable soup.

Zwiebelbrot or onion bread, with its sour-sweet flavours of rye and malt, is excellent with (or in) soup, meats and cheeses of all kinds, and particularly good toasted with melted cheese.

Of the 100 per cent rye loaves available on a fairly wide basis, Kolos bakery's Bavarian loaf is a weighty brick for the fully converted – to my mind more East European than Germanic in style. Supermarkets countrywide sell an oval loaf baked by Bakoven. This is characterised by ridges imprinted by proving baskets and by a sprinkling of whole grains. Very different in style from the Bavarian bread, it is very fine-textured, moist, and with a sour note quite distinct from Russian-style ryes.

The loaf I would recommend as an introduction to the finest aspects of German-style bread is a rye-wheat loaf with a very fine, smooth, grain-free texture, gentle sourness and a remarkable degree of moistness. Its gentle rye flavour will not overwhelm any food apart from the most delicate of creams or mousses. This is baked by Bakoven and is most often sold simply as German rye bread. You will recognise it by its square (not rectangular) shape, and cross-hatched upper crust.

Most of these breads are good keepers, thanks largely to their sourdough content. If you want to use them in recipes calling for stale bread it is sometimes better to slice and dry them in a low oven rather than wait around for a few days. Most are suitable for recipes calling for rye or sourdough breads; do, however, avoid any breads containing whole, hard grains, as these do not grind down properly and will not disintegrate on soaking.

· GLUTEN-FREE BREAD ·

Gluten is a stretchy substance formed when certain grain proteins link up after the flour is mixed with water and agitated by kneading. Of all the grains, wheat has the highest potential gluten content and is the prime substance to be avoided by anyone who suffers from gluten intolerance. Those with only slight sensitivity may be able to enjoy 100 per cent rye breads, oatcakes and buckwheat pancakes, as the gluten content of rye, oats and buckwheat is very low. The majority, however, need to restrict their consumption of baked goods to those made from rice, tapioca, chickpea and maize flours, all gluten-free.

A number of companies produce gluten-free loaves. These fall into three basic categories, all of which, alas, bear a somewhat spurious resemblance to leavened bread as most of us know it. Judging by the comments I have come across from sufferers of coeliac disease (as gluten intolerance is known), most are unhappy with the products on the market and may be better off baking their own bread from the gluten-free flours available. Commercially made gluten-free breads are not entirely unpalatable, however, and the various types deserve a closer look.

SOURDOUGH LOAVES

These are generally based on maize and rice flours, with added grains or seeds to give textural interest. The pronounced sourdough aroma blends quite attractively with that of maize, which dominates all these breads, and the total effect is not unlike tinned sweetcorn dressed in yoghurt. The compact texture is quite challenging but this undergoes a dramatic change on toasting. Heated through, the breads release an almost overwhelming, but not entirely unpleasant, aroma of friar's balsam, and become very moist and somewhat crumbly.

Sourdough gluten-free loaves are available from wholefood shops both freshly-baked and long-life, the latter wrapped in gas-flush packaging. The difference between the two styles is less marked than is the case with loaves made from gluten-rich flours, as they are both essentially heavy, compact and firm yet moist in texture.

WHEAT-BASED LOAVES

These are designed to resemble thickly sliced sandwich loaves as closely as possible – an important consideration for children's packed lunches. Made from gluten-free wheat starch and whey powder, they are raised by a number of agents, including yeast. They include, of necessity, various stabilisers and preservatives and, in common with all British white bread, are reinforced with vitamins and minerals.

The bread emerges from its gas-flushed packaging with the rigid, stale feel of a week-old loaf but once it is heated it becomes soft and moist, if somewhat rubbery, and stays that way for a couple of days. The flavour comes closest to that of real bread, perhaps a sourdough bread, though the aroma is disappointingly cellulose-vegetal. Butter and jam help matters considerably. Cooking limitations are identical to those for hypoallergenic bread, described below.

HYPOALLERGENIC BREADS

These tend to be not only gluten free, but wheat, yeast, soya, milk and egg free, too, and are generally based on either tapioca or rice. Invariably wrapped in heavy, gas-impermeable packaging containing sachets of oxygen-absorbing crystals, they resemble a plain white wheaten loaf. Aroma and texture, however, immediately bear witness to the complex processes that have produced this extraordinary foodstuff. We might joke about mass-produced white bread resembling styrofoam but nothing could come closer than this. The aroma – oddly for a yeast-free loaf – is of mushrooms, the texture unrelievedly dry and the flavour mostly marked by its absence. Toasting, however, results in a dramatic improvement once again and the bread becomes soft and moist in the centre, if still rather bland in flavour.

There is little to choose between the hypoallergenic breads produced by different manufacturers. Any of them are a better choice at breakfast or teatime, with marmalade or jam, than the vegetal sourdough loaves, even though the latter bear more resemblance to real food. They make very fine crumbs which can be used for coating and for gratins and will also fry and crisp fairly successfully. While the bread absorbs liquids readily, the crumb tends to disintegrate and form a floury paste, so avoid recipes that rely on moistened crumbs.

· GRANARY BREAD ·

As a life-long seeker-out of good granary bread I was both surprised and disappointed to discover that granary meal is a proprietary mix (from Rank Hovis McDougall) and that all bakers are supplied with the same formula. I have traced a number of my favourite loaves to their sources and asked the bakers if they really are using the same mix as everyone else. Invariably the answer has been in the affirmative – the extra ingredient is their skill, which owes little to fast-rise machinery. Some use a 'sponge and dough' overnight fermentation, while a very few subject the mix to sourdough.

Granary meal is a mixture of fine wheatmeal, rye flour and malted grain. A wholemeal granary, also created by Rank Hovis McDougall, has recently joined the old-established white flour base. The malting gives the loaf its very specific aroma and flavour, plus a certain natural sweetness. It also contributes to a certain stickiness of texture, the degree of which varies from baker to baker. This combination is as popular with children as with adults and a good argument against the belief that they would eat nothing but fluffy white if given a free hand.

BUYING GRANARY BREAD

So, how do you find your ideal granary loaf? Its appearance gives little clue to its contents; some have glazed, shiny, crackly crusts, others matt and floury ones. Loaves come in large or small rounds, or in tin shapes, sticks, and, of course, as plastic-wrapped, pre-sliced packs; and there are as many shapes and sizes of rolls as of larger loaves. Just about all the unwrapped examples have the mien of a British 'country' loaf, a built-in buy-me factor. No telling if they will be moist and malty, or light and easy; salty, sweet, or even sour. The only thing to do is buy your loaf and see. Once you have decided which you prefer (my own favourites tend to be moist, on the dense side of airy, and not over-salty), try and discover the source, or at least note the supplier, and stay with them. And if you already knew that all granary loaves are made with the same meal and haven't bothered trying different examples I recommend you do so; the variations are little short of startling.

USES OF GRANARY BREAD

Delicious on its own, granary is the bread *par excellence* for a plough-man's lunch or sandwich – if only because we associate it with

granaries and harvests. My own preference is for sandwiches with mashed avocado or butter-fried flat mushrooms; best of all is granary toast coated with bitter marmalade. I rarely use stale granary bread in cooking, simply because I find the grains intrusive, but you could of course make a granary bread-and-butter pudding. Crumbs, as you might expect, turn out lumpy and grainy rather than fine, but you could use this to good effect in a gratin.

· GREEK BREAD ·

The basic, everyday loaf baked in Britain for Greek communities is large, round and two-tiered, like a floppy hat. It is markedly crusty and usually has a slight olive oil content, and occasionally a scattering of sesame or poppy seeds. Supermarket shoppers might be surprised to learn that Greek bakeries sell more of this basic loaf than the distinctive daktyla or even the ubiquitous pitta (see entries). Try one and you will find that this generally well-made, satisfyingly crusty bread is an excellent mopper-up of oil-rich dips, grilled vegetables and casseroles, which are often mistakenly teamed with dominatingly oiled and flavoured Mediterranean-style breads. I find, too, that the crumb is excellent in virtually all recipes that call for stale white bread as it has a good, light, structure and is neither too salty nor intrusively oily.

Greek bakeries often produce sweet festive breads such as the Easter *tsoureki*, a round or oval spiral featuring a hard boiled egg in the centre with a bright red shell. I have also come across plaited sweet breads scented with bitter orange zest and orange flower water, not unlike a chollah (see entry). A delicious accompaniment to sweet, black coffee (or dipped into it) these make a good base for bread puddings.

Look out, too, for freshly made sesame-coated bread sticks (see entry), crisper, crumblier and altogether more delicious than the boxed sticks on offer at most supermarkets.

· GRISSINI ·

See **Bread Sticks**.

· GUERNSEY GACHE ·

Two very different breads claim the honour of being the true gache. Unsurprisingly, one is French in origin, the other British. Neither is as yet widely distributed in mainland Britain but I daresay the British variant will appear in supermarkets in the wake of the current interest in regional breads and buns.

While the French loaf is brioche-like, lightly spiced and has raw apples mixed into the dough, the British gache is fruited and unspiced, enriched with Guernsey milk and butter. Unfortunately, commercial versions of the British bread are indistinguishable from the general run of mass-produced fruit loaves. Properly buttery, well-made loaves are produced on a small scale by bakers on the island, but none are at present equipped to supply major chains. Let us hope that commercial traducements do not win the supermarket race.

· HOT CROSS AND SPICED BUNS ·

Like Christmas decorations, commercial hot cross buns appear in the shops months before the event. Worse, they are barely distinguishable from the glossy, overblown spiced buns that sit fatly on supermarket shelves all year round.

Historically, hot cross buns and spiced buns do share the same basic recipe, with the former distinguished only by the cross cut or pasted on to the upper crust at Easter. What did distinguish both styles from other breads and buns was the use of once-costly spices – sheer economics restricted their sale to times of indulgent festivity.

Traditional spiced buns, with or without a cross, should be quite compact and light, moist, enriched with milk, a little butter and egg, lightly or richly fruited (once by currants alone but now by a mixture of dried fruits) and judiciously spiced. They should be delightful eaten plain on the day of baking, or split, toasted and buttered for up to three days thereafter. In short, they should be a rich, high-quality festive treat.

HISTORY AND SIGNIFICANCE OF SPICED AND CROSSED BUNS

Restricting the sale of treats has always proved difficult. A decree published in 1592 by the Clerk of the Markets asserting that no bakers must sell spiced breads 'except it be at burials, or on Friday before Easter, or at Christmas' was being roundly flouted by the time of James I and has been ever since.

Something we learn from the edict is that spiced 'Lenten bunnes' have been with us for several centuries. As with a good many Easter customs, the crossed bun preceded Christianity, appearing at pre-Christian Greek and Roman festivals. The round bun shape, perhaps already glazed and golden, represented the sun, and the division of the circle into four could be said to represent the sun's passage through the four seasons of the year. Pagan-worshipping Saxons celebrated the feast of Eostre, goddess of Spring, with crossed Eostre bread, signifying the year's rebirth. The Christian calendar naturally exerted its influence in due course, and Good Friday baking became endowed with mystical or medicinal properties. Fishermen took Good Friday buns to sea with them, while housewives preserved them to ward off illness.

THE PROBLEM WITH COMMERCIAL SPICED BUNS

Chemically engineered moist puffiness is irritation enough, but the truly offensive feature of most commercial buns is their aggresive spicing. In the case of wholemeal buns, the overblown spicing has a particularly drying effect on the palate. While this can be softened by generous application of butter it surely should not be necessary to butter an already enriched bun to render it palatable.

Blame can generally be laid at the door of liquid spice, which has many seductive advantages for a baker: it is easily distributed through-out the dough, it does not mark the bread with dubious speckles, it is more reliably consistent in its effect, and it can be added at the last minute – spices restrict the rising action of yeast. Even more impor-tantly, strength of flavour does not necessarily spell higher costs.

BUYING HOT CROSS AND SPICED BUNS

Avoiding factory-baked buns may be a partial solution; unfortunately slips of hand or judgement can occur in the use of ground spice as well as liquid, and in buns of the soundest craft-bakery pedigree. Much depends on your personal expectations, of course – whether butter content is important to you, for instance, or whether you relish these buns for their spiciness rather than the flavour of wheat or fruit. Once you have established your personal preference you should refuse to settle for anything less.

· HERB BREAD ·

See **Flavoured Breads**.

· HOVIS ·

British television viewers could be forgiven for believing that the roads of Pennine villages were once cobbled with Hovis loaves: or at any rate that Hovis was, and still is, the epitome of the good old-fashioned loaf we dimly remember and hope to find again.

Its genealogy is certainly interesting. Hovis was probably the first patented flour mix created in reaction to roller-milled flour, which threw out the wheatgerm along with the bran. The 1880s consumer had little doubt that bran was undesirable, but there was certainly something missing from the flavour of the newly emerging loaves. A certain Richard 'Stoney' Smith worked out that the way to replace the flavourful germ without its attendant problems of rancidity was to process it by steaming and then stabilise it further by salting. The salted, steamed wheatgerm was then mixed with the roller-milled white meal.

In truly modern style a competition was held to decide on a name for the innovative flour mix, and won by a student named Herbert Grime, who hit upon a snappy foreshortening of the Latin *hominis vis* – the life of man. It was widely understood that the vitality of the grain lay in the germ; Fittons of Cheshire, the first manufacturers of Hovis flour, proudly declared that the 'World's Best Bread' contained 'no chemicals or anything but the best of the wheat grain, without the bran or other waste products'. Not a claim that would hold good today. Hovis has billowed to match the size of other emulsifier- and improver-boosted loaves, and it has been joined by a tribe of pre-sliced, overwrapped travesties, from white to wholemeal to the inevitable 'country grain' (back to bran with a vengeance!). Rank Hovis McDougall, the current millers, do produce something very akin to the original flour alongside the modern mixes. Cheeringly, as with granary bread, it is still possible to find small bakeries producing a well-crafted loaf with an attractive flavour and texture. You might even come across the miniature loaves, distinctively emblazoned with the Hovis name, that I recall excavating and filling with strange mixtures during my Lancashire childhood.

· INNES ·

Innes has come to symbolise Britain's answer to the French Poilâne loaf (see **Pain Poilâne**). Both are hefty, 2kg/4½lb cartwheels of chewy, organic wheat bread leavened by a natural sourdough and baked in wood-fired French ovens; but in the case of the Innes loaf the oven is situated in Staffordshire, not Paris.

The Innes bakery produces an ever-growing range of carefully crafted breads with sound pedigree but its most famous product is the original brown sourdough bread, known to aficionados simply as Innes original. This must take longer to make than any other loaf baked in Britain. The dough relies entirely on airborne yeasts and active enzymes for leavening; only purified water and sea salt are added to the flour, which is milled from English wheat using French crystal burr stones. Following a five-day rise the dough is divided and moulded – the original shape in a wicker basket, smaller loaves in tins – to undergo a final rise. The loaves are then consigned to the

200-year-old wood-fired igloo-shaped stone oven, bought in France and reconstructed by the owner, Hugh Lillingston. After a lengthy bake the loaves are rested for a considerable period – twelve hours in the case of the cartwheel loaf – before being wrapped and despatched. Thereafter they have a life of around ten days, developing in flavour as a result of still-active sourdough cultures.

Both crust and crumb are quite smoky in flavour, and distinctly sour, particularly when a few days old. The larger loaf has a deeper, more complex flavour than the smaller versions but it is none the less more gentle than a rye-based sourdough, making this bread a more versatile accompaniment to English foods.

COMPLEMENTARY FOODS

Hugh himself produces one of the finest accompaniments to his bread – an unpasteurised hand-made goat's cheese, perfect for spreading on thinly sliced sourdough when fresh and soft but also wonderful as mature *crottins*, sliced, grilled and served molten-edged on toasted Innes. The bread is equally at home with other British, Irish, and not a few French cheeses, and indeed any foods that are either creamily bland or, at the other end of the scale, sufficiently assertive to stand up to the smoky sourdough.

To accommodate British palates the company has developed a light sourdough loaf, which takes the original soured dough and leavens it further with a little fresh yeast. The new loaf is then baked for a shorter period in an electric oven. It is certainly easier to make sandwiches with this light-textured bread but, eaten by itself, I find it considerably less satisfying than the heavyweight original. It does toast rather better and is probably a wiser breakfast option, near-perfect when spread with a tawny marmalade.

· IRISH BREAD ·

See **Soda Bread**

· ITALIAN BREAD ·

This entry is devoted to the unnamed, crusty loaf you are likely to pick up at your local Italian deli. For ciabatta, focaccia and other Italian breads, see individual entries.

As ever, loaves vary from baker to baker, and the large industrial bakeries that supply many delis tend to produce unsatisfying bread.

Nevertheless, simple, well-made, chewy white loaves can be found in Italian delis and good Continental bakeries the length and breadth of Britain. Seduced by pesto swirls, tomato chunks and libations of olive oil, we tend to forget how admirably plainer, oil-free loaves soak up dressings, marinades and sauces. The breads of the Mediterranean, as of the Middle East, are often designed to soften the impact of oil, spice, salt and rich assemblies of ingredients rather than supply a riot of flavour themselves. For this, a plain, generally wheaten, bread is of the essence, whether it be close-textured and reasonably impervious to oil or absorbent and with a thick crust.

BUYING ITALIAN BREAD

A somewhat irregular, rough-hewn crust on a loaf that seems neither featherlight nor brick-heavy is what I look for, although these features do not necessarily guarantee good flavour. As we know already from the hugely popular British-made ciabatta, not all outstandingly good Italian-style breads are shaped by the hand of an Italian baker. One particularly crusty, chewy, almost sweet-flavoured loaf is produced by a Polish bakery in Manchester, while Philip Jackson of the Star Continental Bakery in Glasgow is famed for a brick-oven-baked Italian loaf long declared inimitable by members of Glasgow's Casa di Italia club. Don't hesitate to explore beyond the obvious, and above all, do give plain breads a chance to shine as an accompaniment to oil-rich foods.

· KUGELHOPF ·
(koughloff, gugelhupf)

This rich, yeasted festive bread is a speciality of Alsace but is equally popular in Germany and Austria – most famously Vienna – and is finally making welcome inroads into the UK. Although there are many variations, the key to its unique appeal is a combination of the lightest possible texture with considerable richness derived from butter and eggs, and of sweetness offset by the refreshing acidity of vine fruit and lemon zest.

Instantly recognisable by its shape, kugelhopf is traditionally baked in a deep, fluted mould with a funnel in the centre. Lamb and fish moulds take over at Easter time in Alsace but the bread you buy in Britain will almost certainly be fluted. It is still rather scarce but one reason I include it here is that the *koughloff* produced by the Bagatelle bakery in London (and currently distributed to specialist outlets in

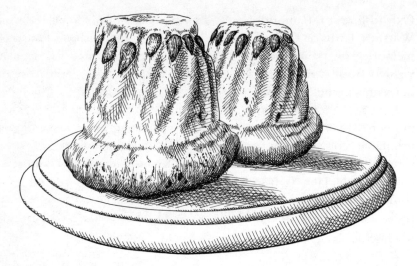

the capital) is the equal of the finest I have tasted in Strasbourg, and indeed better than most. I trust distribution will soon grow wider. If you live near a French, German or Austrian bakery it may well be worth enquiring whether they produce a kugelhopf, as it does often feature in the repertoire of such bakeries on festive occasions.

USES OF KUGELHOPF

Fresh kugelhopf is a delight served plain with a cup of coffee, though you could also treat it as a dessert accompanied by soft or poached fruit and chantilly cream. Lighter styles of the bread will stale within a day or two but butter-rich ones will keep for a number of days if wrapped in foil and stored in a cool place. If you have an entire bread left over, or a number of smaller ones, you can turn them into baba-style desserts by warming the foil-wrapped bread in a low oven, then soaking it in hot kirsch or rum-laced syrup (you could use light syrup from a jar of bottled fruit). Fill the central hollow with fruit and/or whipped cream when cool. Stale slices can be toasted – butter first if the bread is a light one – and served with fruit compote, or turned into a bread pudding.

· LARDY CAKE ·

These round, flat, sticky-topped loaves have somehow retained more individual character than most other British fruit buns. This may be due to regional pride: the use of lard in baking was popular in pig-farming country, roughly defined as the area from Wiltshire, through

Oxfordshire to Cambridge – hence the occasional appellation of Wiltshire lardy or Oxford lardy. There again, my husband has fond memories of Hampshire lardy cake, Harrods procures its popular version from Dorset, and I encountered 'dough cake', similar in all but name, in the North of England.

I suspect the survival of lardy cake in all its calorific glory has more to do with the dietary terrors that prevent it becoming a profitable commercial proposition: refined flour, white sugar or syrup and, the ultimate *bête noire*, lard. I doubt many of us would dare concur with Jane Grigson's pronouncement that 'no tea table is complete without it after a winter's walk', but would sympathise instead with Elizabeth David: 'Every lardy cake should carry a health warning.'

Those very same qualities render a well-made lardy cake almost irresistibly appealing. Try it warm (it reheats well in a moderately hot oven), with the crust crunchy, the sugar part caramelised, the dough soft as down, yet flaky, the acidity of the fruit cutting through the sweetness, the pronounced aroma of lard mingling with that of the wheat – and you may feel personally bound to ensure its survival.

There are two main qualities to look for in a lardy cake: the lard (it should *not* be vegetable fat) should taste clean and leave little after-taste, even while enriching the dough noticeably; and an overall lightness should almost mask that richness. Beyond that, the balance of sweetness, fruit, spice (if used), and rich dough should not be cloying. Baking a well-balanced lardy cake is a good test of a baker's skill and deserves recognition. Keep up the winter walks.

· LAVASH ·

Much less familiar to most of us than pitta bread, lavash, or markouk, is perhaps the most widely eaten bread in the Middle East and also the most ancient. Thin, brittle and somewhat crisp, it is traditionally baked in a clay oven or on a *saj*, an open-air dome-covered oven fired by wood chippings and camel dung. Commercially available lavash carries no hint of camel dung (nor, sadly, of wood smoke) and is most likely to have been baked on the factory equivalent of a griddle pan. Nor is the bread crisp, though it becomes brittle on exposure to the air. It is, however, both versatile and good to eat.

Like pitta, lavash comes in both white and wholemeal versions. Unfolded from their air-flushed packets, the breads form 60cm/2 foot rounds but are designed to be torn into rag-like pieces and used to pick up chunks of roast meat, stew or salad. The bread can be warmed, either under the grill, in the oven, or even in the microwave (folded!); dampen it if you do not want it to crisp overmuch or if it seems at all dry and stale. It will heat through in moments.

USES OF LAVASH

Lavash makes a good sandwich, or at any rate a parcel: simply roll a piece of the bread round your chosen filling, ensuring you end up with two or three layers of bread. As the flavour of the bread is fairly neutral, just about any filling will be fine. Similarly, you can make a parcel designed for serving hot – think of the lavash as a kind of pancake, and wrap moist fillings securely. Cover with foil and warm through in the oven, or coat in a sauce and sprinkle the surface with crisp crumbs or cheese, before baking in an uncovered dish.

Given the generous dimensions of lavash, you can afford to think expansively: use it to wrap freshly cooked picnic foods, perhaps an entire roasted chicken (you might need two breads for safety). The bread will absorb the juices and make a good accompaniment for the bird. Or fold your lavash towel-like under a barbecued joint both before and after carving; once again, the juice-soaked morsels of bread should prove as delicious as the meat. Tear off pieces of unsoaked bread to hold chunks of grilled meat, fish or vegetables.

Finally, a tip for the cook: lavash makes a better 'tent' to place over a resting bird or joint of meat than does the customary foil, which encourages condensation that softens crisp skin or crackling – the bread absorbs some of this steam. Admittedly, it may just collapse on to the roast, but even this is an advantage: you can at least eat the lavash afterwards.

· LINCOLNSHIRE PLUM BREAD ·

Plum bread has become as ubiquitous as any fruit loaf yet remains linked with the county of Lincolnshire. Unfortunately the name is no more a guarantee of finesse than that of Cheddar attached to cheese.

All too often, plum breads are barely differentiated from fruited loaves. The following definition is based on what is widely considered to be the finest example of a Lincolnshire plum loaf, that baked by Derek Myers at his shop in Horncastle. This soft, brown-crusted loaf is rich, moist and aromatic – none too dense, nor fluffed up and rapidly staling through the use of emulsifiers. That richness may well come from a blend of fats but these should not have a pronounced aroma, nor an assertive flavour. The crumb should be an attractive shade of brown, from light spicing and the possible use of brown sugar. Above all, the fruiting should be rich and moist, and should help preserve the bread for a good few days after baking.

Interestingly enough, a number of loaves termed simply 'plum loaf' in deference to their non-Lincolnshire origin, bear a fair resemblance to the ideal, while supermarket-distributed examples unequivocally described as Lincolnshire loaves do not come close.

Like a rich fruit cake, Lincolnshire plum bread needs no buttering to accompany a cup of tea or coffee; it is, however, happy in the company of salted English butter or, as Derek Myers suggests, a wedge of sharp farm-made cheese.

· MAIZE BREAD ·

See **Cornmeal Bread**.

· MALTED GRAIN BREAD ·

Similar in appearance to granary bread (see entry) and often barely distinguishable in flavour and texture, malted grain breads are in fact a little more varied. Some are based on a proprietary mix similar to granary and in these instances the name of the loaf should reflect that of the mix – malted crunch, for example. Others, however, are products of small specialist bakeries aiming to bake a highly individual, perhaps organic loaf.

THE MALTING PROCESS

Rank Hovis McDougall trace the malting process to fifteenth-century Benedictine monks. However, it only became popular in the late nineteenth century, in reaction to the loss of flavour resulting from over-refined roller-milled flour. A variety of grains can be malted successfully, though barley is the usual choice for the manufacture of extracts, and wheat for the grains added to meal mixes. In the malting process, cleaned grain is soaked in water until it absorbs about half its weight in moisture; it is then stored at a temperature that encourages germination. It is allowed to sprout for around ten days under controlled conditions until the shoot is two-thirds the length of the grain. The sprouted grain is then dried in a kiln for about three days, at successively hotter temperatures. The degree of drying or roasting determines the final flavour of the malt.

THE EFFECT AND FLAVOUR OF MALT

Malt in whatever form is a good flour improver; amongst other properties it encourages a good, relatively quick rise, and moisture retention in the finished loaf. When used purely as an improver its presence is barely detectable, but in larger amounts it contributes an uncloying sweetness and a moist, almost sticky texture.

The flavour and texture of a malted grain loaf depend on the type and quantity of malted grain or meal employed, as well as the degree of malting of the grain, the basic mix of flours and meals, the addition of fats – and indeed all the other variables that determine the nature of a baked loaf. Common factors should be a perceptibly nutty aroma, a flaky or grainy, somewhat chewy texture, sweetness and an attractive moistness. The desirable degree of any of these qualities is really a matter of personal preference; personally I don't enjoy loaves at the light, wan end of the spectrum and feel there are too many with undistinguished or even barely detectable wheat flavour.

USES OF MALTED GRAIN BREAD

Along with granary, this is the style of bread we imagine to be the archetypal ploughman's lunch base, and malted breads are undeniably delicious with a chunk of farm Cheddar cheese and a sweet-sour pickle or chutney. A number of sandwich manufacturers are using lightly malted bread to enclose an endless variety of fillings; it does seem to tone in, chameleon-like, with most foods, and is a popular choice for children's lunch boxes. A powerfully malted bread is perhaps best served at breakfast with marmalade or honey, and preferably toasted which effectively roasts the grain even further. As with granary, or any bread containing sizeable chunks of grain, stale malted grain bread is not particularly versatile, though you might try it in a simple Bread and Cheese Pudding (see page 242) or a savoury casserole.

· MALT LOAF ·

Malt loaf is something of a peculiarity, since it rarely appears in the company of other breads, nestling down more happily among sponges and fruit cakes. It is often hard to recognise the bread dough base of these dark, sweet, sticky, squashy confections.

These cake-breads are the ultimate expression of malted (sprouted, then roasted) grain and the extracts derived from it. They are likely to be made from proprietary pre-mixes (all the well-known commercial names are produced this way) and so there is little to choose between them, although degrees of sweetness and, to a lesser extent, intensity of malting, vary a little. Recent developments have included high-fibre versions and loaves flavoured with walnuts and honey but they make little impact on the basic character of the loaf.

Wholefood shops may carry one of the long-life loaves produced from scratch by companies such as Sunnyvale using wholesome ingredients and no chemical additives. These are firmer and less sticky than the pre-mix loaves, noticeably higher in fibre content but with a good, clean flavour. A very few craft bakeries produce a malted fruit loaf from their own customised blend of the appropriate ingredients; these can be refreshingly different from the sticky norm but are generally available only from the bakery's own shop. One widely distributed loaf that is closer to a light teabread than a cake is the Gleneagles loaf, baked by Goswell's under licence from Gleneagles–Veda Maltings. This is sold pre-sliced and, unlike its stickier cousins, toasts readily. If you enjoy sweet-salt contrasts of flavour this is an intriguing base for cheese on toast. Stale slices convert readily into richly flavoured bread puddings.

· MANKOUSH OR MANNAEESH ·

These rich, spicy rounds of flat bread are produced mainly by Lebanese or Mediterranean-style bakeries as a variation on pitta. Their distinguishing feature is a topping of sesame seeds, thyme and sumac blended with olive oil – in other words a paste of *zahtar*, a smoky-sour spice mixture also popular in North Africa and Turkey.

In flavour the bread is curiously similar to Cilician bread (see entry), even though the topping is somewhat different. Above all, it shares the same oil-tempered pungency. Similar again is the near identical-looking thyme bread produced by Abel Bakeries, which is more obviously geared to a British market – the sumac is replaced by the more familiar mint and dill. Sumac comes from the dried red berry of a bush that thrives in the Middle East and in Sicily and has a fruity, sour, somewhat astringent flavour – something of an acquired taste, perhaps, but one I find rather addictive. I would therefore choose a bread that included sumac over one that does not.

In common with other spice-topped Middle Eastern breads, mankoush is good on its own, or with salads and simply cooked vegetables dressed with olive oil. It is a bread you should seek out if putting together a *mezze* spread – even a supermarket-based selection would benefit, though you will almost certainly need to look further afield for the mankoush.

· MARKOUK ·

See **Lavash**.

· MEDITERRANEAN SUNSET LOAF ·
(*manoucher bread*)

This extravagantly named bread is no more and no less than a focaccia jam-packed with designer flavours and colours. Two features demand its inclusion under a separate heading: it is, at the time of writing, flown over from Canada and is consequently breathtakingly expensive, and it has become a near-reverential point of reference in any discussion about the contemporary bread scene.

The bread itself is one of the richest you are likely to encounter. Using the American method of pressing together chunks of dough, it incorporates generous quantities of olive oil, basil and sun-dried tomatoes. Virtually a meal in itself, it will not, to my mind, happily share space with anything other than a fairly plain salad.

Its mastermind is an Iranian poet turned hugely successful business-man by the name of Manoucher Ettminan, who realised what fortunes beckon along the path of breads designed in ostensibly Mediterranean style. Attuning poetic inclinations to baking and to skilful marketing, he set out to prove that his creations – there are six breads in the range, with the Sunset Loaf the jewel in the crown – would 'change the way you think about bread – *forever*'. To set our thoughts on the right path, the wrapper claims for the bread 'a taste like sunshine' with 'power to transform deepest winter into a warm, mellow Mediterranean day'.

Protests at the extravagance of the claim have been surprisingly few. Fashion exerts a firm grip, and no top store and few supermarkets dare be without the Sunset Loaf. Those that don't stock it have contrived to commission own-label imitations, and even craft bakeries are not immune – Innes, for instance, produces a near-identical loaf incorporating their sourdough culture. Perhaps the Sunset Loaf has mystical qualities after all.

You must judge for yourself. I suspect, however, that it will not be long before some fashion-innocent consumer suggests that this emperor has a somewhat expensive and ponderous suit of clothes.

· MUFFINS ·

Like crumpets, English muffins are designed to be toasted and buttered. These smooth, flat-surfaced griddle-baked buns are, however, richer, softer, lighter and generally more bread-like than their holey cousins (the *Oxford English Dictionary* connects 'muffin' with the old French *moufflet*, a general term for soft bread). A centuries old treat in England – though no longer, alas, purveyed by an itinerant muffin man – muffins have recently become hot sellers in supermarkets in France, where, rumour has it, they are enjoyed, like crumpets, straight from the packet.

BUYING MUFFINS

Muffins produced by small specialist bakeries tend to be much better than the mass-marketed item – crunchier-crusted, softer and more flavourful within, perhaps due to enrichment of the basic bread dough with a little milk. Some are made by a long-fermented 'sponge and dough' method, giving them an attractive nuttiness and barely perceptible sour tang, and helping explain why the British tradition is one of very plain, unfruited muffins.

Most of our muffins come from large industrial bakeries (generally via supermarkets), however, and can be creditable attempts – look out for unbleached flour and an absence of unnecessary additives. It is to supermarkets that we owe muffins in various flavours, most notably raisin, bran and molasses. These are decidedly untraditional but attractive to many consumers on two counts: they have a moister, stickier texture and a more assertive flavour, and they have a 'high fibre and healthful' appeal.

USES OF MUFFINS

To the traditionalist there is just one acceptable treatment – toasting and buttering in a highly specific way, which runs thus: open the muffin slightly at the middle seam, either by pulling it apart with forks or snipping it with scissors or a knife; toast it on both sides, then pull it apart completely; place thin slices of butter over the hot, squashy inner surfaces (don't spread it) and then close the muffin up again. In the true spirit of genteel gourmandise you should then place the muffin in a warmed dish, cover it, and turn it over after a couple of minutes so that the butter soaks through both halves.

Like most people, I slice my muffin in two, toast all four surfaces and eat it rather too quickly while still hot and slightly crisp. For two very un-English indulgences see the recipes for Eggs Benedict and Oysters Benedict on page 186.

· MULTIGRAIN AND SOFT GRAIN BREAD ·

The number of these is legion, and although they often go by different names, such as: three-seed bread, mixed grain with kibbled wheat, softgrain white sliced, and so on, there is a palpable sameness about the majority. This seems barely credible, given the almost infinite combinations of different grain meals (wheat, rye, barley, oats and so on), of whole or cracked grains in varying degrees of hardness or softness, and of seeds such as sesame, linseed, poppyseed and pumpkin. Less curious, though, when you consider that most of these breads have been created only in the last ten years or so and that no special skills or technology are needed. To me, this suggests a certain fashion-led desperation which, I fear, is reflected in the flavour and texture of too many of these breads.

Some multigrain and soft grain breads – particularly those of Germanic origin – do follow a well-established tradition and have been specifically mentioned elsewhere in this directory (Swiss Bread, Vogel, Turkestan, etc.). Others are produced by inspired craftsmen for whom flavour is a major consideration; almost invariably, these have very local distribution. A few are welcome attempts by whole-food bakeries to provide much-needed variation on the plain whole-meal loaf; of these, one or two are achieving wide distribution. The vast majority of these breads, however, are mass-produced by large industrial bakeries to satisfy a vague public perception of the desirabil-ity of increasing dietary fibre and to feed the huge sandwich market. Most of the pre-sliced, plastic-wrapped loaves are scarcely more flavourful or texturally interesting than their white, brown or in-between base loaves. Small bakeries are not entirely immune to lapses of taste either. All too often, the most 'worthy' of multigrain loaves taste dry and dusty, betraying a search for novelty rather than a genuine concern for good eating qualities. Or breads may be created from the noblest of motives but turn out to have a positively uncomfortable integrity, a wealth of husky, gum-rasping seeds provid-ing more challenge than pleasure. Truly a rocky road.

· NAAN BREAD ·

No commercial version of this Punjabi flat bread can compare with one fresh from the tandoor, hot and aromatic, with its inimitable contrasts of crisp and soft sections. The traditional naan is a simple mixture of white flour, salt, oil, and yoghurt or yeast, but exposure to the scorching heat and water-absorbent clay of the tandoor oven gives it a number of unique features: a characteristic teardrop shape, produced by the pull of gravity on the vertically hanging dough; a light, slightly bubbly texture, and a flavour lifted by the tang of slight surface scorching.

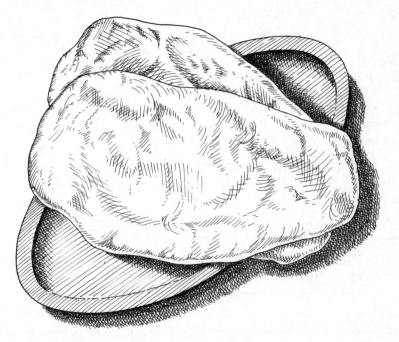

Compromises are unavoidable in mass production. Commercial naan has to withstand plastic packaging, several days' shelf life (or extensive freezing) and reheating. Shape is perhaps the most obvious compromise. Mass-produced naan tends to be baked flat, pre-shaped by hand into the recognisable teardrop; consequently it lacks some of the uneven thickness and the bubbling and charring of the original bread. More flavour-destructive is the combined use of yeast and raising agents, as the latter seem to link up with the oil (generally a hydrogenated one) to produce a heavy, dull, almost metallic flavour. While this is quite easily masked by the spicing and oil content of much of the Indian food the bread normally accompanies, it does not disappear so readily with the kind of simple raita the manufacturers themselves often recommend. As I have encountered this problem in all the commercial naans I have tasted I find little to choose between the products currently available. More obvious choice lies in the area of flavoured naans, such as plain garlic, garlic with herbs, and the newer peshwari naan, sweetened with apple, sultanas, coconut and almond. Despite my reservations, it must fairly be said that all the varieties appear to be selling like hot cakes.

USES OF FRESH AND STALE NAAN

The range of Indian foods traditionally accompanied by naan breads is so vast there is little point in listing individual dishes. The majority of supermarket-purchased breads no doubt see duty alongside cook-chill Indian-style dishes. Hotels, though not yet sandwich bars, have latched on to the chicken-tikka-topped naan, which appears to be relentlessly popular, or the Italo-British-Indian smoked salmon naan.

The keeping qualities of commercial naan breads are one of their greatest strengths – a quick sprinkle with water, a shot of heat from grill or oven, and they are almost as good as new. Very stale breads can be split and crisped to eat with dips or added to salads, though I feel that the simpler pitta breads fare better in this context.

· NATURVIE ·

This is a formula bread, one of a whole crop of 'real' breads that has sprung up in France during the past ten years. This one has found its way to Britain and is at present licensed to the Bagatelle bakery in London.

The idea of a formula bread sounds far from enticing but can (and in this case does) ensure bread of the highest quality. Broadly speaking, the patenting company provides a flour mix and technical advice and determines the method of production. Naturvie flours are stoneground and produced to the highest organic standards; fermentation is slow, and the loaves are formed by hand.

The Naturvie loaf at present available in Britain is organic to the point of using *biologique* Guérande marsh salt (it is also sold as *pain biologique* in some outlets). It is fermented by the sourdough method, although a tiny percentage of compressed yeast is permitted. The thick, crunchy crust is quite powerfully flavoured and the crumb has a characteristic sourdough grey tone, but its aroma is sweet and the texture firm and moist. The loaf keeps well, although the crust softens with time. Altogether a good all-purpose bread and a welcome addition to the array of French breads available in Britain.

· NEWCASTLE BROON ·

Just one example of this bread – produced by J. & F. Thomson & Son of Newcastle – is widely distributed, claiming to be 'the one and only'. This hint at tradition is interesting, as historical references to Newcastle bread do crop up here and there. In *Food in England* Dorothy Hartley comments cryptically, 'This was brown, and had caraway seeds in it,' and Eliza Acton gives a recipe for 'Brown Caraway, or Newcastle Bread' in *The English Bread Book*.

I doubt the Thomson loaf bears much resemblance to Miss Acton's wheaten milk loaf with caraway seeds, as it is made from the proprietary Harvester flour mix supplied by Allied Mills. In its present incarnation it is a fluffy malted grain bread with the addition of Newcastle Brown ale, which must contribute some richness, though this is not apparent, and a degree of bitterness, which certainly is. Not a hint of caraway seeds, which must have disappeared like the comfits on the original Bath buns.

Devotees of light malted grain breads may enjoy this loaf, perhaps with cheese and pickle and a pint of ale, but I must say I find it disappointingly undistinguished. I can't help feeling that Newcastle Brown might have been put to better use.

· OAT BREAD ·

Oatmeal does not announce its presence as assertively as rye; it is much gentler, nutty in a manner akin to wheat grain, and in no way sour (unless suffering from a degree of rancidity, which can be a problem). This is partly due to the lack of gluten, which means that it is added to wheat flour in fairly small proportions, and partly to its intrinsically gentle flavour.

It is well worth finding out if a loaf contains oatmeal or oatflakes and in what proportion. Many breads and rolls ranging from oaties to pane avena (from La Fornaia bakery) contain little, if any, oatmeal in the dough but have a scattering of crushed oat flakes instead – sometimes on the crust only. The flavour of these is, as might be expected, lightly porridgey. Simply by association these breads seem to be well matched with marmalade and with British cheeses.

Wheat loaves with some oatmeal content are rather more interesting, though the flavour is difficult to define. It is somehow both mealy and lightly nutty, dry on the palate in a manner not unlike oatcakes, yet moist on account of the relatively high oil content of oats – an oat loaf keeps better than a plain wheat one. There is an added richness of flavour and if the basic loaf is a white one the colour will be pleasingly golden with a touch of grey – a very natural look. This bread is equally at home with preserves (strawberry jam as much as marmalade) and with soups, cheeses and salads.

Oat bannocks, or fairly flat griddle cakes, are of course another thing entirely and taste rather like oatcakes. Bannocks are rarely found south of the Scottish border and are not especially common even within Scotland. The traditional accompaniments to warmed bannocks are butter, honey and cheese.

USES OF OAT BREAD

Oat breads keep quite well and make particularly good toast, spread with lavish quantities of butter and honey or marmalade, or served with soup and toasted cheese. If you like the basic flavour, you can use stale oat bread in any recipes specifying basic white bread.

· OLIVE BREAD ·

See **Flavoured Breads**.

· PAESANO ·

In the UK this is a loaf from the same stable as ciabatta and Pugliese (see entries), a large squat wheel divided into farls, containing less oil than the other two, and with a much denser and softer crumb. The term paesano simply suggests something cooked 'in the peasant manner', and in this instance it describes a plain, all-purpose loaf. Certainly it would make a good sopper-up of sauces, its dense texture marrying well with hearty stews, despite something approaching sweetness in the flavour. While a thick slice of paesano would serve as an admirable trencher it is not as versatile as the lighter-textured Pugliese. On the other hand it is no doubt the ideal loaf to see a large family gathering through a long, hearty meal, or to cart along (almost literally), semi-indestructible, to a rough and ready picnic.

· PAINS AU LAIT ·

See **Bridge Rolls, Vienna Rolls, Pains au Lait**.

· PAIN AU SON ·

This is the French bran loaf, as coarse and disappointingly dry as any bread produced for dietetic rather than gustatory reasons is likely to be. I have yet to find a French text extolling the bran loaf's eating qualities; even the wrapper confines its eulogy to '*Riche en fibres ... conseillé par le corps médical ... pour faciliter le transit intestinal*' – none of which should need translating. But the loaf undoubtedly has its fans in the UK where it is increasingly available, and does, at least, provide a reasonable foil for bland and creamy foods.

· PAIN AUX NOIX ·

See **Walnut Bread**.

· PAIN DE CAMPAGNE ·

In the UK this basically signifies 'the other sort' of French bread and can range from a small cob-like loaf with a slightly vinegary taste, a coarse texture and a thinnish, chewy-crunchy crust, to a gigantic cartwheel, thick-crusted, grey-crumbed, moist and pronouncedly sour. Supermarket instore bakeries tend to churn out the former style, while French-run bakeries furnish their own retail outlets, adventurous delis and specialist food departments with variations on the cartwheel.

So what exactly is a pain de campagne, or 'country bread'? There is no legal definition in France any more than in Britain; it is simply the antithesis of the refined baguette, which is a 'city' bread designed for quick consumption. The campagne, by contrast, is a *pain de ménage*, a household bread, a staple designed to sustain a family through a number of meals – the peasant farmer through a week, perhaps; the urbanite through a country weekend.

The flour used in a campagne loaf is invariably somewhat coarse – it may contain a modest proportion of wheatbran, rye meal, or both. The bread will also seem less sweet than a standard white loaf; indeed, some are baked using a sour (wild yeast) culture as well as compressed yeast, or a six-hour-fermented starter dough. In the UK, it is almost invariably round, while in France, and the occasional British-based French bakery, it may take the form of a sturdy long loaf from which a kilo or a half kilo is cut to order.

BUYING AND USING CAMPAGNE BREAD

Most supermarkets sell a vinegary, branny, lightweight loaf labelled pain de campagne, but some are also beginning to carry a 'French country' loaf made by a craft bakery using a more painstaking method. This essentially means slower fermentation from a starter dough or wild yeasts and a longer baking time, resulting in a sour (but not vinegary) aroma and flavour, a more compact and moist crumb with a greyish colour, and a thicker, chewier crust. The loaf will feel heavier for its size than the instore equivalent – this is as it should be, and generally promises moistness and good keeping qualities. If you buy a loaf from a good French bakery in the UK you are virtually guaranteed a thick-crusted, chewy, moist, satisfying bread packed with an amalgam of nutty and yoghurt-like flavours.

At the opposite end of the spectrum is the much smaller *campaillou*. Rough-hewn and rather shapeless, with a rugged, crunchy crust, this is a considerably lighter and gentler style of campagne. The crumb has more holes than a ciabatta, and is gently nutty in flavour – hardly sour at all: an excellent daily staple, unchallenging but far from insipid. Along similar lines, but more powerfully flavoured, is the *canaillou* produced by Bagatelle, a London-based French bakery.

One or two essentially British bakeries make what must be considered a British interpretation of the French country loaf. In London, for instance, Sally Clarke produces a campagne that is a small, squat loaf with a lightly crunchy, cross-hatched crust, an almost white, fine-textured wheat flour crumb and a barely perceptible acid tang. If you are looking for a loaf suitable for an English picnic but with a touch more character than a standard white loaf, this style is ideal.

COMPLEMENTARY FOODS

The noticeably coarse texture of most traditional-style campagne breads can be a good foil to robust flavours and resilient textures such as a garlicky pork terrine or a thickly sliced dry-cured or smoked ham, while the slightly sour taste marries well with any number of powerfully flavoured cheeses. I found the advice printed on a French bread wrapper rather appealing: it prescribed '*buffets campagnards*', evoking an image of simple, sunny, bucolic festivity.

KEEPING QUALITIES

The heavier type of pain de campagne stales very slowly; generally the larger the loaf, the thicker its crust, the better its keeping qualities. The sourdough process also has a preservative function. Most will keep for about seven to ten days and you are unlikely to need to 'refresh' this kind of loaf. Staleish slices toast well, however, and form the basis for some of the finest croutes (see pages 183–5). You can also dry out the slices in a slow oven; they will then keep almost indefinitely and can be used in traditional country recipes, from casseroles to sweet puddings. More interestingly, perhaps, they are actually rather delicious to eat as they are. Very satisfying and flavourful – and far more interesting than crispbreads.

The lighter style of campagne loaves, particularly the ones from instore bakeries, do stale within a day or two; they can be temporarily revived as you would a baguette or ciabatta (see entries). I find a three-day-old *campaillou* is almost as good as new if it is given a quick blast in a very hot oven with a little water placed in a tray on a lower shelf. This even works with half a loaf (place cut side down on a tray). Stale chunks of these lighter campagne breads can be crumbed, made into croutons, or frozen whole, just as you would for any British loaf.

· PAIN D'ÉPICES ·

Most of us will have encountered this spice bread in its sliced, plastic-wrapped Dutch incarnation, sold in health-food stores. This is honey-sweet, extraordinarily light in weight, almost dry in texture – and decidedly more cake than bread.

The origins of this style of spice bread are most likely Flemish but French bakers made it their own from the fifteenth century onwards. Until the advent of baking powder, the universal raising agent was some form of yeast; the most painstaking methods still make use of a starter dough derived from semi-fermented honey mixed with wheat and rye flours. The majority are, however, chemically leavened. French pain d'épices is imported into the UK at Christmas time. Apart from the simple bread, sold either as a loaf or more commonly as overwrapped 'fingers', there are a good number of *pains fourrés* – fingers or round cakes filled with marmalade or with plum or prune preserves. The finest use a subtle dose of a complex spice mixture that includes cinnamon, ginger, aniseed, coriander, fennel, nutmeg, cloves and orange zest. Choice between the brands comes down to personal preference but one producer worth looking out for is the reknowned Dijon firm of Mulot et Petitjean.

USES OF PAIN D'ÉPICES

There is a certain vogue among French chefs for serving toasted spice bread with goose liver, which demands a rather fine balancing act of sweet and savoury elements. Dessert use is much simpler. Fresh spice bread can be wrapped in foil, warmed through in a moderate oven and served with sautéed apples, honey parfait or vanilla or ginger ice cream. On wintry days you might team it with a warm, spiced dried fruit compote. Or treat the warmed bread as a sponge pudding and douse it in hot home-made custard spiked with crystallised ginger. The drier varieties are quite absorbent and take readily to bread puddings of all kinds. Or try the variation of *pain perdu* on page 296.

· PAIN DE MIE ·

Selling this thin-crusted, rectangular sandwich loaf to the English must seem to French bakers like selling ice to Eskimos – *pain de mie* is also known in France as *pain anglais*. Unlike the British sandwich loaf, however, a good *pain de mie* has some kinship with a brioche, being enriched with milk, butter and sugar, and sometimes with malted flour. The *pains de mie* I have bought from French bakeries in the UK have been delicious, much closer to a rich, golden British teabread minus the fruit than anything dazzlingly white and de-natured. If you find one – they are easy to identify by dint of being baked in a long, rectangular tin closed on all four sides – do try it: quite apart from making terrific sandwiches it is a useful base for hot charlottes, summer puddings or simple fruit croutes. One bonus is that the loaf is rarely sold pre-sliced, so you could also use the nicely compact crumb to make canapé boxes (see page 177). And this is *the* loaf to use for a Parisian-style croque monsieur (see pages 207–8).

· PAIN AU SEIGLE, PAIN DE SEIGLE ·

French rye by another name (see also **Rye Bread**). It probably does not occur to most of us blessed with a French-run bakery nearby to pay much attention to the words *au* and *de* once we are informed that *seigle* means rye. We either like the loaf or we don't. In case you are shopping in one of those large stores that pride themselves on printing mystifyingly accurate names, it is useful to know that *pain au seigle* – bread *with* rye – is supposed to contain a minimum of 10 per cent rye flour, and will hover around this mark: in other words it is a light rye loaf. A *pain de seigle* – bread *of* rye – on the other hand will be at least 65 per cent, if not 100 per cent, rye.

Most French bakers in the UK tend to produce the latter kind of loaf, with a fairly high, but rarely total rye flour content. Often a sourdough or starter dough method will be used to complement the rye, but a *pain de seigle* may well be less sour than the bakery's *campagne* – it may be worth asking about the degree of sourness if this concerns you.

USES OF FRENCH RYE LOAVES

To the French, rye bread is the ideal accompaniment to oysters, shellfish and certain powerful cheeses such as Munster and Roquefort. More interestingly, however, *pain de seigle* (the heavier of the two breads) is often employed as the base for a *pain décoré*, as the dough is easy to work into fantastical shapes or letters which are then attached to the rounded crust before baking. An equally splendid use of large round rye loaves is *pain surprise*: the upper crust (sometimes decorated) is sliced off, the centre hollowed and formed into a multitude of tiny sandwiches which are then piled back into the loaf-shell, and the lid replaced. The filled loaf might be beribboned and decked with flowers to form the centrepiece of a celebratory buffet. These can generally be made to order by adventurous French bakeries but you could quite easily make up a 'surprise' loaf yourself; the crust-lid is an effective way of keeping canapé-sized sandwiches moist.

· PAIN PARISIEN ·

See **Baguette**.

· PAIN POILÂNE ·

For a good few years the hefty, thick-crusted Poilâne loaf was the only example of French country bread to be found in the UK, and its Parisian pedigree and rough-hewn chic rendered it desirable at a level beyond considerations of flavour. Now there are rivals aplenty, both French- and British-baked, but somehow Poilâne maintains its legendary status.

What lies behind this esteemed, if not inimitable loaf? Principally the determination and dedication of its creator, the Parisian baker Lionel Poilâne; secondly, high-quality organic wheat flour; and thirdly, time-honoured skills – the nurturing of a sourdough starter, a slow fermentation period, hand shaping of the dough (which is mixed mechanically but gently – no hint of high-speed agitation), and baking in purpose-built wood-fired ovens. The size of the loaf ensures high-quality crust and crumb as well as considerable longevity: the 2kg/4½lb cartwheels develop a thick crust in the oven without endangering the moistness of the crumb, while the natural rise method keeps the bread 'alive' – it develops flavour over a number of days and makes hugely flavourful toast once properly stale. The resultant flavours and textures are immensely satisfying: an intriguing amalgam of fresh wheat flavour, moist sourness and slight smokiness, all emphasised by the lengthy chewing demanded by that thick crust. There is no disputing that this is a challenging bread, nor that it engenders addiction – to the extent that some fans will not even consider eating any other bread.

What cannot be claimed for the Poilâne loaf is assured perfection: the sourdough method responsible for the bread's individuality also creates inconsistencies, to the point where, due largely to variable atmospheric conditions, this most hallowed of breads can seem dull and dry, entirely devoid of magic. The master baker himself readily admits that this is the name of the game, and devotees of the bread accept it, undeterred.

There is little point in giving guidelines to purchase. Taste and texture may differ dramatically from loaf to loaf, but the appearance is more or less identical (and the loaves are for the most part sold wrapped in the legend-bearing paper bag). Moreover a 'poor' Poilâne loaf is inferior only by its own unique standards and is still well worth eating. It is, however, worth mentioning that one close imitator could hardly come closer: brother Max Poilâne, whose loaf is flown over to an enterprising London delicatessen, Villandry, and may well make it to the rest of the UK before long. Aficionados can tell the difference between the two loaves – Max's is arguably a little moister and sweeter – but the loaves of both producers vary from week to week and the similarities outweigh the differences.

USES OF POILÂNE

In common with all wheaten sourdoughs (see entry), the fresh bread makes a superb accompaniment to coarse-textured pâtés, cheeses, salads and bistro fare of all kinds. Thinly sliced and toasted it is a good foil to lighter pâtés and mousses, soups and main-course salads. If you have never tried the bread, I would suggest a weekend brunch with toasted Poilâne to accompany scrambled eggs and then honey or marmalade. Above all, do try it – it is usually available in manageable and affordable quarter-loaves; even if you find it is not to your taste you will have some idea of why Poilâne has become a legend, and a measure of excellence.

· PANE AL CIOCCOLATO ·

The only example of this chocolate bread I have come across is made by the Fornaia bakery. It is easy to forgive the numerous stores and delis that tacitly pass it off as their own since the bread is so delicious. It is surprisingly unsweet, richly flavoured with dark chocolate, moist with olive oil, yet light and uncloying. Excellent (unbuttered) with an espresso, it is also good spread with unsweetened mascarpone and accompanied by a glass of wine – ideally, a rich, sweet Recioto della Valpolicella, but even a glassful of unfashionable Lambrusco will work well. Once convinced, you could extend the idea to party canapés. Or try making thin sandwiches filled with a good, fluffy cream cheese. For a sophisticated children's lunch-box treat, add sliced ripe banana to the equation; if the banana is not as ripe as it might be, drizzle some runny honey over it.

Chocolate bread toasts well, even when somewhat stale. If you like the combination of chocolate and peaches, try hot toasted chocolate bread with chilled peaches in Sauternes, or in the Recioto mentioned above. Chocaholics who claim a penchant for plain chocolate digestives with blue Cheshire cheese are guaranteed to enjoy toasted chocolate bread with cool slivers of Dolcelatte and fresh pear. Also, don't forget to try *pain perdu* made in the usual way (see page 295), with Marsala added to the soaking liquid; serve with mascarpone whipped with an equal quantity of fromage frais, lightly sweetened and scented with vanilla. As the bread has a light, unpappy crumb, it makes an excellent base for wildly indulgent bread puddings.

· PANE CON NOCI ·

See **Walnut Bread**.

· PANE DI MAIS ·

See **Cornmeal Bread**.

· PANE INTEGRALE ·

This is wholewheat bread, though not necessarily 100 per cent extraction. As there is nothing particularly distinctive about any such loaves in Britain (nor is it a particularly popular style in Italy), treat it as any wholewheat bread. (see **Wholemeal and Wholewheat Breads**).

· PANETTONE AND PAN D'ORO ·

There is no longer any need to beat the Christmas and Easter queues at Italian delis in order to secure one of these inimitably rich yet light festive breads, nor to stockpile supplies way beyond a mid-season sell-by date. In the UK, as in Italy, year-round supply has become the norm in many shops.

Perhaps one reason this particular celebratory bread has won a place amidst the puddings and pies is its extraordinary lightness – the last quality you would expect from a confection coloured deep gold with the richness of egg yolk and butter and generously speckled with dried and candied fruits. At the same time it offers a wealth of exotic but uncloying flavours and even manages an impression of moistness, though it is dry enough to last a matter of weeks rather than days after the first wedge is cut. All in all, the perfect bread to last through the festive season.

THE STORY OF 'TONY'S BREAD'

Everyone seems to agree about the origin of the name – a story so charming it is worth retelling. In the Middle Ages, a *pan grande*, a huge but rather less luxurious loaf, was the order of the day. In Milan there lived a poor baker named Toni, who had a beautiful daughter. The girl attracted the attentions of a young aristocrat, who decided to surmount the social gap between them by becoming an apprentice to her father. So eager was the young man to win his master's approval that he set about creating a rich and luscious loaf embellished with vine fruits and citrus peel. The monied aristocracy of Milan flocked to buy the new bread, which became known as *'pan di Toni'* and eventually panettone.

SHAPES AND SIZES

Less is known about the various changes in the panettone's shape over the centuries, though the popular domed top is plausibly said to resemble the cupolas of Lombardy churches. The Easter version of the bread, shaped like a dove and known, naturally enough, as a *colomba*, is said to have its origins in the twelfth century, when a pair of doves presaged the defeat of the Holy Roman Emperor, Barbarossa, by the Milanese army. As this event precedes the life and times of Toni by some three centuries, a little doubt might be cast on one or other story. On the other hand, the *colomba* is generally unfruited, and it may have been expedience that eventually determined a common base for the breads.

Slightly different in shape again is the unfruited pan d'oro (often simply spelt pandoro), or 'golden bread'. This is designed to slice neatly into star shapes when cut horizontally and resembles a particularly tall, ridged dome before slicing.

Novelty shapes come and go, the latest being a British-inspired Christmas turkey. I suspect it will prove of minority interest despite the scope for inventive stuffings. The enduring dome shape, most commonly in the form of a tall cylinder (a development of the 1920s) is certainly the most versatile, as the bread can be cut into cake-like wedges or dessert-base rounds, or the entire dome can be hollowed, stuffed with a creamy filling, and served up as a gâteau. It also lends itself to production in a wide range of sizes, from a 1.5k/3¼lb extended family model to a dainty 100g/3½oz individual serving.

BUYING PANETTONE

Commercially produced imported examples are both more easily available and more successful than any home-baked versions, which taste entirely different. I have tasted creditable (and perfectly delicious) British-baked imitations, but they somehow remain imitations, and also stale considerably faster.

Brands vary in quality, of course, and only a minority use pure vanilla rather than vanillin in the flavouring. Since all imported panettone are overwrapped you can check the ingredients for yourself. It certainly pays to read the label since, apart from the basic fruited version, panettone is also available enriched with chocolate chunks or layered with rich Marsala-based creams and robed in chocolate. These are generally heavier for their size – and pricier – than the basic loaf. From a creative cook's point of view they are somewhat less versatile than the eminently gildable basic panettone or pan d'oro. They also make less likely companions to a cup of tea or a glass of Vin Santo, both of which would be overwhelmed by the added sweetness and richness. They are, however, indisputably luscious, and perfect with a double espresso.

USES OF PANETTONE

A number have already been mentioned, including the obvious accompaniment, at any time of day, to a cup of tea or coffee, or a glass of Vin Santo, Marsala or Madeira. Dessert possibilities are legion, from hot panettone toast coated with chilled mascarpone, or slices of panettone covered with sugared, sliced plums or peaches and baked, to whole breads hollowed and filled with fruit, rich creams, ice-cream or zabaglione (see page 299).

· PAN GALLEGO ·

Allegedly a Spanish-style loaf, this is a factory-baked white flour bread, partly batch-baked and plumped up through the action of emulsifiers, so it is rather softer, more refined and squashier than any Spanish country bread. It does, however, have a discernible aroma of virgin olive oil, and in its plainness it makes a rather more acceptable base for salty tapas-style morsels than do the plethora of multi-flavoured Mediterranean-style loaves.

From the same source comes a seeded pan gallego. This is a blend of white and wholemeal flours and a host of seeds, a less likely complement to serrano ham but rather delicious with many of the exciting goat's and sheep's cheeses arriving on the British market. It is particularly toothsome thickly sliced and toasted, when the pumpkin and sunflower seeds and millet take on a powerfully nutty aroma and a noticeable crunch. Depending on the source of your loaf you may find the wrapper suggesting honey as a likely spread; for once, this is a perfectly sensible suggestion – that savoury nuttiness cuts the sweetness and provides a balance for even the heaviest and richest of honeys.

· PAN QUEMADO ·

More usually spelt as one word, panquemado, this is a Spanish-style player on the sweet bread scene. I can hardly better food journalist Michael Bateman's description of its appearance: 'something like a punctured football or a shiny leather tam-o'-shanter'. Fortunately it tastes rather more delicious than such a mangled aspect would have you believe.

In fact, it resembles a brown, glossy-topped brioche, though given the usual rough treatment on supermarket shelves one would imagine that this brioche had been used as a punchbag. This cosmetic problem is a result of the loaf's essential lightness, due partly to the use of olive oil rather than butter as an enriching agent, and the discreet, if noticeable, use of egg. The aroma is both yeasty and lemony and the flavour is markedly sweet. Bear this additional sweetness in mind whenever you use the panquemado in recipes. Once slightly stale, its open, fluffy texture ensures rapid and even absorption of liquid, and this makes it a good choice for most pudding recipes.

· PAN SCIOCCO ·

Also sold under the name *pane toscano*, this unsalted (or, in the UK, low-salt and oil-free) bread is regarded in Tuscany as the ideal accompaniment to anything from Pecorino to prosciutto. Eaten on its own, the bread undoubtedly seems strange – not so much sweet as somehow flavourless, even stale (one supermarket version has tried to combat this by adding lemon oil to the dough). Spread it with a smear of salt-rich sun-dried tomato or olive paste, or munch it with a platter of savoury *antipasti*, and you may soon find yourself in agreement with the gourmets of Tuscany. It is also an arguably better medium for tasting the nuances of an extra virgin olive oil than any of the breads already containing oil, and would make a terrific bruschetta, sprinkled perhaps with a few flakes of crunchy Maldon salt.

· PARATHAS AND PURIS ·

At the time of writing these Indian breads are available only in restaurants or takeaways. Packaging them in a way that preserves their essentially puffy texture seems well nigh impossible, but word is that the paratha, a speckled, flaky, ghee-layered chapati, is set to be the next flat-bread success story. The cushion-like deep-fried puri (yet another treatment of chapati dough) is designed to be enjoyed moments after it leaves the pan and may prove a touch more difficult to package for high-street sale. See also **Chapati**.

· PETIT PAIN ·

See **Baguette**.

· PIKELETS ·

See **Crumpets and Pikelets**.

· PITTA ·

If popularity is the equal of pedigree, the Middle Eastern pitta has become as British as the bloomer. Odd to think that as recently as 1978 Jane Grigson felt compelled to give readers of her *Vegetable Book* a recipe for pitta bread so they could avoid a trek to specialist shops and bakeries. Three years later, however, Claudia Roden announced in her book, *Picnic*, that 'by now everyone has discovered its versatility'. Which indeed we have, and the flat moccasins put in an appearance at every conceivable occasion, from brunches to dinners, party nibbles to picnics, and children's lunch boxes to city sandwich bars.

What makes this Middle Eastern bread so versatile that it outsells all other foreign imports, with the possible exception of the Anglo-Italian ciabatta? Most pittas are simple breads, made with plain white or wholemeal flour and containing only flour, water, yeast and salt (some have preservatives added). They have not escaped the search for novelty – granary pittas are a recent innovation, along with lines such as sesame, garlic, 'hot'n'spicy' and barbecue, but these are fringe sellers. Essentially pittas are more neutral, cleaner tasting and certainly less rich than the Far Eastern family of naan breads. The texture straight from the pack is quite soft and easy to eat, which endears the bread to children and the elderly; moreover, it does not dry out as long as the bread is kept wrapped.

What really sets the pitta apart from other flat breads, however, is its ready-made pocket, which results from the traditional baking method and can accommodate any number of smooth or chunky fillings. Add to this a dizzying variety of shapes and sizes, from cartwheel rounds sometimes sold as *khoubz*, the Arabic name for all such breads (*pideh* comes from the Armenian) to 15cm/6 inch ovals, half-size mini pittas and tiny cocktail pittas, and you have an easy-fill bread for every occasion, as well as for all ages.

USES OF PITTA

Likely uses of both standard pitta and cartwheel *khoubz* are seemingly endless, as Claudia Roden suggests in *A New Book of Middle Eastern Food*: 'Bread is eaten with every meal. Sometimes people break off a piece and double it over to enclose and pick up a morsel of meat or vegetable, or dip it in a sauce or cream salad, holding it delicately between the thumb and the first two fingers. Sometimes it is cut in half and the pocket is filled with hot shish kebab and salads or ful medames ... Some people, my father among them, claim that they cannot truly savour sauces or juices, or anything in fact, without a piece of bread.' Pitta can be filled with virtually anything, and if you wish to imitate sandwich bar practice and chicken tikka is what you fancy, go ahead. I find myself nibbling my way through a pack of pittas without putting them through any paces, and for anyone else impatient of fillings I would recommend trying the traditional, aromatic and self-sufficient Middle Eastern spice dips such as *dukkah*.

Cocktail pittas are designed for filling with any number of spreads and dips, from Hummous to Provençal-style olive and anchovy pastes and tapenade, to herbed and flavoured soft cheeses or butters. Or you can blend cooked, finely diced mushrooms, flaked fish and shredded meats with mayonnaise, mustard-spiked cream or gravy. A fun idea for a children's party (and rather popular with adults) is to split the little ovals, or halve the rounds, and insert slivers of cooked sausage, such as spicy *merguez* or *luganega*, and a dab of chutney or ketchup – doubly hot dogs.

REVIVING AND USING STALE PITTA

Slightly stale pitta can be revived by sprinkling it with water and heating it through in a moderate oven for a very few minutes or by grilling, though this will tend to crisp the crust. In fact this crisp crust is rather attractive, particularly with a soft filling – fried aubergine, perhaps, or a simple tomato salad. Wedges of crisp-grilled pitta are a welcome accompaniment to hummous and taramasalata dips. A further extension of the idea, useful for very stale and dry pitta, is to pull the bread apart and bake or grill it to a crisp. Shards of pitta prepared in this way can be sprinkled into soups or salads or over steamed vegetables. Crisped pitta can also be remoistened – in fact, remade into a new kind of bread entirely – by placing it in the base of a salad bowl (see the recipe for Fattoush on page 220).

As commercial snack manufacturers have been quick to discover, pitta can also be deep-fried to make pitta chips. This is best done, extravagantly but deliciously, in virgin olive oil, and with only slightly stale rather than dried-out pitta. Once again, the chips or crisps can be used as a salad or vegetable garnish but they are likely to disappear rapidly as a snack – sprinkle with salt, and with paprika or cayenne if you like.

· PIZZA BASES ·

Almost any supermarket or convenience store, and a fair number of Italian delis, can be relied on to supply DIY pizza bases in a range of sizes, plain, oiled, even partially topped. If you are a fan of Hovis you will find the bread transmuted into pizza dimensions; if your ideal pizza is actually a focaccia your choice could not be wider.

Authenticity is a futile pursuit; as Marcella Hazan comments in *The Essentials of Classic Italian Cooking*, 'although some formulas are certainly better than others, none may credibly claim to be the ultimate one. What matters is knowing what you are looking for.' The tomato-sauce-smothered bread embellished with a wide variety of toppings is a fairly modern (eighteenth-century) Neapolitan development, but there is little correspondence between commercially produced bases (which most are) and the artisan product baked on stone in a Neapolitan wood-fired oven.

For my money, the finest pizza bases are the simplest; fairly flat, a little irregular, dimpled with good olive oil and sprinkled simply with coarse salt, maybe pepper. Sometimes, these go by the name of *pizza bianca*, though this might also imply a topping of thinly sliced white onions. A recent development in terms of commercial production is a reasonably thin, crispy stone-baked and hand-finished base. Alternatively, you might be best served by buying a good, basic focaccia (see entry) and perhaps brushing off a little of the salt, depending on the savouriness of your chosen toppings.

· PLATZELS ·

These soft little rolls are part of every Jewish baker's repertoire, but are not widely available outside Jewish bakeries. Recipes differ but one constant feature is that the fat is vegetable, not animal based. The platzels produced by bakeries that do distribute them to a few supermarkets and large stores are chewy-crusted, light, soft and well risen. Good to eat when fresh, they are a sound choice for all recipes requiring stale bread.

· PLUM BREAD ·

See **Lincolnshire Plum Bread**.

· PORTUGUESE BREAD ·

Portuguese bread is not easy to come by in the UK. I have found little trace of the famous cornmeal *broa*, or of the heavy, chewy, coarse-ground sourdough loaves you are likely to encounter in Portugal.

The few Portuguese bakeries that do exist are mainly London based and turn out a sound basic loaf, crusty and well risen, which is almost interchangeable with the Spanish (see **Spanish Bread**). The recently established Brixton-based bakery, Funchal, produces a small but excellent range, with pride of place going to the *alentejano* and the *rosquilha*. Both are made from the same basic white dough but the latter, a ring-shaped loaf, has more of the desirable crust. These breads are chewy, rather salt-sour, and with a contrast between the moist crumb and dense crust that is quite addictive.

One supermarket chain has had some success with a *castelo blanco*, actually a brown loaf made with a mixture of rye and wholemeal flours. This is a pleasant bread with a reasonably coarse texture which could be used instead of cornmeal bread in certain recipes, but it is not distinctively different from other rye and wheat mix breads on the market.

If you cannot find Portuguese bread but would like to make *Migas* and *açordas* (see pages 253 and 228), the next best thing is a Spanish loaf, then the basic Italian loaves quite widely available at numerous delis (see **Italian Bread**), or turn to Paesano or Pugliese (see entries). A reasonable substitute for the famous *broa*, or cornmeal loaf, would be the commercial *pane de mais*, while chollah or pan quemado can be used as *pan doce*, or sweet bread (see entries).

· PRETZELS (SALZBREZELN) ·

We all know pretzels as thin, crisp, salty little biscuits sold in packets alongside crisps. The majority are imported from Germany, some from the United States or Israel; all are immediately recognisable by their shapes: very thin, twisted sticks (which should really be known as *Salzstangen*), simple rings, and the characteristic twisted knot. This distinctive knot shape is the sign of the baker's shop in North European cities from Copenhagen to Riga, and hints at the pretzel's *alter ego* as a yeasted bread. In fact, the yeast-raised, bun-sized pretzel is something of a hybrid, chewy like a bagel, as crisp-edged as a bread stick, and very salty, like the little biscuits. In contrast to the biscuits, however, its smoky, crunchy crust is offset by a soft, sweet crumb.

Pretzels and bagels have a number of features in common, including the origin of their names, from the Middle or Old High German word for circular armlets. Pretzels are formed by moulding a fairly plain, firm dough into the characteristic knot shape, then dipping it into brine before baking. As with the bagel, the starch of the crust is rapidly gelatinised and sets to a bright glaze, while the dough remains dense-textured and chewy. However, unlike bagels, pretzels are often baked as soon as they have been moulded, or from a chilled state, and at extremely high heat. The crumb is thus even more close-textured than that of a bagel, the crust teak-coloured, deeply varnished and crunchy, particularly where the shape is at its thinnest. Some are slashed before baking and the slashes filled with crushed salt. During the dough's brief but rapid expansion in the hot oven the slashes open out dramatically, creating more crisp edges. Some are sprinkled all over with salt crystals before baking, or with sesame seeds or spices such as fennel or caraway. Sweet versions exist, too, though these are rarely encountered in the UK.

BUYING PRETZELS

At present only a few companies in Britain make pretzels or 'finish' imported unbaked ones. Pretzels imported as frozen dough from Germany tend to emerge rather soft and flabby after a British bake-off, easily recognisable by their somewhat puffy appearance. It may be, of course, that this style appeals to you, so you should probably go ahead and try them anyway.

The best I have tasted are everything a pretzel should be, and are produced in North London by Bakoven, a company originally set up by a German-trained baker specifically to produce pretzels. The same company now produces very fine German-style rye loaves but has maintained the pretzel tradition. Distribution may well follow the course of the breads and become nationwide before too long.

USES OF PRETZELS

Despite being a beer-drinking nation, we are not yet as accustomed to pretzel nibbling as the northern French or Germans (pretzels are great thirst-inducers). The stalls that line the streets of Strasbourg and Paris do a fair trade in pretzels filled with cheese, charcuterie, salad and even choucroute, as well as dozens sold plain. Perhaps the American dip-and-dunk system will suit us better. Jars of American pretzel dips (rather sweet, mustard-based affairs) designed for use with piping hot pretzels are already imported into the UK, presumably with crisps, tortilla chips or bread sticks in mind. I find that a light cream cheese, or the slightly sweet-tasting mascarpone, make the best dips, either plain or seasoned with herbs and spices. Or try whipping unsalted butter, then seasoning it with salt, pepper and cayenne, or with salt and a grainy, perhaps honey-sweetened mustard; or, more powerfully, with finely chopped shallots, crushed garlic, parsley, salt and pepper. The pretzels should be crisp and, ideally, warm.

USING STALE PRETZELS

Pretzels are undoubtedly at their best fresh from the oven, as the crust softens gradually thereafter. However they can be refreshed very successfully up to a couple of days after purchase by placing them for three to five minutes in an oven preheated to its maximum setting. Eat them within two hours. With staler pretzels, you could slice the thick sections and make baked croutons (see page 171), baking the thin, crisp bits at the same time and treating them as a biscuit.

An alternative tactic for stale pretzels is to dry them out completely in a moderate oven (the time taken will vary depending on staleness – you may need to cut one open at the thickest section to check) and use them as biscuits – they will keep for a good while in this state, even if stored simply in a sturdy paper bag. One enterprising American company is marketing full-size pretzel biscuits baked by the sourdough method, judging perhaps that the British will happily take to anything packaged as a crisp snack, whatever our reservations about trying a curious category of bread.

· PUGLIESE ·

Second only to ciabatta in Italophile affections, a true Pugliese loaf would probably come top of the tree. The southern Italian region of Apulia has everything going for it agriculturally: Marcella Hazan claims that some of the best flour in the world is produced here, while Anna del Conte avers that Pugliese olive oil competes with Tuscan and Ligurian for quality. Unfortunately, the Pugliese loaves baked in Britain generally employ a lesser flour (the better ones are made from strong Canadian flour) and all too often an oil that is far from virginal.

None the less, fine loaves are available nationwide – taste will have to be your guide, as the pale gold crust looks remarkably similar in all loaves. The crumb should be soft, moist and sweetly aromatic, less holey than ciabatta, but still light and almost springy to the touch. In many ways, Pugliese, with its more compact crumb and wider slices, is more suitable for bruschetta, or as a base for pungent vegetable spreads, than the more popular, but holey, ciabatta.

· RICE BREAD ·

Although it has been much praised by the likes of Eliza Acton and Elizabeth David, very little rice bread is sold commercially. Only two types are at all widely available: the first of these is dealt with in **Gluten-free Breads** and the second is a sourdough loaf produced by Natural Rise Foods in North London.

As it has no gluten content, rice cannot be used by itself to produce leavened bread. Rice bread is basically a wheat-based or mixed grain bread to which a small amount of cooked rice has been added, usually short grain. The rice obviously adds texture to the loaf but its main contribution is moistness, and a consequent improvement in keeping quality. If organic, unpolished rice is used it will increase the nutritional value of the bread.

Cooked rice is a useful medium for a sourdough starter, which may be another reason you are most likely to come across rice bread in the form of a sourdough loaf. In the breads I have sampled the sourness has been so pronounced that it was difficult to detect any rice flavour, though the texture was quite pleasant. I imagine there is scope for a subtler form of rice bread which could make a splendid accompaniment to soups, salads and stir-fries. Perhaps it will be a welcome development in the constant search for new styles.

· RYE BREAD ·

We associate rye bread with Scandinavia, Central and Eastern Europe, Jewish baking tradition, the occasional French baked loaf – just about every northerly European country apart from Britain. Despite the fact that rye grain has always been an easier crop than wheat in our cool, damp climate, rye bread is still regarded with suspicion, even distaste, by the majority of Britons today.

A STAPLE BUT SUSPECT GRAIN

Probably introduced by Viking settlers in the sixth century AD, rye was a staple in Britain throughout the Middle Ages. The Brown Bread Guild was principally concerned with producing 'maslin' or monk's corn – mixed grain bread containing rye in various proportions, depending on the harvest in any particular year. Unfortunately, this dependable grain was prone to ergot infestation: cattle died from grazing on the fungus-affected grain, while in humans contaminated bread induced hallucination and madness, frequently proving fatal.

Small wonder that rye has always been regarded with some distrust. However, the recent reaction against over-refined white flour has, to some degree, reinstated rye along with wholewheat, most obviously in mixed grain or granary breads.

THE FLAVOUR OF RYE – A TASTE FOR THE SOUR

Rye meal itself is not noticeably sour – in fact it is quite alkaline, although you would notice a sweet-sour element if you were to taste it alongside wheat meal. It does taste richer and slightly earthier than wheat and for this reason is often added in barely detectable quantities to wheaten loaves to improve the flavour.

A rye loaf raised by conventional baker's yeast via a fast-rise method tastes surprisingly bland. A sourdough ferment, on the other hand, 'lifts' the rich, earthy flavour of the grain beautifully. Using sourdough has a number of positive advantages: it ensures a good crumb structure, moist but uncakey; it causes the flavour to develop for a number of days after the loaf has been baked; and the lactic acid resists contamination and inhibits mould – so a rye loaf made from sound grain by a sourdough process is actually one of the safest breads you could eat.

There are different styles of 'sour' available to the baker, ranging from a rehydrated 'dried sour', usually added to fast-rise doughs, to carefully nurtured cultures. In my experience the ready-mixes deliver a rather startling, one-dimensional shot of sourness, while use of cultures ensures the most interesting and integrated set of flavours. But labelling, where it exists, is unlikely to give you this kind of detail. The best clue – apart from finding out how a particular bakery operates – generally lies with the price: bread made from carefully nurtured dough is more costly to produce.

BUYING RYE BREAD

Despite their marginal share of the market, the range of rye breads available in the UK is very diverse and it is difficult to give a catch-all guide to quality. Some people will always prefer a light-textured, mild-flavoured loaf while for others only the darkest, densest, sourest example will do.

If a particular style of rye is not to your taste, try another style before you give up on the grain. If you have never tried rye bread, I would suggest you start with a middle-range example, perhaps a smooth-textured, gently sour German-style loaf with some wheat content – the Bakoven range is gradually being taken up by a number of supermarkets. I find these breads much more intrinsically attractive than the often dry, mealy, light ryes, yet considerably less demanding than deeply sour, 100 per cent rye blockbusters.

Here are some guidelines on rye breads available in the UK. For Bavarian/Germanic rye and Danish rye, see **German Bread** and **Danish Bread**.

Black rye is not necessarily high in rye content, nor black in colour. The precise rye content, shade, texture and flavour vary considerably from one national style to another. I have come across some virtually inedible examples of black-coloured rye bread, harsh and bitter as a mouthful of coffee grounds, but almost without exception these have been produced by British bakeries attempting to emulate a tradition with insufficient skill to hand. Polish black rye breads look scarcely different from light ryes, and in fact the Polish name means dark rather than black. They are made with coarse rye and wheat meal rather than the more refined, fine milled rye used in other styles of Polish rye. These 'dark' ryes taste quite gentle, if coarse-textured, and are rarely very sour. Try them with coarse, garlicky sausages.

Almost all black breads or black ryes produced by Jewish bakers, bagels included, are near-black in colour and part-rye in composition. Very occasionally their colour comes from molasses, which contributes a rich, somewhat bitter flavour. More often, caramel is used, which gives surprisingly little flavour or sweetness. These torpedo-shaped loaves are usually light-textured and remarkably gentle in flavour, unless generously dosed with caraway. It is perhaps the most widely distributed style of black rye, its colour dramatic, its flavour underwhelming; arguably versatile, but I find it rather unexciting.

Caraway rye features one of the spice world's classic love-it-or-hate-it flavours. While sweetening and softening up sourness, caraway superimposes its perfumed, pungent character on the flavour of the grain. Subtle use is difficult, if not impossible, to achieve – even two or three seeds in a loaf will magically assert themselves. You might well imagine that no food could possibly survive its onslaught, but caraway rye bread seems a natural partner for a variety of Germanic and Danish cheeses, smoked meats and cabbage dishes sweet or sour.

Rather often the use of caraway masks a bread of poor quality or indifferent flavour. At the same time, a judicious blend of rye and wheat flours, sourdough and caraway seeds can achieve a perfect synthesis of fascinating flavours; such loaves, albeit too rare, are being baked in Britain.

Estonian rye, a dense, rye-heavy loaf with a hint of sweetness, is produced by the Ukrainian Kolos bakery in Yorkshire, who inherited the recipe from an Estonian baker. It is perhaps more typical of the Kolos style than of a Baltic rye bread.

Light rye loaves are light in both colour and flavour, and contain a fairly low proportion of rye flour. They are not usually markedly sour, but may have caraway added to lend a distinctive flavour. You should have little trouble finding a light rye loaf – it is the most popular style of rye in the UK and supermarkets have started adding examples to their standard range. The majority are competently (if, to my taste, unexcitingly) executed.

Polish rye presents real problems of definition. Although Polish bakeries are long-established in Britain, a number of bakers have combined Polish and Jewish traditions. Moreover, 'Polish' rye is often a convenient label for East and Central European-style ryes, and to cap it all, the bread currently sold by a good many Polish delis in the UK is in fact a Ukrainian rye produced by a Ukrainian bakery!

The most widely distributed example is Goswell's Polish-style rye, a rather light loaf with a somewhat coarse texture, punctuated by cracked rye grain. Yeast-raised, it is quite sweet tasting with little sour bite. Stefan Najduc of the Polish Barbakan bakery in South Manchester bakes a loaf that is again far from heavy, though made with coarse rye and wheat meal (more rye than wheat) and scented with caraway. In common with other Continental bakeries, Barbakan's loaves have changed over the years and are still being anglicised – for which read lightened – to suit modern tastes. The Yorkshire-based Kolos bakery feels that a 50/50 split between rye and wheat is 'best for the English taste' and this is the mix of the Ukrainian loaf that has been adopted by many a Polish deli.

The picture that emerges of Polish rye is of a light-crumbed but coarse-textured loaf, not sour in the way of full-blown Germanic or Russian-style ryes, but with a slight sweetness sometimes emphasised by the use of caraway. These breads are ideal with the dried, smoked or boiling sausages and smoked, rather fatty *speck, sopocka* and similar pork products beloved of the Polish community.

There are two main **Russian rye** loaves on the British market, neither of which attempts to emulate the famous *borodinski* of Moscow nor the bread of Riga, which is reputedly admired by Russians even more than their own. The St Petersburg Khleb from the Fornaia bakery is made with baker's yeast and has a sweet-sour flavour, highlighted by dill. It contains a fair proportion of rye flour but is boosted by improvers and hydrogenated vegetable oils, in somewhat un-Russian fashion. The Village Bakery's version, called simply Russian rye, contains only organic rye flour, salt, and a sourdough starter gleaned from Kostroma on the Volga. It is dramatically moist, dark and sour, with a patina of woodsmoke. A number of consumers with Russian roots confirm it is pretty close to the kind of bread they enjoyed in the past.

Foods ideally matched with Russian rye are, naturally enough, the ones we tend to associate with Russia: sour pickled vegetables and mushrooms, cured and smoked fish, fatty pork dishes of all kinds, and also soured cream, perhaps as a dressing for salad or a mediating sauce for other foods; and of course cream cheese. A good way of sampling the bread might be in a simple open sandwich of cream cheese and sliced, salted radishes.

Scotch Sourdough Rye is really a bit of a misnomer, albeit baked in Scotland. It is in fact a Polish-style rye produced by Philip Jackson of Star Continental Bakery in Glasgow, one of a number of Scottish bakers continuing the work of East European bakers who settled north of the Border. A hefty loaf with a starch-glazed, shiny, crackled crust, it makes a weekly journey to London, where it has proved remarkably popular. The name applies in London only; in Scotland it is sold as 'Polish'. Yet another indication that you can rarely judge a loaf by its name alone.

· SAFFRON CAKE ·

This is usually sold as Cornish saffron cake, since production of the highly aromatic, moist, fruited tea bread is traditionally centred in Cornwall, once renowned as a producer of the world's most expensive spice. Devon versions of the bread exist, and Elizabeth David noted that it was not always exclusive to the West Country – after all, Britain's greatest centre of saffron production was Saffron Walden in Essex. Proud Cornish bakers have always insisted that their saffron cake predates other counties' 'imitations', back to the days when Phoenician traders exchanged spices for Cornish tin; contemporary historians maintain the Phoenicians never travelled that far.

Nowadays, however, the truth of its pedigree is of less urgent concern than distinguishing between the genuine, yeast-raised, saffron-scented article and cheaply produced, artificially coloured travesties. Some saffron cakes have flecks of saffron filament as evidence of authenticity; other producers possibly feel this protests too much, or deters customers unaware of local tradition. At any rate, the aroma of true saffron is unmistakable, particularly when used in the generous dose demanded of a true saffron cake.

The better examples also have a rich moistness which is responsible for the bread's excellent keeping qualities – so much so that you need to wait several days before consigning the bread to a pudding, or even toasting it. Warming the bread does, however, strengthen the saffron aroma to an almost delirium-inducing level. Warm or cold, it takes happily to butter, preferably slightly salted, although cold clotted cream served with hot saffron cake is also a great treat.

Unfortunately, genuine saffron cake is hard to come by; both mail-order Cornish-baked cakes, and those produced elsewhere are usually boosted chemically, to the detriment of flavour, texture – and the skills of those bakers who turn out the genuine, costly article. Always demand to know the ingredients – and be prepared to pay a fair price for a great luxury.

· SALLY LUNN ·

Almost the most interesting aspect of this large, soft, butter-rich teacake is the dispute over the origin of its name, though a fresh and well-made Sally Lunn – lighter than any brioche – is a great treat.

FRENCH OR ENGLISH?

It seems that French recipes for a rich bread known as '*solilemme*' or '*solilem*' have been in existence for some centuries. One plausible theory is that the bread-cake originated in Alsace as a kind of kugelhupf without the fruit. A particularly appealing suggestion is that the name is a corruption of '*sol et lune*' (sun and moon) – either because the golden cake had a whiter, more silvery base at some stage, or through the tradition of serving it layered with white, scalded cream.

None of these theories appeals greatly to the proprietors of Sally Lunn's Refreshment House in Bath, who maintain that the eponymous lady really did live and bake her unique buns in Bath's Lilliput Alley at the close of the seventeenth century. They suggest, however, that the Huguenot Sally Lunn brought with her from France a favourite recipe for a brioche-style bread and then adapted it to the British oven (which is still open to view in the basement of the Refreshment House in what is now North Parade Passage).

THE IDEAL SALLY LUNN

Recipes from the eighteenth and nineteenth centuries differ quite widely – some add cream to the dough, while others use butter or eggs; spicing may involve saffron, mixed spices or lemon zest. In *The English Bread Book* Eliza Acton suggested adding caraway seeds, currants and candied peel to the basic dough. The bun served at the tea house in Bath is very light and spongy, contains no fruit, and is neither overly rich nor noticeably spiced, though it does have a very fresh aroma with a waft of something citrussy. This is a matter of guesswork, as the recipe is secret and the modern kitchens decidedly not open to view. Recent supermarket copies appear to accept the Refreshment House's Sally Lunn as a model, although the crumb may be denser and heavier and the flavour lemony.

USES OF SALLY LUNN

The Refreshment Room in Bath serves a motley assortment of toppings, hot and cold, savoury and sweet, on split and toasted bun halves, and the leaflet that accompanies plain take-home buns suggests cheese or pâté toppings. My feeling is that these savouries are generally too weighty or too coarse for so delicate a bread. Rather more apt and delicious is the leaflet's recommendation that the bun should be split and toasted, spread liberally with butter, then topped with strawberry jam and cream. There is no suggestion that the bread might be served plain and unadorned, yet a fresh Sally Lunn is so delicious that it is worth recalling Elizabeth David's advice in *English Bread and Yeast Cookery*: 'I find that when freshly cooked this kind of brioche-type cake . . . is much nicer without the spread of butter or cream. It is so delicate, and so light, that a slice or two goes beautifully with a fruit dessert such as a cooked apple dish or baked apricots, and even instead of biscuits or wafers with an ice cream, fruit fool or syllabub. The time to toast and butter the cake is next day when it has already begun to get dry.'

· SCHIACCIATA ·

In Italy this is simply the focaccia of Tuscany and the central regions – in other words a flat bread, dimpled and salted, anointed with olive oil and perhaps scattered with herbs. A number of breads going by rather different names, such as schiacciata, *padina, crescentina* and *gnocco* are in reality very similar.

British bakers have not yet adopted any of the other names, but a version of schiacciata is currently produced by the Innes bakery, of sourdough fame (see **Innes**). Their loaf is characteristically sourdough raised and differs from their focaccia by dint of containing much less olive oil (though its presence is noticeable). It has herbs aplenty, and the balance of lactic acid and herb gives a very distinctive, 'bright' taste, alongside a soft, gentle eating quality. Innes also produce a cheese schiacciata (see **Flavoured Breads**). This is a long way from the original Italian bread but perhaps not so distant in spirit, being hand shaped and wood-fire baked. Doubtless the name will be seized on and exploited in a spirit of industrial enterprise, with rather less pleasing results. On the other hand, the schiacciata might prove a source of plainer alternatives to the flavoured focaccia that have recently seized every baker's fancy.

· SCOTCH BREAD ·

So-called Scotch, or Scottish, bread as purveyed south of the Border almost invariably has only a notional connection with anything that might be termed a typically Scottish loaf. The connection, such as it is, is at least entirely complimentary – a bakery's Scotch bread is likely to be its finest loaf, made from a plain white dough subjected to a relatively long fermentation, since the Scots still have a reputation for being the finest bakers in Britain and are invoked as a stamp of quality. Another possible feature is a fairly heavy dose of salt, to reflect the dietary preference of Glaswegians and Western Scotland in general. Occasionally you may come across a loaf that reflects both traditional baking methods and a Scottish pedigree, but generally the bread does not live up to its name.

· SCOTS BAPS ·

Everyone is familiar with a bap – the word itself (from the sixteenth century, origin uncertain) sounds soft and basic, shorter even than bread or loaf. A bap is, of course, a flat, soft roll, usually dusted with flour. The dough might be white, 'wheatmeal' or wholemeal, but it should be neither rich nor austere, noticeably salty if made in true Scots tradition, and with an unmistakable aroma of lard.

I suspect that few of us south of the Border actually associate baps with Scotland. If your baps come from a packet the lard will probably be absent and the flour dusting thin, while there will be no sign of a dimple – the traditional thumb press which ensures that the crust remains smooth and unblistered. There again, you will probably not encounter many dimples in the baps you find in Scotland, even the largely excellent examples served at breakfast alongside bitter marmalade in fine guest houses. But as the dimple does not perceptibly alter the eating quality of the bap we can probably forget about this.

Sadder perhaps is F. Marian McNeill's lament: 'unfortunately the post-war baker's bap, which is baked on an iron plate, lacks the delectable flavour of the pre-war bap, which was baked on an honest stone sole, and is now hard to come by' (*The Scots Kitchen,* 1929).

The essential thing about baps is that they should be soft (ensured by a mixture of milk and water in the dough) and very fresh: they lose their charm at the first hint of staleness and are at their best warm from the oven, or quickly reheated. Factory-made baps have moisture retainers and anti-staling agents added, and are designed for sandwiches, not for rewarming.

· SELKIRK BANNOCK ·

This fruited loaf with a rich, buttery flavour could claim to be Scotland's answer to Ireland's barm brack and the bara brith of Wales (see entry) but prefers to declare itself a rather more 'purist' product – no dried or candied fruit other than sultanas and no spicing (or other flavouring).

Its precise origin is lost in the mists. The word bannock appears in written form in 1572. F. Marian McNeill suggests in *The Scots Kitchen* that it derives from the Latin *panicum*, doubtless through the influence of the Church and constant reference to Communion bread. The earliest styles of bannock were flat girdle cakes made largely of barley or of mixed grain, eventually soda-raised in the manner of scones (a sectioned plain bannock cuts into scones). The luxurious, fruited, yeast-raised loaf we now call a Selkirk bannock most likely developed from the fine 'manchet' breads familiar in fifteenth-century Edinburgh as in England, rather than from the staple girdle-baked flat bread. Be that as it may, its enduring popularity was ensured by a Robbie Douglas, who opened his bakery in Selkirk market place in 1859. A perfectionist who insisted on very particular local butters and the finest Turkish sultanas, he evidently produced loaves of such finesse that his fame, and that of his bannock, quickly spread countrywide, finding favour even with Queen Victoria. After that, there was no looking back.

A number of Borders bakeries claim that they bake to the original recipe but all have rejected the traditional lard in favour of vegetable fat – which at least does not compete with the flavour of butter. Sultanas traditionally comprise about half the weight of the loaf, which still leaves it light enough for toasting and buttering, or spreading with chunky marmalade. The shape is round and domed, rather like a cob loaf. It is difficult to choose between the products of various bakeries: look for the claim that no preservatives, colouring or artificial flavouring have been used, and that the fat has not been hydrogenated (a taller order, this). After that it is a question of personal preference. One of the finest loaves I have tasted happens to be a supermarket own-brand item (but commissioned from a Borders bakery).

I have kept bannocks for a couple of weeks and still enjoyed them toasted. Once stale, they make an excellent basis for a bread-and-butter pudding – I would dispense with butter but add vanilla, and perhaps cinnamon, in the usual way.

· SFILATINO ·

The Italian answer to the French baguette is a recent arrival in the UK, courtesy of La Fornaia, producers of the original ciabatta. The logical successor to the soft-eating ciabatta, the sfilatino is very much a case of *crosta* (crust) winning out over *mollica* (crumb).

The sfilatino you are likely to encounter in the UK is very similar to a baguette but does not display the characteristic slashes on the upper crust. Unlike its French rival it contains olive oil, giving it a different texture and aroma from French bread. The wheat flour used is rather harder than the French, reflected in a crumb with very small, regular holes, while the crust is firmer but less flaky than that of a baguette.

At the time of writing, the fine sfilatino loaves available in certain British supermarkets and specialist food stores do not yet jostle with grey, wan and cheap imitations, so selecting your sfilatino is not a problem. This is the bread to break alongside bitter-leaf or chargrilled vegetable salads, or to crumble into Italian-style soups. Thinly sliced, it provides perfect canapé-sized crostini. Pesto-filled sfilatino allows the garlic-butter baguette a respite, and where the holey ciabatta caused untold grief to the bread-and-butter brigade, the compact-crumbed sfilatino is far better equipped to hold even melted butter. Finally, it is even easier now for Italian bread enthusiasts to boast of consuming an entire loaf, plain and ungarnished, at a single sitting.

· SODA BREAD ·

The popularity of soda-raised breads in all corners of the UK has always surprised me, since most of the finer features of yeast-raised bread appear to be absent: there is no yeasty aroma; the bread has no soft spring but is resilient and crumbly; the texture is rather rough on the palate; and the flavour is all too often dominated by the soda, with chemical or bitter overtones. That, at least, is my experience of the majority of commercially available soda breads; home-made and hot from the oven is another matter. But I am aware that for every bread-lover who nods in agreement there will be plenty more who feel positively outraged. I do recognise certain positive aspects to soda breads, and must confess that there is one commercially pro-duced loaf (described below) which confounds almost all my earlier criticisms.

Soda breads, white or brown, are certainly less pappy than any cheap, pre-sliced, yeasted loaf and the majority have some wheatgerm and bran content, which also ensures at least a modicum of flavour. They make good, rough, chunky accompaniments to vegetable soups and certain cheeses, while soda farls (round loaves with a division mark splitting the bread into four wedges) can double up as scones if served with good jam and plentiful cream or butter. Soda-raised breads are also a saving grace for anyone avoiding yeast-fermented products – though you need to read labels carefully as certain 'scofa' breads made from a proprietary flour and soda mix occasionally have yeast added.

With the exception of certain Irish soda breads, and perhaps the Melrose loaf described below, most soda breads sold in Britain are remarkably similar in flavour and texture. Small craft bakeries are likely to offer a finer product, but there are few guarantees. This is one bread where the home-baked product generally excels over the commercial. You might, however, care to try the following.

THE MELROSE LOAF

The Melrose loaf is produced by the Houston Bakery in Hawick, Borders country, and distributed quite widely south of the Border. It is likely to be most Sassenachs' only encounter with a Scottish soda loaf, though a number of small craft bakeries in England make a rather similar product (often to be found in the bun and cake section). A malted wheatmeal loaf with a very dense, somewhat dry texture, the Melrose loaf makes no bones about declaring itself essentially a breakfast bread. It tastes somewhat mealy, with a touch of sweetness and a hint of richness, and provides a perfect foil for sticky, aromatic marmalade. It is also excellent with heather honey, but unless you find a very fresh loaf, toasting is almost essential.

Although the wrapper does not suggest it, that dense texture and nutty, yet mild, wheatgerm flavour make an ideal accompaniment to the runny cheeses that are gaining ground throughout the UK. If you have the chance, you should try it with perfectly ripe, scoopable Pentland and the Jersey-milk Bonchester from nearby Borders country.

IRISH SODA BREADS

Ireland's damp, mild climate favours a soft wheat, low in gluten content and not ideal for yeast-raised bread making. Fortunately, acid-containing buttermilk has always been plentiful and combines effectively with soda to leaven unyeasted bread dough. Centuries-old skills make light work of soda bread, usually a 50:50 blend of white and wholemeal flours (known in Ulster simply as 'wheaten bread' or 'scone', and even more simply as 'brown bread' in the South). A few loaves are exported to Britain: look for one that is reasonably light and moist, and without an overpowering slap of soda on the palate.

Since it is difficult to attain a tolerably light texture without excessive use of soda, 100 per cent wholemeal soda loaves are rare. However, an outstanding wholemeal loaf is produced by London-based Margaret Joyce of the Loaves and Fishes Company, who imports both Irish-milled flour and rich Irish buttermilk. The result is a dense, yet very moist bread, almost startlingly oil-rich (though no fat, apart from that of the buttermilk, is added), chewily coarse-textured, with a naturally sweet, wheaten aroma and flavour. The soda element is remarkably subtle, if unmistakable. Moreover, the bread stays moist and delicious for a number of days. No other commercially produced soda loaf available in Britain comes close to this at present.

The white soda farls imported from Northern Ireland or baked under licence in England are almost in another category. In contrast to the Yorkshire farl, which is a round marked into quarter divisions, these triangular wedges are cut before baking. They are high-rise and light, with a distinct soda tang, devised for toasting and splitting rather like an English muffin. There is very little difference between any of the brands currently available.

Fruited loaves and scones range from the pre-sliced, round loaf from the Ormo bakery, which is crumbly rather than dense, to white buttermilk scones barely distinguishable from any English scone baked in a round, to the occasional richly fruited, densely textured wholemeal loaf. A number undoubtedly cross the nebulous borderline between bread and cake.

A true Irishwoman, incidentally, would spread her bread with salted butter, regardless of accompaniment. This works well with the fruited breads, and with the Loaves and Fishes loaf; beyond those I am unconvinced.

STALE SODA BREAD

With very few exceptions, freshness is absolutely of the essence: after twelve hours most soda bread is only good for toasting, and after two days it may as well be crumbed. The assertive, salty flavour of the crumbs is fine for highly savoury stuffings or cheese-based puddings but generally undesirable in the case of sweet puddings or delicately flavoured dishes. A possible exception to the rule – particularly if the bread is a gentle or sweet one, is Brown Bread Ice Cream (see page 315), and the fruited version of the Loaves and Fishes bread makes an excellent bread pudding.

· SOURDOUGH BREAD ·

See **Wheaten Sourdough**.

· SPANISH BREAD ·

As elsewhere in Europe, breads in Spain vary from region to region and indeed from village to village, according to all the usual variables. Wholemeal, rye and cornmeal breads are found mainly in the north-west, but it is the good, crusty, fine white bread that has been famed from Roman times, whether in the form of *bollo* (roll) or *pan* (loaf). There are fine sweet breads, too.

Unlike their Italian and French counterparts, however, Spanish breads are poorly represented abroad. The only commercially produced Spanish-style loaves on sale in the UK at present are pan gallego and the sweet pan quemado (see entries). Both of these are soft-crusted, unlike the majority of loaves baked in Spain.

If you happen to live near a delicatessen serving a local Spanish community or one of the few Spanish bakeries in England, you will probably be able to buy a large, very crusty and well-risen loaf which may contain olive oil in the dough but generally does not. The best examples resemble the Castilian *hogaza* – somewhat flat and with a challenging, but delicious crust. The crumb of these loaves should then be your first choice for *tapas* or *hogazas* (see pages 191–2), for bread-thickened soups and stews and for *torrijas* (Spanish *pain perdu*). But the basic crusty loaves available on a more widespread basis at Italian delis will serve well in the absence of Spanish-baked bread.

· SPELT BREAD ·

A newcomer from the past, this powerfully flavoured, simple wholemeal loaf could claim to remind us of 'how bread used to be'.

Spelt is an ancient, hardy member of the wheat family, mentioned in the New Testament and grown throughout Europe (including Great Britain) for centuries. Production has not been considered cost effective in recent years but is now on the increase as natural hardiness is once more considered desirable. Most spelt production is organic. The nutritional qualities of the grain are remarkable: it is particularly high in protein and has a greater vitamin and mineral content than commonly used wheat. Genetic differences between the two varieties are pointed up by the insolubility of some of the gluten-forming spelt proteins, which has cheering implications for sufferers of coeliac disease (see **Gluten-free Bread**). At the time of writing, this aspect is still undergoing investigation.

Something of the robust nature of the grain is captured in the texture and flavour of the bread: it tends to be quite dense and chewy, with a hint of huskiness, while the nutty flavour has a noticeable touch of acidity and even bitterness. This is partly due to the fermentation method, which tends to be an overnight 'sponge and dough'. To some extent, it looks and tastes like many a stone-ground wholewheat loaf, but more so. Spelt bread is a perfect complement to nutty and mildly acidic British cheeses, robust vegetable soups and substantial salads, and one of the few breads that can hold their own against rich, dark honeys.

At present, only a very few bakers are producing tentative batches of spelt bread; if you do manage to find it, however, bear in mind that it is possible to make a well-risen, attractively textured loaf, and reject anything brick-like.

Spelt bread stays reasonably moist for up to five days. Like any wholemeal loaf it toasts quite attractively, and tastes even more powerful after such treatment.

· SPICE BREAD ·

See **Flavoured Breads** and **Pain d'Épices**.

· SPROUTED GRAIN BREAD ·

These back-to-basics loaves, composed of compacted, unleavened, barely baked sprouted grain are suddenly gathering devotees at roller-coaster speed. Under the labels Essene and Manna, they have been around for a number of years but failed to attract mass popularity, partly due to the need for refrigerated display and storage. Now that long-life versions in specialised packaging are widely available the popularity of these Flintstone diet precursors seems assured.

The simplest are compacted cakes of organically grown germinated wheat grain, with no other ingredients, 'baked' at extremely low temperatures that arrest the sprouting and develop the merest hint of a crust. One producer claims that the recipe was used by the Essene peoples, who inhabited a region near the Dead Sea some 2000 years ago, and was recorded in a first century Aramaic manuscript stored in the Vatican. Others claim that this is the original Staff of Life, or Manna, the recipe given by God himself.

The bread's nutritional value is probably greater than that of any other simple bread – it is naturally high in fibre and the protein and vitamin content is further increased by allowing the grain to sprout. Sodium levels are barely traceable, while starches have been converted into readily digestible sugars.

While its virtues are beyond doubt, I cannot help wishing that God had granted the Essenes a more toothsome recipe. It may be that my tastebuds and expectations are jaded by yeast and salt, but after chewing more than a tiny chunk an overriding impression of moist matting takes over (even the aroma is reminiscent of a coir mat left out in the rain). A kinder comparison would be with grated carrot, as the grain shares something of the carrot's natural sweetness. Laden with salted butter and smothered in honey or chunks of bitter marmalade this might be a very acceptable breakfast bread, but the added fat, sodium and sugar are precisely what its producers proudly avoid. More acceptable, to my mind, are the loaves with added fruit and malt, which are rather similar to conventional malted fruit loaves. Other flavours available are multigrain, onion, carrot and stem ginger. There is little to choose between the different brands, though you might find that the short-life loaves taste fresher while the long-life ones are more convenient.

This is one bread that favours refrigeration: once open, even the long-life loaves go mouldy quickly at room temperature. It is too moist to make into crumbs, too compact to absorb liquids, and too assertively flavoured to make a versatile pudding base – but if you become a devotee I doubt you will have a 'leftovers' problem to speak of.

· STAFFORDSHIRE OATCAKES ·

A product of the Staffordshire potteries and barely heard of outside its home county until recently, this curious, floppy, yeasted pancake is now engendering mild addiction throughout Britain, thanks largely to supermarket distribution.

A Staffordshire oatcake is not a jot like the crumbly Scottish biscuit; soft, moist and pliable, it resembles a large flattened pikelet; local names include 'Potteries poppadums', 'Tunstall tortillas' and 'clay Suzettes'. Its origins are difficult to determine; it may date back to the first successful cultivation of wild oats, sometime after the Roman conquest of Britain. Historian C. Anne Wilson notes in *Food and Drink in Britain* that by the Tudor era numerous styles of oatcakes had become established in the North of England: Kitcheness bread, 'thin oatcakes made of thin batter'; and riddle cakes, which were thick and 'leavened with ale-barm or sour leaven'. Soft oatcakes still make an occasional appearance in Yorkshire and South Manchester and are established in pockets of Derbyshire. In neighbouring Stafford-shire, the Industrial Revolution that created the potteries also brought about a 'front-room' oatcake-baking industry run by pottery wives, which survives to this day.

BUYING STAFFORDSHIRE OATCAKES

The ingredients are as simple as the baking process: the dough/batter is made of fine oatmeal, white flour, occasionally a little wheatgerm, and skimmed milk or half-milk, half-water. The slack mixture is yeast-raised, poured on to a griddle, then baked and racked to dry slightly. The finished oatcake has a mealier flavour than pikelets or crumpets and does not need to be smothered in butter before it displays its virtues.

All oatcakes aspire to the same ideal but details such as salt level and degree of pliability vary from producer to producer, and locals have fierce preferences. The rest of us are not afforded such luxury of choice: although oatcakes from one or two of the front-room concerns can be ordered by mail, the oatcake that is commercially distributed is made by a single (in fact the only) factory. Dismissed by locals as 'cardboard cutouts' the oatcakes available in supermarkets are actually rather delicious. Oatcakes I ordered by mail from Glenn Fowler, baker at the front-room oatcake shop in Hanley, were indeed more fine and delicate, but rather too salty for my taste.

USES OF STAFFORDSHIRE OATCAKES

An oatcake fresh from the bakestone has a hint of crispness that is lacking in the packaged examples. Staffordshire-born-and-bred aficionados will not touch a day-old specimen; the rest of us, however, have to make do. Try one straight from the packet and the chewy, resilient texture may stop you mid-bite. Take a moment to warm it, either in the microwave, a dry frying pan or under the grill, and the texture softens considerably to that of a thickish, freshly made pancake. If you toast it over or under a fairly high heat the oatcake will re-acquire crisp edges, a nice contrast with the basic softness. This is just as effective with refrigerated oatcakes, which is how they should be stored if not eaten within a day of purchase. They freeze well and reheat quickly from frozen, but should be separated by layers of waxed paper, like any pancake.

As its nicknames suggest, the Staffordshire oatcake does share certain qualities with both chapatis and crêpes – it can simply be torn into rough pieces and eaten hot or cold (though not straight from the fridge) with a fried breakfast or with steamed vegetables; or it can be warmed, rolled round anything from a sausage to a mushroom ragoût, and sauced, baked or gratinated. Neal's Yard Dairy in London sells them as a complement to their British cheeses; Glenn Fowler, shocked that I sampled his oatcakes neat, suggested firmly that I microwave them with a bit of cheese and perhaps tomato sauce. Steve Dixon, oatcake chronicler and author of a recipe booklet, suggests spreading them with grated Cheddar or Cheshire cheese, or perhaps goat's cheese and bottled brown sauce. The North Staffordshire Hotel in Stoke serves an 'Oatcake Arnold Bennett' named after the novelist, who had oatcakes sent to him in London by overnight train: the 'Arnold Bennett' is filled with smoked haddock and mackerel and coated with cheese sauce, and is somewhat distanced from the popular Pottery fry-up. In his *Oatcake Cookbook*, Steve Dixon lists recipes for tostadas, dosa, lasagne, and even Club sandwich, and breaks the savoury rule with a 'Hanley Forest Gateau'. I would hesitate to layer my oatcakes with morellos, cream, kirsch and chocolate but am secretly relieved at this sanction of a sweet recipe: I have always thoroughly enjoyed Staffordshire oatcakes spread with a thin layer of strawberry conserve.

· STOLLEN ·

The Dresdner stollen is now as much a feature of Christmas in the UK as its Italian equivalent, the panettone. A mark of its acceptance is its year round availability; while the large loaves linger for months past Christmas in big stores, a number of supermarkets have capitalised on demand by producing British-made 'stollen sticks', usually sold, as the rich little cakes they are, on the cake counter.

There are many versions of stollen within Germany and a good few within Dresden, which is acknowledged as the source of the richest version. The shape – a long, ridged loaf with tapered or rounded ends – is said to represent the Christ child in swaddling clothes and the bread is more properly known as Christstollen. The main variation on this dense, fruit-laden, vanilla-scented yeast cake, apart from proportions of butter and fruit, is the inclusion or otherwise of marzipan (a relatively light almond paste, not the dense yellow stuff found on British Christmas cakes). Where it is rolled into the bread, marzipan undoubtedly adds an extra dimension of moistness and richness; apple-filled stollen (generally British baked) achieve the moistness without the high sugar dose.

British bakers have copied the essential features of the stollen quite successfully and we now have whisky and brandy versions competing for shelf space with the original rum-flavoured loaf. Most, it must be said, are a real treat and I would as happily buy a good British product as a stollen from Dresden. As with panettone, it is worth checking that true vanilla rather than the artificial, rather thinner flavour of vanillin has been used.

USES OF STOLLEN

Stollen keeps well wrapped in foil and stored in a cool place – the fridge if you want to keep it for a month or more. The starch will harden a little but the bread can be revived by heating it in a moderate oven (still wrapped in foil but slice it into portions first). Like most breads, stollen can be frozen for at least three months – again it is wise to slice it first.

Ideally, stollen should be enjoyed as it is, with a cup of coffee. Most versions of the bread are too dense to make successful puddings, and the marzipan layer is problematic. One possibility is to soak the stale slices – toasted first if you like – in dessert wine or Madeira and layer them with bottled fruit or apple purée and cream to form a trifle.

· STOTTIE, GEORDIE STOTTIE ·

A flat disc of a bread once confined to North-east England, the Stottie has suddenly been seized on by the revivalist consciences of supermarket bread buyers. Originally a crunchy-crusted, oven-bottom bap made from leftover dough perked up with a pinch of pepper, the stottie allegedly gained its name from the practice of bouncing, or 'stotting' the freshly baked bread to check its texture.

I doubt whether J. & F. Thomson of Newcastle, producers of the widely distributed commercial stottie, test the bounceability of their pizza-sized half-pound 'flour cake', despite their claim of generations-old Tyneside tradition. This stottie has a fluffy, insubstantial consistency and an unsatisfying flavour that lags some way behind a fairly pleasant aroma. I suspect even a freshly baked specimen would fall flat on its face.

The very same stottie has none the less been seized on with alacrity by sandwich bars up and down the country: where the North majors on pease pudding stuffings, southerners appear to have adopted the stottie as a 'light' alternative to the ciabatta – lighter even than a regular bap. Prepacked sandwiches usually consist of just a quarter of a stottie but the whole bread does seem an ideal size for a *pan bagnat* (page 198), the Niçois sandwich stuffed with vegetables and doused in olive oil, if a more appropriate bread cannot be found.

· STRADELLA COLORATA ·

This is a distinctively shaped (split, tapered oval) and coloured (swirls of spinach- and tomato-stained dough) bread from La Fornaia. Slices of this green and red zebra of a loaf make a dramatic impact in the bread baskets of smart restaurants. They are also much employed for startling 'look at me' sandwiches, which unfortunately don't have an equally dramatic 'eat me' quality. The bread itself has a firm, dry crumb from which the flavours of tomato and spinach are curiously absent.

Although somewhat disappointing in flavour, the *stradella* can be used to make dramatic and imaginative canapés or crostini. You could add moisture and richness with a layer of mascarpone and pungency with vibrant Italian-style relishes – a finely diced medley of green olive and sun-dried tomato echoes the colour of the bread as well as providing sympathetic flavours.

· SUN-DRIED TOMATO BREAD ·

See **Flavoured Breads**.

· SUNFLOWER AND HONEY BREAD ·

A sweet, nutty style of bread which could almost be classed as a multigrain bread (see entry), except that it has become a hugely popular and surprisingly varied category in its own right.

Generally speaking, the use of seeds in bread falls in one of two camps: sprinkled over the crust, or added to the dough of mixed grain breads where the seeds fight for space with flaked, kibbled and malted grains of different denominations. Sunflower seeds, however, differ from others such as sesame and poppy in that they are natural dough improvers and will help loaves to achieve an open texture; a number of sunflower loaves incorporate a meal ground from the seeds in addition to the whole seeds. The aroma of sunflower meal is powerful, almost overwhelming, and the flavour may be too austere for many people unless tempered by other ingredients.

Perhaps it was German bakers, with their passion for packing breads with nuts and seeds, who first discovered the happy alliance of sunflower seeds and honey, the dry nuttiness of slightly roasted seeds acting as a foil for the honey's rich sweetness. The experiment may well have been prompted by concerns of health – certainly the wholesome image of both sunflowers and honey partly accounts for the bread's lasting appeal. Whatever its origin, sunflower and honey bread is now a firmly established category in the UK.

Some loaves are simply produced by adding seeds and honey to a granary mix. This can be quite successful, as the seeds echo the nuttiness of malted grain, but all too often the level of honey is cloyingly high. More successful are breads that temper the sweetness further with a proportion of rye in the dough, and perhaps incorporate some form of sourdough, too, to give a keen edge. Many of these are German inspired, while one or two are made from German-produced pre-mixes. The level of honey added to the dough varies considerably; loaves in which the use of honey is so subtle as to be barely noticeable (some even declare themselves '*not* sweet') are certainly the most versatile and can be used in virtually any context.

Finally, there is a tribe of stoneground, often organic, wholemeal breads. These can be most successful of all, with the seeds and honey simply augmenting the wheat's natural nuttiness and sweetness. Good on their own, they are perfectly delicious with British farmhouse cheeses, from salty Cheshire to biting Cheddar.

Ways of using stale bread are more or less determined by the basis of the loaf (granary, white, rye, wholemeal and so on) and the amount of seeds. Most work particularly well in stuffings.

· SWEDISH BREAD ·

Perhaps the most widely distributed Swedish-style bread in Britain is the one in the Kelderman range – a Dutch-baked bread, very similar to compact Danish rye loaves. With little competition from Swedish-originated breads, this is somewhat misleadingly shaping British understanding of the genre.

Some Swedish-baked breads are sold at fairs held in London at Easter and Christmas, and in occasional store promotions. With the imminent acceptance of Sweden into the European Community, these should rapidly become more widely available in Britain. Amongst the most popular are the sweet-sour limpas and kavrings, the latter being the richer of the two. While limpa simply means loaf, both types tend to comprise a blend of wheat, rye and malt flours and to be enriched with margarine and sweetened with corn syrup. More festive loaves might be spiced with aniseed, fennel and bitter orange peel – a good match for sweet-cured fish, such as the famous *ansjovis*, as well as hams, smoked game and sweetish yet powerful cheeses. Many white loaves are similarly sweetened and lightly spiced, though there has been a health-conscious trend towards unsweetened basic breads.

POLAR FLAT BREAD

One style of bread that has recently arrived in Britain is Polar Flat Bread. This is actually Lapp in origin, its nationality claimed as fiercely by Finns as by Swedes. Whatever the issue, both shapes (thin, flat squares and rather puffier rounds) make a welcome and interesting addition to the range of breads sold in the UK. Polar Thins and Polar Rounds look for all the world like soft crispbreads, and taste not dissimilar: both are made from a typical blend of fine wheat and rye flours enriched with margarine and dried milk and slightly sweetened. They also appear to have a slight scent of fennel or caraway, though this is not declared on the English packaging.

USES OF POLAR FLAT BREADS

These breads are very good eaten 'neat' but are in fact designed for making sandwiches, either split or rolled. Interestingly, both Thins and Rounds have been scaled down for the British market – partly for reasons of economy, no doubt, but also, one suspects, to render them more manageable to British culinary imagination (or, perhaps, its absence). Where Swedish wrappers illustrate split and toasted Rounds filled with cheese, egg and dill; cheese, ham and mustard;

sardines in tomato sauce; and liver pâté, *ansjovis* (substitute anchovy) and parsley, the British wrapper concentrates on simple open sandwiches, and the inevitable pizza. The wrapper for Thins similarly suggests simple cones and lasagne, where the Swedes would favour spreading, rolling and slicing.

The sweetness of the breads and their overtones of rye and spice make them perfect for a Swedish buffet table or *smorgåsbord* as well as with British smoked meats and cheeses, and the sweet-cured rollmops and gravad lax that we have more or less adopted as our own – in fact, any foods that have at least a hint of sweetness.

· SWISS BREAD ·

Switzerland boasts over 200 types of bread and an exemplary bakery school in Lucerne, yet only two basic styles are currently represented in Britain, and – if you discount the commercial Vogel loaf (see entry) – neither of those is widely available.

British loaves calling themselves Swiss basically build on the healthy muesli image seen on cereal packets: wholesome wholemeal with a touch of grit and fibre. Amusingly enough, this rather approximates to the infamous *Graubrot*, or grey bread, the least desirable grade of pre-prosperous days. The present-day British crop are, however, modern versions on the theme, and a welcome contrast to both the British wholemeal loaf and the sour full-grain rye loaves of Germanic tradition.

Perhaps the finest of the loaves are from the North: Bettys tearooms in Yorkshire, founded by a Swiss confectioner, still send their bakers to train at Lucerne and have perfected a palatable 'Swiss peasant loaf', dense and attractively moist, more wheat than rye in flavour, but with cracked rye and chopped walnuts for textural contrast. Swiss Emmental certainly acquires a fresh dimension when eaten in the company of this bread, which could have been designed with cheese in mind.

The innovative Kroustie company, which purveys a wide range of European-style breads via gazebos in West Yorkshire shopping malls, includes in its range a 'Swiss healthy wholemeal' – once again a mixture of wholemeal, wheat and rye flours but this time with a marked sourdough tone. Like the Bettys loaf (and in contrast to the Vogel) this is free form, oven-bottom baked and a fair representative of a certain style of Swiss baking. It, too, works well with Swiss cheeses, and with dried beef and mountain hams, as well as most soups and salads. Neither of these loaves is distributed in the South at present, though a number of bakeries produce 'Swiss muesli bread' in vaguely Germanic style.

Better known, perhaps, is the zopf, a milk-and-butter-enriched plaited loaf, again produced by craft bakeries. Unfortunately the zopf is not invariably sold by name but often simply sited next to brioches and chollahs in larger bread departments. It differs from these by being at base a milk bread; it may also contain kirsch. It is generally so light, despite a noticeable butteriness, that most people would have no problem in consuming an entire loaf – which would be a shame, as it makes excellent puddings, whether of the bread-and-butter, steamed or souffléd varieties.

· TARTE TROPÉZIENNE ·

A rare creature amongst the *pâtes brisées*, *sucrées* and *feuilletées* of the French patisserie counter, this bread-based 'tarte' is little known outside St Tropez but has none the less made a certain mark in the UK.

Similar in concept to the German *Bienenstich* (usually sold in the UK under its direct translation of 'bee sting' – see entry), the Tropézienne is composed of a large, round cake-sized bun made of an enriched dough and coated in toasted, flaked almonds. After it is baked it is split and filled with a rum-flavoured Chantilly cream or *crème patissière*. The blend of lightly enriched bread and custard-based cream is surprisingly delicious, and considerably less cloying than even a light sponge. It is very much a Continental concept, but not so far removed, perhaps, from Cornish splits.

The tarte Tropézienne makes an excellent dessert served with a simple, sharp fruit compote; when slightly stale it can be used to make a light trifle – moisten the tarte with sweet wine and top the cream with a low-sugar preserve, or compote: more of a tipsy cake than a trifle, perhaps, but none the less light and delicious.

· TEACAKES ·

Teacakes are made for toasting. So unthinkable is the notion that anyone might nibble their teacake ungrilled and unbuttered that the majority of British bakers get away with little short of murder. The problem is that the route to maximum butter absorption is strewn with emulsifiers: most teacakes consist of poor-quality bread dough with good air-trapping quotient, 'enriched' with a little fat – generally a hydrogenated oil – and a scattering of indifferent-quality dried fruit. Once the starches have been softened by heating, the surfaces browned by toasting and the crumb soaked in butter, the standard teacake's unappealing aspects are easily ignored.

Although teacakes were always meant to be eaten toasted, toasting was not, of course, always designed to disguise. In Yorkshire, indisputably linked with the teacake, the tradition was of rich un-fruited teacakes made from a milk dough, but the vast majority to be found there now are of the mass-produced, bland variety. However, there is nothing bland about the buns sold at Bettys tearooms in Yorkshire. Were you to buy any of the currant, wholemeal or spiced teacakes on offer at the shop you would have trouble saving any for the toaster. None the less, toasted and buttered they really are a delight.

To a bleary-eyed breakfaster popping a mass-produced teacake in the toaster, nothing could seem more amusing, even precious, than Dorothy Hartley's advice on the matter in *Food in England*: 'Toast bottoms and tops first; split and toast insides; *lay* (do not poke or spread) bits of butter on the lower half; cover with the top half; and invert. Keep hot for 3 minutes, then turn right side up, polish the top with a suspicion of butter, cut in quarters, and send to table.' No mere show of course – the process was designed to do its best by a decent bun and turn it into a perfect treat. I suspect we generally regard the humble teacake as unworthy of our concern, but if we care at all about our basic bread this is as shortsighted as reasoning that a sandwich loaf has only one necessary function – and that function has little to do with questions of quality or taste. It is surely worth ensuring that an indulgence is a real treat.

· TORTILLAS ·

The flat breads of Mexico have long been familiar to devotees of Tex-Mex cuisine and even to snackers on corn chips, which are simply deep-fried shards of tortilla. Now they are available at the bread counters of every multiple they can fairly claim to be established in the UK in their own right.

Tortillas come in two varieties: corn and wheat (or flour, as the latter are sometimes known), and are both imported and produced in this country. Corn tortillas are much the more venerable of the two, being the staple food of the Mayan Indians. The Mayas cultivated many different strains of maize, from which they formed as many different styles of breads. As these proved quite unpronounceable to the Spanish conquistadors they named the lot tortillas, or 'little cakes'; they also introduced wheat and used it in similar fashion.

Corn tortillas emerge from their airtight plastic packet looking like a cross between soft cardboard and stiffened chamois leather. They soften considerably on heating but are much more palatable when fried until crisp. Wheat tortillas are tougher than yeast-leavened breads but are fine once warmed and filled with a moist mixture. The flavour of wheat tortillas is not wholly dissimilar to that of the corn ones but the texture is smoother and more pliable.

Although a number of companies are competing for the market, their products are very similar. Imported tortillas tend to be packed with improvers and preservatives. Corn tortillas are the purer of the two, despite traces of the lime with which the fresh corn is treated to produce *masa* and *masa harina*, the dried flour. Wheat tortillas contain fats, usually hydrogenated, dextrose and raising agents; soya flour may be used as an enriching agent.

USES OF TORTILLAS

Manufacturers tend to suggest that wheat tortillas can be eaten plain with savoury accompaniments, rather like flat breads. I feel they are a little too tough for such use and work better as pancake substitutes. One or two producers market salsas and dips to encourage the customer to convert their corn tortillas into *nachos* or *tostaditas*. This involves cutting each tortilla into quarters and deep-frying them in corn oil until crisp. It is cheaper and easier to buy a packet of corn chips, but there are plenty of other uses for tortillas:

Tostadas are deep-fried whole corn tortillas, usually sandwiched with spicy, savoury fillings and stacked in a pile.

Tacos shells are shaped *tostadas*; special wire moulds exist, or you can fold the tortilla into shape with tongs. *Tacos* are filled with almost any combination of savoury ingredients and crisp salad.

Taquitos are made by softening corn tortillas by frying them in oil for a few seconds only. They are then filled, rolled into cigar shapes and fried again until crisp and golden. *Taquitos* can also be made with wheat tortillas and wrapped round a *fajita* filling (usually grilled, marinated meat or chicken), in which case they might be left soft.

Enchiladas are *taquitos* or *fajitas* that have been covered with a sauce and baked in the oven.

Quesadillas are again best made with wheat tortillas, although corn could be used and fried until crisp. Tortillas are softened briefly in a dry or oiled griddle, filled with a cheese-based mixture, then folded and warmed or fried.

Burritos are made from wheat tortillas which are filled and then folded like envelopes. These are usually left soft but may be crisp-fried, in which case they are known as *chimichangas*.

· TRESSE ·

This describes a three-strand plaited loaf which can be made from various styles of bread, although the ones available do not differ greatly. If you find it at a French bakery it will almost certainly be made in the style of a baguette (or *pain ordinaire*), and will most likely be scattered with poppy seeds. If you buy it elsewhere as a poppy seed plait it is likely to be a little more dense, and perhaps enriched with milk. A loaf of this type can be found at a small number of Danish-style bakeries.

I recall from 'Danwich' days the near-perfect combination of light crumb with the crunch of almost acrid poppy seeds and the creaminess of scrambled egg; I also find the poppy-seed plait a good foil for the smooth, soft texture of smoked salmon.

· TURKESTAN BREAD ·

'An unforgettable taste from a faraway land' runs the legend on the wrapper that covers the widely distributed loaf baked by H. Stokes & Sons of Gloucestershire. A good few centuries up on Dr Vogel, the pedigree claimed by the Turkestan loaf is on a footing with that of Essene bread (see **Sprouted Grain Bread**).

We read on the packet that the Turkoman tribes have inhabited the Turkestan region of Asiatic Russia 'since Biblical times' – the suggestion is that their bread, like their nomadic lifestyle, remains unchanged. Somewhere there is an admission that Turkoman bread is in fact unleavened; this would make it rather different from the modern squishy, emulsifier-boosted loaf. Somehow, I doubt ancient availability of wheat flakes or nomadic use of soya flour. Of course it is easy to poke fun and, to be fair, the bread only claims to be *based* on traditional Turkestan recipes. It is packed with grains and notches up a creditable fibre content. If only it felt like an honest chew, one might not be tempted to cavil at all.

More attractive and convincing is the scattering of Turkestan loaves produced by small specialist bakeries throughout the UK (under licence from the millers, Spillers). One such is made by the Yorkshire institution, Bettys. Perhaps it takes Swiss training, as undergone by Bettys bakers, to understand the potential of a healthy grain-packed bread. Their Turkestan is baked free-form and has a dark, crunchy crust. Its aroma is more mealy than sweet, its texture pleasingly compact, and the flavour, while undeniably on the austere side, leaves no bitter tang (a problem with the more commercial loaf). Once again, craft shines through a pre-mix.

Supermarket instore bakeries generally produce a tin loaf version as lightly disappointing as that of the Stokes bakery. To set the bread in context, however, it is undoubtedly more interesting than the softgrain tribe, and certainly worth trying if high-fibre bread is an important consideration for you. If you find you enjoy this particular mix of grains and flakes, do none the less check whether a small-scale craft bakery near you might not be producing a more satisfying loaf.

· TURKISH BREAD ·

Visit a Turkish bakery in London and the pre-eminent status of bread in the Middle Eastern diet becomes clamorously evident. A wide range of breads, flat and leavened, cartwheel- and snack-sized, pour on to shop shelves from the adjacent bakery and disappear into bags and baskets almost as fast. Shoppers – Greek and Cypriot as well as Turkish – stagger out impossibly loaded; those with a free hand (principally children) waste no time in tearing off a chunk from a steaming hot loaf. As Nevin Halici notes in her *Turkish Cookbook*, 'a Turk will eat as much bread in a day as an English or American person would eat in a week'.

Many of the breads sold in Turkish bakeries are as Greek or Cypriot, or indeed Syrian or Lebanese, as they are Turkish: pitta and lavash among the flat breads, daktyla and the round, capped Greek loaves, plain and seeded. Others are not unlike the oval Iranian *barbari*, scattered with sesame seeds. The basic, most popular bread, simply *ekmek*, weighs 500g/1lb 2oz, is 25cm/10inches round, leavened and light, but no more than 4cm/1½inches thick, and dimpled like an Italian focaccia. This is very simple and plain, made of standard white baker's flour and delicious hot from the oven. Being fairly flat it stales quite quickly, but remains fine for serving with dips and perfect for making Turkish bread pudding (*ekmek tatlisi*) for which a recipe is given on page 281.

Almost invariably you will find a range of seeded sticks, including the Egyptian-style *semit* – crisp rings of bread dough coated in sesame seeds. Occasionally the dough is enriched with butter and egg and well on the way to joining the ranks of celebrated Turkish pastries – which is where you should look for them if they fail to appear on the bread shelves.

· VIENNA ROLLS ·

See **Bridge Rolls, Vienna Rolls, Pains au Lait**.

· VITBE ·

Like Hovis (see entry), the proprietary VitBe flour mix was devised in response to the demand that flavour be added back to white loaves produced from roller-milled flour. In this case, too, wheatgerm was separated from bran, cooked to stabilise it, and mixed in with the white flour. The basic mix is still similar to the original, but the Allied Bakeries VitBe wheatgerm loaf is now very much in the wrapped, pre-sliced, emulsifier-boosted league. However, it still has its fans, despite the general trend towards grain and bran packed breads – to which Allied Bakeries have swiftly responded by producing VitBe Hi-Bran. This is now outselling the wheatgerm loaf. It still has a cooked wheatgerm content and something of its characteristic aroma and flavour but its real aim is to win the palatable bran game: the wrapper declares that the loaf is 'specially baked to be lighter than most other bran breads' and tells the consumer precisely how many slices will be required to meet recommended dietary fibre levels. To anyone unblinded by the drive to fibre, it makes for harsh eating, allied to an insubstantial texture and an unfriendly aftertaste; those pursuing fibre through thick and thin will probably welcome that lightness, along with the instant flavour-awareness secured by the use of salt, sugar and vinegar. None the less, more of a palatised pill than a delight for the senses.

· VOGEL LOAF ·

The Swiss equivalent of Hovis and VitBe (see entries), this multigrain, high-fibre loaf has been going strong for some thirty-five years. Remarkably enough, it preceded the F-plan diet, government-endorsed fibre counts, and the current spate of softgrain breads – a tribute to the prescience of the Swiss nutritionist Dr Alfred Vogel.

Less to the loaf's credit is a rather wan flavour and a somewhat dry and over-light texture. I imagine it may have altered over the years to suit changing tastes, though the firm of Goswell's, who bake the bread commercially and distribute it widely throughout the UK, claim their methods are faithful to the original conception. Certainly instore versions of the Vogel loaf seem rather lighter still.

Whatever my reservations, the Vogel loaf has a dedicated following, and certainly this highly textured bread (plenty of kibbled wheat and rye grain, plus bran) is a much better proposition than the cheap bandwagon softgrain loaves. If it is toothsome grain you are after, it is worth giving the Vogel a trial.

· WALNUT BREAD ·

Strange that a bread that goes so well with Cheddar and Stilton cheese should be so little represented in British bread-baking tradition, that British supermarkets should be well stocked with *pain aux noix, pane con noci* and German 'goldgrain' walnut breads, but rarely afford a glimpse of an English walnut loaf.

If you hunt hard in delis and specialist bread departments, or buy from small, independent bakeries, there is at least a fair chance that you will come across a walnut bread in English style – or rather two distinct styles, both different from the Continental. The walnut bloomer is usually made with a base of unbleached white flour but looks russetty-brown when sliced, simply from particles of nut; this is usually crusty and light. The walnut granary loaf is usually baked in a cob shape with walnuts added to the proprietary flour mix, and is softer and moister, with chunkier pieces of nut throughout. A few bakers add dried fruit such as apricots or raisins to a basic white or wholewheat walnut loaf; these usually have more of a sweet fruited loaf or tea loaf character than that of a savoury bread.

PAIN AUX NOIX

French walnut bread has been granted a stab at widespread appeal by technology that allows dough to cross the Channel in a part-baked, frozen state. This has enabled supermarkets and large stores to 'bake-off' what can truthfully be described as French bread, even if the question of quality is not addressed as firmly as it might.

Freshly baked *pain aux noix* can be a great treat; the crisp, toasted nuggets of walnut that poke through the crust add considerably to the crunch and have a smoky sweetness brought about by exposure to fairly high heat. In a loaf with a high proportion of wholewheat flour the nuts almost magically point up the intrinsic nuttiness of the grain. Some bakers add a little rye to the dough to balance the richness but this is barely perceptible. More obvious is the incorporation of walnuts into a country-style loaf, usually made with some proportion of sourdough. These loaves can be almost brick-like in weight and tend to taste earthy and noticeably sour.

Pain aux noix can also be shorthand for breads containing a mixture of walnuts, hazelnuts (*noisettes*) and even raisins. Some French bakeries in the UK as in France are experimenting with different nuts, principally pecans, in which case the loaf should be known as *pain aux noix de pecan*.

PANE CON NOCI

This generally refers to three different types of Italian-style nut bread: a tin-baked loaf, British in style apart from the addition of olive oil; a ciabatta studded with sultanas as well as walnuts; and a long log of a loaf, more compact and rounded than a ciabatta, richly packed with both sultanas and raisins and hence more correctly known as *pane di uva con noci*.

USES OF WALNUT BREAD

All of these are good accompaniments to cheeses of various kinds. Light *pain aux noix* and English walnut bloomers are best served with fresh, soft cheeses or fairly young, moist, crumbly or flaky versions of Lancashire, Caerphilly or Cotherstone, but Stilton works well too. Try light *pain aux noix* with simple vegetable soups. The sweeter, richer granary-style breads are perhaps better with more mature, firm, salty cheeses – Cheddar is a favourite. The country-style *pains aux noix* suit French cheeses, from slightly tangy *triple crème* examples to young and mature goat's cheese, to Roquefort, and are perfect with sorrel soup.

Walnut breads containing dried fruit are perhaps best served toasted and spread with honey or marmalade or, in the case of *pane di uva con noci*, mascarpone cheese.

Slightly stale walnut bread toasts well and is good coated with melted cheese as an accompaniment to vegetable soups. Thoroughly stale and dry bread is best used in stuffings.

· WHEATEN SOURDOUGH ·

This is a distinct and delicious category of bread, and increasingly popular – but rarely, if ever, sold under its proper name. The closest you may come is to a loaf simply described as 'sourdough' or 'sour bread' which usually implies that it is made largely or entirely of wheat. As a rule, however, wheaten sourdough loaves masquerade under a variety of French and English names.

One exception to the Anglo-French dominance is the Italian-baked bread imported by Patricia Michelson of La Fromagerie in North London. This heavy-crusted, soft-crumbed goliath of a loaf (some 4kg/9lb in weight, but sold in manageable sections), smoky and sour, is sold simply as a *pagnotta*, a generic Italian name for country bread. This is one of a kind, however, and not as yet widely available.

WHAT'S IN A NAME?

The best approach is to treat the name as a bakery or shop code. For instance, the 'San Francisco sourdough' sold by numerous London stores is produced by Bagatelle, a London-based French bakery. If you buy direct from the bakery shop you will be informed that the loaf is a *pain au levain*, or yeast free. This in fact means that it is free of baker's (i.e. compressed) yeast; it relies on a sour culture and natural airborne yeasts to effect fermentation.

Another wheaten sourdough loaf sold as *levain* by certain London shops is none other than the *campaillou* (see **Campagne**). This could hardly be more distinct from the Bagatelle loaf: where the *campaillou* is small, light, crusty and holey, sweet and gentle in flavour, the *pain au Levain*/San Francisco bread (which is available in various sizes) is weighty, compact, chewy-crusted, moist and deeply sour. At least both loaves are wheaten, and of a medium extraction (what used to be known loosely as wheatmeal); fortunately, both are excellent loaves of their kind, and unlikely to disappoint an experimental or confused purchaser.

More serious is the problem of short-cut loaves produced by factory bakeries in order to satisfy growing consumer interest in breads with a lactic tang. Taking a minimum-effort, maximum-profit route, a bag of powdered pre-mix 'sour' is poured like spice into a dough almost identical to that of the plastic white sandwich loaf. What comes out at the other end is, unsurprisingly, poor-quality bread with a separate shot of harsh acidity. I have come across such a loaf described as a San Francisco sourdough. If this constitutes your first experience of a so-called wheaten sourdough there is some danger it will also be your last. The only remedy is to cast names aside and buy a loaf made by a craft bakery – or several, in different styles – which you are assured is a wheaten sourdough; and to remember that the outstanding Poilâne and Innes loaves (see entries) are wheaten sourdoughs, too.

USES OF WHEATEN SOURDOUGH

For addicts, all other wheat bread is insipid and rye too earthy: wheaten sourdough is their staple, for strawberry jam as for goat's cheese. The unconvinced may find the bread ideal in just one or two contexts.

With such variation in textures and flavours, it is rather difficult to suggest a catch-all range of complementary foods. Suggestions made under separate entries (Innes, for example) will hold good for that bread and similar styles. As a general guideline, it is useful to think of the lactic sourness as parallel to the use of vinegar or lemon juice in salad dressings and sauces; if you think the food in question would be given a fillip by a touch of acid it will probably take happily to sourdough bread. Texture comes into the equation as well, of course, but this is an easy aspect to consider: you would not pile cottage cheese or fromage frais on to a soft white bread, sour or not, but a firm, slightly coarse-crumbed bread would do the soft, bland cheese considerable favours.

Toasting boosts the perception of sourness – if you are using bread that is a few days old, the chances are it will anyway have soured a little more from the time of purchase. And, as the Croque Max (see page 208) illustrates, even a simple cheese and ham sandwich can be given extra zest by that touch of lactic sourness in the bread.

Strongly sour bread is not ideal for gentle or relatively bland bread puddings but is generally fine for most savoury recipes. Crumbs can be used, like the bread itself, to 'lift' the flavour of crumb-coated fried foods, and there is no harm in adding a small proportion of sourdough crumbs to any fresh or dried crumb mixture.

· WHEATGERM BREAD ·

The legal definition of this bread is simple: it must contain not less than 10 per cent dry matter weight of added processed (stabilised) wheatgerm, the highly nutritious and powerfully flavoured core of the grain. Like brown bread (see entry), wheatgerm bread may contain caramel as a colouring agent, but in all other respects it may resemble white bread. As described elsewhere (see **Hovis**) processes for reinstating stabilised wheatgerm (less prone to rancidity) were devised soon after the introduction of roller milling, and a number of millers patented flour mixes in which a proportion of this processed germ was added back.

If your main concern is that there should be plenty of attractive, rich, nutty flavour and a modicum of fibre, you need only look for a 'wheatgerm bread' claim on the wrapper or shelf. If you are concerned about the exact composition of your loaf, or looking for a specific flavour and texture beyond that supplied by the wheatgerm alone, things get a little more difficult. The problem, as with brown bread, is knowing what else you are getting with your wheatgerm; whether the bread is composed of predominantly highly refined flour with a low extraction rate (no bran at all), or is something approaching wholemeal in composition. Colour alone can be misleading: you need to read the label. Most wheatgerm breads have a proprietary brand name attached, e.g. VitBe or Hovis and a label listing the majority of ingredients. If you buy an unwrapped loaf from a bakery, you will need to ask about its composition.

While I feel that the best wheatgerm flavour is found in the context of a coarsely stoneground wholewheat flour, you may be unwilling to make the transition from plain white to bran-rich wholewheat. If you have never tried wheatgerm bread, you may well find it attractively, but not aggressively, more flavourful than your usual white, and just as versatile.

· WHITE BREAD ·

If you have skimmed through this directory alphabetically you will have a good idea of the range of white breads available and, if you have sampled a few, a fair grasp of what makes white bread good or bad, delicious or dismal, and differentiates one white loaf from another. This entry is mainly concerned with the legal definition of white bread and the desirable qualities of white bread in general, including the plastic-wrapped sandwich loaf.

WHAT IS WHITE BREAD?

Who better to provide a definition than the National Association of Master Bakers? According to their *Book of Breadmaking*, 'white bread shall be composed of dough, made from flour, yeast and water, which has been fermented and subsequently baked'. Somewhat un-challenging, and with no provision for unleavened bread. Salt is not included as an essential – it appears in the list of permitted additives.

It may be more instructive to look at the list of permitted ingredients, summarised as:

salt; edible oils and fats; milk and milk products; sugar; enzyme active preparations; rice flour and soya bean flour in restricted quantity; wheat gluten and wheat germ; various seeds and cracked, kibbled and/or malted wheat grain; cracked oat grain, oatmeal and oat flakes; yeast stimulating preparations; acetic acid, vinegar, monocalcium phosphate, acid sodium pryophosphate, lactic acid, potassium acid tartrate and sodium diacetate; lecithin; permitted bleaching and improving agents; dispersing agents; permitted pre-servatives; permitted emulsifiers and stabilisers.

It takes a mere glance at this list – or indeed at the labels on white loaves available in any supermarket – to realise that there are many hundreds of possible permutations, whether you are buying a British bloomer or a sliced white.

There is simply not sufficient space here to examine closely the role and implication of each permitted ingredient (the deeply curious should consult either the *Master Bakers' Book of Breadmaking*, published by Turret Press; or apply to the Flour Advisory Bureau at 21 Arlington Street, London SW1A 1RN). The effects of seeds, grains and the like are mentioned within individual entries in this directory such as **Sunflower and Honey Bread**; the various functions of preservatives, emulsifiers, improvers and so on are discussed briefly in the Introduction.

WHAT IS GOOD WHITE BREAD?

What makes a really good white loaf? Most of us have firm priorities and preferences. It is, however, interesting to turn to a professional perspective, and the Master Bakers' manual has an instructive section on breads baked for competitions. These are the qualities their judges look for:

A wholesome, yeasty aroma
A clear, bright crumb without variations in brightness
An absence of cores, streaks and steam discoloration
A soft springiness, indicated by a crumb surface which is strong yet resilient

A velvety texture
A well and evenly baked crust.

These may not all feature strongly in our private list of priorities. Good aroma, texture and crust seem fair enough: but what do we make of a 'bright crumb', 'cores' and 'streaks' or a 'resilient' crumb surface? We are not, after all, evaluating washing powder.

But of course these concerns are linked: cores and streaks indicate all manner of unskilled mixing and moulding, which will in all likelihood lead to a 'weak' crumb and poor texture – the most common cause of complaint from consumers. A crumb that slices and butters well is a valid virtue and one we probably take for granted.

The list of professional requirements is not so distant after all from our own main concerns. On the other hand, not all professional bakers would agree with even the initial premise, that 'wholesome, yeasty aroma'. Personally, I rather like a modicum of yeastiness on white bread as on champagne, but plenty of people object to the aroma on either; many a miller would claim you should be able to smell the wheat, particularly when the bread is made from fine, soft, aromatic English wheats. Certainly it is the lengthier, more painstaking fermentation methods, in which a minimum of yeast is allowed to do its work at a gentle pace, that produce loaves where the wheat aroma is predominant. Sourdough aficionados would claim that neither wheat nor yeast should predominate, but a different aroma altogether. And if you favour bread baked in a wood-fired oven your preferred aroma will be smoke-tinged.

For every baker who regrets the passing of bromides as permitted flour bleach there are others who would wince at the idea of brightness, looking instead for the creaminess of a naturally aged, unbleached flour. A white loaf made from stoneground, sifted flour will contain flecks of bran which give a far from velvety texture. An 'evenly baked crust' may not be the priority of a baker producing hefty oven-sole-baked free-form loaves, where part of the joy is the contrasting sections of thick and chewy or light and crisp-eating crust.

All in all, however, those competition virtues constitute a sensible list of qualities to consider when judging the quality of a loaf for ourselves, even allowing for differences in perception and priority (one person's 'soft spring' will always be another's rubbery bounce).

JUDGING QUALITY AT A GLANCE

Can you tell at a glance how your loaf will be? Well, probably not. Even if you can handle the loaf (with tongs, or your hand wrapped in one of those cellophane bags) and discreetly rap or even sniff the crust, little may be revealed.

Fine baguettes are fairly easy to spot, just difficult to come by. Bloomers, by contrast, sit proudly on almost every baker's shelf, but reveal little of their innermost secrets. Bloomers and the ever-enticing cottage loaves have occasioned me more disappointment than any other shape and style of bread. Free-form crusts of a certain category of bread, from the holey, light-crumbed ciabatta to the firmer-crumbed, deep-crusted *pain de campagne* styles, *are* generally reliable indicators of quality (though not of flavour). An attractive crust somehow commends itself immediately, partly by sheer contrast with pale, wan tin loaves. Still no guarantees, but you are in with a fair chance. Tin loaves tend to look simply pale or dark, and the dimensions between loaves of a statutory weight barely differ. Here it is simply a question of trial and error and discovering a reliable bakery or source of supply – some of the finest craft bakeries produce simple tin loaves.

SLICED WHITE

You might imagine yourself on safer, if more mundane ground with wrapped, sliced white loaves. They come thin, medium and toaster-sliced, small and large – and then what? Well, two recent developments have gathered considerable force in the last year or so. In response to a growing call for flavour and finesse as well as convenience, sliced loaves from organically grown flour, or baked by more traditional slow-fermented methods, are claiming a good deal of supermarket shelf space.

Organic loaves came first, not always the shining beacon they might be; a number are still emulsifier boosted, fast-fermented and with suspect hydrogenated oil content. The organic flour in no way guarantees the final flavour and texture. On the other hand, carefully made loaves such as that by Doves Farm are a delight, as ideal for desserts such as charlottes or summer puddings as for sandwich or toaster use.

Just about every supermarket has brought out at least one 'traditionally raised and baked' sliced white loaf. The names – Baker's Choice is typical – mean very little, but the wrappers usually explain what sets these breads apart from the run of the mill. Sensibly enough, the producers of the breads are banking on improved flavour to win converts. Decidedly a move in the right direction.

· WHOLEMEAL AND · WHOLEWHEAT BREAD

In the minds of most people these two are synonymous but legally they need not be: wholemeal bread can be made of any grain, not just wheat, as long as all parts of the grain are used. So it is technically possible to have a wholemeal rye loaf. However, in this case the bread would be clearly named a rye loaf; if the label simply says wholemeal it is safe to assume it is a wholewheat loaf.

ADDITIVES IN WHOLEMEAL BREAD

Wholemeal then, means bread 'wi' nowt taken out', in the words of the advertising jingle. What the term does *not* necessarily mean is nowt put in. The list of permitted additives is too long to reproduce here but basically includes edible fats (including hydrogenated oils), enzyme active preparations, yeast-stimulating preparations, lecithin, preservatives, emulsifiers and stabilisers, any number of seeds and malted grains and caramel colouring. There is a whole host of additives here we simply don't imagine will be allowed houseroom in a 'wholesome' loaf. These perform many different functions: they make it easy to produce an even-crumbed, light-textured, long-keeping loaf, one that can be sliced and packaged just like a white sandwich loaf; they enable modern machinery to produce a fast-rise loaf virtually untouched by human hand – in fact the same functions they fulfil in the case of white or brown or 'fancy' breads, though they have to work harder in the case of wholewheat with its gluten-inhibiting bran content. Some would claim that these additives are essential to the production of a desirably light wholemeal loaf but I have sampled loaves that seemed perfectly light enough (though not, I admit, springily squashy), the good rise achieved by the use of sourdough leaven in combination with baker's yeast. But of course, like any bread, wholemeal loaves can be produced with no additive other than water, and perhaps salt and baker's yeast. This simple, additive-free loaf is what a good many consumers imagine they are buying, particularly when the loaf is bought loose, with no wrapper information to contradict the assumption.

STONEGROUND OR ROLLER-MILLED?

Wholemeal/wholewheat breads may be produced from roller-milled or stoneground flour, or a mixture of the two. Roller milling flattens and shears away the wheatgerm along with the bran and separates them completely from the starchy white endosperm. Wholewheat flour made by the roller-milling process has the bran and germ added back so that the flour can claim to contain the whole wheat. Stoneground wholewheat flour is produced by crushing all parts of the grain at the same time, usually resulting in a coarser grind, and most people claim that bread made from stoneground flour tastes better.

The question of how to know whether a loaf is produced by stonegrinding or roller milling is not easily resolved – though most loaves produced from stoneground flour will advertise the fact. You will probably discover the coarseness of the grind only on cutting into the loaf, though certain categories of loaf are likely to use a specific grind: a genuine Irish wholemeal soda bread, for instance, is likely to contain very coarsely ground flour, a craft bakery's organic stoneground wholewheat will probably be fairly coarsely ground, a 'soft-eating' mass-produced wrapped and sliced sandwich loaf is likely to contain the finest grind of flour.

THE IDEAL LOAF

What makes an ideal wholemeal loaf? Assuming purity of ingredients, there is little that divides opinion so hotly, apart perhaps from the broader question of 'white versus brown'. I had an argument on the matter with a baker whose breads I generally admire a good deal: I confessed to a preference for moist, dense wholewheat loaves; he could see no point in any professional baker producing such an unskilled affair. He would not himself rely on improvers but would use all his skills to bake a nicely risen, neatly slicing, even-crumbed loaf. Another baker regularly flattens his well-risen, carefully crafted 'sponge and dough' fermented loaves as they go into the oven to fit in with his customers' image of a decently solid wholemeal loaf.

A style of loaf that I do find appealing is wholemeal raised with a proportion of sour fermented dough. The slight acid tang of this kind of bread makes its relative lightness seem absolutely right. Very few wholewheat loaves are produced along these lines, however. Some are produced entirely by sourdough fermentation and the majority of these I find too heavy, their sourness too intense; all too often, it seems, the flavour of the wheat is completely masked and barely distinguishable from rye. Others may feel differently: if this is the kind of loaf that appeals to you, look out for 'natural rise' or 'sourdough' on the label.

Another style of wholemeal bread is termed 'Continental' – a rather loose term that can mean whatever the manufacturers wish (some claim to be Dutch inspired) but tends to indicate a particularly sweetly nutty flavour, often produced by the addition of honey and, occasionally, butter. Such breads have an extremely appealing aroma, a moderately light texture and are perhaps the most user-friendly of wholemeal breads, as happy spread with jam or honey as when served with savoury foods. Not for purists, however.

BRAND NAMES AND OTHERS

A number of brand names have longstanding fame and following: Allinson's, Prewett's and Cerea for example, and Benaura in Scotland. The brand names in fact apply to the flour and, occasionally, a recommended recipe. You may find on close inspection that the same bakery has produced the differently named loaves under licence. A licence for a particular flour may be granted to a number of bakeries, with the result that the style of, say, an Allinson's loaf will vary quite markedly, in the manner of the original Hovis. The styles of these breads are, however, basically similar – sweet, nutty tasting and reasonably light – although the balance of textures and flavours will vary a little. Disappointingly, the majority have a soft crust due to the inevitable plastic wrapping for nationwide distribution.

More recent labels are Doves Farm, Cranks, and Whole Earth (again, one bakery – Goswell's – has a licence to produce all of these, which leads to some uniformity). They are all made of organically produced stoneground flour, the Whole Earth loaf containing a range of organic seeds, carrots and kelp, too, which makes for a highly distinctive flavour and texture you may love or hate.

Loaves with brand names, organic or no, may contain additives or hydrogenated fats. This may not worry you one jot if what you are looking for is something as close as possible to mass-produced white sandwich loaves – soft, springy and long-lasting. As such loaves would not be my first choice, however, I am bound to suggest that you try a craft bakery loaf at some stage. A well-made organic stoneground loaf is arguably more wholesome and its firmer texture allies better to a wide range of foods, particularly British farmhouse cheeses, from crumbly Lancashire to a firm Cheddar. It would be fair to claim that only here will you find the finest, fullest flavour of wheat. It could be the bread you have been searching for all your life without knowing it. That said, there are only a few wholemeal loaves that I truly enjoy and I have to admit your search may be a long one.

· ZOPF ·
See **Swiss Bread**.

· RECIPES ·

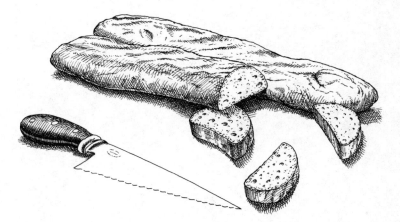

·A NOTE ON QUANTITIES AND· INGREDIENTS

Most of the recipes are designed to serve four, apart from sandwiches and savouries based on a single slice, roll or loaf, and certain desserts where serving size may depend on the diners' figure-consciousness. I should say also that a number of vintage bread-based recipes were evidently designed for trencherman appetite . . .

Although you should follow either Imperial or metric measurements and not combine the two, exact quantities are rarely, if ever, crucial – your own preferred texture or flavour balance is much more important. In any case the bread you use will vary in staleness and dryness – treat quantities as a variable, if tried and tested, guide.

Good bread deserves the company of good ingredients, whatever the recipe or occasion – and so do you, and anyone who sits at your table. The recipes may not always specify in detail, but I would make a plea for the use of meat from humanely reared and decently fed animals, properly free-range eggs, and organic milk and dairy produce if you can find them. Organically grown fruit and vegetables generally have a better concentration of flavour than their mass-produced counterparts. All the recipes in this book call for plain, in other words soft, 'all-purpose' flour – here, too, I try to use organic, certainly unbleached flour. The sugar I use is raw cane, which is only part refined, but you may prefer the more neutral flavour of white sugar. I have no hesitation in recommending Maldon sea salt with its large, fragile crystals, but to simplify matters measures in recipes are based on fine crystal salt. Pepper is black and freshly ground. Herbs are fresh unless otherwise stated.

In the final count, use whatever tastes right to you.

· CRUMBS, CROUTONS ·
AND BREAD CASES

· BREADCRUMB TACTICS ·

For most of us most of the time, breadcrumbs come out of a back-of-cupboard packet, and we need a good reason or two before going through the hassle of making our own. Here are a few: first of all, it's not a hassle – not in these days of food processors and blenders. Second, you can control the quality of your crumbs, as you choose the loaf from which they are made and any butter, oil or aromatics that are added. You can have a good deal of fun experimenting with crumbs from variously flavoured breads. Also – a compelling reason, this – *fresh* crumbs don't yet come in packets.

There is a good deal you can do with fresh or semi-stale crumbs: whip up quick and easy-going soufflés, dainty dumplings and the lightest of steamed chocolate puddings; add butter or oil, spices or herbs to make a simple stuffing for vegetables; or fry the crumbs in butter to add crunch to steamed vegetables or to sweet and savoury gratins; or caramelise them for quick puddings.

Here are various suggestions for producing and storing different styles of breadcrumbs.

MAKING LIGHT WORK OF FRESH BREADCRUMBS

Crumbs have been collected as long as bread has been baked, and methods of producing them have hardly varied over the centuries – grating, sieving, or pounding in a mortar were the only choices in pre-processor days. Now, however, a food processor or blender has much to recommend it if you want a reasonable quantity of fresh, fine crumbs.

Basic Food Processor or Blender Method for Fresh Breadcrumbs
You can use frozen bread to make crumbs, either defrosted, or straight from the freezer if the bread is already in small chunks. Cut off the crusts and tear the bread into rough chunks about

2.5–5cm/1–2 inches square and drop half a dozen into the food processor bowl or blender goblet. Place the lid on, switch on the machine, then feed a steady stream of chunks through the feed tube until the bowl or goblet is about half full, after which it will start to process unevenly.

Grating

The most common suggestion, grating, is fairly laborious and only works with fairly stale and dry chunks of bread. Use the largest holes on the grater (this will still produce fine crumbs) and hold the grater deep inside a mixing bowl, stock pot, or large plastic bag – the staler the bread, the further the crumbs will fly. The grated crumbs will be rather uneven and will need pushing through a wide-mesh sieve to refine them – even then, only half will make the grade.

The breadcrumbs will keep in a sealed container in the fridge for a couple of days or in the freezer for a couple of months. If freezing, label them with the type of crumb (brioche, walnut bread and so on). Frozen crumbs stay more or less free-flowing, which means you can keep a large tubful, adding or scooping out at will. Remember to have a clear-out some two months after the first lot goes in, however.

Fresh or Stale?

Many cookery books recommend that bread should be a couple of days old before crumbing but I find that this is rarely necessary. The aroma of really fresh crumbs adds an extra dimension to any savoury or sweet dish – a simple baked tomato, for instance, or sweet dumplings made with brioche crumbs. Most of the bread we buy is, in any case, at least half a day old at the time of purchase.

Some rye breads are difficult to crumb when fresh; try processing a chunk and see what happens. If you need to stale the bread, the best way is to dry it in a microwave: place a thick slice on a layer of kitchen paper and microwave on High for 1–2 minutes, then let it stand for a further 2 minutes before processing. If you do not have a microwave, dry out your bread, sliced or in chunks, in a low oven. Removing thick or bitter rind before slicing will save extra effort later, and speed the staling.

Most recipes that specify fresh breadcrumbs can be made with either very fresh or semi-dried crumbs, perhaps five or six days old.

DRIED BREADCRUMBS

Dried breadcrumbs have two main uses: to line soufflé and savarin dishes and to coat fried foods where very little fat or oil should be absorbed. Escalopes or rissoles coated in dried crumbs rather than fresh ones have a finer, more elegant finish, simply because dry bread grinds down more finely than fresh. Another use is as a crisp topping for gratins.

Dried crumbs can be made from any bread but plain white is the most versatile. The bread should be completely dry before processing; alternatively, fresh crumbs can be allowed to dry out and then reground for a finer texture. The bread or crumbs can be left to dry out naturally, dried in a very low oven, or microwaved on High for a few minutes.

Browned crumbs, by contrast, are produced by baking fresh or stale bread or crumbs at a higher temperature – 350°F/180°C/Gas Mark 4 – for about 15 minutes or until golden brown. Leave the bread to cool and then process it in a blender or food processor, or coffee grinder, or put it in a folded tea-towel or a heavy-duty plastic bag and crush it with a rolling pin (much less noisy, and avoids scratching the processor bowl). Dried crumbs keep well in a sealed container for a few weeks – taste before using if in any doubt. They can also be frozen, well sealed, for 3–4 months.

BUTTERED CRUMBS

I generally find that half the weight of butter to crumbs is enough to add butter-drenched crispness to simply cooked foods such as steamed fish or vegetables. Melt the butter in a saucepan over a moderate heat. As soon as it starts to foam, add the fresh bread crumbs and fry, stirring constantly, until the butter is absorbed. Keep frying over a brisk heat until the crumbs are crisp and brown.

Spices such as nutmeg, allspice, garam masala and cayenne add further interest. Sprinkle them on to the crumbs shortly before they are done, to allow spices to toast and release their aroma.

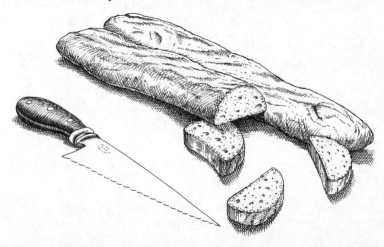

MADEIRA BUTTERED CRUMBS

Butter-laden crumbs and a spicy, creamy bread sauce (see pages 272–75) are good complements to roasted pheasant and guinea fowl with their tendency to dryness and also add a festive air to the ubiquitous Christmas turkey.

125g/4oz unsalted butter
125g/4oz fairly dry white
   breadcrumbs

100ml/3½fl oz Bual (medium dry)
   Madeira
salt and pepper

Heat the butter in a wide frying pan until it foams. Tip in the crumbs and stir around with a fork (use a heat-resistant plastic fork if your pan is non-stick). Continue to fry over a moderate heat until the crumbs are golden brown, then pour in the Madeira. Keep stirring until the liquid has evaporated and the crumbs are crisp once more. Season and serve – keep them warm until the roast is ready, if necessary.

OLIVE OIL CRUMBS

This Italian version of buttered crumbs is rich, simple and versatile (you can reduce the amount of oil to 5 tablespoons for use with richer foods), as delicious on steamed vegetables or fish, as with simply sauced pasta (see Sicilian Pasta on page 169). Lemon zest and finely chopped flat-leaf parsley can be included to brighten the crisp richness of the crumbs.

120ml/4fl oz extra virgin olive oil
1–3 cloves garlic, halved or sliced

125g/4oz crumbs from a ciabatta or
   Pugliese loaf or any good bread

Heat the oil gently in a frying pan with the cloves of garlic – sliced for a more pungent effect – until the garlic is golden and the oil well-flavoured. Discard the garlic and fry the crumbs in the oil until crisp and golden. Drain on kitchen paper if you like.

HERBED CRUMBS

This is a useful guideline recipe for anyone who has only a few sprigs in their herb garden or is resigned to buying little packets from supermarkets. The combination of herbs can be adjusted to suit the recipe and your circumstances – in years when I beat the slugs to the basil I've put by a freezer shelf-full of basil-and-olive oil crumbs.

Herbed crumbs do freeze well; store them in small cartons or heavy-duty plastic bags.

You could create an array of flavours by adding a small amount of finely diced sun-dried tomato, anchovy, olive, caper, lemon zest, crumbled bacon, and so on to the crumbs. Raw garlic quickly turns musty when frozen, so for a gremolata topping add lemon zest and chopped garlic only when you come to use the herbed crumbs.

If you allow the crumbs to absorb only a quarter their weight in butter, or in oil, they will be left thirsty, and become a useful stuffing for vegetables that release moisture on heating – mushrooms and tomatoes are obvious examples.

125g/4oz day-old white bread without crusts
15g/½oz flat-leaf parsley
15g/½oz basil

15g/½oz tarragon leaves
2 tablespoons extra virgin olive oil or melted unsalted butter

Put the bread and herbs in a food processor and process until fairly fine. You can then use the pulse button to combine the crumbs and the oil or butter but it is simpler to toss them lightly but thoroughly with your hands.

CARAMELISED CRUMBS

Like praline, these crumbs can form the basis of a number of instant desserts – layered with lightly cooked, tart fruit or stirred into thick, strained yoghurt.

To make caramelised crumbs, add caster or demerara sugar to buttered crumbs (see page 163) after they have been coated in butter and fry until crisp and caramelised; use the same weight of sugar as butter. To make spiced caramelised crumbs, sprinkle in ground cinnamon or freshly ground nutmeg or allspice half a minute before the end of cooking (for 125g/4oz breadcrumbs, 1 teaspoon cinnamon or ¼ teaspoon allspice or nutmeg is usually sufficient).

SWEET OLIVE OIL CRUMBS

As I was wondering whether oil-fried crumbs might usefully be sweetened to serve with fruit or in desserts I came across just such a use in a book of Spanish recipes promoting olive oil. It suggested layering lightly cooked apple slices and sherry-soaked raisins with the crumbs; they would also work well with pears poached in a sugar syrup enriched with Pedro Ximenez sherry or Moscatel wine.

The meeting of oil and sugar at high temperature does unpleasant things to pans, however, so it is best to mix the sugar into the crumbs off the heat – the result will not be caramelised but will give a good crunch; you might try using raw cane demerara sugar to maximise the effect.

150ml/5fl oz extra virgin olive oil
125g/4oz fresh white breadcrumbs

50g/2oz golden granulated sugar or
    demerara sugar

Heat the oil in a deep frying pan until fairly hot but nowhere near smoking. Fry the crumbs over a moderate heat until crisp and golden. Quickly drain on kitchen paper, then tip into a mixing bowl and stir in the sugar. Use soon after making.

· SIMPLE RECIPES USING · BREADCRUMBS

GARLIC-CRUMBED GREEN BEANS

A number of simple dishes can be finished rather neatly by throwing in a handful of plain or flavoured breadcrumbs to soak up oils and juices and provide an attractively crisp texture. This recipe and the two that follow give some idea of the versatility of this treatment.

The idea for this particular dish comes from Jacques Médecin, the colourful and controversial one-time mayor of Nice, who compiled a seminal volume on the cuisine of the area, *La Cuisine du Comté de Nice*. It does demand really fresh, crisp green beans.

225g/8oz very fine green beans
3 tablespoons extra virgin olive oil
1 large clove garlic, crushed with a
    pinch of salt
75g/2½oz fresh breadcrumbs
    (sourdough bread works well)
salt and pepper

Optional additions:
12 oil-cured black olives, stoned
1 small crottin or other mature goat's
    cheese, rind removed if necessary
    and crumbled

Blanch the beans in rapidly boiling, slightly salted water for 3 minutes – this can be omitted if the beans are very young and fresh. Drain well. Heat the oil in a frying pan and add the crushed garlic. When it turns transparent but before it starts to brown, add the beans and cook, stirring constantly, over a moderate heat until they are crisp-tender and have become dark green and mottled. Stir in the crumbs, then increase the heat and keep stirring until the crumbs are deep brown and crisp. If using olives and cheese, add them half a minute before the end of cooking, so that the olives heat through and the cheese just begins to melt. Tip into a dish and serve immediately.

CUMIN AND CAPER-CRUMBED SKATE

Here crisp crumbs contrast pleasingly with the soft flakes of the fish.

4 × 175g/6oz pieces skate wing
salt and pepper
125g/4oz unsalted butter
1 tablespoon ground cumin
juice of ½ lemon

1 tablespoon salt-packed capers, rinsed, dried and chopped
2 tablespoons finely chopped flat-leaf parsley
100g/3½oz fresh white breadcrumbs

Season the fish on both sides. Heat half the butter in a large frying pan and, when foaming, add the fish in a single layer. Fry gently for 2 minutes on each side, then add the cumin and cook for 2–3 minutes more per side, or until the fish is opaque in the thickest section. Squeeze a little of the lemon juice over the fish, then remove from the pan and keep warm while preparing the crumbs.

Melt the remaining butter in the pan, stir in the capers, parsley and remaining lemon juice and add the crumbs, with a little seasoning if you only seasoned the fish lightly. Increase the heat to fairly high and keep stirring the crumbs briskly until brown and crisp. Pile the crumbs on to serving plates, and top with the skate.

FRIED APPLES WITH CINNAMON CRUMBS

A richly buttery dish, rather faster to put together than a crumble, and with a pleasing contrast between tender apples and crisp crumbs. Brioche crumbs would be particularly fine.

450g/1lb well-flavoured eating apples, peeled, cored and sliced or diced
a little lemon juice
90g/3oz unsalted butter or clarified butter (see page 178)

2–3 tablespoons caster sugar
90g/3oz fresh white breadcrumbs
1 rounded teaspoon cinnamon
single cream, to serve

Toss the apples with a little lemon juice as you prepare them. Melt half the butter in a large frying pan and sauté the apples until golden brown – do not stir too enthusiastically or they may break up, but do flip them over once one side is brown. When almost done, stir in half the sugar and transfer the apples to a warm platter.

Melt the rest of the butter in the pan and add the crumbs. Stir to coat thoroughly in the butter, then add the remaining sugar and the cinnamon, increase the heat and stir until the crumbs are brown and crisp. Tip the hot crumbs over the apples and either pour cream in rivulets over the crumbed apples or serve in a separate jug.

ASPARAGUS WITH BUTTERED CRUMBS

This simple recipe is a development of the Polish chopped egg and breadcrumb coating and combines soft crumbs soaked in melted butter with the crunch of brown, butter-crisped crumbs. Salsify or scorzonera could be presented the same way – or any soft braised vegetables such as fennel or chicory.

450g/1lb fresh green or white asparagus spears, trimmed and peeled	125g/4oz very fresh butter
	50g/2oz fine fresh breadcrumbs
	50g/2oz coarse fresh breadcrumbs
salt and pepper	

Rapidly boil or steam the asparagus until just tender, then drain thoroughly, preferably on kitchen paper or a towel. Transfer to a serving dish, season and keep warm while you prepare the crumbs.

Melt half the butter in a pan until foaming, add the fine crumbs and fry briskly, stirring constantly, until they are brown and crisp – about 5 minutes. Spoon the crumbs over the asparagus.

To make the soft crumbs, melt the remaining butter (preferably in a separate pan) until just foaming, add the coarse crumbs and quickly stir around until coated in butter. Remove from the pan at once and tip over the asparagus, along with any butter remaining in the pan. Serve immediately.

CALF'S LIVER WITH PAIN D'ÉPICE

This is an adaptation of a *foie gras* treatment created by Christian Constant at the Crillon in Paris. It must be one of the simplest dishes in the great chef's repertoire, paying due respect to a luxury ingredient. This slightly humbler recipe is delicious, equally simple and almost as fast.

For the spinach salad:
225g/8oz very young spinach leaves
25g/1oz butter
1 tablespoon extra virgin olive oil
salt and pepper

For the liver:
4 × 100g/3½oz thin slices calf's liver

salt and pepper
150g/5oz pain d'épice crumbs (you will
   need 9–10 slices)
50g/2oz unsalted butter
2 tablespoons extra virgin olive oil
good splash of fine balsamic vinegar
   or juice of ½ orange

To make the warm spinach salad, melt the butter and oil in a large frying pan. When foaming, add the rinsed and dried spinach leaves and rapidly toss them until they are coated in oil and just wilting. Transfer at once to warmed serving plates and season.

Season the liver fairly generously, then coat it in the crumbs. The best way to do this is to press them on firmly by hand and gently shake off any surplus.

Melt the butter and oil over a moderate heat in the same pan you used for the spinach. Add the escalopes in a single layer. Turn them over after 1½ minutes and cook for a further minute or so to leave the liver pink-centred. Arrange the liver so that it overlaps each bed of spinach. Deglaze the pan at once with the vinegar or orange juice; it will take only a few seconds to foam up and reduce considerably. Swirl the pan, then drizzle the juices over the exposed salad. Serve while at the peak of perfection.

SICILIAN PASTA

This popular way of serving oil-crisped breadcrumbs can be adapted according to your taste and your storecupboard. You could fry the crumbs in the oil from anchovies, olives or sun-dried tomatoes, and if you prefer just a hint of chilli, sauté the chilli with the garlic and discard both before crisping the crumbs. The crumbs also make a fine dressing for steamed cauliflower or broccoli.

4 tablespoons extra virgin olive oil
2 fat cloves garlic, sliced
125g/4oz fresh breadcrumbs from
   ciabatta, pain de campagne or
   cornmeal bread
1 large fresh red chilli, seeded and
   finely diced
4 anchovy fillets, rinsed and chopped

2 tablespoons chopped, stoned black
   olives
2 tablespoons chopped flat-leaf
   parsley
salt and pepper
225g/8oz dried tagliarini or spaghetti
   (or 350g/12oz fresh pasta)

Heat 3 tablespoons of the oil in a frying pan and sauté the garlic until it begins to brown. Discard the garlic, add the breadcrumbs and fry over a medium to high heat, stirring constantly, until crisp and brown. Either scoop out the crumbs into a bowl or use a separate pan to sauté the chilli in the remaining tablespoon of oil. When softened, add the anchovies and olives, cook for 30 seconds, then add this mixture to the crumbs. Finally stir in the parsley and seasoning. Cook the pasta in plenty of boiling salted water until *al dente*, then drain quickly, allowing the pasta to retain a little of its cooking water. Place the pasta in a heated serving bowl and toss with the crumb mixture. Serve at once.

Variations

Replace the chilli with 1 tablespoon finely diced sun-dried tomato and use some of the tomato oil in cooking; add 2 or 3 fresh plum tomatoes, skinned, seeded and diced (and seasoned separately); toss in a handful of lightly cooked skinned young broad beans with the crumbs, or add any diced, crisp-cooked, fresh green vegetable to hand.

SPEEDIEST APRICOT BAKE

This is one of those simple and delicious dishes that are born only when needs must – in this instance, to transform a bag of wan and woolly fresh apricots to a joyous dessert.

100g/3½oz fresh white breadcrumbs	4 plump, firm apricots, halved and
50g/2oz unsalted butter, melted	stoned
50g/2oz caster sugar	
sprinkling of powdered vanilla (or stir	
some vanilla extract into the	
butter)	

With a fork, stir the melted butter and sugar through the crumbs until they are coated. Spoon a good half of the crumbs into a buttered baking dish and arrange the apricots cut-side down over the crumbs. Sprinkle the remaining crumbs on top and bake at 190°C/375°F/Gas Mark 5 for 30–40 minutes, until the surface is browned and crisp.

The bottom layer of crumbs will have soaked up the apricot juices to delicious effect, while the upper layer forms a crisp contrast, slightly caramelised and smoky. Ridiculously good served with pouring cream.

· MAKING CROUTONS ·

There are three basic ways of making croutons and each is more suitable for certain dishes than others. Fruit soups, crystal-clear consommés and delicate fish or vegetable mousses usually favour light croutons, which simply contribute crunch rather than rich flavour and leave no streak of oil or butter on the surface of the dish. Cream soups, oil-dressed salads and rich ragouts take well to lightly fried, perhaps spiced or garlic-rubbed croutons which are not in themselves over-rich. Vegetable purées and soups, lightly dressed salads, tomato-based pasta sauces, and thinly sauced meat, fish or poultry will probably welcome the crunch of richer oil- or butter-replete croutons.

Croutons are also variously shaped: besides the usual cubes they might also take on the role of croutes – thin slices of *ficelle* or baguette – or be cut into slim triangles or stamped out as fanciful heart shapes. Here are the basic methods.

BAKED CROUTONS

Thinly slice *ficelles*, slim baguettes, bridge rolls or individual brioches. Or cut crustless bread into 1cm/⅓ inch cubes. For a garlic flavour, rub sliced but not yet cubed bread firmly with the cut sides of a halved garlic clove; sliced croutons can be rubbed after baking.

Place the bread shapes in a single layer on a baking sheet and bake at 180°C/350°F/Gas Mark 4 for about 15 minutes or until dry, crisp and lightly golden. Cool completely and either use at once or store in an airtight jar for 2–3 weeks. To make buttered or oiled croutons, brush the bread lightly with melted butter or olive oil and bake until golden. These are best used within a few hours. If you want to serve the croutons immediately they can be baked for 7–8 minutes in a hotter oven (220°C/425°F/Gas Mark 7).

PART-BAKED, PART-FRIED CROUTONS

Cut the bread into shapes or cubes as described above. Place in a single layer on a baking sheet and bake in the oven at 160°C/325°F/Gas Mark 3 for about 15 minutes or until dried out but not coloured. Cover the base of a frying pan with a thin film of oil or clarified butter. Place the cubes of bread in the pan in a single layer and sauté over a moderate heat, shaking the pan from time to time and tossing the croutons until golden. If the fat is absorbed before this stage, add a little more. Drain the croutons on kitchen paper and serve soon after making. They can be frozen; reheat and recrisp them after thawing by placing them in a moderately hot oven for a few minutes or in the microwave on a fairly high setting for a few seconds.

FRIED CROUTONS

For these you will need about 50g/2oz clarified butter, or 4 table-spoons oil, or butter and oil mixed, for 4 small-to-medium slices of bread. But that is a rough estimate. The important thing is that the pan should contain fat to a depth of 1cm/⅓ inch.

Shape the bread as before (this method is best suited to smallish cubes). Heat the fat in a frying pan and cook the croutons briskly, stirring constantly, until brown. Drain on kitchen paper. The fat can be infused with garlic before frying; to flavour the croutons with herbs or spices, toss them in the mixture immediately after draining. Serve soon after making, or freeze and then recrisp them as described above.

TOASTING

You can also make a form of crouton by toasting and buttering bread and then cutting it into squares. These croutons will probably be a little chewier and they should be used straight away.

MELBA TOAST

This is half-way between toast and crouton or croute and is decidedly the best use for ready-sliced bread – although you can of course use a good-quality loaf. Toast slices of medium-thick bread at a moderate heat until lightly golden. Remove the crusts and cut the slices in half horizontally. To do this, keep the palm of your hand flat on the crustless slice of bread and use a long-bladed, serrated knife to cut through the soft centre. Now either toast the thin slices under a moderate grill or (easier) dry them out in the oven at 180°C/350°F/ Gas Mark 4 for a few minutes until completely crisp and curled up. Good with pâtés and creamy dips.

CAJUN CROUTONS

Hotly spiced croutons for zipping up soups and salads.

125g/4oz stale French bread – baguette, *ficelle* or a loaf with crust removed
4 tablespoons olive or vegetable oil

2 teaspoons Cajun Spice Mix (see page 202)

Slice the *ficelle* or baguette thinly; slice and shape or cube the loaf. Heat the oil in a frying pan until fairly hot but not smoking and toss the bread in it until golden brown. Drain briefly on kitchen paper, then toss in the spice mixture to coat. Serve within an hour or two.

· SIMPLE RECIPES USING CROUTONS ·

WARM MUSHROOM SALAD WITH WALNUT BREAD CROUTONS

Make the walnut bread croutons by any of the methods outlined on pages 171–2. You could use walnut oil for this but as it has a fairly low smoking point I tend to use extra virgin olive oil; clarified butter would also be fine. If you make the croutons in advance, warm them gently just before tossing them into the salad.

225g/8oz assorted young seasonal vegetables, such as French beans, asparagus tips, sugar snap peas, etc.	1 tablespoon Bual (medium sweet) Madeira
125g/4oz cherry tomatoes, halved	2 tablespoons walnut oil
15g/½oz unsalted butter	25g/1oz walnuts, toasted
1 small shallot, finely diced	1 teaspoon well-aged balsamic vinegar
1 clove garlic, crushed with a pinch of salt	50–75g/2–2½oz walnut bread croutons
150g/5oz oyster mushrooms, sliced or torn	25g/1oz Parmesan cheese, in thin shavings
salt and pepper	

Warm a salad bowl or a mixing bowl in a low oven. Trim the vegetables and steam or blanch them for 3 minutes, then place them in the bowl along with the tomatoes and return the bowl to the oven.

Heat the butter in a pan and gently cook the shallot and garlic in it until softened. Add the mushrooms and a pinch of salt and cook, stirring, until softened, then increase the heat to drive off excess liquid. Add the Madeira to the pan and allow to reduce for a moment, then stir in the walnut oil and immediately remove the pan from the heat.

Remove the bowl from the oven and tip in the mushroom mixture along with the walnuts, balsamic vinegar and a little seasoning. Toss thoroughly, transfer to a serving bowl if necessary, and mix in the croutons and cheese. Serve immediately while everything is warm and aromatic.

OMELETTE GRAND'MÈRE

Serves 1

This simple dish somehow avoided adoption by zealous proponents of '*cuisine Grand'mère*', despite its generations-old pedigree and its simplicity. Perhaps it was just too simple. While a ready supply of triple-reduced veal stock would come in handy, the idea is to use up juices left over from the Sunday roast in a sensibly light supper.

50g/2oz pain de campagne or other country bread, without crust, cut into 1.2cm/½inch cubes
40g/1½oz unsalted butter
2–3 tablespoons seasoned roasting juices (or flavourful veal stock)

3 eggs
salt and pepper
a scattering of finely chopped flat-leaf parsley or chervil

Fry the bread in 25g/1oz of the butter until brown and crunchy, stirring constantly. Remove from the heat, add the roasting juices or stock and stir quickly until absorbed. Beat the eggs with seasoning. Melt the remaining butter in an omelette pan. When it foams, add the eggs and stir briskly over a moderate heat in the usual way. Once the base is set, tumble the hot croutons on to the omelette, sprinkle over the herbs and serve at once.

CROUTON FRITTATA

Serves 1 hungry person or 2 as a light meal

Frittatas are becoming as fashionable as focaccia but are no less delicious for it. Now that no restaurateur dare be without shelves full of oil-cured Mediterranean vegetables, a frittata along these lines is obvious bistro fare. They are simple to make at home, and ingredients can be varied to include any good leftovers you have to hand.

You will need an ovenproof frying pan for this. If you only have a large one, double the ingredients and eat the rest of the frittata cold with salad. Or you could, at a pinch, finish off the dish under a medium grill instead of in the oven.

2 teaspoons extra virgin olive oil
15g/½oz unsalted butter
1 medium slice wholemeal, country or good white bread, crusts removed, cut into 1.2cm/½inch cubes
1 sun-dried tomato, chopped

3–4 chargrilled artichoke hearts, chopped
3 eggs, beaten
1 scant teaspoon pesto
1 teaspoon chopped fresh herbs, such as parsley, chervil and tarragon
salt and pepper

Heat the oil and butter in an ovenproof frying pan until the butter foams. Add the bread cubes to the foaming butter and sauté until golden, stirring gently, then add the sun-dried tomato and artichokes. Stir the pesto, herbs and seasoning into the beaten eggs, pour into the pan and cook on a medium heat for a few minutes, lifting the edges of the omelette so that liquid egg can run underneath. When the base of the omelette appears just set, transfer the pan to the oven and cook at 160°C/325°F/Gas Mark 3 for about 10 minutes or until completely set and a little puffy and brown. Cut into wedges and serve.

· BREAD CASES ·

Bread cases, or croustades as they are sometimes known, are a blessing to anyone with few pretensions to being a pastry chef. They range from crusty hollowed-out rolls – an obvious cop-out but more than forgivable if the bread is delicious – to tiny, shallow tartlet shells which will lighten the burden of all reluctant entertainers.

TARTLET CASES

Makes 48–72 cases, depending on size of cutter

I large white loaf, thinly sliced and crusts removed	175g/6oz clarified butter (see page 178) or unsalted butter, melted

Flatten the bread by rolling over the slices with a heavy rolling pin, then cut out rounds with a 5–7.5cm/2–3inch cutter. Dip the circles of bread quickly into the butter so that both sides are coated and allow the excess to drip back into the bowl. Line shallow miniature muffin tins with the bread and press a second tin on top of each lined tin – the bread rounds should overlap the hollows slightly as they shrink when cooked. (If necessary, you can first cut rounds from unflattened bread, then flatten the rounds to fit your tins.) Bake at 190°C/375°F/Gas Mark 5 for about 15 minutes, until the cases are brown and crisp (lift the upper tin to check this). If the edges brown quickly while the base remains pale, reduce the oven temperature a notch and continue baking until the base is crisply golden brown. Tip out of the tins and either fill at once with a hot mixture, or allow to cool and fill with a cold cream or paste. Unfilled cases can be stored in an airtight tin for up to 2 days and then reheated.

Fillings

Fillings should be finely chopped and bound with a creamy mixture such as béchamel or reduced cream sauces or mayonnaise. Scrambled eggs work well too.

DEEP BUN CASES, OR 'TULIPS'

Makes 24 cases

I small white loaf, thinly sliced and crusts removed	125g/4oz clarified butter (see page 178), or unsalted butter, melted

Roll the bread out thinly as for tartlet cases. Coat both sides of each slice with the butter, then press them into deep bun tins. Press a second matching bun sheet on top and bake at 180°C/350°F/Gas Mark 4 for 20–25 minutes, until crisp and golden brown. Use hot, cold or reheated as for tartlet cases.

Fillings

These can be much chunkier than the fillings for tartlets but should still be moist and creamy. Most croute or crostini toppings will be fine (see pages 185, 187–9), as will richly sauced seafood, poultry and game. This is definitely knife-and-fork food, however, not a dainty party nibble.

BREAD ROLL CASES

No longer chic dinner party fare except, perhaps, for filled brioche buns (see page 38) but very welcome at breakfast or supper. You can also prepare a whole loaf in this way, fill it with salad or a seafood fricassée and cut it into thick slices to serve (a flattish loaf makes slicing easier).

4 standard breakfast or dinner rolls	125g/4oz unsalted butter, melted

Cut a slice from the top of each roll and scoop out the crumb with a grapefruit spoon or your fingers (freeze or dry this for another use), leaving a shell at least 6mm/¼inch thick. Brush the hollowed roll and its lid with butter, generously on the inside and lightly round the outside. Place on a baking sheet and bake at 180°C/350°F/Gas Mark 4 for 20–30 minutes or until thoroughly crusty outside and golden brown inside.

Tiny rolls can be baked at a slightly higher temperature for 10–15 minutes.

Fillings

Tiny rolls are best with the same type of filling as tartlet cases: small quantities of rich or palate-awakening morsels. Larger rolls are more of a meal-in-a-bun affair: fill with scrambled eggs or mushrooms fried in butter for breakfast and anything from ratatouille to steak and kidney casserole for supper.

COFFYNS AND SNUFF BOXES

Makes 20–24

Pretty names for yet another kind of bread case, this time shaped from a large loaf with a knife or pastry cutter. For the sake of (relative) simplicity, I am giving a method that involves as little fiddle as possible. If you are a keen disciple of Eliza Acton you might use two pastry cutters to shape the box and a lid. The following are lidless, and thus should, I suppose, simply be considered as boxes.

I day-old large, square tin loaf (white is usual, but choose a loaf to suit your filling)	175–225g/6–8oz clarified butter (see page 178) or unsalted butter, melted

Remove the crust from all sides of the loaf and cut the bread into slices 5cm/2inches thick. Now cut each slice into quarters to make cubes. With the tip of a small sharp knife, score a square on one side of each cube, about 6mm/¼inch in from the edges. Cut down to within 6mm/¼inch of the base and very carefully pull out the crumb. Brush all sides of the boxes with the butter, place on a baking sheet and bake at 200°C/400°F/Gas Mark 6 for about 10 minutes or until crisp and golden all over. The boxes can be stored in an airtight tin for 2 days and then reheated. Fill just before serving.

Fillings

This is yet another vehicle for presenting creamed wild mushrooms; the contrast of crisp, buttery bread and the mushrooms' soft earthiness works as well as ever, with the added advantage that a scant tablespoonful fills the cases generously. On the same theme of stretching luxury items, use the boxes as containers for asparagus tips, scallops, lobster or crab, sweetbreads, smoked quail's eggs and smoked salmon. The filling should in all cases be moist, but need not be overly rich: well-seasoned, creamy fromage frais is fine.

· CANAPÉS AND TOASTS ·

TRUFFLE BUTTER CANAPÉS

These had proved their worth at several parties before I came across the very idea in Eliza Acton's *Modern Cookery* (1845). Indeed, her method of truffle butter production was very similar to one I had evolved before I discovered that a rather superior version was imported from Italy by one enterprising company. There are now a number of truffle butters on the market, the majority, sad to say, rather disappointing and packed with superfluous ingredients.

Here is my interpretation of Eliza Acton's recipe for potted truffles and for extra butter, followed by a note about the canapés. You could, of course, vastly simplify the whole thing by tracking down a jar of good truffle butter.

250g/8½oz very fresh unsalted butter	salt
90g/3oz fresh or frozen firm black winter truffles, cleaned and sliced	pinch each of mace and cayenne ½ nutmeg, in one piece

Clarify the butter by melting it, simmering it gently for 3 minutes, then, once it has settled, pouring the clear golden liquid through muslin, leaving most of the whey at the bottom of the pan. I usually melt the butter in a glass jug in a microwave so I can easily discern the two layers.

Put the clarified butter in a clean saucepan and add the truffles, salt and spices. Simmer as gently as possible for 15–20 minutes, then remove the truffles with a slotted spoon (discard the nutmeg), dry them on kitchen paper and place in a small pot or jar. Chill the butter until any juices exuded by the truffles separate off from the fat. Pour off the juices and reserve them to flavour a sauce or gravy.

Melt the butter again, pour just enough over the truffles to cover them and pour the rest of the butter into another small jar. Cover both jars and store in the fridge.

The potted truffles can be added to all manner of canapé fillings or toppings, from creamed mushrooms to potted chicken to scrambled eggs; but the butter provides an even greater pleasure, simply because it is a bonus. It can be used for cooking scrambled eggs, frying quail's eggs, or as the base of a miraculously flavourful béchamel – but the canapé that has proved such a success is one that Eliza Acton also recommended: simply spread thin slices of *ficelle* (or stamp out or cut small rounds from a wider loaf) with the truffle-infused butter, then bake them in a hot oven until browned. Serve hot, and keep your guests guessing: most people think it a rather fragrant form of garlic.

PANETTONE CANAPÉS

Makes about 12

For the seventh or eighth day of Christmas, when a little richness is welcome again and a mid-afternoon glass of Vin Santo seems perfectly in order. I am assuming you will have leftover panettone, leftover marrons glacés, leftover rum ... But you could also use sweetened chestnut purée, available year-round, candied ginger in syrup, or even candied apricots or bitter cherries.

50g/2oz broken marrons glacés or 2 tablespoons sweetened chestnut purée
2 tablespoons rum
150g/5oz panettone, sliced and cut into medium-thick rounds with a 5cm/2inch biscuit cutter

175g/6oz ricotta or drained fromage frais
a few drops of vanilla extract
dusting of cocoa powder

Soak the marrons glacés in the rum for at least 4 hours or overnight. If you are using chestnut purée simply blend it with the rum shortly before putting together the canapés.

Beat the ricotta or fromage frais until smooth (I invariably use a food processor for ricotta), then beat in the vanilla. If you are using marrons glacés, remove them from the rum. Mix the rum, or rum and chestnut purée, into the cheese.

Toast the panettone on both sides until golden brown. Quickly transfer to a serving dish, spoon some of the cheese mixture on to each, sprinkle with rum-soaked marrons glacés, if using, and dust with cocoa powder. Serve warm with a glass of sweet Vin Santo or a cup of espresso coffee.

SESAME PRAWN TOASTS

Makes 24 large or 48 small canapés

This popular canapé is surprisingly quick and simple to put together. Although white bread is the norm, it works well with brown or wholemeal, too, as long as you avoid loaves with nuts, seeds or grains.

Deep-frying produces the crispest, richest results but the toasts can also be baked in the oven at 220°C/425°F/Gas Mark 7 for 12–15 minutes. In this case the bread should be toasted, and spread with a smear of butter if you wish, before topping it with the prawn mixture.

125g/4oz cooked, peeled prawns (preferably not frozen)
125g/4oz skinless lemon sole fillet
1 egg white
1 teaspoon cornflour
1 teaspoon soy sauce
1 teaspoon lime juice
1 small clove garlic, sliced
pinch of cayenne

salt (optional)
3 × 2.5cm/1 inch chunks fresh ginger root, peeled
6 large thin slices white or wholemeal bread, crusts removed
50g/2oz white sesame seeds
olive or groundnut oil for deep-frying (see above)

Place the prawns, lemon sole, egg white, cornflour, soy sauce, lime juice, garlic, cayenne, and salt if using, in a food processor. Squeeze the juice from the ginger using a garlic press, discard the debris and add the juice to the processor bowl. Blend everything until smooth and sticky – you will need to scrape down the sides of the bowl two or three times. This mixture can be kept, covered, in the fridge for 12 hours. Pile the prawn mixture on to the bread and cut each slice into 4 triangles; cut these in half again if you want particularly dainty canapés. Sprinkle the triangles with the sesame seeds.

Heat the oil to a fairly high temperature – the bread should sizzle immediately on immersion. The oil should not, however, start smoking at any stage. Fry the canapés in batches. It should take 2–3 minutes for the bread to become golden and the prawn side puffed up; turn the triangles over while frying, if necessary. Drain on kitchen paper and then serve either hot or at room temperature. The toasts can be reheated and crisped in a hot oven but will not taste as fine as when freshly made.

WELSH RABBIT

Serves 1

Rabbit or rarebit? It seems that rabbit came first, as a joke at the expense of the Welsh. Lizzie Boyd, in the British Tourist Association's huge compendium, *British Cookery*, favours rarebit in the sense of rare meaning soft – softened cheese. Whatever the origin – at least 600 years ago, and probably as old as bread, cheese and ale – it makes a satisfying and delicious supper dish. It seems apt to use a Welsh cheese and I favour Leon Downey's Llangloffan, a delightful, organically produced Jersey-milk cheese, but any crumbly, easy melting cheese would be fine.

1 teaspoon butter	salt and pepper
50g/2oz Llangloffan cheese, crumbled or grated	1 slice white or wholewheat bread toasted on one or both sides
2 tablespoons dark ale	
1 scant teaspoon English (or Welsh!) mustard	

Preheat the grill. Melt the butter in a small saucepan, add the cheese and ale and allow the cheese to melt very gently, stirring from time to time (this can be done in a microwave on Low). When the mixture is smooth, stir in the mustard and seasoning to taste. Place the hot toast on a heatproof serving dish and pour the rabbit mixture into the centre of toast. It will quickly spread to the sides. Brown under the grill for a few seconds, and eat at once, before the cheese hardens. A good British dish that calls for beer as an accompaniment.

English Rabbit

English Rabbits sound altogether more sophisticated, with the bread soaked in as much red wine as it will absorb, either before or after toasting. The cheese can be prepared as above, with red wine substituted for the ale, or simply crumbled on top of the wine-soaked toast and grilled. I would use a good Lancashire cheese or Appleby's Cheshire, though Single or Double Gloucester or Cheddar would also fit the bill.

ROASTED CHEESE

An after-dinner or supper savoury dating back to Georgian times. This is basically Mrs Rundle's 1807 recipe, quoted by Elizabeth Ayrton in *The Cookery of England*.

90g/3oz Cheshire cheese, grated
90g/3oz fresh white breadcrumbs
2 egg yolks
I teaspoon English mustard

salt and pepper
4 slices white or brown bread,
    toasted

Beat together the cheese, breadcrumbs, egg yolks and mustard with a little salt and plenty of pepper. Cut each slice of toast into 3 fingers and cover with the paste. Place on a baking tray, cover with foil and bake at 200°C/400°F/Gas Mark 6 for 10 minutes. Uncover and allow to brown for a minute or two. Serve immediately.

GLOUCESTER CHEESE AND ALE

A dish dating back to the Middle Ages.

225g/8oz Single or Double Gloucester
    cheese, grated
2 teaspoons good-quality English
    mustard

600ml/I pint brown ale
4 large slices brown bread, toasted
    and crusts removed

Put the cheese in a flameproof dish or a frying pan. Dab the mustard over it, then pour on all but 4 tablespoons of the ale and stir over a low heat until all is smooth and bubbling. Heat the reserved ale. Place the hot toast on warmed plates and moisten each slice with a spoonful of ale. Spoon the cheese mixture over the toast, allowing it to run over the edges, and serve at once.

BUCKINGHAM EGGS

Serves 1

I confess I had not heard of this seventeenth-century snack, attributed to George Villiers, Duke of Buckingham, until I came across a glowing recommendation from that little-known gourmet but widely admired doyen of horror pics, the late Vincent Price. In the Sixties, Vincent and his wife Mary published their *Treasury of Great Recipes*, a gem of a collection gleaned from wide-ranging travels and polished by subsequent home experiment. As Vincent says (well he would, wouldn't he), this dish is 'perfect . . . for a midnight supper'.

I slice good bread, such as white,
    wholemeal, walnut or granary,
    toasted
I teaspoon softened butter
½–I teaspoon anchovy paste
a little English mustard

I large or 2 small eggs
I teaspoon thick cream
salt and pepper
small knob of unsalted butter
a little grated Cheddar cheese
a few drops of Worcestershire sauce

Trim the crusts from the toast if you prefer. Cream together the butter, anchovy paste and mustard to taste and spread it over the toast. Keep the toast warm. Beat the eggs with the cream and seasoning, then scramble them slowly in the butter. Remove from the pan while still creamy and pile on to the toast. Sprinkle with the Cheddar and Worcestershire sauce and grill under a high heat until the cheese bubbles. Serve piping hot.

ALEXIS SOYER'S MUSHROOMS ON TOAST

A serendipitous recipe from *Shilling Cookery for the People*, published in 1854 by that great chef and culinary champion of the poor, Alexis Soyer. This very simple little savoury was prompted by the chance discovery of fine field mushrooms during a pre-breakfast stroll in Devonshire. Here, with a few minor adjustments, is Soyer's creation.

butter for spreading	salt and pepper
4 thick rounds good white bread, fresh or slightly stale	4 large flat, brown-cap mushrooms or field mushrooms, stalks
100g/3½oz clotted cream	trimmed

Spread butter over a baking dish or foil-covered tray, or generously butter the base of the four bread rounds. Spread half the clotted cream over the unbuttered side of the four bread rounds and season lightly. Position the mushrooms on the cream-coated rounds, stalk-side up, spoon the rest of the cream into each mushroom cap, then season generously. Invert 4 small ovenproof dishes, preferably Pyrex ones, over each toast and place the assembly in the oven at 200°C/400°F/Gas Mark 6. Bake for 25 minutes, then remove the inverted dishes and serve at once, while the base of the toasts remains crisp.

JURASSIEN LEEKS ON TOAST

Plain white bread would seem all wrong here, the texture too soft and dense. Pain de campagne would be used in the Jura but British wholemeal would also work well.

4 medium leeks, green part discarded, whites cut into 2·5cm/1 inch slices	grating of nutmeg salt and pepper
25g/1oz unsalted butter	4 thick slices pain de campagne
1 heaped teaspoon plain flour	25–50g/1–2oz Comté or Gruyère
1 glass dry sherry (or Vin Jaune)	cheese, grated
150ml/5fl oz crème fraîche	

Simmer the leeks in a pan of boiling salted water for about 10 minutes or until tender but still slightly resilient. Drain thoroughly, then place in a saucepan with the butter and cook for 2 minutes, until turning golden. Sprinkle with the flour and cook gently, stirring, for a further minute or two, then remove the pan from the heat and add the sherry or wine. Return to the heat and gradually stir in the cream. Allow to bubble for 2–3 minutes, then season to taste (be generous with the nutmeg and pepper).

Toast the bread under the grill or in a hot oven (it is traditional, but not essential, to butter the bread first). When lightly golden, pile the leek mixture on to the toast, cover with the grated cheese and grill or bake until bubbling and golden. Serve at once.

POACHED EGGS GAMBRINUS

An extraordinary and unexpectedly delicious snack from the brasseries of Brussels. Gambrinus is the patron saint of brewers and appears to have lent his name to a fair range of dishes incorporating beer of all complexions. This dish uses the unique Kriek Lambic – a slightly sweet beer in which wild cherries have been macerated. Kriek is now quite widely available in the UK at wine shops and some supermarkets.

4 thick slices pain de campagne, crusts removed	1 rounded tablespoon plain flour
50g/2oz clarified butter (see page 178), or butter and oil (optional)	4 tablespoons double cream
	¼–½ teaspoon sugar
250ml/8fl oz Kriek Lambic beer	grating of nutmeg
4 eggs	salt and pepper
15g/½oz butter	1 tablespoon chopped flat-leaf parsley

Fry the bread gently in the butter, or butter and oil, on both sides until golden brown. Try and time it so that the bread is hot at the same time as the sauce is ready. (If you prefer, you can simply toast the bread without butter.) Bring the beer to the boil in a wide saucepan, then slip in the eggs – breaking them into a cup first is helpful. Poach for 3–4 minutes, spooning the simmering liquid over the yolks as the eggs cook – the yolks should really remain runny. Remove the eggs with a slotted spoon, drain them on kitchen paper and trim off the knotted edges if you like.

Strain the beer through a fine sieve into a jug. Melt the butter in a saucepan, add the flour and cook, stirring, for 1–2 minutes.

Gradually add the hot beer, stirring or whisking briskly at each addition to make a fairly thick, smooth sauce. Stir in the cream, then add the sugar, nutmeg, salt and pepper. Simmer gently while adjusting the seasoning, then stir the parsley into the sauce.

Place each slice of bread on a warmed serving plate, slip a poached egg on top, then spoon the sauce over the egg and bread. The only accompaniment should be a refreshing glass of Kriek.

JURASSIEN CROUTE

This is a poor man's version of that more famous, and extravagantly delicious, Jurassien dish of Bresse chicken with morels – though maybe not such a poor man, if he can afford morels at all. I have suggested using the dried fungus, not only because the season for fresh morels is so short, but because dried morels have a magnificent, concentrated smoky flavour and their soaking water substitutes well for rich stock.

8 dried morels
225g/8oz wild, field or oyster and
    browncap mushrooms
2 shallots, finely diced
15g/½oz smoked bacon fat or butter
salt and pepper
2 tablespoons Vin Jaune or dry sherry

2 tablespoons veal stock and/or
    mushroom liquid
2 tablespoons crème fraîche
1 tablespoon chopped flat-leaf
    parsley
1 teaspoon finely chopped tarragon
4 thick slices campagne or other
    'country' bread

Soak the morels for a good hour in 6 tablespoons of warm water. Strain the liquid through filter-paper or muslin to trap any grit, and set aside. Rinse the morels well under running water and squeeze dry. Cut in half and remove any further traces of grit, then drain on kitchen paper.

Wipe and slice the mushrooms. Sauté the shallots in fat or butter until translucent. Add the fresh mushrooms to the pan with a pinch of salt, cover and cook until the juices run. Remove the cover, add the morels, stir round and drive off the excess liquid. Add the Vin Jaune or sherry and cook until no liquid is visible. Add stock and/or soaking liquid, reduce until syrupy, then stir in the crème fraîche. Season and add half the herbs.

Toast the bread on one side, place on a heatproof dish and spoon the mushroom mixture over the untoasted sides. Grill or bake in a fairly hot oven at 200°C/400°F/Gas Mark 6 until bubbling – about 5 minutes. Sprinkle with the remaining herbs and serve at once.

EGGS BENEDICT

For those moments when the cholesterol clock stops ticking. This brunch snack is an American invention but designed with English muffins in mind – ham, poached eggs and hollandaise sauce on any other bread base is simply not eggs Benedict.

2 muffins, split in half
25g/1oz butter
4 small, thick slices roast ham
4 eggs, freshly poached
salt and pepper

For the hollandaise sauce:
3 egg yolks
1 tablespoon water
125g/4oz clarified butter (see page 178) or unsalted butter
1–2 tablespoons lemon juice

Toast and butter the muffins. Trim the ham slices to fit the muffin halves and lay them on top of the buttered sides. Put a poached egg on top of the ham and season lightly. Spoon over a generous helping of warm hollandaise sauce, made as follows.

This is the blender method for hollandais sauce – rather simpler and faster than the conventional method. Warm a blender (or food processor) by filling it with hot water, then draining and drying it. Place the egg yolks and water in the blender, cover and process for 30 seconds. Bring the butter to the boil in a small saucepan and, with the motor running, trickle it through the feeder funnel. When all the butter has been added drizzle in the lemon juice, then pour into a warmed jug and season to taste. Use warm.

Variation: Oysters Benedict

Not quite as classic a recipe, but an equally great one. Toast the muffins until they are very crisp and brown and then butter them. Omit the ham and when you have removed the eggs from their poaching water, slip in 4 freshly shucked large oysters. Poach them very gently for just one minute, then drain on kitchen paper. Place one egg and one oyster beside each other on each muffin half, season lightly and douse with hollandaise sauce that has had 6 tarragon leaves and a sprig of chervil or dill blended in with the other ingredients. Serve immediately.

CINNAMON TOAST

The first cinnamon toast I tasted was rather late on in life, at Bettys tearooms in Harrogate where it remains one of the most popular items on the menu. I did not for a moment imagine, as I subsequently buttered and dusted my granary toast at home, that there might be any particular formula to follow but food writers have many an instruction to issue (unlike Bettys, who claim a secret recipe).

In her cookery column in *The Times* Shona Crawford Poole recommended making cinnamon sugar in the ratio of four parts caster sugar to one part cinnamon, spreading it generously on lavishly buttered toast and grilling it until the sugar melts. The toast could be white or brown, dainty fingers or crunchy chunks. Jane Grigson suggested using 1 tablespoon sugar to 1 teaspoon cinnamon and mixing it with enough claret to make a spreadable paste. The bread is then toasted again, just to heat through. Others have made something approaching French toast, dusting fried bread with the cinnamon and sugar.

I must say that I rather favour granary toast but I know people for whom it's Mighty White or nothing. You can't really go far wrong – a couple of experiments and you will have determined your favourite method and ideal quantities.

· CROSTINI AND BRUSCHETTA ·

Crostini, of Tuscan origin, have much the same meaning as the French *croutons* and can be made in the same way (see page 171), using olive oil rather than butter, and served as an accompaniment to creamed soups. They are popular as canapé bases, spread with various piquant toppings.

The Italian bruschetta consists simply of country bread seasoned with olive oil and salt. Garlic and pepper are modern flourishes. The name is derived from the Latin *bruscare*, to roast, or the Roman dialect *bruciato*, meaning burnt; in other words bruschetta is always roasted or chargrilled.

BASIC CROSTINI

The ideal bread to use is a sfilatino, as rounds of the thin stick will be just the right size. A baguette is also suitable, or shapes can be stamped out from slices of larger loaves; square slices can be toasted and quartered to form squares or triangles. The crostini can be prepared a couple of hours in advance, but no more or they will begin to seem stale and overdry.

Cut whatever bread you are using into slices about 1cm/⅓inch thick. If you wish, brush the slices generously with extra virgin olive oil. Now either grill them quickly on each side until lightly coloured, or bake in the oven at 200°C/400°F/Gas Mark 6 until golden brown – about 5 minutes.

THE SIMPLEST CHEESE CROSTINI

All three of these ideas come from promotional leaflets, which are often a fine source of quick and clever ideas.

Boursin Crostini

Spread the crostini with garlic or pepper Boursin and toast until melted and browned. Serve floating in soup or on top of salad.

Rambol Crostini

Arrange a sliced strawberry over each crostino and dust with black pepper. Put a thin slice of Rambol walnut cheese on each strawberry-covered toast, grill gently until melting and browned, then serve at once.

Parmesan Crostini

Mix together 3 tablespoons extra virgin olive oil, 2 crushed cloves of garlic and 1 tablespoon chopped basil. Brush this mixture over the crostini, sprinkle with freshly grated Parmesan and place on a baking tray. Bake at 200°C/400°F/Gas Mark 6 for about 10 minutes, until crisp and golden. Serve with soups or salads, or as a canapé.

CROSTINI WITH BROAD BEAN PURÉE

This is a good way of using up older, plumper broad beans. If you have only a few beans, stretch them with ricotta or fromage frais.

Plain sfilatino is fine for this recipe but you could add interest and colour by using tomato- or olive-flavoured ciabatta.

½ sfilatino or ciabatta loaf
1 clove garlic, halved
extra virgin olive oil, to drizzle

4 or 5 mint leaves
4 tablespoons extra virgin olive oil
juice of ½ lemon
salt and pepper

For the broad bean purée:
350g/12oz broad beans (shelled
    weight)

Slice the bread thinly and grill it lightly, then rub it with the garlic and drizzle with a little oil. Cook the broad beans in boiling, salted water for 5–8 minutes, depending on size, or half that time if frozen. Drain and cool the beans, then pop them out of their skins (this is important!). Place in a food processor with the mint and reduce to a purée, then trickle in the oil and the lemon juice with the motor running and season to taste. Spoon on to the crostini.

CROSTINI WITH RICOTTA

Tuscan favourites for topping crostini are purées of chopped olives and sautéed chicken livers, but I rather like the crostini bianchi in Marcella Hazan's *Essentials of Classic Italian Cooking*. These have a simple topping of firm ricotta blended with anchovies, butter and pepper, but any number of piquant additions to the ricotta work well. Here is a basic formula.

225g/8oz sfilatino loaf, or equivalent, made into crostini
225g/8oz ricotta, drained if very moist
salt and pepper
finely chopped flat-leaf parsley (optional)
a little extra virgin olive oil

one of the following:
50g/2oz sun-dried tomatoes, finely diced

50g/2oz black oil-cured olives, finely diced
8 anchovy fillets, finely diced
25g/1oz Parmesan or Pecorino cheese, grated
2 teaspoons pesto
2 teaspoons of *salsa ghiotta* (or other piquant relish)
3–4 teaspoons walnut or artichoke purée

Blend together the ricotta, seasoning and parsley, if using, with one of the piquant ingredients (or a mixture), just until the ingredients are blended together – flecks of colour look attractive. Add a little oil if the mixture looks dry. Spoon a little of the topping on to each toast and serve soon after making.

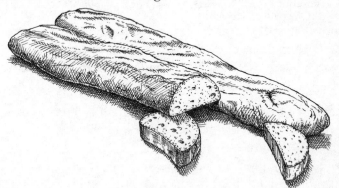

CROSTONI WITH ROASTED GARLIC AND PANCETTA

Serves 6
A simple but powerful snack, with interesting contrasts of texture. Crostoni are double the size of crostini.

1 ciabatta loaf	salt and pepper
1 head garlic	150g/5oz pancetta rottelata (rolled
3 tablespoons extra virgin olive oil	and very thinly sliced pancetta)

Cut the ciabatta into thirds, then halve these horizontally. Either bake in the oven at 190°C/375°F/Gas Mark 5 for 10 minutes, in which case you can do this in advance, or grill them gently, at the furthest remove possible from the heat, shortly before serving.

Peel off the outer layer of papery skin from the garlic and trim the top to expose the cloves slightly. Blanch (not so necessary for new season's garlic) in boiling water for 5 minutes, drain and coat in a spoonful of the oil. Wrap in foil or place in a small, covered dish and bake at 180°C/350°F/Gas Mark 4 for 45–60 minutes, until tender. Squeeze out the flesh from the cloves and purée with the remaining oil and the seasoning.

Spread the garlic purée over the cut surfaces of the ciabatta toasts. Divide the pancetta between the toasts, draping it over the edges. Grill under a moderate heat until the pancetta is crisp and then serve immediately.

GARLIC BRUSCHETTA

4 slices good crusty bread, such as	4 cloves garlic, slightly crushed
ciabatta, Pugliese or a simple oil-	4 tablespoons extra virgin olive oil
free loaf, about 1.2cm/½inch thick	salt and pepper

Barbecue, chargrill or grill the bread on both sides. Immediately rub one side with the garlic. Place on a plate, garlic side up, and spoon over the oil. Season with coarse salt and pepper and eat while warm.

Variations

For a tomato bruschetta, peel, seed and mash 4 plum tomatoes, add a few torn basil leaves and season. Pile on to the garlic-rubbed bread then drizzle with the oil.

Other toppings need be limited only by your imagination, though grilled or bottled Mediterranean vegetables and some piquant element such as olives, anchovies, capers, sun-dried tomatoes, goat's cheese or feta are the most obvious candidates. Bruschetta can be constructed rather like pizza, with a pile of toppings culminating perhaps with cheese, but it is good to return to first principles from time to time and enjoy simply roasted bread rubbed with garlic or tomato.

· HOGAZAS, BOCADILLOS AND TAPAS ·

The Spanish equivalents of bruschetta are much less familiar to us than the range of Italian grilled breads presented at almost every bistro. Perhaps this has much to do with the runaway success of pizza and ciabatta; or perhaps the *hogazas* of Spain – tomato-rubbed thick slices of crusty country bread that may or may not be toasted – seem more austere, more demanding of the finest authentic ingredients.

Bocadillos are little different from filled baguettes; if you were to slice open a demi-baguette and insert a few furled slices of serrano ham – no butter – you would have a *bocadillo*, more or less. Other likely fillings are chorizo, manchego cheese and wedges of tortilla.

Tapas are more of a household name – and a somewhat maligned one, thanks largely to the misguided efforts of the first sprinkling of so-called tapas bars set up in the UK. These little nibbles are generally served with bread rather than on it but many would in fact make excellent finger-food snacks if served on a bread base. If you want to do this, simply seek out good Spanish cheeses, hams, chorizos, olives, anchovies, tuna and bottled *piquillo* peppers, cut them into little chunks, douse them in Spanish extra virgin olive oil and arrange each item separately on small rounds of bread or toast.

On the basis that it might be salutary to note the simplicity of the most favoured bread-based snacks, here are recipes for Catalan garlic- and tomato-topped breads. These are so basic they vary only with the ripeness of the tomatoes, the garlic of the season and the vintage of the olive oil.

PA Y ALL

The oldest, most basic snack in all Catalan-speaking areas. Bread, garlic and oil are undoubtedly the three great essentials of all Mediter-ranean cuisine while tomatoes, now an inextricable fourth, are relative newcomers on the scene.

4 generous slices fresh crusty country
   bread
4 fat cloves garlic, peeled and halved
   or mashed

salt
about 4 tablespoons extra virgin
   olive oil

Rub the bread with the garlic halves or spread mashed garlic on each slice. Sprinkle with coarse salt, then drizzle with the oil. That really is that, though you could serve it as an accompaniment rather than a meal in itself.

PA AMB TOMAQUET

This moistened bread can form the basis of a meal. Likely accompaniments are any fine Catalan products – anchovy fillets, sardines, mountain hams and cheeses, *butifarra* sausage (a little like black or white puddings). Prominent Catalan figures, reports Colman Andrews in his treat of a book, *Catalan Cuisine*, have been known to eat ripe figs or bitter chocolate with their daily tomato bread.

8 slices crusty country bread	salt
4 ripe, juicy tomatoes	6 tablespoons extra virgin olive oil

Barbecue, chargrill or toast the bread lightly on both sides. Cut the tomatoes in half and, cupping each half in turn in the palm of your hand, squeeze hard while rubbing each slice of bread with the cut surface of the tomato – some seeds and flesh and a lot of juice should soak into the bread. Sprinkle on salt to taste, then drizzle with the oil and serve without delay.

Traditionally the bread is soaked and oiled on both sides but it is easier to eat if you flavour one side only.

PAN CON TOMATE Y JAMON

This takes the concept one step further, covering the bread with crushed tomatoes and adding a layer of cured ham. There are many styles and grades of *jamon*, the finest, which you will find in only a very few delicatessen in Britain, coming from a fully acorn-fed Iberian black-footed pig – rare, expensive, but one of the most delicious such foods you will ever eat. A good, basic serrano ham, available in most supermarkets, is perfectly fine for the purpose; the next task is to ensure that the tomatoes are sun- and vine-ripened. You may not find Spanish bread, but any fine loaf will serve well.

225g/8oz good country bread	2–3 tablespoons extra virgin olive oil
1 clove garlic, halved	salt
500g/1lb 2oz ripe tomatoes, peeled, seeded and chopped, then drained in a sieve	50g/2oz (4 slices) serrano ham, cut into strips

If the bread is very fresh, simply slice it into manageable pieces; if it is somewhat stale, cut it into neat rounds with a large biscuit cutter and toast lightly on both sides. Rub the fresh or toasted bread with the garlic. Mix the tomatoes with the oil and salt to taste. Divide the mixture between the pieces of bread and cover with a pile of ham strips.

· SANDWICHES ·

In 1925 Mrs Hilda Leyel noted with some amazement in her book *The Gentle Art of Cookery* that 'fortunes are made in the City of London out of sandwiches'. Seventy years later they still are, and not only in London: the four contenders for the 1994 Sandwich Bar of the Year had established their emporia in Liverpool, Croydon, Birmingham and Crewe. We consume in excess of 200 million sandwiches each week in the UK, accounting for a £1.5 billion industry. Rather a pity the 4th Earl of Sandwich could not profit more from his creation – but then he would probably have gambled away his fortune, as unwillingness to leave the gambling table allegedly prompted that first sandwich.

There is little doubt about the reason for the sandwich's phenomenal success – convenience. More interesting is the question of what makes a good sandwich. One of the Sandwich Bar of the Year contenders emphasised the importance of faultless quality and interesting fillings. The director of the British Sandwich Association, which runs the competition, specifies variety and depth of filling. Another judge highlights the role of bread. For Mrs Leyel, whose own recipe collection displayed variety and interest, it was plenty of butter – and grating the majority of fillings. Personally I have little problem with sliced fillings (admittedly we no longer have to worry about besmirching white kid gloves) and, if a filled baguette is a sandwich, no cavil at the absence of butter on occasion. But I have every sympathy with the Flour Advisory Board's suggestion – in another context – that we should select the bread to match our food as carefully as we might a glass of wine. And of course the ingredients should be generous and of impeccable quality.

The Flour Advisory Board issues a very sensible sandwich guide for caterers which should be standard issue – and would not come amiss in any household. To summarise its step-by-step guide to a perfect sandwich:

1. Begin with a chopping board, a sharp cook's knife, a palette knife and a serrated knife.
2. Prepare fillings and garnishes and place these next to the bread, next to the softened butter.
3. Butter the bread (with the palette knife) right to the edges.
4. Spread the filling to the edges so it is visible. Always fill generously and don't forget the seasoning.
5. Cut and display in different ways.
6. Eye appeal is important: try to achieve a contrast in colour, flavour and texture. The type of bread and filling, the napkin, garnish and choice of plate are all important to a winning sandwich.

The range of possible combinations is more or less infinite, so I have concentrated on listing the world's really great sandwiches in this chapter. I have sadly left out a wealth of intriguing documented examples, with fillings ranging from frog's legs and lamb's brains to codfish cheeks and green pea purée, as well as most of the really familiar staples, from Cheddar cheese to prawn mayonnaise. I have allowed myself one or two personal discoveries, mainly rye bread based, with the partial excuse that they may be of interest to anyone unfamiliar with rye (and we certainly don't encounter many rye bread sandwiches at supermarket counters). I do hope that you will experiment, even with the classics.

THE BLT AND CLUB

Serves 1

Perhaps the most striking feature of both these American classics is that the bread should be toasted and, ideally, still warm when eaten. If the toast seems like an Americanisation of a British invention, it is worth noting that the *Oxford English Dictionary* describes the very first sandwich (the one allegedly constructed by the 4th Earl of Sandwich) as 'some slices of cold beef placed between slices of toast'.

The definition does not say how *many* slices of toast, but we can reasonably assume that there were just two – exactly as there should be for the Club. What makes the Club a chunky affair is that it adds chicken to the BLT's essential ingredients.

For the BLT:

2 medium-thick slices white bread
softened butter
2 or 3 Cos lettuce leaves, torn
4 rashers very thinly cut streaky
    bacon, fried until crisp
1 ripe tomato, thickly sliced
salt and pepper

1–2 tablespoons Hellmann's or
    home-made mayonnaise

For the Club:

50–100g/2–3½oz freshly roasted
    chicken, sliced
paprika

For a BLT, lightly toast both slices of bread and then butter them. Layer the lettuce, bacon, well-seasoned tomato and mayonnaise on to one slice of toast. Put the second slice on top, press together and eat while the toast (and bacon, if possible) is warm.

For a Club, make the sandwich in exactly the same way but add the chicken, well seasoned with salt, pepper and paprika.

Variation

If you want to add another layer of bread, make it a slice of brown or wholewheat toast; you could then also add a layer of well-seasoned sliced, hardboiled egg and increase the amount of mayonnaise.

OYSTER LOAVES AND PO'BOYS

There is something of an international dispute about the origins of this glorious invention. Most authorities consider it a New Orleans classic, created in a waterfront bar in the Depression years when oysters came cheap and a French stick slathered with mayonnaise and packed with deep-fried oysters would fill up the poorest worker. Later the 'Po'Boy' turned into a 'Peacemaker' (or perhaps it was always a '*pourboire*', or tip), offered to angry wives by wayward husbands who spent their nights and their money on hooch and jazz; the hot sandwich picked up for a few pence at the market on the way home seemingly kept the peace.

Others point to the 'Boxed Oysters' of Connecticut, or the 'Squarer' loaf of San Francisco. It was the latter – a filled loaf, baked crisp in the oven, that M. F. K. Fisher described in *Consider the Oyster* as 'exquisitely hot and comforting'. English food historians, meanwhile, maintain this was an eighteenth-century dish – a pan-fried, stuffed 'manchet' – that crossed the water.

Certainly a common circumstance was, as Dickens' Sam Weller noted, that 'poverty and oysters always seem to go together'. Oysters are no longer poor man's fare, of course, so the Po'Boy has become a luxurious treat. A splendid 'nouveau pauvre' version I came across involved cod cheeks rather than oysters – unfortunately, these are somewhat more difficult to come by, if less expensive; but if you do find them, treat them in exactly the same way.

Here are the basics, with two different ways of frying the oysters.

I baguette or short French stick
50g/2oz butter, melted
150ml/5fl oz mayonnaise
a few gherkins or capers, finely
    chopped (optional)
3–4 crisp lettuce leaves such as iceberg
    or Cos, shredded
12 freshly shucked oysters
2 tablespoons plain flour, seasoned
    with salt and pepper

For oysters in batter:
cayenne
50g/2oz plain flour

I teaspoon groundnut or corn oil
I egg white
pinch of salt
vegetable oil for deep-frying

For oysters in a crumb coat:
I large or 2 small eggs, beaten
50g/2oz fine dry breadcrumbs from a
    cornmeal loaf or a plain white
    loaf
50g/2oz clarified butter (see page 178)
    or unsalted butter
4 tablespoons corn oil

Slice about a third off the top of the loaf and pull out as much of the crumb as you can (reserve this to make breadcrumbs). Brush inside the lid and the base with the butter and place in the oven at 220°C/ 425°F/Gas Mark 7 for 5 minutes or until golden and crisp. Cool a little and then spread two thirds of the mayonnaise in the bottom half of the baguette and one third in the top, adding the gherkins or capers if using. Press the shredded lettuce into the lower half of the baguette.

For the oysters in batter, pat the oysters dry and dust them with the seasoned flour, adding a little cayenne. Make the batter by whisking or blending the flour and oil with 3 tablespoons cold water. Whisk the egg white with the salt until stiff, then fold it into the batter. Dip the oysters in the batter then deep-fry them in hot oil; if using a deep-fryer set the temperature to 190°C/375°F; if using a saucepan check that a slightly stale cube of bread crisps and browns in 30 seconds. Cook just until golden – about 3 minutes. Drain well on absorbent paper then place in the baguette, close up and serve.

For the crumbed oysters, pat the oysters dry and dust them with the seasoned flour. Dip the oysters in the beaten egg, then the breadcrumbs and shallow-fry them in the butter and oil, which should be very hot but not smoking. Cook for no more than 3 minutes, turning once to brown both sides, then press them into the baguette, close up and serve immediately.

MUFFULETTA

Less controversial than the Po'Boy, this New Orleans sandwich was made famous by the city's Central Grocery and is heavily Italian influenced. The bread itself should be a plain, round flat loaf such as you might use for *pan bagnat* (see page 198) – a sesame-seeded flat Turkish bread would be ideal. Rather than compromise with poor quality bread, you could substitute a lightly herbed focaccia and go a little easier on the olive dressing.

One interesting variation I have come across uses chargrilled tuna steaks instead of the meats and cheese, and substitutes mayonnaise for the olive oil in the dressing.

I large round flat loaf of bread (see above)
4 slices provolone cheese
4 slices cooked ham or mortadella
12 thin slices salami

For the olive dressing:
50g/2oz oil-cured black olives, finely diced
100g/3½oz green olives, finely diced
100g/3½oz mixed pickled Italian vegetables or 2 anchovy fillets, finely chopped, plus 2 teaspoons

salt-packed caper fillets, rinsed, drained and chopped
I clove garlic, very finely chopped
2 tablespoons chopped flat-leaf parsley
I tablespoon chopped marjoram or oregano
100ml/3½fl oz extra virgin olive oil – rosemary-scented if possible
pepper

Mix together all the ingredients for the dressing (this can be prepared days in advance and stored in the fridge). Slice the loaf horizontally in half and remove a little of the crumb. Spread both halves generously with the dressing, then pack in the provolone, ham and salami, adding more dressing if you wish. Press on the lid and cut into wedges like a cake to serve.

THE HERO (OR SUB)

This is rather like a torpedo-shaped Muffuletta, though without the olive salad. There should be four contrasting Italian cured meats or salami, and at least one cheese – two contrasting cheeses makes for more excitement. You can of course roast your own peppers, but I like the idea of assembling this in a jiffy while still fresh with inspiration from a visit to the deli. A ciabatta is the ideal receptacle to my way of thinking, though not quite the right submarine shape. A long English Vienna roll may be a more appropriate shape; you would need two for this amount of filling. If you disregard the shape, a wide choice of loaves, long or round, presents itself. When using a heavily oiled and flavoured bread, go easy on the olive oil, though not on the garlic.

1 large loaf, long and tapered if possible, or 2 smaller ones	100g/3½ oz salami
	100g/3½ oz prosciutto or bresaola
extra virgin olive oil	100g/3½ oz peperoncini or chargrilled
1–2 cloves garlic, halved	peppers, drained
90g/3 oz Gorgonzola cheese	a few anchovy fillets (optional)
100g/3½ oz provolone, or a similar soft, fairly mild cheese, thinly sliced	a few crisp Cos lettuce leaves (optional)
100g/3½ oz mortadella	a sprinkling of wine vinegar
100g/3½ oz coppa	black pepper if needed

Split the loaf or loaves horizontally in half and remove a little of the crumb if you wish. Brush the insides of the loaf with olive oil and rub vigorously with the garlic. Spread the Gorgonzola over one half and then pile in the remaining ingredients – the meats will look best if folded to fit. Season as needed to produce a slightly piquant effect. Press the loaf closed, wrap in foil and refrigerate until needed (this is ideal picnic fare). Slice on the diagonal to serve.

PAN BAGNAT

Serves 1–4, depending on appetite

In common with most of the world's great sandwiches, the Pan Bagnat of Nice was never the subject of great culinary debate in its place of origin: rather it was a matter of remoistening the previous day's *pain de ménage* (household loaf), slapping in some local ingredients and squashing the whole thing up to render it portable. Ideal sustenance for a day spent working in fields or olive groves, or a weekend game of boules.

Inevitably, perhaps, this Mediterranean make-do classic has been seized on eagerly by City brasseries and become a receptable for any ingredient with a Mediterranean image. This is not necessarily a bad thing but it does tend to dazzle us out of contemplating a humble, homely version. Before I chart the steps to a simple Pan Bagnat, whose one essential is that the bread be bathed (*baigné/bagnat*) in olive oil, here is a listing of the ingredients likely to find their way into one of chef Antony Worrall-Thompson's glorious creations: extra virgin olive oil; balsamic vinegar; garlic; red onion; tapenade; pesto; grilled aubergine; grilled pepper; grilled courgette; sun-dried tomato; buffalo mozzarella; black olives; basil; rocket; baby spinach.

1 large, round flat white loaf, or a
    baguette, or a simple herb
    focaccia, slightly stale
4–8 tablespoons extra virgin olive oil
1 clove garlic, halved
4 large, ripe, sweet tomatoes, peeled
1 tablespoon red wine vinegar, or to
    taste
2 yellow peppers, roasted, peeled and
    sliced, or bottled chargrilled
    peppers drained and sliced

100g/3½oz oil-cured black olives,
    finely chopped
50g/2oz capers, gherkins, or anchovy
    fillets, rinsed, drained and finely
    chopped
salt and pepper

Cut a lid off the flat loaf or halve the baguette or focaccia. Hollow out the loaf, reserving the crumb. Douse the insides with olive oil and rub with the garlic.

Seed the tomatoes over a sieve to catch the juices, then mix the juices with the wine vinegar and use to moisten the crumb; add more oil if required. Chop the tomatoes roughly and mix with the peppers, olives, capers, gherkins or anchovies, and seasoning. Pack into the hollowed-out bread and replace the lid, or press the halves together. Wrap tightly in foil, place in the fridge and weight down with a couple of cans or jars.

Chill for at least 6 hours and up to 48 hours, as convenient. This makes great picnic food, as it will slice easily when unwrapped. It may not be traditional but there is no reason why you should not add some protein in the form of good tuna, cured ham, or semi-hard goat's or sheep's cheese.

PASTRAMI ON RYE

Serves 1

Still chic after all these years, pastrami is a more recent sandwich filler than one might imagine, dating from just before the Second World War. The name is Yiddish (derived from Romanian) and the sandwich should be kosher: bread, beef, no butter, a smear of mustard, perhaps a pickled cucumber.

Pastrami distinguishes itself from salt beef (or corned beef in the US) by being smoked after curing. If you have any choice, go for the round, peppercorn-coated New York style rather than the brick-shaped, paprika-dusted pastrami. The next important thing is that the beef should be hot. It is hardly practical to freshly steam pastrami at home but I have found that thickly cut pastrami can be heated quite successfully in the microwave.

2 thin slices light rye bread	100g/3½oz pastrami, thin or thick cut
I teaspoon American-style mustard	I mild dill-pickled cucumber

Spread the bread with the mustard. If you are using thick-cut pastrami, place it in a microwave-proof dish, cover, and warm through in a microwave on Low for 15–20 seconds. Sandwich the hot pastrami, or cold thin-cut pastrami, with the bread and serve with the cucumber on the side.

Non-Kosher Variation:

And not even on rye. The successful blend of flavours in this Prêt à Manger sandwich shop creation so surprised me that I feel bound to list the components: pastrami, dill pickle, sour cream and mustard sauce – on walnut and raisin bread.

THE REUBEN

Serves 1

The Reuben appears to have an older pedigree than its pastrami-on-rye cousin. Though no one knows precisely who Reuben was (it may have been Reuben Kulakofsy of the Blackstone Hotel in Omaha, Nebraska, or the owner of Reuben's Deli on Manhattan's 58th street), examples of the sandwich can be traced back to the early 1900s.

2 thin slices dark rye bread	2 thick slices salt beef
2 tablespoons Hellmann's or home-made mayonnaise	2–4 tablespoons soft-cooked sauerkraut, well drained
2 thin slices Gruyère or Emmental cheese	

Spread one slice of bread with a little of the mayonnaise and cover it with a slice of cheese, followed by a slice of salt beef. Now cover it with the sauerkraut – I warm this first in the microwave – and top with the remaining mayonnaise. Press on the second slice of beef, the second slice of cheese and finally the second slice of bread (spread this first with a little mayonnaise, if you like). Press together firmly and toast on both sides until the cheese has melted. One way of doing this is to dry-fry one side of the sandwich in a frying pan or ridged steak pan over a low flame, then place the pan under the grill to toast the upper side. Another trick is to serve the sandwich open faced, as at Minsky's American Bar in London – cover the beef with the sauerkraut, followed by the beef and cheese and grill until the cheese has melted and the sauerkraut heated through. Toast the second slice of bread separately and perch it on the molten cheese.

HOT HAM AND SPINACH SANDWICH

Serves 6

This is such a good combination, the sandwich so satisfying a meal in itself that it deserves to be added to the Reuben hall of fame. Stinco di Prosciutto al Forno, to give the soft-cooked ham shank its full name, is available (under the Fiorucci label) in some Italian and Continental delis, as well as the specialist food departments of large stores. It is a vacuum-packed product – one of the world's best boil-in-the-bag dishes – housed in a colourful box.

500g packet of Stinco di Prosciutto (see above)	12 medium-thick slices moist, light but compact rye bread (I prefer bread without caraway seeds for this sandwich)
500g/1lb 2oz fresh spinach	
salt, pepper and nutmeg	
50g/2oz butter	3–6 teaspoons German mustard

Reheat the ham according to the instructions on the packet, making sure to retain the rich juices. Meanwhile, prepare the spinach. Wash it thoroughly and remove any tough stalks, then plunge it into a large pan of boiling salted water for 2 minutes, until just tender. Drain well through a sieve and squeeze dry, pressing down hard on the sieve. Turn the lump of compacted spinach on to a board and chop roughly. Season generously, then warm it through gently in a saucepan with the butter.

Slice or pull apart the ham and keep it warm in its juices. Toast the bread on one side only (a few slices at a time), then spread the untoasted side with mustard. Divide the ham and spinach between half the slices, spooning a little of the juices over each. Cover with the remaining toast, pressing down firmly, and serve at once.

The juice-soaked layer of bread is the flourish that makes this sandwich so good, hence the need for a bread with a compact crumb, and the absence of butter. Most rye breads will fit the bill.

CAJUN-SPICED CHICKEN ON FRENCH BREAD

Serves 2–4

You can buy ready-made Cajun spice mixes but as I have a dread of dried onion and garlic I make up my own – it is very quick.

I have purposely not called the chicken 'blackened' because it is perfectly interesting without such extreme treatment. So if you prefer not to frighten the cat and alarm the neighbours, simply fry the chicken briskly, but more gently, for 4–5 minutes per side, until completely cooked. If you are cooking on a barbecue, fling it on the hottest spot with impunity.

2 chicken breast fillets
25g/1oz butter, melted
4 heaped tablespoons mayonnaise
2 heads chicory or fennel, or some
    crisp lettuce leaves, thinly sliced
1 French stick, or 4–8 slices of light
    pain de campagne

1 teaspoon pepper
1 teaspoon cayenne
1 teaspoon paprika
1 teaspoon ground cumin
1 teaspoon ground coriander
1 teaspoon caster sugar
½ teaspoon dried oregano
½ teaspoon dried thyme

For the Cajun Spice Mix:
1 teaspoon salt

Put the chicken fillets between sheets of freezer layering tissue and beat them out flat, using a heavy rolling pin. Coat the chicken with the melted butter, then with the spice mixture, which you make by simply stirring or shaking all the ingredients together. Mix together the mayonnaise and chicory, fennel or lettuce.

Turn off smoke alarms and open all doors. Heat a griddle pan (or the barbecue) until searingly hot, throw the spiced breasts on to the pan and press down with tongs for a minute. After 2 minutes, turn over and cook for 2 minutes more. Test with a sharp knife: if the flesh is still pink in the centre, reduce the heat a little and cook for a further 2–4 minutes.

Slice the French stick in half, crisping first in a hot oven if necessary, or toast the sliced bread on one side only. Top with a spoonful of the salad, then cover with a portion of chicken breast (you can slice this into strips for ease of eating if you like). Cover with more salad and the remaining bread and serve immediately.

RANNOCH RYE SANDWICH

Thinly sliced cold-smoked wild venison from Rannoch is at last available in some supermarkets, as is its perfect sandwich partner, the natural-rise, woodfire-baked Russian loaf from the Village Bakery. Both are North Country products; could this account for their complementary flavours?

8 thin slices Russian rye bread (see
   above)
a little butter (optional)
½ teaspoon grated horseradish
4 tablespoons crème fraîche
100g/3½oz wafer-thin cold-
   smoked venison

I small, or ½ large ripe
   avocado, peeled and thinly
   sliced
salt and pepper
squeeze of lemon juice

Butter the bread lightly if you wish. Mix together the horseradish and crème fraîche and spread half of it over the bread, then cover with slices of venison, trimmed to fit. Spoon the remaining horseradish cream over 4 of the slices of bread. Season the avocado with salt, plenty of pepper, and lemon juice and arrange on top of the cream-coated venison. Cover the avocado-topped slices with the plain slices and press together. Cut each sandwich into 4 small squares to serve.

You could of course rearrange this to make open sandwiches – use only 4 slices of bread, perhaps cut a little more thickly, and fold the venison attractively rather than laying it flat. The colour contrasts look suitably dramatic.

AVOCADO, ROQUEFORT AND WALNUT BREAD SANDWICH

Serves 1

small avocado, preferably Hass
pepper
¼–½ teaspoon well-aged balsamic
   vinegar

25g/1oz good-quality Roquefort
   cheese
I tablespoon crème fraîche or thick
   Greek yoghurt
2 fairly thick slices walnut bread

Mash half the avocado with a little pepper and the balsamic vinegar; mash half the Roquefort with the cream or yoghurt. Spread one piece of walnut bread with the avocado mixture and the other piece with the Roquefort mixture. Slice the rest of the avocado and sandwich, with the Roquefort, between the slices of bread.

HUNGARIAN-STYLE GRILLED CHICKEN ON RYE

This is a terrific blend of flavours in which light caraway rye bread comes into its own. If you have a jar of bottled grilled peppers to hand it is also very quick to prepare.

2 chicken breast fillets
5–6 tablespoons crème fraîche
1 tablespoon grainy mustard
2 teaspoons sweet paprika
½ teaspoon light honey

salt and pepper
1 large red pepper or 175g/6oz bottled
    peppers in olive oil
4 large or 8 small thin slices caraway
    rye bread

Beat the breast fillets flat; I use a marble rolling pin and enclose the fillets in freezer layering tissue. Mix together the crème fraîche, mustard, paprika and honey with ½ teaspoon salt and some pepper and spread it over the chicken. Set aside to marinate at room temperature for 2 hours, or in the fridge overnight, bringing it back to room temperature before cooking.

Just before cooking the chicken, grill the fresh pepper until charred, then peel and slice it, or slice the bottled peppers and warm them through in the oil, either in a microwave or under the grill.

Grill the chicken breasts, still coated in the marinade, under a medium to high heat for 4–5 minutes per side, or until no pink shows when you cut into the centre of the fillet with a sharp knife. Rest the chicken for a moment while you toast the bread on one side. Place a whole or half chicken fillet on the untoasted sides of half the bread, spooning on any juices. Top with the pepper and press on the remaining slices of bread, untoasted side down. Serve at once.

CUCUMBER SANDWICHES

Most of the great classic sandwiches are American in origin; cucumber sandwiches, however, must surely be universally acknowledged as quintessentially English.

The only trick to these is that you must salt the cucumber or you will end up with a very soggy mess rather than a neat pile of crisp triangles or soldiers.

2 cucumbers
handful of salt
1–2 teaspoons white wine vinegar

1 large white or brown loaf, thinly
    sliced
plenty of softened butter

Peel the cucumbers very thinly with a swivel-bladed potato peeler. If they are very large, halve them lengthways and discard the seeds. Otherwise, simply slice them very thinly, preferably on a mandoline. Pile the slices into a colander and mix in some salt and the wine vinegar with your hands. Leave for 1–2 hours, then rinse, drain and squeeze dry – either with your hands or in a clean tea towel. The cucumber can be refrigerated in a plastic bag until ready to use.

Butter the bread generously, sandwich with the cucumber, press the slices together and trim off the crusts. Cut into triangles or fingers.

Variations

Add a few finely torn or chopped mint leaves to the cucumber, along with a small pinch of caster sugar.

Mix the drained cucumbers with 100ml/3½fl oz pot of thick crème fraîche, 1–2 tablespoons snipped chives and a dusting of white pepper. This is better with brown bread rather than white.

SHOOTER'S SANDWICH

Not many people have encountered this alternative *boeuf en croute*, with the crust that of a loaf of bread rather than pastry. The idea seems to have been born in the Thirties, while in 1955 Elizabeth David commented in *Summer Cooking* that she found it invaluable when packing, moving house, or going on picnics or journeys.

My version is quite elaborate, adding spinach and a mushroom stuffing to the filling. It looks most dramatic when sliced, fit to grace any dinner-party table, although equally apt for a plan-ahead picnic, whether Glyndebourne or the local park. Its blessing is that it is remarkably foolproof and, despite appearances, really quite simple to prepare. I doubt most of us would attempt it when moving house, however.

1 × 400g/14oz white bloomer loaf
750g/1½lb piece beef fillet, trimmed
    of fat and sinew
1 tablespoon good olive oil or melted
    butter

salt and pepper
1 tablespoon Madeira
2 teaspoons Dijon mustard
2 tablespoons crème fraîche
1 tablespoon finely chopped tarragon

For the mushroom duxelles:
15g/½oz dried ceps or 'forest mix'
    mushrooms
225g/8oz oyster or field mushrooms,
    finely chopped
15g/½oz unsalted butter

For the spinach wrap:
500g/1lb 2oz large spinach leaves,
    stalks removed
grating of nutmeg
2 tablespoons crème fraîche
1 tablespoon grainy mustard

Slice the bloomer in half lengthways; I usually leave the other side intact to act as a hinge but this is not essential. Hollow out the loaf a little by removing the crumb with your fingers – you should remove about (200g/7oz). Process about 50g/2oz of the crumbs for the mushroom stuffing and freeze or dry the rest for another recipe.

Soak the dried mushrooms in a little warm water for at least 1 hour, then drain, rinse and squeeze dry, retaining the soaking water. Chop the soaked mushrooms finely if large. Place in a frying pan with the fresh mushrooms, butter and ¼ teaspoon salt; cover and cook until the juices run. Remove the lid, add the Madeira and mushroom soaking water and cook, stirring from time to time, until the juices have almost evaporated. Stir in the mustard and crème fraîche and allow to bubble away for a minute or two, until thick. Add the tarragon and season with pepper, adding more salt if needed. Mix in the reserved crumbs and set aside to cool.

Cook the spinach in a large pan of rapidly boiling, salted water for about 2 minutes, until just tender. Drain, refresh under cold water and drain again thoroughly, pressing down hard without tearing the leaves. Lay out the leaves carefully on a double layer of absorbent kitchen paper to dry. When fairly dry, arrange them on a sheet of freezer-layering tissue or cling film in a rectangle large enough to enclose the beef. Sprinkle with nutmeg and some salt and pepper, then mix together the crème fraîche and mustard and spread it over the spinach.

Cut a deep pocket through the beef fillet using a sharp knife: start 1cm/⅓inch from one end, cut two thirds of the way widthways through the fillet and stop 1cm/⅓inch from the other end. Using a meat bat or a heavy rolling pin, pound the edges of the slit surfaces lightly to open out the pocket. Season the fillet fairly generously inside and out with salt and pepper and coat with the oil or butter. Pack the mushroom stuffing into the pocket, close up the slit as best you can and tie the fillet quite firmly with string at 2.5cm/1inch intervals. Roast in the oven at 240°C/475°F/Gas Mark 9, allowing about 30 minutes for medium-rare roast (if the roast is very rare, the blood is likely to seep through the meat and into the bread). Remove from the oven and allow to rest for 15 minutes.

Remove the string and place the fillet in the centre of the spinach rectangle. Pat the spinach round the fillet, with the help of the tissue or cling film, then place the fillet inside the hollowed-out loaf. Close up the loaf firmly, wrap it in foil and place in a large, rectangular terrine, loaf tin or other firm container into which it will just fit. If the container is too wide, fill the gaps with crumpled foil or newspaper. Place a brick or other heavy weight on top of the loaf and leave it to cool completely before refrigerating it for at least 6 hours or overnight (leave the weight on if space allows).

If you are taking the loaf to a picnic keep it wrapped in its foil (but don't attempt to haul the brick with it!) until serving. Slice fairly thickly with a sharp, long-bladed knife. This really needs no accompaniment but a simple tomato salad with a tarragon vinaigrette would not go amiss. Or simply wash and dry a few sprays of cherry tomatoes 'on the vine'.

KNIGHT IN BLACK ARMOUR

A make-do recipe, but as easy to find an excuse for as its sweet milk-and-jam counterpart, *pain perdu* (see page 295). Adapt it to the ingredients you have, but make sure to use a cheese that does not string or harden too quickly. I have suggested Leerdammer – a good melting cheese, and with a flavour that melds well with the beer and rye – but Gouda would also be suitable.

2 slices (about 75g/2½oz) black rye bread	5 tablespoons beer
	l egg yolk
l teaspoon German mustard	3 tablespoons milk
2 thin slices (about 40g/1½oz) Leerdammer cheese	good knob of unsalted butter

Spread the bread with the mustard, then make a sandwich with the cheese. Pour the beer, warmed if the bread is rather dry, into a soup plate wide enough to hold the bread and dip each side of the sandwich into the beer. It should all be absorbed quite quickly; if not, leave the sandwich to soak for a few minutes.

Beat together the egg yolk and milk and pour this into a second soup plate. Heat the butter in a frying pan until it foams. Quickly dip each side of the beer-soaked sandwich into the egg mixture, then transfer it to the frying pan and fry gently for about 3 minutes per side, shaking the pan now and again, until the bread is crisp round the edges and the cheese melted. Eat hot.

CROQUE MONSIEUR

For such a simple dish, this has a bemusing number of variations. It made its first appearance in Paris in 1910 and is still to be found in every café, street stall and seemingly every freezer cabinet. Cheap and nasty versions abound, but so do good ones. Here is a classic version.

1 teaspoon Meaux mustard
25g/1oz unsalted butter, plus extra for
    frying
2 fairly thin slices *pain de mie* or plain
    white sandwich bread

40g/1½oz Gruyère cheese, thinly
    sliced
40g/1½oz slice cooked or roast ham

Blend the mustard with the butter and spread it over the bread (if you are using enriched *pain de mie* you could omit the butter and spread with mustard only). Press the cheese on to both pieces of bread, top one piece with the ham, then sandwich the bread together, pressing down.

Melt a knob of butter in a frying pan until foaming and fry the sandwich over a very gentle heat for about 5 minutes or until the base is golden and the cheese beginning to melt. Turn the sandwich over carefully and remove it from the pan while you add another knob of butter. Return the sandwich to the pan and fry gently for 5 minutes until the cheese is oozing. Serve immediately.

A Note on Grilling

I am convinced that gently frying the sandwich is the best way to prepare a closed Croque Monsieur but if you want to cut down on the butter a reasonable result is arrived at this way: toast the bread on one side and spread the untoasted sides with mustard. Cover one half with all the cheese, the other half with the ham. Return to the grill, filling-side upwards. Once the cheese has melted press the halves together and serve.

CROQUE MAX

Serves 1

Max Poilâne is the lesser-known brother of Lionel (see **Pain Poilâne**) but is possibly even more of a bread fanatic, claiming to eat 'bread with bread' and carrying his own bread to restaurant meals. The Croque Monsieur served in his modern café in Montparnasse has a sourdough base. I could not imitate it exactly but it is essentially very simple and is perfectly successful with any good, dense sourdough, with which Gruyère and smoked ham have a great affinity.

50g/2oz slice thinly cut sourdough
    bread
50g/2oz thinly sliced smoked ham

50g/2oz Gruyère cheese, grated

Toast one side of the bread. Sprinkle a little of the cheese on the untoasted side, then cover with the ham, folded as necessary. Sprinkle the rest of the cheese over the ham and grill under a moderate heat until the cheese bubbles. Serve at once, perhaps with a simple tomato salad.

LEMON SANDWICHES

Serves 1

It took me a long time to persuade myself to try this unlikely idea, which I first encountered in Jane Grigson's *Fruit Book*. A firm convert, I shall now always endeavour to serve these delicate, piquant little sandwiches alongside slices of 'traditionally' smoked (i.e. with a pronounced aroma of wood smoke) Scottish salmon.

2 thin slices good, compact
    wholewheat bread
unsalted butter

3–4 very thin slices peeled lemon
    (a thin-skinned lemon is
    best)

Spread both slices of bread liberally with butter, then remove the crusts. Generosity with butter is essential. Make sure no stray pips or pith adhere to the lemon and sandwich it between the bread. Cut into small squares and serve with slices of your favourite smoked salmon and black pepper.

LEMON CURD SANDWICHES

A much more likely combination than the one above is Frances Bissell's home-made lemon curd sandwiches with fruit salad. This is rather neat picnic fare, avoiding the problems of transporting cream – though there is much to be said for lemon curd sandwiches with raspberries *and* cream. Generally speaking, thinly cut white bread is the thing with raspberries, though a compote of blackberries and blueberries could take more assertive brown bread. Blueberries, incidentally, positively benefit from the alliance with lemon curd, while cream of any description does little for their rather retiring flavour.

There is no need for a recipe for lemon curd sandwiches – simply slice your chosen bread thinly, and spread it as thickly or thinly as you wish with lemon curd. Instead, here is my favourite formula for lemon curd, which is fairly tart. If you prefer something gentler, increase the sugar by 50g/2oz, the butter by 25g/1oz and add one more egg.

| zest and juice of 2 large, juicy unwaxed or organic lemons | 125g/4oz caster sugar |
| 90g/3oz unsalted butter, cut into small pieces | 3 large eggs, beaten |

The simplest method is to whisk together all the ingreadients (straining the eggs through a sieve) and microwave on Medium, stirring every 30 seconds, until the curd thickens. For the more conventional method, place the lemon zest and juice in a bowl with the butter and sugar, place the bowl over a saucepan of simmering water and stir gently until the butter and sugar have dissolved. Strain the eggs into the mixture and continue to heat gently, stirring frequently, until the mixture is thick. It should not be allowed to boil at any stage. Pot, cover, and store in the fridge for up to 3 months.

THE BAGEL CLASSIC

Serves 1

Lox is brine-cured, extremely salty, lightly smoked salmon and it is allegedly the reason for the *schmear* of salt-cutting cream cheese in this popular bagel sandwich. Nova is mild-cured and more pronouncedly smoked and its presence in a bagel would be frowned upon by the traditionalists. Use whatever smoked salmon you prefer but remember to choose a sweet cream cheese if the salmon is rather salty.

| 1 freshly baked plain bagel | 1 thick slice smoked salmon |
| 1 *schmear* cream cheese (in fact, a good helping, *not* a meagre smear) | a sprinkling of snipped chives |

Halve the bagel and spread each half generously with cream cheese. Press the salmon, folded as necessary, on to one half of the bagel, and sprinkle a few chives over the other half. Press together.

CARAWAY-RYE BAGEL WITH MELTED MÜNSTER

Serves 1

This is a perfect combination and whether through childhood memories or sojourns in Alsace, my addiction to it was instant.

| 1 caraway-rye bagel | about 90g/3oz mature Münster cheese (a baby Münster will do), thinly sliced |
| 2 tablespoons mild salad sauerkraut (optional) | |

Halve the bagel and toast both sides until golden. If using the sauerkraut, heat it in a microwave or small saucepan and quickly pile it on each bagel half. Arrange the cheese on top right up to the edges of the bagel, and flash under a moderately hot grill for about 30 seconds, until the cheese is just melting. Even more perfect with a glass of beer.

CINNAMON BAGEL APPLE PIE

Serves 1

If this speedy alternative to apple pie appeals it may be worth reserving a corner of your freezer for a bagful of cinnamon-raisin bagels and storing a jar of apple sauce in the fridge. You can, of course, sauté and purée apples from scratch for a less fast, but potentially even more delicious concoction.

1 stale cinnamon-raisin bagel	1 good tablespoon thick Jersey cream
3 tablespoons thick apple sauce	or strained Greek yoghurt

Preheat the oven to 220°C/425°F/Gas Mark 7 and place a tray of water near the bottom. Slice the top third off the bagel and pull out as much crumb as you can from the base without damaging the sides or centre. Replace the lid on the base and heat in the oven for 5–10 minutes, depending on how stale the bagel is. When it is crisp on top, remove the bagel from the oven and fill the base with the apple sauce. Put it back in the oven, with the lid at its side, for 3 minutes to allow the filling to warm through, then remove from the oven, spread the chilled cream or yoghurt over the sauce and replace the lid. Serve at once, with a knife and fork and napkin as the cream will ooze out of the bagel.

ALL-AMERICAN MAPLE-PECAN CINNAMON RAISIN BAGEL

Serves 1

1 cinnamon-raisin bagel	a few drops of vanilla extract
3 pecan halves	1 teaspoon maple syrup
25g/1oz cream cheese or fromage frais	

Heat the bagel and the nuts in the oven at 200°C/400°F/Gas Mark 6 for about 5 minutes, until the bagel is crisp and the nuts toasted. Lightly stir together the cream cheese or fromage frais, vanilla and maple syrup. Chop the toasted nuts and add to the mixture. Halve the bagel and spread with the cream cheese mixture. Eat at once. You will need a napkin!

BAGUETTE SANDWICHES

There is very little you can't put into a baguette. A rather splendid French guide to sandwiches proposes warm *boudin, gésiers confits* (potted gizzard) and leftover boiled beef, not forgetting sliced frank-furters with sauerkraut, or '*tranches de corned-beef avec piccalilli*'. It also has a few suggestions for adding interest to that great classic, *baguette au jambon de Paris* – horseradish butter; tomato butter with slices of Gruyère; hardboiled eggs and tarragon mayonnaise; Roquefort blended with softened butter.

Here, among a wealth of possibilities, are some personal favourites. Each makes enough for a standard 225g/8oz baguette, unbuttered.

Fig and Prosciutto

extra virgin olive oil, for drizzling
100g/3½oz finely sliced prosciutto
100g/3½oz torta dolcelatte (dolcelatte cheese layered with mascarpone)

2 large or 4 small ripe figs, cut into wedges
a very few basil or mint leaves

Slice the baguette in half and drizzle with olive oil, then add layers of all the remaining ingredients, sprinkling with more olive oil if you wish.

Spinach, Bacon and Tomato

a handful of baby spinach leaves
1 teaspoon extra virgin olive oil or walnut oil
90g/3oz cream cheese
4 rashers streaky bacon, fried until crisp, then crumbled

grating of nutmeg
2 ripe firm tomatoes, thickly sliced
salt and pepper

Toss the spinach leaves in the oil. Mix together the cheese, bacon and nutmeg and spread thinly on both cut sides of the baguette. Season the tomato and arrange it in the baguette with the spinach.

Herbed Omelette

Make a 3-egg omelette in the usual way but in a large pan so that it can be rolled up to fit the baguette. Add plenty of fresh herbs – basil, chervil, chives and so on. Split open the baguette and remove a little of the crumb. Douse the cut sides of the baguette with a flavoured herb oil – a slightly spicy, chilli-flavoured oil would work well, too. Roll up the omelette and place inside the baguette. Close up and cut into slices. Eat soon after making.

Roast Beef and Onion

75g/2½oz softened butter
1–2 teaspoons Dijon mustard
dash of Worcestershire sauce or
 mushroom ketchup
1 mild onion, finely diced
1 tablespoon olive oil
salt and pepper

½ teaspoon soft brown sugar
1 teaspoon well-aged balsamic
 vinegar or a little less of red wine
 vinegar
4 medium-thick slices rare roast
 beef

Blend 50g/2oz of the butter with the mustard and sauce or ketchup and spread it over the cut sides of the baguette. Cook the onion very slowly in the remaining butter and the oil with a pinch of salt until completely soft and collapsed. Add the sugar and vinegar and cook for a few minutes longer. Leave to cool, then spoon into the baguette. Add the beef, season, and close up the sandwich.

MEDITERRANEAN LAMB BAGUETTES

This is a simple and versatile recipe for a stuffed picnic loaf which will also sit happily on the buffet table.

2 baguettes
50g/2oz unsalted butter
2 tablespoons extra virgin olive oil
2 cloves garlic, very finely chopped
500g/1lb 2oz lean minced lamb
150g/5oz courgettes, blanched and
 grated
2 tablespoons sun-dried tomato
 paste or 25g/1oz sun-dried
 tomatoes in oil, finely diced

1 rounded tablespoon tomato
 purée
25g/1oz black olives, finely diced
25g/1oz salt packed capers, rinsed
 and chopped
1 teaspoon summer savory leaves or
 ½ teaspoon dried summer savory
salt and pepper

Cut each baguette open length ways, leaving it joined along one side. Hollow them out somewhat, reserving the crumb. Butter the insides of the baguettes.

 Heat the oil in a heavy frying pan, add the garlic and cook over a gentle heat until soft – about 5 minutes. Add the lamb and cook, stirring frequently to break up any clumps, until no pink meat remains – about 12–15 minutes. Add the courgettes to the lamb along with the tomato paste, tomato purée, olives, capers and savory. Cook gently for 3 minutes, then season with salt and pepper. Set aside to cool to room temperature.

Process the reserved bread crumbs until fine and stir into the cooled filling, then divide it between the baguettes and close them up so that the filling is completely enclosed. If the baguettes are too long to fit in the fridge, halve them at this stage. Wrap them tightly in foil and chill for 2–3 hours or overnight.

Serve cold and cut into slices for a picnic or, if you are serving them at home, crisp the foil-wrapped parcels in the oven at 220°C/ 425°F/Gas Mark 7 for 10 minutes. The stuffed baguettes can also be frozen for up to 2 months, thawed gently, then heated through as described.

THE CIABATTA SANDWICH

Sandwich bars and supermarkets have not been slow in exploiting the possibilities presented by this universally pleasing bread. The usual fillings are Italian cured meats and marinated vegetables, with the ubiquitous sun-dried tomato making a customary appearance, but there is very little you can't put into a ciabatta – even British roast ham and farmhouse Cheddar snuggle down happily inside the plain, unflavoured original. The following are a few simple favourites. Each makes enough for a third of a ciabatta loaf or one ciabatta roll.

Tomato Salad

4 tablespoons extra virgin olive oil, oregano-flavoured if you wish

I fat clove garlic, halved

3–4 ripe, firm plum tomatoes, thickly sliced

a few leaves each of basil, flat-leaf parsley and mint

1–2 teaspoons balsamic or red wine vinegar

salt and pepper

Use half the oil to brush the cut sides of the loaf then rub vigorously with the garlic. Arrange the tomatoes on the base of the loaf, drizzle on the rest of the oil and sprinkle with the herbs. Season with vinegar, salt and pepper then press the two halves together tightly.

Fresh Asparagus and Parmesan

100g/3½oz freshly cooked asparagus, cut into 7.5cm/3inch lengths

25g/1oz Parmesan cheese, thinly shaved with a potato peeler

2 tablespoons truffled olive oil or walnut oil

a squeeze of lemon juice or 1 teaspoon balsamic vinegar

salt and pepper

Arrange the asparagus and Parmesan over one side of the bread, perhaps with the asparagus tips poking out. Whisk together the oil, lemon juice or vinegar and seasoning and drizzle it over the filling. Press on the top half of the bread. For the best flavour the asparagus should be at room temperature or warm, but not chilled.

Artichoke Hearts and Prosciutto

90g/3oz bottled grilled artichoke hearts in olive oil

40g/1½oz wafer-thin prosciutto slices

a few drops of balsamic vinegar

pepper

If the artichoke hearts have not already been chargrilled, place them on a foil-lined tray under a very hot grill and turn to char slightly all over. Slice them thickly and arrange on one side of the bread with the prosciutto, folded to fit. Drizzle over the vinegar and grind on pepper. Press on the top half of the bread.

DANISH OPEN SANDWICHES

What we know as an 'open sandwich' is rather significantly called a *smørrebrød*, or 'butter bread', in Denmark. Butter acts as both a mediator of powerful flavours and a barrier between the bread base and the juices from the toppings. Thus rule number one of open-sandwich production is to butter the bread generously.

The next most helpful thought is that each sandwich should be a meal in miniature, consisting of bread, butter, a savoury element of fish, egg, meat or cheese, a little salad or vegetable (more than a token flash of green) and, where appropriate, a generous helping of mayonnaise, remoulade, or similar sauce. Combinations may be simple or elaborate, to suit the occasion: in Denmark the *smørrebrød* is a lunchtime staple (wrapped in greaseproof and carried in a special lunch box to school, office, field or building site), a Saturday supper tradition, a breakfast and evening snack option – and the perfect centrepiece for a party of any kind.

Construction:

Packaged pre-sliced rye bread and a fresh white poppyseed twist make ideal bases. Cut the bread into 5 × 10cm/2 × 4inch rectangles (white bread should first be sliced 1.2cm/½inch thick) and coat one side generously with slightly salted butter.

Plain, soft lettuce leaves, if used, should form the next layer and overlap the bread. Subtly flavoured toppings such as shrimps or roast pork should be served on white bread; strong or bland items such as herrings or egg on rye. Fish and meat could be marinated, roast or fried. Roasted meat and salami should be sliced very thinly and folded as necessary to overlap the edges of the bread. Likely garnishes include strips of scrambled egg, curried egg, and macaroni salad, cucumber and tomato twists, onion rings, radish slices, and sprigs of parsley and dill. Sauces are generally based on a properly prepared, thick mayonnaise.

Try to provide a selection of at least three types of sandwich, and supply knives, forks and napkins. Here are three suggestions as a starting point.

Amager Sandwich

This workman's sandwich from the island near Copenhagen consists simply of 1 thin slice of dark rye bread and 1 medium-thick slice of white bread sandwiched together with 15g/½oz salted butter! It tastes surprisingly interesting.

The Hans Christian Andersen Sandwich

This sandwich is perhaps the most classic in the Danish repertoire and is reputed to have been a favourite of the famous fairytale creator. Spread rye bread with slightly salted butter, then arrange crisply cooked bacon, sliced liver pâté, diced jellied beef consommé and sliced tomato on top so that a line of each is visible. Spoon on freshly grated or creamed horseradish and sprinkle with chopped parsley.

Do-it-Yourself Prawn Pyramid

Still unsure about construction? Here is the perfectly traditional answer: let people make their own sandwiches. Pass round light, crusty white bread, salted butter, and shelled, cooked prawns, followed by a small jug of melted butter, plus lemon wedges and sprigs of dill.

· Salads ·

Armenian Aubergine Salad with Pitta

A personal favourite among the many vegetable salads of the Mediterranean. This should be served warm, either in pitta, as here, or with crisp shards of pitta (see Fattoush on page 220), crumbled into the salad just before serving. Toasted flaked almonds can also be added for a good contrasting texture.

2 firm aubergines, about 350g/12oz each, cut into 2.5cm/1inch cubes
salt and pepper
about 150ml/5fl oz extra virgin olive oil
1 clove garlic, peeled
1 small red onion, finely diced
1 tablespoon red or white wine vinegar
½ teaspoon caster sugar
1 teaspoon cinnamon
2 sprigs mint, torn or chopped
4 pitta breads

Place the aubergine cubes in a colander, sprinkling each layer generously with salt, and place a weighted plate on top. Leave to drain for 2 hours, then rinse off the salt and pat dry.

Gently heat about 90ml/3fl oz of the oil with garlic, then discard the garlic once its flavour has suffused the oil. Gently sauté the aubergine in the oil for about 30 minutes or until thoroughly soft and browned all over, adding more oil if necessary. Meanwhile, fry the onion separately in 2 tablespoons of the oil until translucent – 15–30 minutes.

Mix together the vinegar, sugar and cinnamon and add to the cooked aubergine with the onion. Mix thoroughly and taste for seasoning – it may need a little salt and pepper. Stir in the mint when serving the salad – preferably warm, although it is fine when cool, but less attractive chilled. Heat the pitta breads and fill with the salad.

CHICKEN PITTA, FATTET-STYLE

Fattet is a pitta-based salad of countless variations, described by Claudia Roden in her seminal book, *Middle Eastern Cookery*. The name apparently refers to the manner of breaking up crisp bread into pieces in the hands, and the bread that is used is generally a form of pitta, crisped in the oven and crumbled. Most of these dishes are surprisingly complex, so I have extrapolated something of the method to make a simple filling for pitta.

2 chicken legs
stock for poaching the chicken (or use water and aromatics – see page 222)
salt and pepper
1 small mild onion, finely chopped
15g/½oz unsalted butter
½ teaspoon cinnamon

¼ teaspoon allspice
seeds from 1 cardamom pod
200ml/7fl oz thick Greek yoghurt
1 clove garlic, crushed with ½ teaspoon salt
25g/1oz pine nuts, lightly toasted
4 pitta breads
salad leaves, to serve (optional)

Poach the chicken legs in the stock until the flesh is very tender, about 45 minutes. Strip the meat off the bones, season and put into a mixing bowl. While the chicken is cooking, sauté the onion very gently in the butter for about 45 minutes or until very soft and golden, adding the spices 5 minutes before the end. Add this mixture to the chicken in the bowl.

Mix together the yoghurt and crushed garlic and stir into the chicken and onion mixture, along with the pine nuts. Pile into split pitta breads (which you can warm and even crisp slightly), adding some salad leaves if you like.

Variation

If you want to make a Fattet salad, layer all the ingredients in the following manner: first toasted, crumbled pitta (see Fattoush, page 220), moistened with some of the cooking stock, then chicken and onion, followed by yoghurt topped with toasted pine nuts. I have tried it and it is indeed a rather intriguing and delicious dish.

PANZANELLA

This simple dish born of *cucina povera* has been seized on by restaurants sporting a fashionably Mediterranean gloss and has joined the ranks of designer dishes. If the ingredients are fine, it is food for the gods – but easier to achieve in Tuscany than Britain. Perhaps Panzanella, like all tomato-based salads, should be restricted to the summer months.

Rather than give a highly specific recipe I have noted a basic formula and included a number of options. There are many obvious choices for the bread – ciabatta, Pugliese, *pan sciocco* – but it need not be Italian; any well-made country bread will be fine. The bread can either be simply moistened with wine or water, or toasted first and, if you like, rubbed with garlic. You could even turn the whole thing into a bruschetta, by piling the salad ingredients on to a single, toasted and garlic-rubbed slice of bread.

4 thick slices good country bread (see above)

about 1 glass wine or use water

1 clove garlic, halved (optional)

2 tablespoons extra virgin olive oil

½ red onion, thinly sliced (optional)

2 firm but ripe tomatoes, peeled, seeded and chopped, (add the juice to the bread-soaking liquid)

1 small ripe yellow pepper, diced

1 small or ½ large cucumber (or 4 young courgettes), sliced into matchsticks

handful of oil-cured black olives

a few basil leaves, torn

For the dressing:

Either

3 tablespoons extra virgin olive oil

1 tablespoon well-aged balsamic vinegar

salt and pepper

Or

2 anchovy fillets, drained

12 salt-packed capers, rinsed and dried

3 tablespoons extra virgin olive oil

1 teaspoon red wine vinegar

salt and pepper

Soak the bread in the wine or water and tomato juices until thoroughly moist – you can toast it or bake it in the oven first if you wish and then rub with the garlic. Squeeze dry, crumble roughly, and sprinkle with the oil. If using the onion, for a milder flavour soak it in salted water for 1 hour, then drain. Put the onion and bread in a bowl with all the remaining salad ingredients.

If you are making the first dressing, simply whisk the oil, vinegar and seasoning together; for the second, pound the anchovies and capers with the oil before whisking in the vinegar and seasoning. Toss the salad in the dressing. If you have time, chill for a while to allow the flavours to meld but return to room temperature for serving.

FATTOUSH

This very simple, fresh-tasting Syrian salad is open to many variations without departing from the spirit of the dish. This recipe is a basic formula which you can use as a guideline. Even the nature of the bread can be varied. After it has been toasted you can either soak it or scatter it over the salad at the last moment so it retains its crispness. Or you could soak half and scatter half.

I white or brown pitta bread
juice of I large or 2 small lemons
2 small ridge cucumbers, diced
4 small, ripe but firm tomatoes, diced
I bunch of spring onions, finely sliced
I Little Gem or Cos lettuce heart, shredded or I bunch of purslane, leaves only
2 tablespoons chopped flat-leaf parsley
I tablespoon finely chopped mint or I teaspoon freeze-dried mint
I tablespoon chopped coriander leaves (optional)
I fat clove garlic, crushed with a little salt
salt and pepper
8 tablespoons extra virgin olive oil
I teaspoon powdered sumac (optional)

Split the pitta bread and grill it or bake it in the oven at 200°C/400°F/ Gas Mark 6 until brown and crisp. Crumble it into shards with your hands. If you wish to soak some or all of it, simply sprinkle it with cold water or with a little of the lemon juice diluted with water.

Mix together all the ingredients except for any pitta you want to keep crisp and toss well, adding any reserved pitta just before serving.

CAESAR SALAD

Caesar Salad dressing can now be bought ready made in little sachets or as a powder mix; neither bears much resemblance to the unctuous coating devised by Caesar Cardini on 4 July 1924 for his Tijuana restaurants. The stroke of genius that assured instant popularity may well have been the use of an egg as in a hangover cure; be that as it may, the near-raw egg is an essential element. Ensure your egg is very fresh (and fully free range) and use it with aplomb.

If you are keen to toss up a salad replete with croutons, parmesan and a punchy dressing, but fearful of the raw egg, you could try substituting a spoonful of concentrated, syrupy veal stock plus one of thick soured cream for the egg, but I think you should give your creation another name. That said, seventy years of Caesar salads have seen many a variant, not least in the choice of bread for croutons: walnut bread is a likely candidate, and wheaten sourdough a current trend. I have even come across versions using pumpernickel or dark rye for dramatic colour impact. A good, plain white remains the classic.

2 fat cloves garlic, sliced
6 tablespoons extra virgin olive oil
2 medium-thick slices stale bread
    (see above), cut into 1.2cm/½inch
    cubes
2 romaine (Cos) lettuce hearts
I large, very fresh free-range egg

juice of I small lemon
I teaspoon Worcestershire sauce
2–4 anchovy fillets, drained and finely
    chopped (optional)
salt and pepper
25g/1oz Parmesan cheese, freshly
    grated

Put the garlic in the oil and leave for 2 hours or more to infuse, then discard the garlic. Fry the bread in half the oil until crisp and golden. Drain and set aside. Wash and dry the lettuce leaves thoroughly, tear long leaves into bite-sized pieces and place in a large salad bowl.

Place the egg in a saucepan with cold water to cover, bring to the boil and cook for 1 minute, then cool quickly under the cold tap. For an easily made dressing, break the egg into a blender goblet and add the remaining olive oil, lemon juice, Worcestershire sauce, anchovy, if using, and seasoning. Blend briefly then pour over the lettuce leaves and toss. Finally toss lightly with the croutons and scatter with the Parmesan cheese. To do things the proper and showy way (a source of great pride and competition among waiters of a largely bygone era), take the salad bowl to the dining table, coat the leaves evenly with oil, then toss with everything apart from the egg. Break the egg directly into the salad bowl, swiftly retrieve any bits of shell, and toss adroitly well away from the laps of your diners.

CIRCASSIAN CHICKEN

A highly individual and delicious Middle Eastern recipe. I have used the sauce to stretch two chicken legs or breasts to make a salad or filled pittas for four, but the recipe can readily be adapted to suit a whole poached chicken if you double the sauce ingredients. If you don't have chicken stock sitting patiently in the freezer, cook the chicken in water with aromatics (onion, carrot, celery, parsley, bay and so on) rather than resorting to a stock cube.

A point to watch is the freshness of the walnuts; take note of the use-by date on the packet or buy from a supplier with a rapid turnover.

2 chicken legs or breasts
stock for poaching the chicken (see
    above)
salt and pepper
50g/2oz stale white bread without
    crust
100g/3½oz walnuts
1 clove garlic, chopped

½ teaspoon salt
pinch of cayenne (optional)
1 teaspoon paprika
1 tablespoon walnut oil
1 tablespoon finely chopped flat-leaf
    parsley
4 pitta breads (optional)

Poach the chicken in stock to cover, or use water and aromatics as for stock making. Cook until the flesh is falling off the bones. Reserve 150ml/5fl oz of the stock. Strip the meat off the bones, season and place in a mixing bowl.

Soak the bread in half the reserved stock for about 10 minutes, until moist and soft. Place the walnuts, garlic, salt, cayenne, if using, and half the paprika in a food processor and grind until powdery. Add the bread and blend to a firm paste, scraping down the sides of the bowl as necessary. Gradually add most or all of the remaining reserved stock to form a thick sauce and use this to coat the chicken.

If you are making a salad, transfer the chicken to a serving dish. Mix together the walnut oil and remaining paprika and drizzle over the chicken, then sprinkle with the parsley. Or simply add the oil, paprika and parsley to the chicken and sauce and use to fill warmed and split pitta breads. Sliced tomatoes or green salad leaves can be added to the pitta filling, or dressed and served separately.

· SOUPS ·

We tend to define soup as a more or less liquid food, generally eaten at the start of a meal, maybe a meal in itself when accompanied by plenty of bread. Yet the root meaning of the word soup is a soaked morsel of bread. Think of 'sop' – as in 'to sop up' or 'sopping wet' – and the old link with soaked bread becomes obvious. Soup is as ancient a food as bread itself, often no more than bread and water, though flavourings, from bitter herbs to bouillon, have always been sought after to cheer the palate.

Bread-and-water or bread-and-milk soups have all but died a death in Britain; I am not sure anyone in Devon or Cornwall still eats 'kettle broth', a boil-up of bread, hot water and onion fried in dripping, nor does the nursery treat of bread and milk any longer find favour. Elsewhere in Europe the story is rather different, and the less affluent areas of Eastern Europe and the Mediterranean have preserved their simple soup traditions. Now that our choice of good breads is improving and it is fashionable to go on a 'back to basics' quest for the simplest of dishes, it may be that we will adopt these unsophisticated soups with the zeal of fresh discovery.

AÏGO BOULIDO

This is Provençal dialect for *eau bouillie* – boiled water. The water is, of course, flavoured, with garlic and herbs, and rendered substantial by bread; in times of plenty, or when the chickens were laying well, egg would be added for protein and enrichment.

I litre/I ¾ pints water	salt and pepper
2–6 cloves garlic, crushed	I egg yolk (optional)
I bay leaf and/or 4 sage leaves	4 thick chunks country bread, slightly
I tablespoon extra virgin olive oil	stale

Put the water, garlic, herbs, oil and a little salt in a large saucepan, bring to the boil and simmer for 15 minutes. Beat the egg yolk in a large jug and gradually strain on the flavoured water (discarding the herbs), whisking all the time. Adjust the seasoning, adding pepper if you wish. The bread can either be grilled, placed in warm soup bowls and the soup ladled over, or torn into chunks and stirred into the thickened soup – in which case you might whisk the soup into the egg in a warmed tureen, dispensing with the jug.

SOPA DE AJO

The garlic and bread soup of Castile and Aragon differs little from similar soups in France and Italy. Once again the garlic, as well as paprika and perhaps oregano or cumin, is simmered in salted water and poured over bread. Modern (mainly restaurant) practice is to fry the seasonings and the bread; this is the method used below.

4 cloves garlic, chopped	I litre/I ¾ pints hot water
I teaspoon paprika	salt and pepper
100ml/3½fl oz extra virgin olive oil	100g/3½oz serrano ham, finely diced
4 slices country bread, crusts removed	I–4 eggs (optional)

Sauté the garlic and paprika in the oil until the garlic is golden. Remove the garlic with a slotted spoon and set aside. Cut or tear the bread into small cubes and fry it in the oil until crisp and golden-red. Return the garlic to the pan and add the water with a little seasoning. Simmer for a few minutes until the bread starts to break up.

Divide the ham between 4 warmed bowls and, if using the eggs, either break one into each bowl before pouring over the soup or whisk a single egg into the prepared soup before ladling out. Wait a couple of minutes for the egg to cook slightly, then serve hot.

ACQUACOTTA

This Tuscan soup exists in a thousand rich and flavourful, somewhat aristocratic versions, all of which include, as one would expect, the ubiquitous tomato. But shepherds and their travelling pots preceded the arrival of the tomato, and an old saying indicates the basic constituents of the soup: '*Mi manca la mentuccia, l'olio, e sale; farci l'acquacotta se ci avessi il pane*' (I lack mentuccia [a wild mint], oil and salt; but I will make *acquacotta* if you have bread). Wine or even crushed grapes might have been included before the advent of the tomato, and eggs were used to enrich the 'cooked water' whenever possible.

In certain areas, fresh ceps are used to make a superior but still fairly simple soup; you could substitute flat mushrooms and dried ceps, or simply flavour the water with dried ceps alone.

450g/1lb fresh ceps, or 225g/8oz flat mushrooms plus 25g/1oz dried ceps, or 50g/2oz dried ceps alone
2–4 cloves garlic, chopped
4 tablespoons extra virgin olive oil
salt and pepper
225g/8oz ripe tomatoes, peeled, seeded and diced
1 litre/1¾ pints hot water
a few basil leaves
8 fairly thin slices Italian bread (originally unsalted Tuscan bread), toasted
2–3 eggs (optional)
25g/1oz Parmesan or Pecorino cheese, freshly grated

Soak dried ceps in warm water for 2 hours, then drain, rinse and squeeze dry; reserve the soaking water and strain it through muslin or a coffee-filter paper. Wipe, trim and slice fresh mushrooms.

Cook the garlic in the oil until softened, then add the fresh mushrooms, if using, with a little salt and sauté for about 10 minutes, until soft and yielding their juices. Add the dried mushrooms and their liquid (if using dried mushrooms alone, sauté these in the oil before adding the liquid). Add the tomatoes and water, bring to the boil and simmer for 10–15 minutes, until all the mushrooms are tender. Adjust the seasoning, adding pepper to taste, and stir in the basil leaves, torn if you wish.

Divide the bread between 4 warm soup bowls. If using the eggs, whisk these together with the cheese and stir into the hot soup, then pour immediately over the bread in the bowls. Otherwise simply pour the soup over the bread and sprinkle with the cheese. Serve at once.

PANE COTTO

This Italian soup is interesting in that it is no longer water that is credited in the name but bread. In fact the basic proportions of bread and water are little different from the previous soups but instead of garlic the main flavouring is bay leaves. Feel free to use a good chicken or vegetable stock here; the quality of the stock and the bread make a considerable difference to the final result.

I litre/1¾ pints of good stock
salt and pepper
4 fresh bay leaves
4 tablespoons extra virgin olive oil
4 thick slices good Italian-style or
    country bread, crust left on if you
    wish

4 tablespoons grated Pecorino or
    Parmesan cheese

Season the stock to taste and put it in a large casserole with the bay leaves. Simmer for 10–15 minutes, then discard the leaves. Add the oil and the bread, torn into chunks, and simmer for about 5 minutes until the bread has swollen and starts to break up. Ladle into hot bowls and sprinkle immediately with the cheese so that it starts to melt. Serve piping hot.

CATALAN OLIVE OIL SOUP

I have adapted this Minorcan speciality, known there as *Oliaigua*, from the recipe given by Colman Andrews in his fascinating book, *Catalan Cuisine*. Like all the others, this soup originally consisted of nothing more than oil, salted water, garlic, parsley and bread (*oliaigua* means oil and water). This version admits onion to the equation, along with tomato.

I large onion, chopped
2 cloves garlic, finely chopped
100ml/3½fl oz extra virgin olive oil
225g/8oz ripe, red tomatoes, peeled,
    seeded and chopped

I litre/1¾ pints hot water
salt and pepper
2 tablespoons chopped flat-leaf
    parsley
4 slices country bread

Sauté the onion and garlic very gently in the oil until the onion is golden and collapsing. Add the tomatoes and hot water with a little seasoning. Simmer for 10 minutes, then add the parsley and simmer for a few minutes longer. Toast the bread and place a slice into 4 warmed soup bowls. Ladle the soup over the bread and serve hot.

Pappa Al Pomodoro

This robust soup is a step or two up from the simple 'cooked water' versions. The link with our current understanding of 'pap' as undemanding, undistinguished mush is rather unfortunate – what this soup should *not* be is pappy, even if the bread is completely disintegrated.

Ensuring an attractive texture is a simple matter of buying good bread (ciabatta is fine) and making sure it is stale. I once made the mistake of using too fresh and soft a bread and, yes, the end result was pappy – unfortunately I was cooking for some 30 people at the time. I learnt my lesson.

Finally, a word about Parmesan cheese. Anna del Conte insists in *The Gastronomy of Italy* that Pappa 'is never eaten with Parmesan'. However, flakes of just-melting cheese floating on the surface of the soup are undeniably attractive, so I include it as an option.

350g/12oz stale ciabatta or
    country bread – wholemeal works
    quite well, too
150ml/5fl oz extra virgin olive oil
1 mild onion, chopped
4 cloves garlic, finely chopped
1 kg/2lb 4oz ripe tomatoes, peeled,
    seeded and diced, or 2 × 400g/
    14oz cans Italian tomatoes

salt and pepper
1 litre/1¾ pints hot water or stock
pinch of cayenne (optional)
1–2 tablespoons tomato purée
    (optional)
small handful of basil leaves, torn or
    shredded
flakes of Parmesan cheese (optional)

If the bread is not thoroughly stale and dry, place it in a low oven for about 15 minutes. Break it into small pieces.

Heat about half the oil in a large, heavy-based pan and sauté the onion and garlic in it until soft and golden. Add the tomatoes and seasoning and simmer for 15 minutes, stirring from time to time. Purée this mixture in a blender, then sieve it if you prefer a smooth texture, but tradition suggests you should not do so.

Return the purée to the pan, add the bread, the water or stock and the cayenne, if using. Bring to the boil and simmer for 15 minutes, stirring occasionally and checking the bread is not catching on the bottom of the pan. Break the bread up with a wooden spoon if you prefer, and add the tomato purée if it seems too wan in colour.

Check the seasoning, stir in the basil and most of the remaining oil, then ladle into serving bowls. Pour a slick of oil on the surface and add a few flakes of Parmesan if you wish. Serve hot if using Parmesan or at cool room temperature without the cheese (but never chilled).

AÇORDA

The food of Portugal remains something of a closed book to most of us. Enthusiastic reports of local cuisine filter through from those who venture beyond the confines of holiday villages and coastal hotels, yet the basic produce remains beyond our reach in the UK. I doubt the extraordinary bread soup or porridge that is Açorda will ever make it to supermarket cold cabinets. For one thing it won't cook, chill and reheat easily. For another, it may be simply too weird a concept for most Britons to swallow. And yet, notorious lovers of nursery food that we are, and keen adventurers into the once-strange realms of garlic and coriander leaf, there is no reason why we should not find Açorda deliciously addictive.

There is little point in attempting absolute authenticity, or even in making painstaking efforts to produce this dish that pleases partly by its simplicity. What is supremely important is the quality of the bread – a badly made loaf will yield glue instead of a palate-seducing texture. The ideal bread is either a cornmeal loaf or a coarse-textured country one, though not one that is too sour. One solution is to use a mixture of good white bread and coarse wholewheat. I have experimented with numerous variations and have been happy with most, even if the bread has not had the dense, heavy feel of a Portuguese loaf.

225g/8oz stale bread (see above)
1–5 cloves garlic, peeled
pinch of salt
2 tablespoons finely chopped
    coriander leaves

2 tablespoons extra virgin olive oil
600ml/1 pint boiling water or light
    stock
2 eggs, beaten (optional)

Tear up the bread into small chunks – if the crust is not too heavy or dark it can be left on; it is all a matter of taste and preferred texture. Pound the garlic with the salt in a mortar and pestle, then pound in the coriander. Put this mixture in a heavy-based saucepan with the bread, oil and water or stock. Bring to the boil and simmer very gently, stirring, for about 10 minutes. The consistency should be that of a chunky porridge, the bread not so much disintegrated as thoroughly moistened. Either serve the soup immediately or stir in the beaten eggs and cook gently for half a minute more.

It is possible to make a plain Açorda without any cooking at all: simply combine all the ingredients in a large, warmed tureen. In this case you will almost certainly need more water or stock – about half as much again.

ANDALUCIAN GAZPACHO

Most of us make some version of Gazpacho the moment we acquire a blender or food processor; it seems inconceivable that this salad-as-soup could have been invented without puréeing machines in mind. But of course it precedes blenders by several centuries; indeed Gazpacho precedes the arrival of the tomato in Europe. Whereas pounders prize smoothness as proof positive of their skills, we blender operators like to maintain a chunky, rustic look. Which is the more authentic? It depends which country you are in, which area, or village, or family within that village.

A desperate striving after authenticity is bound to be futile; we might have to abandon the tomato; our search for the precise style of bread would prove fruitless; even the sun would fail to beat down with the lack of mercy that makes Gazpacho the only conceivable midday repast on certain days. We can either abandon the recipe altogether or adapt it to good-quality, readily available ingredients and personal preference.

1kg/2lb 4oz very ripe, red tomatoes, peeled and seeded
1 cucumber, peeled, seeded and chopped
2 green peppers, chopped (and peeled with a potato peeler if you have the patience)
½ large, sweet onion, chopped
225g/8oz fresh white breadcrumbs
2 tablespoons white or red wine vinegar

2 tablespoons extra virgin olive oil
1 teaspoon salt
black pepper or cayenne pepper
up to 600ml/1 pint cold water or tomato juice
ice cubes, to serve

Additional garnishes:
black olives, stoned and diced
hardboiled egg, chopped
croutons baked or fried in olive oil
(see page 171)

Reserve a little tomato, cucumber and green pepper for garnish. Blend everything apart from the water or tomato juice and ice cubes to a fine consistency, adjusting the seasoning to taste. Add enough water or tomato juice to give the consistency you favour (if the tomatoes are none too ripe and sweet, tomato juice will help the situation). Chill until ready to serve. Check the seasoning and consistency once more, then ladle into bowls and garnish as you wish. Serve with good bread.

ROASTED RED GAZPACHO

This all-red soup omits greenery, apart from the essential basil, but there is no reason why you should not add cucumber or other herbs.

1kg/2lb 4oz ripe, red tomatoes
2 red peppers
1 mild red chilli
5 tablespoons extra virgin olive oil
4 cloves garlic
175g/6oz slightly stale white country
   bread without crusts
1 tablespoon red wine vinegar
about 600ml/1 pint tomato juice

small bunch of basil leaves, torn
salt and pepper

To serve:
ice cubes
croutons fried in extra virgin olive oil
   (use oregano- and chilli-
   flavoured oils if you have them,
   see page 172)

The tomatoes, peppers and chilli can be left whole and barbecued or grilled, when they acquire an added dimension of smokiness. Alternatively, halve them and roast in the oven at 200°C/400°F/Gas Mark 6 with 1 tablespoon of the olive oil until blackened round the edges – this will take about 30 minutes, but some vegetables may be ready earlier and should be removed individually.

Blanch the garlic for a mellow effect by simmering it in a small pan of water for 10 minutes. Peel the vegetables and remove the seeds; do this over a sieve and catch the juices in a bowl.

Place the bread and the garlic, pressed out of its papery skin, in a food processor and reduce the bread to crumbs. Add the vinegar and blend for a few seconds, then blend in the remaining oil. Next add the peppers, chilli and tomatoes and process once more. Finally blend in the reserved vegetable juices and enough tomato juice to give the desired consistency, then add the basil and process briefly; season to taste. If the soup seems too thick, dilute with iced water and check the seasoning once more. Serve chilled, with ice cubes and croutons.

PALE ALMOND AND GRAPE SOUP

A subtler chilled soup than the previous two, this is popular in the Moorish-influenced Cordoba and Malaga regions of Spain, source of the famous muscatel raisins (and muscat grapes) and of fine almonds. The grapes need assiduous peeling but this can be done in advance of serving the soup, which will itself rest happily in the fridge for a day or two.

75g/2½oz whole almonds
1 clove garlic, chopped
pinch of salt
100g/3½oz fresh white breadcrumbs,
    soaked in 150ml/5 fl oz milk or
    water for 30 minutes
4 tablespoons extra virgin olive oil
1–2 tablespoons sherry vinegar
750–900ml/1¼–1½ pints water

225g/8oz muscat grapes, peeled,
    halved and pips removed
ice cubes, to serve

For the croutons (optional):
100g/3½oz white bread, cut into
    cubes
5 tablespoons extra virgin olive oil
1 teaspoon caster sugar

Drop the almonds into a pan of boiling water, simmer for about 3 minutes, then drain and pop off the skins. Process together the almonds, garlic and salt in a small food processor if you have one – otherwise a coffee or spice grinder works better than a large food processor, or you can pound them together in a large mortar.

Blend in the breadcrumbs, then the oil, and finally add vinegar and water until you reach a flavour balance and texture that you like. Add more salt if needed.

Chill until ready to serve, then add the grapes and a few ice cubes. If serving croutons, fry the bread in the oil until golden and crunchy, stirring frequently, then sprinkle in the sugar and stir until lightly caramelised, turning up the heat if necessary. Do not make these too far in advance of serving as they will soften.

FLANDERS SHRIMP BISQUE

This is a good soup to make if you have odds and ends of prawn shells in the freezer (always keep the debris of shell-on prawns if you have a spare corner in the freezer but use them within a few weeks of freezing). Or you can simply buy shell-on prawns, raw or cooked, plus some potted shrimps and ready-made fish stock – adapt the recipe to whatever you have to hand.

100g/3½oz potted shrimps
1 tablespoon good olive oil
450g/1lb shell-on prawns, raw or
    cooked
1 small glass cognac
1 glass dry white wine
1 litre/1¾ pints fish stock (either use
    home-made or buy half that
    quantity of ready-made stock
    and dilute with water)

about 1 tablespoon tomato purée
100g/3½oz fresh white breadcrumbs
salt, pepper and cayenne
8 thin slices baguette
4 tablespoons crème fraîche

Melt the butter from the potted shrimps, pour 1–2 tablespoons of the butter into a flameproof casserole and reserve the rest. Add the oil to the casserole and heat together with the butter. Place the prawns, in their shells, in the pan. If raw, sauté over a high heat for 5 minutes until cooked through; if already cooked, sauté more gently for 2–3 minutes.

Add the cognac to the pan and ignite it, standing well back. When the flames die down add the wine, bring to the boil and cook for 1–2 minutes to reduce. Heat the stock and pour it into the pan, along with half the shrimps; bring to the boil and simmer for 5–10 minutes. Process the mixture in a food processor or blender until the shells are quite finely ground (if using a processor you will obtain a finer grind by spooning the majority of solids into the bowl and processing before adding the rest of the liquid). Press through a fine sieve back into the rinsed-out pan.

Stir in enough tomato purée to give a good colour and flavour, then add the breadcrumbs and season to taste. Bring to the boil and simmer for a few minutes, then sieve once more. Return to the pan with the remaining shrimps and warm through. Meanwhile, spread the reserved shrimp butter on the bread and then toast it, adding a pinch of cayenne to the butter for added spiciness if you wish.

Ladle the hot bisque into warmed soup bowls, stir a swirl of crème fraîche into each one and top with the toasted bread.

WHITE WINE SOUP

An extremely rich 'après-ski' soup which adapts well to any variety of stock as long as it has a good depth of flavour.

600ml/1 pint good stock	50g/2oz slightly salted butter
1 cinnamon stick	(optional)
200ml/7fl oz dry white wine	6 egg yolks
salt and pepper	200ml/7fl oz thick crème fraîche
½ loaf country bread, torn into 8	125g/4oz Gruyère or Comté cheese,
chunks	grated (optional)

Bring the stock to the boil in a large casserole along with the cinnamon stick. Simmer for 5–10 minutes, then remove the cinnamon. Add the white wine and return to the boil, then season to taste, bearing in mind that a fair quantity of richly bland egg and cream will be added.

Toast the bread, first spreading it with the butter if you wish. Place one chunk in each of 4 warmed soup bowls.

Whisk together the egg yolks and crème fraîche in a bowl and pour a ladleful of stock into the mixture. Whisk this well, then pour it into the rest of the stock, whisking constantly. Warm through over a very low heat, stirring all the time and not allowing the custard-like mixture to approach simmering point. Adjust the seasoning and ladle the soup into the bowls. Float a second chunk of bread in the soup and serve, strewing a little cheese on top if you wish, and serving the rest separately.

LATVIAN RYE BREAD SOUP

The Scandinavian and Baltic countries have a particularly interesting set of soups in which the dominant flavour is rye bread. Only slightly sweet, they may be served at any time, breakfast included, and are something of a light meal in themselves.

This recipe is based on a soup my grandfather used to make in Lancashire, where there were a number of enterprising Ukrainian bakers. The bread he used was always referred to, somewhat disparagingly, as 'Ukrainian bread', not to be confused with the real (and quite unobtainable) Latvian loaf. He would dry the bread in the oven and sometimes keep it for months, at which stage it would need lengthy simmering before breaking up. Being a frugal and proud housekeeper he would also dry and save apple peel for flavouring this and similar soups.

225g/8oz thick, dry slices of dark, dense rye bread
1 litre/1¾ pints water
handful of dried apple peel, if you have it
75g/2½oz light muscovado sugar
50g/2oz raisins
75g/2½oz dried apples
150–300ml/5–10fl oz cranberry juice, to taste
15g/½oz potato flour

Place the bread, water and apple peel, if using, in a large saucepan, bring to the boil and simmer until the bread breaks up. Press through a sieve, return to the rinsed-out pan, and add the sugar, raisins and apples. Simmer gently until the fruit is plump and soft.

Add the lesser amount of cranberry juice to the soup. Blend the potato flour to a paste with a little more cranberry juice and add some of this (you may not need it all) to the soup. Whisk in thoroughly, and allow to bubble for a couple of minutes before deciding whether to add more – the soup should be the consistency of thick cream. Add more cranberry juice if needed to freshen the flavour. Serve cold, with sweetened, thick cream if the occasion warrants it.

PECAN AND PRETZEL SOUP

I first came across the idea of using pecans in soup in one of the excellent booklets compiled by American cookery writer James McNair, while I encountered the extraordinary notion of pretzel soup in William Woys Weaver's remarkable book, *Pennsylvania Dutch Country Cooking*. I am not sure what prompted me to combine the two elements, beyond my enjoyment of both. The result is as delicious as I hoped, sumptuously rich in flavour and texture, with a toastiness that prevents the soup from cloying.

125g/4oz stale pretzels, plain or garlic/ onion-flavoured
125g/4oz pecan nuts
300ml/10fl oz dry cider
1 leek, white part only, shredded
1 small celery stick, diced
15g/½oz unsalted butter
600ml/1 pint flavourful chicken or vegetable stock

1 bay leaf
1 cinnamon stick
1 tablespoon soft brown sugar
1–2 tablespoons medium dry sherry or Madeira
dash of Worcestershire sauce
salt and pepper
150ml/5fl oz double cream

Roast the pretzels and the nuts in the oven at 180°C/350°F/Gas Mark 4 until the pretzels are dried through; they may not need very long, depending on degree of staleness, but the nuts will need 15–20 minutes. Place the roasted pretzels in a bowl, pour over the cider and leave to soak while preparing the next stage.

In a large, heavy-based pan, cook the leek and celery in the butter for 15 minutes or until softened, stirring from time to time. Chop the roasted nuts roughly, reserving a few whole ones for garnish, and add to the vegetables.

Heat the stock separately until almost boiling and add it to the vegetables along with the bay leaf, cinnamon stick and sugar. Finally add the pretzels and cider, bring to the boil and simmer gently, partly covered, for 2 hours, by which time the nuts should be soft and the pretzels completely collapsed. Top up with a little water from time to time if necessary, and give the contents a quick stir.

Remove the bay leaf and cinnamon stick and purée the soup in a blender. Return to the rinsed-out pan, add the sherry or Madeira, Worcestershire sauce and seasoning to taste. Bring to the boil and briskly stir in the cream, check the seasoning once more, then ladle the soup into warmed bowls. Garnish with the reserved nuts.

COLETTE'S CHERRY SOUP WITH CROUTONS

This dessert soup was one of the French writer's favourite dishes for the days 'when one does not cook'. Of course a little cooking is involved, but the deliciousness of the finished soup belies its convenience and speed. I have altered the original recipe a little, adding cinnamon or vanilla and wine as extra enrichment. But you can leave them out without compunction.

680g/1lb 8oz jar morello cherries in juice or light syrup
25g/1oz unsalted butter
1 heaped tablespoon plain flour
5 tablespoons red wine or port
1 cinnamon stick or vanilla pod
2–4 tablespoons caster sugar or vanilla sugar

salt
For the croutons:
125g/4oz *pain de mie*, milk bread or good-quality bridge rolls, cut into 1.2cm/½inch cubes
50g/2oz unsalted butter
1 tablespoon vanilla sugar

Drain the cherries in a sieve, catching the juice or syrup in a jug. Melt the butter in a large saucepan, add the flour and cook, stirring, for 2 minutes. Gradually stir in the liquid from the cherries, then add the wine or port and cinnamon or vanilla. When it reaches boiling point, add the cherries and sweeten to taste; season with a very little salt. Simmer gently for 10 minutes, then remove the cinnamon or vanilla.

To make the croutons, fry the bread cubes in the butter, stirring constantly, until crunchy and golden. Add the sugar and stir around briskly until the croutons are lightly caramelised.

Ladle the hot soup into warmed serving bowls and float the freshly made croutons in it. Cream is not really necessary but you could gild the lily with pouring cream or stirred crème fraîche.

· SAVOURY DISHES ·

CRAB CAKES

These are the simplest of crab cakes which I devised after finding that I have fresh breadcrumbs to hand rather more often than cold mashed potato, the alternative binder. You can of course make the cakes more exciting and individual by adding aromatics – ground cardamom is a personal favourite, or lemongrass, coriander and chilli for a Thai effect.

Ready-prepared crab is blessedly convenient but do make sure it smells fresh as the sea.

225g/8oz fresh crab meat, a mixture of brown and white
50g/2oz fresh white breadcrumbs
2 teaspoons extra virgin olive oil or mayonnaise
1 teaspoon Dijon mustard
1 teaspoon sherry vinegar or 1 tablespoon dry sherry
salt and pepper
1 small egg, beaten with 1 tablespoon water
25g/1oz fine dried breadcrumbs
oil, or a mixture of oil and butter, for frying or grilling
lime or lemon wedges, to serve

Flake the crab meat and mix it with the fresh breadcrumbs, oil or mayonnaise, mustard, vinegar or sherry, and seasoning – go easy on the salt, generous with the pepper. The mixture should be moist but should stick together; you may need to add a few more breadcrumbs.

Form the mixture into 4 large or 8 small cakes and dip them into the beaten egg, then into the dried breadcrumbs (soup bowls are ideal receptacles for both). Fry them gently in a little oil, or oil and butter mixed, (or brush them with oil and grill them) until crisp and hot – about 4 minutes per side for large fishcakes, 2–3 minutes per side for small ones. Serve with lime or lemon wedges and perhaps a light, refreshing salad.

SALT COD SOPA SECA

Sopa seca translates as 'dry soup' but is in reality a thick casserole in which a surface layer of bread absorbs most of the juices. Its apparent simplicity belies a moreish deliciousness. All manner of bits and pieces can be included, from sausage and game to root vegetables, but since salt cod is gradually creeping into the British repertoire, this is the ingredient I have chosen. Chickpeas might also be added in Portugal but I prefer the dish without.

450g/1lb salt cod (a good, chunky middle-cut steak if possible)
2 cloves garlic, peeled
1 large mild onion, chopped
4–5 tablespoons extra virgin olive oil
225g/8oz slightly stale cornmeal bread, or coarse country bread, crusts removed

1 teaspoon mild paprika
pepper
2 tablespoons finely chopped flat-leaf parsley

You will need to desalt the cod by soaking it in several changes of cold water for up to 48 hours (keep it cool, preferably refrigerated, during this time). I find that 3 or 4 days do the fish no harm and ensure there is no danger of salt shock at the end. When ready to cook, simmer the fish very gently in unsalted water with the garlic cloves for 10–15 minutes or until the cod is just cooked and flakes quite easily. Drain well, reserving the water and garlic, cool the fish a little, then flake roughly.

Cook the onion in 3 tablespoons of the oil for about 40 minutes, until golden and very soft. Slice the reserved garlic cloves and add them to the onion shortly before the end of cooking.

Use a little of the remaining oil to grease a wide, ovenproof casserole dish. Cut the bread to fit the dish, cover the bottom of the dish with a layer of bread and spread the onion and its oil over it. Spoon the cod flakes over the onion and season with half the paprika, a little pepper, and most of the parsley. Cover with the remaining bread and drizzle the rest of the olive oil over it. Bring 600ml/1pint of the cod cooking water to the boil and pour it slowly over the casserole – it should reach about half way up the layer of cod. Sprinkle the surface with the remaining parsley and paprika and bake at 190°C/375°F/Gas Mark 5 for 25 minutes, until lightly golden on top; if it is still pale and rather moist towards the end of cooking, either turn up the oven a couple of notches, or grill under a gentle heat. Serve hot or warm, perhaps with a simple salad.

FISH STEAKS WITH A HERB AND PINE NUT CRUST

You can make this with any firm-fleshed fish from cod to monkfish or wild salmon. Pine nuts are difficult to chop finely and processing can reduce them to an oily paste, but if you process the nuts with breadcrumbs, this avoids the problem to a large extent.

4 × 150–175g/5–6oz fish steaks (see above)
salt and pepper
50g/2oz pine nuts
125g/4oz fresh white breadcrumbs
1 tablespoon finely chopped parsley
1 tablespoon finely chopped chervil
1 tablespoon finely chopped tarragon

½ teaspoon finely grated lime, lemon or orange zest
1 teaspoon toasted and crushed coriander seeds
40g/1½oz unsalted butter, melted
2 tablespoons pine nut oil or extra virgin olive oil

Check over the fish and discard any loose bones, then season lightly. Grind the pine nuts briefly with the breadcrumbs; if making the crumbs from scratch, process the bread just until coarse crumbs are formed, then add the nuts and process again. Stir in the rest of the ingredients in the order given, including a generous dash of seasoning. Press this mixture over the fish and place the steaks in an oiled roasting dish. Bake at 200°C/400°F/Gas Mark 6 for 10–15 minutes or until the fish is opaque (check with a sharp knife). If the crust has not coloured and crisped you could flash it under a hot grill.

SICILIAN SARDINES

The raisins, pine nuts and orange mark the brilliant touch of Arabic influence in this dish: the blend of tastes and textures is tremendous, lifting the rich, briny flavour of the sardines to new heights. It is best made when fresh sardines are readily available, although you could try it with large anchovies or small herring.

12 fresh sardines
100g/3½oz fresh white breadcrumbs
6 tablespoons extra virgin olive oil
50g/2oz currants, soaked in warm water for 1 hour
50g/2oz pine nuts, toasted if you wish
6 anchovy fillets, drained, or 3–4 salt-cured anchovies, rinsed and filleted

2 tablespoons chopped flat-leaf parsley
finely grated zest and juice of 1 orange
salt and pepper
4 bay leaves, broken in half
2 oranges, cut into wedges, to serve

First of all you will need to clean and bone the sardines. Remove the back fin and attached bones by pulling it off from the tail end. If the head is still attached you can remove the head and innards in one go by snapping back the head and pulling. Otherwise, slit open the belly cavity right up to the tail and remove the innards. Place the fish, opened out flat and side-skin up, on a board and press your thumb firmly all the way along the backbone. Turn the fish over, loosen both ends of the spine if necessary, and pull it away towards the tail, leaving the tail intact. Rinse the sardines thoroughly under running water then pat dry with kitchen paper.

Fry the breadcrumbs in 4 tablespoons of the olive oil over a fairly high heat until crisp and brown. Place them in a mixing bowl with the drained currants and the pine nuts. Mash the anchovies and add them to the mixing bowl along with the parsley and orange zest.

Lay the sardine fillets out, skin-side down. Season lightly with salt and pepper, then place a heaped teaspoonful of filling near the head end of each and roll up. With 1 tablespoon of the remaining oil, lightly oil a baking dish into which the rolls will fit tightly (to prevent their unrolling). Pour over the orange juice and tuck in the bay leaves. Dust a little seasoning over the surface, drizzle with the remaining oil, then bake at 200°C/400°F/Gas Mark 6 for about 20 minutes. Serve at room temperature with the orange wedges and plenty of good bread.

HOT SOUFFLÉED CRAB

Serves 4 as a first course, 2 as a main course.
If you buy ready-prepared fresh crab (dressed without added seasoning and crumbs) this takes only 5 minutes to prepare before baking.

75g/2½oz fresh light rye breadcrumbs
2 teaspoons unsalted butter
150g/5oz fresh crab meat, a mixture
    of brown and white
2 tablespoons crème fraîche
2 large eggs, separated
½ teaspoon grated lemon zest

1 tablespoon lemon juice
1 teaspoon tomato purée
pinch of cayenne (optional)
salt and pepper
1 tablespoon freshly grated Parmesan
    cheese

Fry 2 tablespoons of the breadcrumbs in the butter until brown and
crisp, then set aside. Mix together the crab meat, crème fraîche, egg
yolks, lemon zest and juice, tomato purée, cayenne, if using, seasoning
and the remaining breadcrumbs. Whisk the egg whites with a pinch
of salt until fairly stiff. Stir a good spoonful of the egg white into the
crab mixture to lighten it, then gently fold in the remaining white.
Pile the mixture into 4 lightly buttered 150ml/5fl oz ramekin dishes
or a 600ml/1 pint soufflé dish or oval baking dish. Sprinkle the
reserved fried crumbs and the Parmesan over the top, and bake at
180°C/350°F/Gas Mark 4 until brown and puffed up – about 10
minutes for ramekins, 15–20 minutes for a soufflé dish, and 12–15
minutes for an oval baking dish. Serve at once with a crisp salad.

LIGHT RYE SOUFFLÉ

This is moist and light with a slight tang – subtler than you might
imagine from a combination of Wensleydale cheese, soured cream
and rye. Unlike béchamel-based soufflés, it tastes rather good cold,
should you have any left over.

150ml/5fl oz beer (I use Dunkel
    Weissbier)
125g/4oz light rye bread without
    crusts, torn into rough chunks
150ml/5fl oz crème fraîche (low fat is
    fine)

125g/4oz Wensleydale cheese,
    crumbled
1 teaspoon English mustard – try a
    beer mustard
2 eggs, separated
salt and pepper

Warm the beer if the bread is very dry and then pour it over the
bread. Leave to soak for about 10 minutes, then break it up with a
fork or give it a quick burst in a food processor. Beat in the crème

fraîche, followed by the cheese – again this can be done in the processor, using a pulse action or short bursts of power. Blend in the mustard and the egg yolks and season with a little salt and plenty of pepper.

Whisk the egg whites with a pinch of salt until stiff. Stir (or process briefly) a quarter of the egg white into the bread and cheese mixture to loosen it, then lightly fold in the remaining white. Spoon the mixture into a buttered (and crumbed if you have the patience) 900ml/1½ pint soufflé dish or casserole and bake at 200°C/400°F/Gas Mark 6 for 20–25 minutes, until well risen and browned. A slightly runny centre is an attractive contrast to the crunchy crust but can't always be gauged. Good with a crisp salad, and thin rye-bread toast.

GLAMORGAN SAUSAGES

A simple but remarkably delicious skinless, meatless sausage. Freshness is of the essence – the mixture will sour if kept uncooked for any length of time. Once cooked, the sausages may be enjoyed piping hot or cooled to room temperature but will not reheat very successfully.

350g/12oz soft white bread without crust
2 tablespoons finely chopped parsley
6 sprigs of thyme, leaves only
225g/8oz mature Caerphilly cheese (Ducketts, if you can get it), crumbled
2 leeks, whitest part only, very finely chopped

1 heaped teaspoon coarse-ground mustard powder
3 egg yolks
salt and pepper
about 50g/2oz dried breadcrumbs, for coating
butter, for frying

If you are using a food processor, process the bread into crumbs and chop the herbs at the same time. Then add all the remaining ingredients except the dried breadcrumbs and the butter and process briefly. If you don't have a processor, make the bread into crumbs and stir in all the remaining ingredients except the dried breadcrumbs and the butter. If the mixture does not cohere easily, you may need to add another egg yolk. Form the mixture into about 2 dozen 5cm/2inch sausages and roll them gently in the dried breadcrumbs. They can also be made half-size, or any size you prefer, for party fare.

Melt the butter in a frying pan until foaming and cook the sausages over a moderate heat for 5–10 minutes, depending on size, until golden brown. Serve hot or cool, with grilled tomatoes if this is to be a supper dish.

BREAD AND CHEESE PUDDING

A simple thrifty dish whose basic ingredients can be varied according to what you have in stock. I sometimes add skinned, chopped tomatoes or olives.

175g/6oz bread slices (wholemeal, granary, light rye or good basic white), crusts removed
15g/½oz unsalted butter
1 small shallot, finely chopped
175g/6oz brown-cap mushrooms, sliced
salt and pepper
1 tablespoon soy sauce

1 tablespoon dry or medium sweet Madeira
175g/6oz crumbly farmhouse cheese
450 ml/15fl oz milk (semi-skimmed if you wish)
1 teaspoon Dijon mustard or ½ teaspoon mustard powder
3 eggs
1–2 tablespoons finely chopped flat-leaf parsley

Cut the bread into triangles and set aside. Melt the butter in a small frying pan and sauté the shallot until soft and golden. Add the mushrooms with a small pinch of salt, cover the pan and cook until the juices begin to run. Remove the lid and continue to cook, stirring, until the juices have evaporated. Add the soy sauce and Madeira and cook over a high heat until the liquid is absorbed, then season to taste. Layer the bread, mushrooms and crumbled cheese in a greased 1.2 litre/2 pint soufflé dish or similar ovenproof dish (there is no need to do this particularly neatly).

Heat the milk and mustard in a saucepan until almost boiling. Meanwhile, whisk the eggs in a mixing bowl and season. Pour the hot milk over the eggs, still whisking, then strain the hot liquid through a sieve over the layered bread. If you have time, leave it to stand for 30 minutes until the bread has absorbed most of the liquid. If not, just leave it for 5 minutes before baking, pressing down any protruding bits of bread with your hands. Sprinkle the surface with parsley, then bake at 180°C/350°F/Gas Mark 4 for about 40 minutes, until puffed up like a soufflé and crunchy and brown on the surface. Serve at once, with lots of crisp salad.

NEUCHÂTEL FONDUE

Does anyone still confess to enjoying fondue away from the ski slopes? One person who does is Patricia Michelson, proprietor of one of the country's finest cheese shops, La Fromagerie in North London, which is also an excellent deli. She does have the advantage of having to hand the finest Alpine cheeses but adds, sensibly, that this is one of the few dishes that uses day-old French bread to advantage – and in some quantity.

Here is the official method sanctioned by the Swiss Cheese Union.

I garlic clove, halved

350ml/12fl oz (½ bottle) Neuchâtel or other dry white wine

I teaspoon lemon juice

500g/1lb 2oz Swiss Gruyère cheese, coarsely grated

250g/8½oz Swiss Emmental, coarsely grated

I small glass kirsch or other eau-de-vie

3 teaspoons cornflour

grating of nutmeg

pepper

I kg/2lb 4oz French bread, cut into bite-sized cubes

Rub a fondue pot with the garlic, then discard it. Pour the wine into the pot and warm gently. Add the lemon juice and cheese and bring slowly to the boil, stirring all the time. As soon as the cheese has melted, blend together the kirsch and cornflour and add to the fondue. Stir thoroughly as the mixture thickens, then season to taste with nutmeg and black pepper.

Place the dish on an adjustable burner. Once you have speared a chunk of bread on to your fondue fork, stir it round the fondue a couple of times before removing. To avoid burning your lips on the dipping fork, transfer the coated bread to a plate and eat with an ordinary fork (though the Swiss instruct firmly that you should 'eat straight from the *caquelon* [fondue pot]'). Serve with white wine, black tea and a glass of kirsch – the traditional Swiss accompaniments.

· SIMPLE VEGETABLE GRATINS ·

There is no great art to creating vegetable gratins. The vegetables are simply steamed or boiled to tenderness, coated in a flavoured white sauce and then dusted with a little cheese and breadcrumbs. If the crumbs are dried they should come from a white loaf; if fresh, a wide range will usually be suitable. I might choose wholewheat bread for white vegetables, for instance, or perhaps a mushroom-flavoured loaf if the flavours of the gratin are generally robust. You might consider a number of the Mediterranean-style flavoured breads appropriate to spinach, mushroom or onion gratins.

Overleaf are two examples of basic vegetable gratins with variations, followed by two close 'cousins', a *tian* and a Brown Betty.

WHITE VEGETABLE GRATIN

Ideal vegetables for this are cardoon, chard, sea kale and salsify, and of course luxurious white asparagus, but braised chicory, celery or fennel are also suitable, as indeed are onions, poached and thickly sliced. In line with the Provençal flavours, and particularly if you include the truffles or olives, you might prefer to use crumbs from a pain de campagne loaf, perhaps even an olive or walnut one.

about 500g/1lb 2oz white vegetables, trimmed (see above)

1 bay leaf, sprig of thyme, a strip of lemon zest to flavour the water (optional)

lemon juice (optional)

25g/1oz unsalted butter or 2 tablespoons extra virgin olive oil

2 tablespoons plain flour

300ml/10fl oz water from cooking the vegetables or home-made stock, warmed

150ml/5fl oz single or double cream

2 fat or 4 thin anchovy fillets, mashed

grating of nutmeg

salt and pepper

25g/1oz Parmesan, Pecorino or Gruyère cheese, freshly grated

1–2 tablespoons fine dried breadcrumbs or 25g/1oz fresh breadcrumbs

Optional additions:

shavings of black or white truffle

1 tablespoon oil-cured black olives, finely diced

Cut up the vegetables as appropriate and cook in lightly salted boiling water until just tender – this may take anything from 10 minutes (for short lengths of cardoon) to 30 minutes (for whole onions). Flavour the water as you wish, bearing in mind that you might use it for the sauce. Lemon juice will help retain the whiteness of certain vegetables, particularly salsify, but will, of course, add acidity and a citrus flavour to the sauce. Drain the vegetables thoroughly, reserving the cooking liquid if you need it for the sauce. Heat the butter or oil in a saucepan, stir in the flour and cook without browning for 2 minutes. Gradually stir in the vegetable water or stock and then the cream. Add the mashed anchovy and leave to simmer and reduce very gently for 15–20 minutes, stirring from time to time. Add nutmeg and pepper to taste, and check if a little salt is needed despite the anchovy. Add the truffle or olives at this stage, if using.

Arrange the vegetables in a buttered or oiled gratin dish, coat with the sauce and sprinkle with the cheese and breadcrumbs. Bake at 190°C/375°F/Gas Mark 5 until bubbling and lightly browned – about 20 minutes. Good with plainly cooked meat, poultry or fish, or simply on its own, with plenty of crusty bread.

GRATED ROOT VEGETABLE GRATIN

Onion and leek are good additions and should be finely sliced before cooking. You could add Parmesan to the topping, particularly if using nutmeg, or 25g/1oz finely chopped cashew nuts.

750g/1½lb root vegetables, peeled and
   coarsely grated
50g/2oz unsalted butter
½–1 teaspoon salt
pepper
garam masala or grated nutmeg, to
   taste
150ml/5fl oz double cream or crème
   fraîche

For the topping:
40g/1½oz unsalted butter
1 clove garlic, peeled
50g/2oz fresh white or brown
   breadcrumbs
1 tablespoon finely chopped parsley
½ teaspoon finely grated lemon zest

Sweat the root vegetables in the butter until softened – about 10 minutes. Onion and leek, if used, are best softened separately, then added to the root vegetables. Season generously with salt, pepper and garam masala or nutmeg and pile into a buttered gratin dish. Pour in the cream.

For the topping, infuse the butter with the garlic by sautéing the garlic gently for a few minutes and then discarding it. Add the breadcrumbs to the pan and stir around to coat with the butter, then stir in the parsley and lemon zest and spoon over the gratin. Bake at 190°C/375°F/Gas Mark 5 for 30–45 minutes, until the topping is crunchy and golden brown. If you prefer a fresher parsley and lemon flavour, reserve some or all of it until the gratin is cooked and simply sprinkle it on top.

THE SIMPLEST SPINACH GRATIN

This Provençal recipe (accurately, a *tian*, taking its name – like the gratin – from the baking dish) is utter simplicity. Like all simple dishes, its success depends on the quality of the ingredients, from spinach to crumbs. The packets of ready-washed young spinach available in supermarkets are ideal, if expensive; use a basil-infused oil for a vibrant effect – the Californian Consorzio brand is vivid in colour and flavour.

225g/8oz prepared young leaf spinach
25g/1oz fresh breadcrumbs (white,
   pain de campagne or wholewheat)
salt, pepper and nutmeg

2 tablespoons extra virgin olive oil
2 tablespoons basil-infused extra
   virgin olive oil
2 tablespoons fine dried breadcrumbs

Chop the spinach finely – processing it for a very few seconds works well. Place in a bowl and mix with the fresh breadcrumbs, seasoning, and half the olive oil and basil-infused oil. Spread the remaining olive oil in the base of a shallow gratin dish (about half the volume of the packet of spinach) and sprinkle with half the dried crumbs. Pack the spinach mixture into the dish, pressing down with your hands. Sprinkle the remaining dried crumbs over the surface and dribble with the remaining basil oil. Bake at 180°C/350°F/Gas Mark 4 for about 45 minutes, until the spinach is tender and the top of the gratin brown and crisp. Serve hot.

TOMATO BROWN BETTY

This is based on a recipe from Margaret Costa's ever-useful *Four Seasons Cookery Book*. Buttering the breadcrumbs gives a welcome added richness – you could substitute olive oil for half the butter if you prefer. You could also experiment with a number of Italian-style breads – even some of the powerfully flavoured focaccie might work well here.

Serve this as a side dish, with an omelette or plain roast chicken, for instance, or as a light lunch or supper in itself, perhaps with more bread and a green salad.

175g/6oz fresh wholewheat breadcrumbs (or see above)
75g/2½oz unsalted butter
1 tablespoon chopped flat-leaf parsley
leaves from 1 sprig of tarragon, finely chopped

25g/1oz Parmesan cheese, freshly grated (optional)
4 rashers smoked streaky bacon
1 mild onion, finely chopped
4 large baking tomatoes, such as Momotaro, peeled and thickly sliced
salt, pepper and sugar

Mix together the breadcrumbs, 50g/2oz of the butter, the herbs, and Parmesan, if using. Derind the bacon and fry until crisp, then crumble it into the crumb mixture. Retain any fat that has run out of the bacon and add the remaining butter to the pan. Sauté the onion until golden brown and then set aside.

To assemble the dish, scatter a layer of the breadcrumb mixture in a buttered baking dish. Cover with a spoonful of onions, then a layer of tomatoes, seasoned with salt and pepper, and sugar if the tomatoes appear unripe. Continue layering, finishing with crumbs. Bake at 200°C/400°F/Gas Mark 6 for 25–30 minutes until bubbling hot.

· STUFFED VEGETABLES ·

STUFFED AUBERGINES TURKISH-STYLE

Not the famous *Imam Bayildi* but simply the result of a visit to a Middle Eastern, mainly Turkish, shop in North London. The mounds of shiny, taut-skinned aubergines had not a wrinkle between them and I needed a likely use for the huge tin of pepper purée I had just discovered there.

I was also in proud possession of an extraordinarily vibrant oregano oil (from California) and the following recipe happened. Of course fresh or freeze-dried oregano would be fine, and a dose of chilli or cayenne added to tomato purée could replace the red pepper paste. It is, however, worth seeking out the paste if you can, as it is bursting with colour and character and is remarkably inexpensive.

2 aubergines, about 225g/8oz each
salt and pepper
I shallot or small onion, finely diced
2 tablespoons extra virgin olive oil
   (oregano-flavoured, if you
   have it)
225g/8oz lean minced lamb

2 tablespoons red pepper paste
50g/2oz fresh white or brown
   breadcrumbs
I teaspoon cinnamon
½ teaspoon ground cumin
I egg yolk

Halve the aubergines from stem to base. Cross-hatch the exposed halves with deep cuts (but avoid cutting through to the skin) and salt them liberally. Set aside for 1–2 hours, then firmly squeeze out the bitter juices, rinse with water and squeeze again. Remove most of the flesh with a spoon and set aside.

Cook the shallot or onion in the oil until softened. Add the lamb and stir around briskly, breaking up any clumps of meat. Cook just until the meat loses its pinkness, then add the aubergine pulp and cook for 2 more minutes. Stir in the pepper paste, breadcrumbs, spices and seasoning, then remove from the heat and set aside to cool. Shortly before stuffing the aubergines, mix in the egg yolk thoroughly.

Pile the mixture into the aubergine shells and arrange them in an oiled, ovenproof dish into which they will fit snugly in a single layer. Bake at 160°C/325°F/Gas Mark 3 for 30–40 minutes, until the filling is completely tender. Serve hot, accompanied by fresh or crisped *khoubz* or pitta bread.

MUSHROOMS WITH GOAT'S CHEESE AND WALNUT BREAD

Juice-absorbing, flavourful croutes and crumbs are the clue to perfect baked mushrooms.

4 large open-cap mushrooms, about
    100g/3½oz each
25g/1oz butter
2 tablespoons extra virgin olive oil
2 tablespoons medium dry Madeira
4 thin circles walnut bread
2 teaspoons walnut oil
salt and pepper

For the filling:
4 mature goat's cheese rounds, such
    as crottins, pelardons or Innes
    Clifton, about 50g/2oz each
4 teaspoons walnut oil
50g/2oz walnut bread crumbs

Wipe the mushroom caps and remove the stalks (these are not needed in this recipe but you could dice and fry them, then use in a sandwich spread, a breadcrumb stuffing or perhaps another mushroom recipe). Heat the butter and oil in a large frying pan and sauté the mushrooms, cap-side down, for 3–4 minutes until golden. Add the Madeira and allow it to bubble up, then turn over the mushrooms and sauté for another minute or two.

Arrange the walnut bread rounds in a lightly oiled or buttered baking dish and drizzle with the walnut oil. Remove the mushrooms from the pan, place them on the bread rounds, stalk-side upwards, and season generously. To make the filling, remove the rind from the cheeses as necessary, then roll each cheese in the walnut oil. Place the crumbs on a plate and roll the cheeses in the crumbs, pressing on any surplus with your fingers. Place each crumbed cheese inside a mushroom cap and season lightly. If any walnut oil is left over, drizzle this over the surface of the cheeses. Bake near the top of the oven at 190°C/375°F/Gas Mark 5 for 20 minutes. The cheese should hold its shape but be beautifully soft inside. If the crumbs do not appear to have crisped very much, flash the dish under a hot grill for half a minute or so. Serve at once.

Variation

If the cheeses you find are very pungent or hard with age, crumble them into a stuffing: prepare the mushroom caps and the walnut bread croutes as above, but this time dice the mushroom stalks and sauté them in a little extra oil and butter once you have removed the mushroom caps from the pan. Mix the stalks with 175g/6oz mature goat cheese, 50g/2oz walnut bread crumbs, 1 fat clove garlic crushed with a little salt, 2 tablespoons finely chopped flat-leaf parsley and 3 tablespoons extra virgin olive oil. Season to taste, then pack this filling into the seasoned mushroom caps and place them on the croutes. Drizzle over 1 tablespoon olive oil, and then bake at 190°C/375°F/Gas Mark 5 for 20 minutes. Serve hot.

ITALIAN-STYLE STUFFED MUSHROOMS

A good way of adding a wild mushroom flavour to stuffed cultivated mushrooms is to use dried ceps in the filling. This means you must either have the prescience to soak a few an hour or two before preparing your mushrooms or have to hand some cep powder. This is almost impossible to track down but you can make your own by grinding some extremely clean and well-dried ceps in a spice mill or coffee grinder.

4 very large or 8 medium firm open-cap mushrooms

4 large or 8 small circles fresh or slightly stale bread, about 1.2cm/½inch thick

4 teaspoons flavoured or plain olive oil, or butter

1 clove garlic, halved (optional)

For the filling:
50g/2oz fresh white breadcrumbs
1 clove garlic, crushed with a pinch of salt
25g/1oz pine nuts, toasted

25g/1oz stoned black olives, finely diced

2 oil-cured sun-dried tomatoes, finely diced

25g/1oz Parmesan cheese, freshly grated

1 tablespoon finely chopped parsley
½ teaspoon powdered ceps (see above)
grating of nutmeg
1 small egg, beaten
3 tablespoons oil from the olives or sun-dried tomatoes
pepper

Wipe the mushrooms, remove the stalks and chop these finely. Mix together all the filling ingredients in the order given, using 1 tablespoon of the oil and stirring in the chopped mushroom stalks. Use a second spoonful of the oil to rub over the mushroom caps, then season them inside and out with black pepper and pack with the filling.

Spread the bread croutes with oil or butter and rub them firmly with the cut sides of the garlic, if using. Place the croutes in an ovenproof dish and arrange the mushrooms on top, stuffing-side up. Drizzle the remaining oil over the surface and bake at 200°C/400°F/Gas Mark 6 for 20–25 minutes, until the mushrooms are tender. Serve hot.

STUFFED PEPPER TRIO

Peppers are a perfect vehicle for oil-soaked crumbs. The combined aromas of sizzling sweet pepper, green olive oil, herbs and pungent anchovy evoke sun and plenty on the greyest winter day – even if, without their stuffing, those peppers would most likely betray the blandness of northern climes. Frying the peppers to tenderness before stuffing ensures there is no need to dull the flavours of the filling through overcooking.

3 peppers, I yellow, I red and
   I green
	3 small anchovy fillets, drained and
	   finely chopped

3 tablespoons extra virgin olive oil	90g/3oz stoned herb-cured
150g/5oz herbed crumbs	black olives, finely chopped
(see page 164)	salt and pepper

Quarter the peppers and remove the stalks, seeds and ribs. Heat the oil in a large heavy-based frying pan until sizzling and arrange the peppers in it, skin-side down. Cook for 10 minutes or until the peppers are just tender, stirring gently or shaking the pan from time to time to prevent sticking. Drain off any juices and add to the crumbs, then stir the anchovies and olives into the crumb mixture.

Arrange the peppers snugly in an oiled roasting dish, season them with salt and pepper and divide the crumb mixture between them, pressing down a little on each pile to help it hold together. Bake at 180°C/350°F/Gas Mark 4 for 15–20 minutes and serve hot, perhaps with some crusty ciabatta.

STUFFED CABBAGE PARCELS

These are from the Languedoc region of France where they are known under the charming if misleading name of *poules vertes*, or green chickens. They are designed to make a meal of a simple broth.

8 large cabbage leaves	I clove garlic, crushed with a little salt
150g/5oz slightly stale pain de	25g/1oz walnuts, finely chopped
campagne or other good bread,	I egg
without crust	I tablespoon chopped flat-leaf
150ml/5fl oz milk	parsley
225g/8oz sausagemeat	salt and pepper
a little bacon fat or butter, for frying	about I litre/1¾ pints light stock

Blanch the cabbage leaves for a few minutes, until flexible enough to flatten. Cut away the tough stem and lay the leaves out flat on kitchen paper.

Soak the bread in the milk, warmed if the bread is very stale, for at least 10 minutes. Meanwhile, fry the sausagemeat in the bacon fat or butter, breaking it up with a fork, until nicely browned. Remove from the heat. Break up the bread, squeezing out any excess liquid, and mix with the sausagemeat, then beat in the garlic, walnuts, egg, parsley and seasoning.

Divide the filling between the cabbage leaves, positioning it near the base of each leaf. Fold over the bottom edge, then the sides of the leaf, and finally roll up into a bundle. Tie each bundle lightly with thread or thin string. Heat the stock in a large pan until simmering, put in the stuffed cabbage parcels and cook gently for 30 minutes. Drain, remove the string and return the parcels to the stock to serve.

Variation

For a Provençal-style variation, omit the stock and arrange the bundles side by side in an oiled gratin dish. Season 400g/14oz canned tomatoes (or 450g/1lb ripe, red tomatoes, peeled, seeded and chopped) and pour them over the stuffed cabbage leaves. Drizzle 2 tablespoons extra virgin olive oil over the surface, sprinkle with a handful of dried breadcrumbs and/or a little grated cheese, and bake in the oven at 180°C/350°F/Gas Mark 4 for about 30 minutes. Serve hot with good bread.

BAKED STUFFED CUCUMBERS

Serves 4 as a main course, 8 as a first course

Cooked cucumbers may be expected to collapse into a watery mush – sliced and exposed to salt they fall into sad limpness at unwarranted speed. But a firm, fresh cucumber will take poaching and baking in its stride with great tolerance, even when stuffed with a soft and creamy mixture such as this rather old-fashioned, moistened-bread filling. If you prefer a firmer consistency, use fresh, unsoaked crumbs to the same weight.

2 firm, plump cucumbers
vegetable stock to cover
200g/7oz stale white bread, broken
    into small chunks
150ml/5fl oz creamy milk
1 tablespoon finely diced onion or
    shallot
25g/1oz unsalted butter
2 tablespoons finely chopped flat-leaf
    parsley

1 large or 2 small eggs, beaten
good grating of nutmeg
100g/3½oz Gruyère cheese, finely
    grated
4 tablespoons thick soured cream or
    crème fraîche
salt and pepper
2 tablespoons fine dried breadcrumbs

Halve the cucumbers both lengthwise and widthways to give eight pieces in all. Scrape out the seeds and soft central portion to leave a channel for the stuffing. Place the cucumber portions in a saucepan, add vegetable stock to cover and poach very gently until just translucent – about 15 minutes, but check after 10. Drain cut-side downwards on a wire rack or kitchen paper.

Put the bread into a mixing bowl, heat the milk to boiling point and pour it over the bread. Stir well, then set aside for 10 minutes. Meanwhile, fry the onion or shallot in the butter until translucent, then add the parsley. Break up the bread with a fork, squeezing out excess milk if necessary, then add it to the pan and stir around so that it absorbs all the butter. Return the mixture to the bowl and beat in the eggs, nutmeg, two thirds of the cheese, half the cream, and a good measure of salt and pepper.

Put the cucumbers in a buttered baking dish, season the cut surfaces generously with salt and pepper, then pile in the stuffing. Sprinkle with the remaining cheese, followed by the dried bread-crumbs. Finally spoon over the remaining cream and bake near the top of the oven at 180°C/350°F/Gas Mark 4 for about 20 minutes, or until the top is crisp and brown and the cucumbers tender. Serve hot with Melba toast (see page 172) or any thin, crisp toast.

· SAVOURY MEAT DISHES ·

PORTUGUESE MIGAS

Do not let a lack of Portuguese charcuterie, or the strange notion of a bread-based pancake, stop you attempting this dish, which is both fascinating and delicious. *Presunto* and *chourico* are scarce in Britain but the Spanish *serrano ham* and chorizo are quite widely available and make perfectly good substitutes.

225g/8oz stale cornmeal bread or coarse country bread, cut into cubes
300ml/10fl oz salted boiling water
1 clove garlic, finely chopped
2 tablespoons extra virgin olive oil
50g/2oz *presunto* or serrano ham, in a piece if possible, quite finely diced

75g/2½oz *chourico* or chorizo (mild or hot), quite finely diced
1 teaspoon mild paprika
1 tablespoon chopped flat-leaf parsley
salt and pepper

Place the bread in a mixing bowl and pour on the boiling water. Stir gently, set aside for 10 minutes and then mash with a fork.

Sauté the garlic in the oil until beginning to brown, add the ham and sausage and sauté for 2–3 minutes, until the sausage releases some of its fat. Stir in the paprika and parsley, then add the bread. Mix the bread and meat together by using a cutting motion with a wooden spoon, then pat the mixture down firmly to form a fat pancake. Cook over a moderate heat for about 5 minutes or until the underside is golden.

Carefully place a plate over the pan and invert the pan and plate at the same time, leaving the Migas on the plate. Now slip it back into the pan for about 5 minutes to brown the reverse side. Cut into wedges and serve hot. It is good with a crisp and pungently dressed salad.

HERBED RACK OF LAMB

A classic use of oil-soaked breadcrumbs and one of the best: the crumbs release the oil to provide a continuous basting of the lamb, at the same time absorbing the juices so that they themselves end up richly flavoured and moist. The lamb needs little further accompaniment – perhaps some redcurrant jelly. I find this a convenient dish to make for large numbers of people, particularly as both elements of the coating can be prepared some while in advance.

2 racks (best ends) of lamb, chine
   bone removed
1 tablespoon flowery honey
1 tablespoon Dijon mustard
2 tablespoons wholegrain mustard
1 tablespoon extra virgin olive oil
2 cloves garlic, crushed with a pinch
   of salt
pepper

For the crumb coating:
50g/2oz fresh white bread without
   crust
1 tablespoon finely chopped flat-leaf
   parsley
1 teaspoon finely chopped tarragon
1 teaspoon finely chopped thyme
a very few tender rosemary leaves,
   chopped, or use rosemary-
   infused olive oil
2–3 tablespoons extra virgin olive oil

Trim the lamb to remove all extra fat. Mix together the honey, mustards, oil and garlic, season with pepper and spread all over the meat. Leave the lamb to absorb these flavours at room temperature while you heat the oven to 200°C/400°F/Gas Mark 6. Position the lamb on an oven rack or, if retained, the chine bones, and roast for 10 minutes.

Make the herbed crumbs while the lamb is roasting (or do this in advance and store, covered, in the fridge). Ideally, use a food processor to make the bread into crumbs (in which case the herbs can be added and chopped at the same time), then add the oil and use a pulsing action until the breadcrumbs and oil are lightly combined. If you don't have a food processor, make the bread into crumbs and combine with the remaining ingredients.

Remove the lamb from the oven and press the crumbs over the meat. Return to the oven and roast for a further 10 minutes. Remove from the oven again and leave to rest for a further 10 minutes before carving into chops (or, if your oven cools rapidly, switch it off as soon as the lamb is done and leave the lamb inside with the oven door open). Spoon up all the juice-soaked crumbs in the roasting tin and serve alongside the lamb.

MILANESE VEAL CHOPS

I hesitated before including a recipe for veal, but now that free-range, grass-fed and suckled veal is becoming widely available we should perhaps take advantage of it. It is surely preferable to buy meat from a properly reared animal than buy a ready-breaded escalope originating from a battery chicken; moreover the veal will have considerably more taste. Pink veal from free-range animals is, unsurprisingly, more flavourful than the ivory-white flesh of an iron-deprived animal.

Although traditionally accompanied by a Milanese risotto, a simple salad is sufficient with the *Costolette*. While the recipe is a well-established one, the tip of starting the cooking in a cold pan is one revealed by writer Anna del Conte.

4 × 175g/6oz trimmed veal chops (tail end of fat and excess bone removed)	100g/3½oz very fine dried white breadcrumbs
2 small eggs, beaten with a pinch of salt	100g/3½oz clarified butter (see page 178) or unsalted butter
	lemon wedges, to serve

Bring the chops to room temperature before coating and cooking. Nick the fat running down one side of each chop, place the chops between plastic layering tissue and pound them with a marble rolling pin to a 1.2cm/½inch thickness, avoiding the bone. Pour the beaten eggs into a soup plate and spread the crumbs on to another soup plate. Dip both sides of each chop in the beaten egg, allowing excess egg to drain off, then press them into the crumbs, using your hands to coat the veal thoroughly.

Press small knobs of the butter on to a heavy-based frying pan. (You may well need to cook the veal in two batches, in which case wash the pan and rinse it under cold water before cooking the second batch. Or, use 2 pans from the start.) Lay the chops in the pan and turn on the heat to moderate. After 2 minutes' cooking, shake the pan to prevent the chops from sticking. Carry on cooking and shaking for a further 3 minutes or so until golden brown underneath, then turn the chops, adding a few more knobs of butter to the pan. Cook and shake the chops for a further 3–6 minutes or until just cooked through: test near the bone with the point of a sharp knife – the flesh should no longer be pink, although I find a slight pinkness ensures the juiciness I favour. If at any stage the butter sizzles furiously and the crumb coating is browning too fast, reduce the heat.

Serve the chops with the cooking butter poured over them and accompanied by lemon wedges.

VIENNESE VEAL ESCALOPES

While Austrians will admit that their great dish originated in Milan, they will also insist that the *Schnitzel* was perfected by the Viennese (they will probably also maintain that it is barely worth eating outside Vienna). It is well-nigh impossible to get hold of the ideal *Frikandeau* cut, which is supposed, once beaten out and cooked, to cover an entire dinner plate. The pink and half-size escalopes I buy from my Q-Guild butcher, however, certainly deserve to be cooked in the manner of a *Schnitzel*, and this is the method.

Use the same method for escalopes of chicken or pork, or slices of aubergine.

4 × 125g/4oz veal escalopes
50g/2oz plain flour
2 small eggs, beaten with a pinch of
    salt and 2 teaspoons extra virgin
    olive oil

100g/3½oz fine, fresh white
    breadcrumbs
pure lard or extra virgin olive oil, for
    frying*
lemon wedges, to serve

*You will need a lot of cooking fat – an initial 100g/3½oz lard or 150ml/5fl oz olive oil, plus more for topping up; the escalope must float easily. The fat really needs to be of the finest – free-range lard or (less traditionally) extra virgin olive oil.

Trim the escalopes if necessary, then pound (see note on pounding chops on page 255, but don't be too fierce with the escalopes) to a 6mm/¼inch thickness. Sift the flour on to a soup or dinner plate. Pour the beaten eggs into another soup plate. Spread the crumbs on to a third soup or dinner plate. Dip each escalope lightly in the flour, shaking off excess, then the egg, letting excess drain off, then into the crumbs. Press both sides down lightly on to the crumbs, but do not press additional crumbs on with your hands.

The fat should be sizzling before the escalopes are added to the pan, but keep the heat moderate once the meat is cooking. You will probably fit only one, possibly two escalopes in your pan, but they cook very quickly. Place the escalopes in the pan and shake the pan gently while cooking – it is fine for a little fat to flow over the upper surface of the escalopes. The escalope should be turned once the base is golden brown – a maximum of 2 minutes. When the second side is golden brown and the escalopes cooked through – test with the tip of a small sharp knife – drain them briefly on absorbent paper, then serve on a warmed plate with a good wedge of juicy lemon, salt and pepper.

RUSSIAN CHICKEN RISSOLES

There is probably a whole bookful of tall stories concerning the origin of these famous rissoles, known as *pozharski kotlety* and immortalised by Pushkin in the early eighteenth century. Generally they concern an act of deception – the meat should have been luxurious veal, not chicken, but the contents of the rissoles were pounded to conceal their identity. There are as many recipe variations as background legends, so I have had little compunction in adding my own.

Traditional Russian accompaniments are mushrooms in soured cream sauce, fried potatoes and peas, but a simple salad dressed with soured cream, dill and chives would also be in keeping.

2 skinless, boned chicken breasts, about 275–350g/10–12oz in total
sprig of tarragon
150ml/5fl oz single cream
75g/2½oz stale white bread without crust, broken into small chunks
50g/2oz softened unsalted butter

1 egg, separated
2 tablespoons Madeira
grating of nutmeg
salt and pepper
40g/1½oz fine dried breadcrumbs
75g/2½oz clarified butter (see page 178), or half unsalted butter and half oil

Mince the chicken with the tarragon, using the pulse action of a food processor, until it is finely ground – almost a paste. Heat the cream until almost boiling, pour it over the bread and leave for 10 minutes, until all the liquid is absorbed and the bread is completely soft. Tip the mixture into the food processor and blend briefly with the chicken. Add the softened butter, egg yolk, Madeira, nutmeg and seasoning and process until well mixed, stopping to scrape down the processor bowl from time to time. Transfer the chicken mixture to a bowl. Whisk the egg white with a pinch of salt until stiff, then stir it thoroughly into the chicken – it is too dense for the egg white to be folded in, but adding the white does give a lighter texture. If you have time to chill the mixture at this stage it will be easier to shape and handle.

When you are ready to cook the rissoles, shape the mixture into 8 oval patties – wetted hands make this easier. Put the dried breadcrumbs into a soup plate and dip the rissoles into them, pressing down lightly. Melt the butter or butter and oil in a large frying pan and cook the rissoles, in batches if necessary, over a moderate heat for 5 minutes, until brown and crisp underneath; turn and cook the other side for 5–8 minutes, reducing the heat a little if the outside browns too quickly (it will take 10–15 minutes for the chicken to cook through safely). Drain on kitchen paper and serve hot.

Venison Rissoles with Gjetost Sauce

This Scandinavian-spirited recipe should of course be made with reindeer meat, as tender and delicious as the finest venison. Almost all cuts of venison have a very low ratio of fat to lean meat, which means that for rissoles a little extra fat will not come amiss. You could use a proportion of fatty pork, as do sausage makers (but ensure it is free range, to match the nature of the venison), or you could soak some breadcrumbs in cream – or both. The following recipe is a guideline.

Gjetost, a curious Norwegian goat's cheese made from cooked whey, resembles a Caramac bar in appearance and, to some extent, in flavour: the caramelised whey has a distinct sweetness to it. It is rather more widely available than reindeer, but you could omit the sauce altogether and serve the rissoles with a generous quantity of lingonberry or even cranberry sauce.

350g/12oz lean minced venison plus
   125g/4oz fat-rich minced pork,
   or 450g/1lb minced venison
1 small onion, finely diced
15g/½oz bacon fat or butter, plus extra
   for frying the rissoles
50g/2oz slightly stale white bread
   without crust, torn into chunks
150ml/5fl oz single cream
pinch of allspice
3–4 juniper berries, toasted and
   crushed (optional)

1 small egg
salt and pepper

For the sauce:
a little Madeira
100ml/3½fl oz water
100ml/3½fl oz crème fraîche
25g/1oz Gjetost cheese, thinly sliced
   or crumbled
1 tablespoon rowanberry or
   redcurrant jelly

Mix the venison with the pork, if using. Fry the onion in the 15g/½oz bacon fat or butter until softened, then cool slightly. Soak the bread in the cream, warmed if the bread is very dry. Break the bread up with a fork once it is thoroughly moistened. Add the onion, bread, allspice and juniper berries to the meat and mix thoroughly, then mix in the egg and seasoning. Form into 4 large or 8 small rissoles and fry in a little bacon fat or butter over a fairly high heat until well browned on the outside but still slightly pink in the centre – 4–5 minutes per side for large rissoles, about 3 minutes per side for small ones. Remove from the pan and keep warm.

To make the sauce, add a splash of Madeira to the pan and cook over a high heat to reduce quickly. Add the water and continue to reduce the liquid, scraping up any pan residues, until only 2–3 tablespoons remain. Remove from the heat. At this stage you can strain the syrupy liquid if you want a perfectly smooth sauce. Whisk the crème fraîche into the reduced liquid and return it to the heat, allowing the sauce to bubble up. Now reduce the heat, stir in the cheese and cook gently until it melts. Whisk in the jelly until that, too, is melted. Taste and adjust the seasoning, or add a little more jelly. This sauce can be cooled and reheated successfully.

Mashed or boiled potatoes to soak up the sauce are good with this. For a touch of colour serve with a spoonful or two of lingonberry preserve.

Meatballs in Soured Cream and Caper Sauce

These uniquely piquant meatballs are popular throughout the Eastern Baltic, where they are known as *Königsberg klops*. This version is close to the original, eighteenth-century East Prussian recipe; in the Baltic states, pickled herring or spiced Baltic sprat would be used instead of the Mediterranean anchovy, while pickled dill cucumber replaces the capers, and is often incorporated in the meat mixture.

In addition, mustard can be stirred into the finished sauce. This piquancy masks considerable richness; serve simply with plain boiled potatoes and a little salad.

1 medium onion, finely diced
15g/½oz unsalted butter
225g/8oz ground veal
225g/8oz ground beef
2 egg yolks
1–2 sprigs marjoram
3 anchovy fillets, rinsed and mashed
75g/2½oz fresh white breadcrumbs,
    (preferably from a light
    sourdough pain de campagne)
zest of ½ lemon (optional)
salt and pepper

For the sauce:
600ml/1 pint light beef or veal stock
50g/2oz unsalted butter
50g/2oz plain flour
1 tablespoon salt-packed capers,
    rinsed and chopped (optional)
2 egg yolks
150ml/5fl oz thick soured cream or
    crème fraîche
squeeze of lemon juice

Sauté the onion gently in the butter until soft and golden. Cool a little, then place in a mixing bowl with all the remaining meatball ingredients and mix thoroughly with your hands. To check the seasoning, poach or fry a little of the mixture and taste before proceeding further. Form the mixture into 16–20 meatballs.

Bring the stock to the boil in a pan and gently drop in the meatballs. Reduce to a simmer and cook until they rise to the surface – about 10–15 minutes. Remove with a slotted spoon and keep warm.

To make the sauce, strain the stock through a sieve and boil over a high heat to reduce by about a quarter. Melt the butter in a separate pan, stir in the flour, then gradually add the stock, stirring continuously, to make a smooth sauce. Add the capers and a little seasoning and simmer for 10 minutes, then add the meatballs and heat through gently for 5 minutes. Remove from the heat. Beat together the egg yolks and cream and stir briskly into the sauce. Check the seasoning, adding a squeeze of lemon juice and more salt and pepper as needed, then return to a very gentle heat and stir continuously until the sauce has thickened; do not let it approach boiling point. Once the sauce has thickened, serve immediately.

The dish can be prepared ahead up to either of two stages: either poach the meatballs, strain the stock and chill both separately until ready to proceed; or work as far as adding the meatballs to the thickened sauce, then cool and chill it; reheat gently but thoroughly before finishing the sauce.

BOBOTIE

I first came across Bobotie while researching foods to accompany a tasting of South African wines. The basic recipe seemed so makeshift, the essential ingredients so unlikely a combination, that I dismissed it as an unappealing curiosity. I was, thankfully, proven wrong by the late great South African gourmet and wine authority Peter Devereux, who prepared the dish in his Johannesburg kitchen before jetting off on a business trip to London, then taxi-ed it over to me along with a his own recipe and a box of Cartwright's Curry Powder. I found it delicious, so here is Peter Devereux's (hardly makeshift) recipe. You can buy both Cartwright's Curry Powder and Mrs Ball's Peach Chutney in the UK – if all else fails, contact Emory St Marcus in West London (tel: 0181 878 1898).

I am so fond of the chutney that I occasionally substitute it for the vinegar and sugar in the original recipe and trust this may not be too inauthentic a deviation.

3 large mild onions, finely diced
2 tablespoons groundnut oil
1½ tablespoons Cartwright's Curry Powder (see above) or other mild curry powder
500g/1lb 2oz minced topside beef
50g/2oz soft white breadcrumbs
4 tablespoons milk
½ teaspoon salt

½ teaspoon ground pepper
1½ tablespoons sugar
1½ tablespoons wine vinegar
For the custard:
1 egg, beaten
120ml/4fl oz milk
½ teaspoon salt

Fry the onions gently in the oil until golden. Stir in the curry powder and cook gently for a further 3 minutes, then leave to cool. Place the meat into a large mixing bowl and mix in the breadcrumbs by hand, then add the milk, salt, pepper and onion mixture, including all the oil. Knead with your hands to mix well. Dissolve the sugar in the vinegar and add to the mixture, distributing evenly.

Pack the mixture into an ovenproof dish (it should be 10–15cm/ 4–6inches deep so it stays moist). Press down to compact it and create an even surface, then pour over a custard made by beating together the egg, milk and salt. Bake uncovered for about 1 hour at 180°C/ 350°F/Gas Mark 4, until the custard mixture is brown in patches. Serve with fluffy rice and Mrs Ball's Peach Chutney, and either glazed carrots (Peter's suggestion) or a simple salad of tomatoes and spring onions.

· DUMPLINGS ·

The *Concise Oxford Dictionary* defines dumpling as a 'mass of dough boiled or baked' or a 'small fat person'. Dumplings in Britain have a decidedly bad press. Not so in most of the rest of Europe, where dumplings might evidence the highest degree of culinary skill and the root of the word, whether it be *knödel, quenelle, gnocchi or knedlakh*, has a rather more delicate connotation – that of the Latin word *nodulus*, or little knot. We have much to learn about the potential delicacy and deliciousness of dumplings.

Bread-based dumplings are lighter than any that are flour-based, making them particularly suitable for light vegetable soups, stews or consommés. Variations in size, shape, flavouring and presentation are endless.

BAVARIAN-STYLE DUMPLINGS

By some tacit agreement the basic formula for savoury dumplings is deemed to be Bavarian, though they arguably reach their apotheosis in Austria and Hungary. This recipe is ideal for making use of a miscellany of breads – white, brown and even flavoured – either roughly cubed or in crumbs; you can even include the crust provided it is not too harsh or burnt. If you want very fine, light dumplings, however, use an enriched bread, and the crumb only.

250g/8½oz stale bread pieces or
    crumbs (see above)
150ml/5fl oz milk
1 small onion, very finely diced
25g/1oz unsalted butter
2–3 tablespoons chopped flat-leaf
    parsley
grating of nutmeg
2 eggs, beaten
salt and pepper
about 1 litre/1¾ pints light stock or
    water for poaching (unless adding
    dumplings to soup or stew)

flour for coating (optional)

Optional additions:
175g/6oz fresh ceps, diced and fried
    in butter
175g/6oz crisply smoked bacon or
    cured ham, fried until crisp
1 teaspoon dried cep powder (see
    page 249)

Break up any bread pieces and place them, or the crumbs, in a mixing bowl. Heat the milk and pour it over the bread. Leave for a few minutes until the bread is soaked through – you may need to add a little more milk, or (less likely) to drain off excess. Break up the soaked bread with a fork or stir through the crumbs.

Fry the onion in the butter over a gentle heat until translucent and then add it to the soaked bread along with the parsley, nutmeg, eggs, seasoning and any of the optional additions. Mix together lightly; if the mixture seems very wet, add some breadcrumbs or a little plain flour or potato flour. If you have time, chill the mixture to make shaping easier.

Bring the cooking liquid to a gentle boil while shaping the mixture. You can either do this with wetted hands, tossing the shaped dumplings in a little flour or, if you are deft with spoons, use 2 wetted tablespoons to form quenelles, dropping them directly into the gently simmering liquid. Simmer for 10–15 minutes or until cooked through (you may need to cut one open to check). Serve at once with a soup or stew, or use for a gratin (see below).

Variation: Gratinated Dumplings

Remove the dumplings from their poaching liquid with a slotted spoon, drain on kitchen paper or a tea-towel, then arrange in a single layer in a buttered gratin dish. Coat with a little melted butter, grated cheese, and crisp buttered crumbs (see page 163) and bake in the oven at 200°C/400°F/Gas Mark 6 for 5–8 minutes. Serve at once.

FRESH CRUMB DUMPLINGS

A simple formula for making dumplings from fresh crumbs which need no soaking. Double up the quantities as necessary, and add aromatics and flavourings to taste (see Bavarian-style Dumplings on page 262).

125g/4oz fresh white breadcrumbs	1–2 teaspoons potato flour or
15g/½oz softened unsalted butter	cornflour
1 large egg	salt, pepper and nutmeg

Beat everything together in the order given; use the lesser amount of flour initially. Test a spoonful of the mixture in simmering salted water – if it breaks up before rising to the surface, mix in the rest of the flour and perhaps a few extra crumbs. Form the mixture into dumplings of whatever size you wish and simmer for 5–10 minutes or until cooked through – the exact time will depend on the size and will usually, but not always, coincide with their rising to the surface. Cut one open to check before removing the rest of the dumplings from the liquid and draining.

BREAD-CUBE DUMPLINGS

These dumplings are made from bread that has been cubed and fried in butter, with flour or breadcrumbs as a thickener. Once again, you can add sautéed onion and other flavourings to taste (see Bavarian-style Dumplings on page 262).

125g/4oz day-old bread, cut into
    small cubes
15–25g/½–1oz unsalted butter
1 large egg
150ml/5fl oz milk

nutmeg or chopped parsley, to taste
salt and pepper
up to 4 tablespoons plain flour or fine
    breadcrumbs

Fry the cubes of bread in as much butter as needed until golden brown, then place them in a mixing bowl. Beat together the egg, milk, nutmeg or parsley and seasoning and pour over the bread. Sift in 2 tablespoons of flour, or stir in the equivalent amount of breadcrumbs, and mix to a soft dropping consistency. Set aside for 30 minutes in a cool place.

Bring a pan of salted water to the boil and test a dumpling (see Fresh Crumb Dumplings on page 263) adding more flour or crumbs to the mixture if necessary. Simmer the dumplings for about 10 minutes or until cooked through, drain and serve as required.

Variation

A favourite Austrian dish is *Knödel mit Ei* – dumplings with egg. This is made by slicing and frying leftover dumplings in butter or lard, then beating 2 or 3 eggs with seasoning and pouring them over the crumbs in the pan. The eggs are stirred gently until set and the dish is served straight from the pan, with a green salad.

WILD MUSHROOM DUMPLINGS

Here is a recipe where preserved Lactaires (*Lactarius deliciosus*, or saffron milk cap) really come into their own. You are most likely to find these in jars, sometimes cans, imported from France. Stock up if you travel to France or Spain, where both fresh Lactaires (in season) and bottled or canned ones (try the hypermarkets) can be remarkably inexpensive. Not only do they maintain a pleasing crunchiness through thick and thin, they also have a peppery bite that makes their presence felt.

If you cannot get Lactaires there is no reason why you should not use fresh, firm brown cap mushrooms and boost the flavour with porcini purée, a versatile product that is rapidly claiming well-deserved space on both deli and supermarket shelves.

1 small shallot, finely diced	225g/8oz fresh white breadcrumbs,
50g/2oz unsalted butter	preferably from pain de
150g/5oz bottled Lactaires, very finely	campagne
diced, or 225g/8oz brown cap	2 tablespoons finely chopped flat-leaf
mushrooms finely diced	parsley
2 eggs, plus 2 egg yolks	generous grating of nutmeg
2 tablespoons potato flour	salt and pepper
180ml/6fl oz crème fraîche	1 litre/1¾ pints light stock
1–2 teaspoons porcini purée (optional)	2 egg yolks

Fry the shallot in a little of the butter until translucent. Add the remaining butter and the bottled or fresh mushrooms. Bottled mushrooms need only be infused with the butter for 2–3 minutes; fresh mushrooms should be cooked through and any juices released driven off over a high heat. Set aside to cool a little. Whisk together the 2 whole eggs and 2 yolks until foaming. Mix the potato flour with 5 tablespoons of the crème fraîche to form a smooth paste and whisk it into the eggs. Combine the mushrooms, egg mixture and porcini purée, then gradually mix in the breadcrumbs, parsley, nutmeg and seasoning. Chill for 30 minutes.

Use your hands to form the mixture into small dumplings the size of a walnut. Bring the stock to the boil in a large pan, reduce to a simmer, and place as many dumplings as will sink out of sight into the simmering liquid – it is important to maintain the liquid at a gentle but noticeable simmer to prevent the dumplings breaking up. After 5–8 minutes the dumplings will bob to the top of the liquid; cut one open to check if it is cooked through and leave the dumplings poaching for another minute or two if you are uncertain. Remove the dumplings with a slotted spoon and drain on kitchen paper.

Strain the poaching liquid through a fine sieve and boil it until reduced by half. Beat together the egg yolks and the remaining crème fraîche and whisk this mixture into the reduced stock. Heat gently, stirring constantly, until thickened. Return the drained dumplings to the thickened sauce and warm through before serving.

CALF'S LIVER DUMPLINGS

Every German-speaking area of Europe takes pride in some version of the little dumplings known as *Leberknödel* or *Lebernöckerl* and there are fiercely distinct differences between them, whether of content or shape. They range from solid and punchy to delicately flavoured, featherlight floaters. These are in the latter category, which officially makes them *Lebernöckerl*.

75g/2½oz slightly stale white bread
90ml/3fl oz milk
1 tablespoon finely diced onion
15g/½oz unsalted butter
150g/5oz calf's liver
50g/2oz softened unsalted butter
1 egg, beaten
1 tablespoon finely chopped flat-leaf
    parsley

pinch of fresh or dried marjoram
finely grated zest of ½ lemon, or a
    little orange zest
50g/2oz fresh white breadcrumbs
salt and pepper
about 1 litre/1¾ pints veal or beef
    stock, for poaching

Soak the bread in the milk for at least 10 minutes, then drain it through a sieve, pressing down well until the bread is dry. Fry the onion in the butter until translucent. Work the liver briefly in a food processor until puréed, then add the bread and onion and process again until smooth. Add the softened butter and egg and process again. Finally add the herbs, zest, breadcrumbs and seasoning and process briefly to combine. Chill the mixture for 1 hour.

Bring the stock to the boil in a large pan. Form the mixture into dumplings by shaping it between 2 teaspoons, dipping the spoons in cold water between each one. This is not as difficult as it may sound – simply turn the mixture a couple of times with each spoon and drop it from a spoon into the simmering liquid. The quenelles are so light they will float almost at once but will not be cooked through until they have simmered for 10 minutes or so – cut one open to check. Serve at once with creamed potatoes and a little salad.

Variation

To produce delectable fritters, heat some unsalted butter in a frying pan and simply drop generous teaspoonfuls into the pan. After a couple of minutes, shake the pan round and see if you can turn the little fritters easily. If not, wait another minute or two before doing so. Both sides should end up brown and crunchy, with the centre slightly pink and soft. Serve at once, dressed with a few drops of sweet balsamic vinegar. For the first course of a dinner serve 3–5 arranged on a mound of dressed salad leaves.

STUFFINGS
· AND SAUCES ·

· STUFFINGS ·

Britain has a remarkably rich tradition of bread-based stuffings and forcemeats, used to moisten and flavour meat, poultry and fish. Open any book documenting the history of British food and you might well conclude that stuffings are the prime medium for British culinary invention.

It is not really in the scope of this book to list a hundred and one inventive stuffings, fascinating as the subject is. Although I have allowed myself a couple of highly specific favourite recipes, I feel the most useful kind of information to pass on where stuffings are concerned is formulae for popular basic mixes, to which you can add a personal touch.

General Principles
Bread is by far the most ancient and still the most popular base for stuffings. One of its great advantages over other starches is the attractive lightness of texture it lends to all manner of stuffings. It is the binding and enriching agents, such as egg, milk and suet, that give density and weight to the mixture: the more bread, the lighter the mix. White bread is commonly specified in recipes but you can vary the bread as you would any other ingredient – with a view to balance of flavour and texture.

Seasoning is of crucial importance; in many ways a stuffing is a means of seasoning a cut of meat or fish from the inside. Apart from the obvious salt and pepper, you could also try herbs and spices, small quantities of anchovies, air-dried ham, olives, fresh chillies, citrus zest and cheese. Piquancy is desirable but overpowering the meat or fish is not; delicate foods demand a fairly delicate stuffing, while robust meats or fish can cope with a relatively powerful one.

SIMPLE SHALLOT AND PARSLEY STUFFING

A useful, basic stuffing to which you can add fruit, nuts, or salty or piquant elements. It is suitable for roast meat, poultry or vegetables.

150g/5oz shallots, finely chopped
50g/2oz unsalted butter
150g/5oz fresh breadcrumbs of your
    choice

small bunch of parsley, finely chopped
salt and pepper
grating of nutmeg
a little egg or milk, to bind

Sauté the shallots in the butter until soft and translucent. Tip into a mixing bowl and add the breadcrumbs, parsley, seasoning and nutmeg. Bind lightly with egg or milk – the latter will give a lighter effect.

BASIC HERB STUFFING

150g/5oz fresh breadcrumbs of choice
75g/2½oz shredded suet
50g/2oz diced ham or streaky bacon,
    cooked and crumbled
1 tablespoon finely chopped parsley

1 teaspoon each herbs of choice:
    thyme, sage, marjoram, crumbled
    bay
salt and pepper
1 egg plus 1 egg yolk

Mix together the breadcrumbs and suet, then mix in the remaining ingredients, binding the mixture lightly with as much egg as needed.

Variation

For a butter-based stuffing, omit the suet and fry 1 large mild onion, finely chopped, in 50g/2oz unsalted butter until soft. Mix with the breadcrumbs and the ham or bacon (omit this if you prefer), then stir in all the remaining ingredients.

SAGE AND ONION STUFFING

Perhaps the most popular and quintessentially English of stuffings, particularly suitable for rich poultry such as duck and goose.

2 large mild onions, chopped
25g/1oz unsalted butter
100g/3½oz fresh white or brown
    breadcrumbs
4–12 sage leaves, finely chopped, or 1–3
    teaspoons dried sage

a little grated lemon zest (optional)
salt and pepper
1 small egg, beaten
100–150ml/3½–5fl oz good flavourful
    stock

Gently cook the onions in the butter until translucent. Leave to cool, then lightly mix in the remaining ingredients, adding sage to taste and using just enough stock to bind the mixture together. This will be enough for a largeish duck; you may well need to double it for a goose.

VICTORIAN OYSTER STUFFING

This was traditionally used for the Christmas turkey, which was then served with oyster sauce – basically a béchamel incorporating the juices of the shucked oysters, which are then simmered briefly in the sauce. The amount given here is enough for a turkey breast or 1 large chicken.

12 fresh oysters
100g/3½oz fresh white breadcrumbs
50g/2oz butter, melted, or suet
zest of ½ lemon
1 tablespoon finely chopped parsley
grating of nutmeg or pinch of ground
   mace

pinch of cayenne
salt
1 egg yolk
a little milk (optional)

Open the oysters and reserve the juice either for the stuffing or for an accompanying sauce. Chop the oysters into large pieces and combine with the remaining ingredients, using the egg and oyster juice or milk to bind the mixture lightly.

Variation: Crab Meat Stuffing
Another Victorian favourite, this time used for mutton; recently cookery writer Frances Bissell has championed a delicate crab meat stuffing for lamb. Follow the recipe above, substituting 150–175g/5–6oz crab meat for the oysters. All white meat gives a delicate result, mixed white and brown meats a considerably more powerful effect. If you use butter rather than suet the mixture is suitable for stuffing white fish.

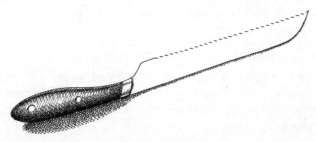

FORCEMEAT STUFFING

Forcemeats are generally defined as containing a high proportion of meat (although the medieval meaning simply implied 'minced food') and are often baked in a separate dish or in little balls alongside the meat. Use this stuffing for meat or poultry or fry small forcemeat balls to accompany soups and stews. Shallots softened in butter could be added to the mixture to enhance the flavour further.

225g/8oz fillet free-range veal or pork
100g/3½oz raw bacon, ham or gammon
100g/3½oz fresh white breadcrumbs
1 tablespoon finely chopped parsley
1 teaspoon finely chopped thyme
salt and pepper
1 egg
a few tablespoons concentrated stock

Mince or process both meats finely, then mix with the remaining ingredients, adding enough stock to bind.

'LOAVES AND FISHES' LAMB STUFFING

This recipe was given to me by Margaret Joyce from Galway, who now lives and works in London, where her bakery, Loaves and Fishes, produces the most wonderful soda bread to be found on English soil (and, some would have it, on Irish too).

This stuffing would enable the Christmas turkey to sit proud on its platter and can also be used to stuff a loin of lamb. I like to add a little honey – no more than a teaspoonful – to the stuffing. Or try using the Loaves and Fishes fruited soda bread. If you cannot get hold of Margaret's bread, the nearest equivalent would be a dense wholemeal loaf.

1 large onion, chopped
50g/2oz salted butter, such as Kerrygold
1 tablespoon finely chopped sage
400g/14oz can of apricots in natural juice
225–275g/8–10oz Irish wholemeal soda bread, made into crumbs
125g/4oz walnuts, chopped
1 egg, beaten
salt and pepper

Cook the onion in the butter until softened, then stir in the sage. Drain the apricots, reserving the juice, dice them and add to the onions along with the breadcrumbs and nuts. Add half the reserved juice, then stir in the egg and season to taste. If the mixture seems a little dry add more, or all, of the reserved apricot juice.

· ELIZA ACTON'S FORCEMEATS ·

The remarkable nineteenth-century cookery writer Eliza Acton had much to say on the subject of forcemeats and in *Modern Cookery* she proffered a fierce corrective to the 'odds and ends' school of stuffing production: 'The coarse and unpalatable compounds so constantly met with under the denomination of forcemeat . . . show with how little attention they are commonly prepared. Many indifferent cooks pique themselves on never doing anything by rule, and the consequence of their throwing together at random (or "by guess" as they call it) the ingredients which ought to be proportioned with exceeding exactness is repeated failure in all they attempt to do.' Feeling severely reprimanded, I was relieved to discover some leeway allowed to those of 'long experience', though quite unsure whether I have the requisite 'very correct eye'.

I don't suppose most of us have the indispensable large marble or Wedgwood mortar Eliza Acton used but we do have other means of pounding 'until not a single lump of fibre be perceptible'.

MUSHROOM FORCEMEAT

Eliza Acton used this 'poached in small balls for soup, or fried and served in the dish with roast fowls, or round minced veal; or to fill boiled fowls, partridges, or turkeys'.

125g/4oz just-open mushrooms, peeled and trimmed	40g/1½oz softened butter
	salt and a hint of nutmeg
40g/1½oz unsalted butter	1 teaspoon finely grated lemon zest
pinch of mace and of cayenne	1 large or 2 small egg yolks
125g/4oz fine fresh breadcrumbs	

Sauté the mushrooms, diced if large, in the butter with the mace and cayenne for 5–7 minutes, until cooked through. Place them in a sieve to drain, reserving the liquid that runs off. When cold, mince the mushrooms finely and mix with the remaining ingredients, including as much of the reserved liquid as the mixture will hold, but making sure to include at least one egg yolk to bind the mass. Add more mace and cayenne, if necessary. Miss Acton preferred this to be completely smooth, in our terms processed, but it will be somewhat lighter if left slightly coarse.

A Good Common Forcemeat

Miss Acton suggests that this 'may be fried in balls of moderate size, for five minutes, to serve with roast veal, or it may be put into the joint in the usual way'.

90g/3oz fine fresh breadcrumbs	I teaspoon finely grated lemon zest
50g/2oz butter	I small teaspoon nutmeg, mace and
50g/2oz lean ham, very finely minced	cayenne, mixed
I dessertspoon finely chopped mixed	pinch of salt
herbs	I small egg or 2 egg yolks

Mix together all the ingredients in the order given. This is a very versatile stuffing.

Stuffing for Roast Wild Duck and Teal

Nothing complex or even very specific here, but an interesting idea worth following when you next bag wild duck or come across mallard or teal in your local supermarket: 'a bit of soft bread soaked in port wine, or in claret'. I would suggest slightly stale white bread, and go for the port with its power and sweetness.

Bread Sauce

Bread sauce is our closest surviving link with the bread-thickened stews and sauces of our Medieval ancestors, which were gradually superseded by flour-thickened, egg-liaised or reduced sauces.

There are three slightly different methods of making the basic bread sauce; if you already have a favoured method you would probably as soon change it as risk ruining your Christmas dinner. For the record, however, you can either a) simmer milk with aromatics for a good long while, strain, then simmer the infused liquid further with chunks of bread or crumbs; b) simmer milk, aromatics and bread together, then remove the aromatics before completing the sauce; or c) simmer everything together, remove the mace, bay and cloves but purée the onion along with the bread. Personally I prefer the subtlest of these, also perhaps the most popular, so here it is.

500ml/18fl oz rich creamy milk – Jersey if possible

1 mild onion, peeled and stuck with 3 cloves

1 fresh or dried bay leaf

1 blade of mace

100g/3½oz slightly stale good white bread without crusts, torn into small chunks

25g/1oz salted butter, cut into small pieces

2 tablespoons thick double cream

salt and pepper

pinch of cayenne (optional)

Place the milk, onion, bay leaf and mace in a saucepan or a double boiler and bring to the boil as slowly as possible. If time permits, keep it on a very low simmer for a further 40 minutes but the infused milk can be strained straight after it comes to the boil.

Put the bread in a non-stick saucepan and strain the milk over it, pressing down hard on the onion to extract juices. Leave for a few minutes, then break up the bread with a fork or whisk. Return to the heat and simmer very gently for about 15 minutes, whisking from time to time. Remove from the heat, stir in the butter and cream and season to taste with salt, pepper and cayenne, if using. If the sauce is rather runny, add more bread in the form of fresh crumbs; if too thick, dilute with more milk or cream. Serve warm with roast poultry or sausages.

BEST OF EVERYTHING BREAD SAUCE

This combines onion, garlic and horseradish sauces in a mild blend with aromatic spices. Serve it with poultry in the traditional manner or with pork or fish.

4 spring onion bulbs, finely chopped

2 cloves garlic, sliced

25g/1oz unsalted butter

450ml/15fl oz creamy milk

100g/3½oz slightly stale white or wholewheat bread without crusts, broken into small pieces

150ml/5fl oz double cream

1 teaspoon grated or creamed horseradish

pinch of freshly grated nutmeg

pinch of freshly ground allspice

salt and pepper

Sweat the spring onions and garlic in the butter for 10 minutes until soft. Add the milk and bring to the boil, then whisk in the bread. Simmer very gently for 30 minutes, stirring occasionally to prevent sticking, then press through a coarse sieve or purée in a blender. Add the cream and return to the heat. Allow to bubble up, then stir in the horseradish and spices and season to taste.

GARLIC BREAD SAUCE

Much more of a Balkan than a British tradition, although food writer Colin Spencer suggested in a recent *Guardian* article that a garlic-based sauce would be a rather sensible Christmas dinner choice, as garlic is reputed to combat cholesterol. His sauce contained a truly Gallic quantity of garlic – 3 whole heads – and I have an idea this might see off the cholesterol in a single serving, as well as any Boxing Day guests. The following Balkan-style recipe is a touch milder, and can be enriched with a little fresh or soured cream before serving.

6–10 cloves garlic, peeled
5 tablespoons extra virgin olive oil
50g/2oz slightly stale white bread
    without crusts

250ml/8fl oz stock (any type)
salt and pepper

Fry the whole garlic cloves gently in the oil for about 10 minutes. Stir in the bread, then pour in the stock, bring to the boil and simmer for 10 minutes, whisking gently, until the bread has broken up and absorbed the liquid. Sieve or purée the sauce and season to taste. Reheat gently before serving.

AJO BLANCO

This is virtually the same as the base for that extraordinary refreshing soup from Malaga, Pale Almond and Grape Soup (see page 230). It seems appropriate to use sherry vinegar in a sauce that stems from Malaga but there is much to be said for tarragon vinegar, too, particularly if the sauce is to accompany fish. It also goes well with a young broad bean salad or other green beans.

2 cloves garlic, peeled
50g/2oz blanched almonds
pinch of salt
125g/4oz fresh white breadcrumbs

6–9 tablespoons extra virgin olive oil
2 tablespoons sherry vinegar or 3
    tablespoons tarragon wine
    vinegar

Pound or process the garlic, almonds and salt until they form a paste. Moisten the breadcrumbs very lightly with water, then pound or blend them into the paste, adding a few more drops of water if necessary. Very gradually work in the oil as for making mayonnaise, until you reach the consistency you like, then beat in the vinegar. Taste and add more salt if necessary.

SALSA PICCANTE

Italy has its pounded bread sauces, too, and this one comes from Genoa. The Genoese would serve it with regional specialities such as roast capon or herb-simmered beans but it will also give a lift to just about any white or boiled meat, fish or vegetable.

50g/2oz pine nuts
2 tablespoons chopped parsley
1 tablespoon salt-packed capers, rinsed
1 clove garlic, chopped
2 salt-packed anchovies, soaked, filleted and rinsed or 4 anchovy fillets in olive oil, drained

225g/8oz ripe, red tomatoes, peeled, seeded and chopped
125g/4oz fresh white breadcrumbs, soaked in 6 tablespoons red wine vinegar
150ml/5fl oz extra virgin olive oil
salt and pepper

Pound or process together the nuts, parsley, capers, garlic and anchovies. Add the tomatoes and process again, then the vinegar-soaked crumbs. Process once more, then gradually blend in the oil and season to taste.

PIQUANT BREAD SAUCE FOR BAKED FISH

This recipe is adapted from one devised by the modern Finnish chef, Eero Mäkelä. It is excellent with fish baked in butter; place a sprig or two of fresh dill in the belly cavity of the fish before baking.

250ml/8fl oz milk
75g/2½oz stale white bread, broken into small chunks
1 teaspoon Dijon mustard
100ml/3½fl oz crème fraîche
15g/½oz unsalted butter
2 tablespoons liquid from the dill-pickled cucumber

1 medium dill-pickled cucumber, lactic-cured if available, finely diced
1 scant tablespoon freshly grated horseradish or bottled horseradish
3–4 tablespoons finely chopped dill
salt and pepper

Heat the milk to boiling point and pour it over the bread. Set aside for 10–15 minutes until the bread is completely soft, then place the bread and any unabsorbed milk in a food processor or blender. Add the mustard, crème fraîche, butter and cucumber liquid and blend in quick bursts until emulsified. Pour into a saucepan and bring almost to the boil, then stir in the cucumber, horseradish and dill and season to taste. If the sauce seems too thick, dilute with a little more cucumber liquid or milk. Serve hot.

ROMESCO SAUCE

This great Catalan sauce has a hundred variations but the essentials are roasted nuts, oil-fried bread, and mildly hot romesco peppers, available in good delicatessen. Generally used for seafood or as a dressing for tuna salad, it is also well suited to chicken and a variety of vegetables.

2 dried romesco peppers or fresh
   medium-hot chillies
4 fat garlic cloves
5–10 tablespoons extra virgin olive oil,
   plus oil for baking and frying
2 large 'stuffing' tomatoes, such as
   Momotaro or Marmande, or
   200g/7oz can or jar of roasted
   piquillo peppers

50g/2oz white bread without
   crusts
24 hazelnuts, toasted and
   skinned
2–3 sprigs flat-leaf parsley
cayenne, to taste
1 tablespoon sherry vinegar
salt and pepper

If using dried peppers, soak them in a little warm water for a few minutes. Brush the garlic with olive oil (and the tomatoes, if using) and bake at 180°C/350°F/Gas Mark 4 for 15 minutes. Fry the bread in oil until crisp and golden, then drain on kitchen paper.

Grate or grind the hazelnuts separately, then pound or blend them with the dried peppers or fresh chillies, peeled garlic and fried bread. Chop and deseed the tomatoes, or deseed canned peppers, and blend them with the nut and bread paste. Now add the parsley and cayenne, if needed, followed by the vinegar. Season with salt and pepper and gradually incorporate the olive oil, as for mayonnaise, until you obtain a consistency you like. Adjust the seasoning before serving.

MUHAMMARA

This is a splendidly colourful Middle Eastern dip to set beside the paler hummous and taramasalata. For the correct, slightly hot flavour, you will need to secure a large tin of Turkish or Cypriot red pepper purée – remarkably inexpensive and very versatile. Alternatively, use bottled peppers and a touch of cayenne.

The other essential is walnuts that are in no danger of rancidity, so buy from a reliable supplier and check the use-by date on the packet. Finally, pomegranate molasses or syrup: this intriguing condiment is increasingly sold in large stores and delicatessens, and a Middle Eastern shop is virtually guaranteed to have it. It is rather like sour tamarind paste, which you could use as a substitute. Failing all else, use lemon juice to lift the flavour of the dip, perhaps adding a very little honey.

125g/4oz walnuts, lightly toasted
2 plump cloves garlic, crushed to a
    paste with a pinch of salt
200g/7oz red pepper paste (see
    above)
50g/2oz fresh white or brown
    breadcrumbs

2 teaspoons pomegranate
    molasses
1 teaspoon ground cumin
1 tablespoon chopped parsley
150ml/5fl oz extra virgin
    olive oil
salt

Grind or grate the walnuts and mix in the garlic paste. Add the pepper paste, breadcrumbs, pomegranate molasses, cumin and parsley. (All of this can be done in a food processor – use the processor to add the oil, too, as for making mayonnaise.) Add the oil in a slow, steady stream, beating or whisking the mixture while doing so. You can add less oil for a thicker dip or spread, and a little more if you want a sauce-like consistency. Taste and add salt if necessary. Serve with pitta bread or as a sauce for chicken or vegetables.

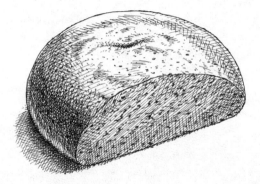

· DESSERTS ·

BASIC BREAD PUDDING

The English bread pudding is one of our most basic and ancient ways of rendering stale bread both palatable and filling. This sweet and sustaining pudding was reputedly most popular in the Midlands and the North of England, or wherever most sustenance was needed at least expense.

Although it can be served hot, with plenty of custard to leaven the density, it would usually be stored in an airtight tin in a cool larder for a couple of days to mature, rather like a fruit cake.

225g/8oz stale white or brown bread
about 300ml/10fl oz water or milk
125g/4oz currants, raisins or sultanas
2 tablespoons dark orange
   marmalade
100g/3½oz soft brown sugar

1 teaspoon mixed spice or vanilla
   extract
1 tablespoon melted butter
1 large or 2 small eggs
demerara sugar, for sprinkling

Break up the bread and cover it in water or milk. Leave for an hour or so until completely soaked through – add more liquid if needed. Crumble up the bread and squeeze it dry, then mash it with a fork until fairly smooth. Beat in the dried fruit, marmalade, sugar, spice or vanilla and butter, followed by the egg. If the mixture is not of a stiff dropping consistency, add a little more water or milk. Turn into a buttered 20cm/8inch square tin, a square roasting dish or a large loaf tin, sprinkle with demerara sugar and bake at 150°C/300°F/Gas Mark 2) for about 1 hour, or until firm.

BARA BRITH BREAD PUDDING

This pudding is a compilation from numerous traditional recipes. Such puddings were popular lunch-box fare for South Wales miners, or the source of pin money for their wives.

350g/12oz wholemeal bara brith,
    sliced or broken into chunks
600ml/1 pint fairly strong cold tea
2 eggs, beaten
1 large or 2 small eating apples, peeled
    and grated

1 teaspoon cinnamon
1 tablespoon light muscovado sugar
1 tablespoon demerara sugar
15g/½oz butter

Soak the bara brith in the tea for about 2 hours or until all the bread is very moist. Drain the bread thoroughly either through a sieve or, to produce a pudding suitable for a miner's lunch-box, by squeezing it dry with your hands. Break up with a fork and stir in the beaten eggs, followed by the apple, cinnamon and muscovado sugar. Spoon the mixture into a greased 900g/2lb loaf tin, which it should fill to a depth of 2.5cm/1inch or so – any baking dish will serve, as long as the final depth of pudding is not much greater than this. Sprinkle the surface with the demerara sugar and dot with the butter. Bake at 140°C/275°F/Gas Mark 1 for 1½ hours or until a skewer inserted in the centre emerges clean and the surface of the pudding begins to crack.

BREAD PUDDING LIÉGEOIS

I don't truly know whether anyone in Liège prepares this particular pudding. I do know that bread puddings are almost as common in Belgium as mussels and chips, and that coffee is just one of a favoured range of bread-soaking liquids, particularly in Liège – *café Liégeois* is world famous as perhaps the last word in iced coffee doused with whipped cream.

This is a nursery pudding for adult palates, dark, aromatic and rather unsweet. Similar in many respects to a British bread pudding, the major difference, richness apart, is that it is eaten hot, while soft and moist-centred.

300–450ml/10–15fl oz very hot
   double-strength ground coffee
225g/8oz slightly stale brioche without
   crust, torn into cubes
1 large egg
90g/3oz light muscovado sugar
1 teaspoon cinnamon

pinch of salt
5 tablespoons thick double cream
75g/2½oz raisins, soaked in 2–3
   tablespoons dark rum for at least
   2 hours
1 tablespoon demerara sugar

Pour the hot black coffee over the brioche: start with the smaller amount of coffee and stir it around; if a number of dry patches of brioche remain visible, add more coffee. Set aside for 2 hours, until the brioche is completely sodden, then tip the mixture into a large sieve and leave to drain for 30 minutes – break the brioche up a little with a fork to help it drain.

Beat the drained brioche with a fork or large spoon until it forms a lumpy paste. Whisk together the egg, muscovado sugar, cinnamon and salt and beat into the brioche paste, then beat in the cream and the rum-soaked raisins. Turn it into a buttered gratin dish and sprinkle with the demerara sugar, then bake at 150°C/300°F/Gas Mark 2 for about 1½ hours, or until a skewer inserted in the centre emerges clean but the pudding is still somewhat soft. Cool for 10 minutes before serving with plenty of cream.

PAIN D'ÉPICES PUDDING

Somewhat spicier and richer than a plain bread pudding, this makes good use of the Dutch honey and spice breads readily obtainable in wholefood shops. Other pains d'épices will also suit; as indeed would the spicy Caribbean bun.

125g/4oz pain d'épices or similar spice
   bread, torn into chunks
zest and juice of 1 orange
125g/4oz stale wholewheat bread,
   torn into chunks
300ml/10fl oz creamy milk
3 tablespoons honey or golden syrup

100g/3½oz muscovado sugar
2 eggs
small pinch of salt
½ teaspoon cinnamon
½ teaspoon ground aniseed
50g/2oz candied orange or citron peel,
   finely diced

Place the spice bread in a mixing bowl and pour over the orange juice made up to 150ml/5fl oz with hot water. After about 5 minutes, break up with a fork. Place the wholewheat bread in a separate bowl. Bring the milk and honey or syrup to the boil and pour this over the wholewheat bread. Set aside until the bread is disintegrating and then break it up with a fork. Combine the two breads.

Whisk together the orange zest, sugar, eggs, salt and spices and work into the bread mixture, then stir in the candied peel. Transfer the mixture to a buttered ovenproof dish and bake at 150°C/300°F/ Gas Mark 2 for about 1 hour or until firm in the centre. Cool, then refrigerate, covered, for 24 hours to allow the flavours to blend and mellow. Serve at room temperature, as a cake or pudding, accompanied by thick cream.

TURKISH BREAD PUDDING WITH MORELLO CHERRIES

Well, yes, this is doubtless best made with fresh morellos but I certainly would not want to forgo such a wonderful pudding simply because I could not buy fresh cherries. Bottled morellos are fine, particularly as the majority are barely noticeably sweetened, and the juice can be used as a syrup base. It *is* important that the cherries are a sour variety, as sweet fruit will not provide sufficient contrast to the syrup-soaked bread.

125g/4oz open-textured crustless white bread, thinly sliced (use Turkish or Greek bread if you have it)
50g/2oz unsalted butter
350g/12oz drained weight of bottled, stoned morello cherries, or stoned fresh cherries

175g/6oz caster sugar if using bottled cherries, 200g/7oz if using fresh cherries
150ml/5fl oz syrup from the cherry jar, or water
300ml/10fl oz double cream, lightly whipped
25g/1oz skinned pistachios or toasted split almonds

Spread the bread with the butter and bake it in the oven at 160°C/ 325°F/Gas Mark 3 until dried out and golden – at least 30 minutes. Arrange the slices in a heatproof dish in a single layer and spoon over the well-drained bottled cherries, if using. Dissolve the sugar in the juice or water, bring to the boil and allow to bubble away for a couple of minutes. Add the fresh cherries, if using, and simmer gently for about 10 minutes, until the cherries have just collapsed. If using bottled cherries, simply simmer the syrup until thick. Pour the syrup (and cherries) over the bread and bake at 160°C/325°F/Gas Mark 3 until the syrup is more or less absorbed – about 20–30 minutes. Leave to cool, then spread the whipped cream over the pudding and sprinkle over the nuts.

BREAD AND BUTTER PUDDING

The original and official nursery pudding – or so claims the book *British Cookery*, produced by Food from Britain and the Tourist Authority. It is far from our most ancient bread pudding – Poor Knights (see page 295) precedes it by several centuries, and instructions for preparing crumb puddings date as far back as the thirteenth century – but bread and butter pudding does have a venerable, three-century pedigree none the less. Here is the basic, simple, rather frugal recipe from which you can develop your own pudding.

8 thin slices slightly stale white bread	50g/2oz caster sugar
50g/2oz butter	300ml/10fl oz milk
50g/2oz currants and sultanas	a few drops of vanilla extract or
2 eggs	rosewater

Butter the bread on one side and slice diagonally in half. Soak the dried fruit in warm water for a few minutes, then drain. Scatter some of the fruit in a buttered pie dish and cover with a layer of bread, butter-side down. Sprinkle with the remaining fruit, then cover with the remaining bread, butter-side up (or make four layers if necessary). Whisk together the eggs and sugar, then whisk in the milk and vanilla extract or rosewater and strain it over the bread. (If you wish, sprinkle surface with extra sugar and dab with butter.) Place in a water bath and bake at 180°C/350°F/Gas Mark 4 for 35 minutes. It should be crisp and golden brown on the top, sides and bottom. Serve hot.

BREAD-NO-BUTTER PUDDING

My name for this favourite pudding, while accurate, could be accused of being misguided. This is blissfully rich and creamy, makes excellent use of rich teabread or brioche and has little to do with frugality. It tastes as good chilled as hot.

125g/4oz sliced fruited or enriched bread, preferably a little stale	50g/2oz caster sugar
2 teaspoons apple and pear spread (from wholefood shops) or 2 tablespoons bitter orange marmalade	*To glaze:*
	1 tablespoon concentrated unsweetened pear juice (from
300ml/10fl oz single cream	wholefood shops) or 2
1 vanilla pod, split	tablespoons bitter orange
3 egg yolks	marmalade, warmed and sieved

Spread the bread with the pear and apple spread or with marmalade and slice diagonally in half. Arrange attractively in a buttered baking dish, spread-side down. Put the cream and vanilla pod in a saucepan, bring slowly to the boil, then remove from the heat and allow to infuse for a few minutes. Remove the pod, but scrape the seeds into the cream. Whisk together the egg yolks and sugar, pour the cream on to this mixture and whisk again, then strain it over the bread. Leave to soak for 1 hour, or for 2 hours if the bread is stale.

Place the dish in a water bath and bake at 150°C/300°F/Gas Mark 2 for 40–45 minutes or until set in the centre. Remove and brush with the pear juice or marmalade. Serve hot, warm or cold.

APPLE-CINNAMON PUDDING

This uses a cinnamon-raisin loaf but for a more rococo effect you could try and find a cinnamon-swirl kosher kuchen, which makes it attractively striated. The maple syrup finish adds yet more gloss and swirl, making a fairly simple pudding perfectly presentable for the smartest dinner party.

350g/12oz flavourful eating apples, such as Cox, peeled, cored and sliced
25g/1oz unsalted butter
125g/4oz cinnamon-raisin loaf, thinly sliced
25g/1oz walnuts or pecans, toasted and chopped

150ml/5fl oz milk
150ml/5fl oz single or whipping cream
½ vanilla pod, split, or ½ teaspoon vanilla extract
5 tablespoons maple syrup
3 egg yolks

Lightly butter a shallow 1 litre/1¾ pint baking dish. Sauté the sliced apples gently in the butter until very tender but not disintegrating, shaking the pan from time to time to prevent sticking. Cut the cinnamon bread into triangles or circles, depending on the shape of the loaf, and arrange it in the dish, interspersed with the apples and nuts. Pour the milk and cream into a saucepan, add the vanilla pod, if using and bring slowly to the boil. Whisk together 4 tablespoons of the maple syrup, the egg yolks, vanilla extract, if using, and the hot milk and strain it over the bread and apple mixture. Set aside for 1–2 hours while the bread soaks up the liquid, pressing it lightly once or twice to submerge the bread. Put the baking dish in a water bath, then bake at 180°C/350°F/Gas Mark 4 for about 30 minutes, or until the custard is just set. Remove the dish from the oven and swirl the remaining maple syrup over the surface of the pudding. Serve hot.

CREOLE BREAD PUDDING

This is adult fare, and for a somewhat indulgent occasion: the quantities of butter, cream, egg, sugar and bourbon are rather immodest. Keep the first course a light one as this pudding and its sauce are best consumed at a single sitting.

When nectarines or peaches are not in season, well-drained bottled or canned fruit works well. Use the syrup to make up part of the liquid for the sauce and cut down on the sugar proportionately.

225g/8oz baguette or *pain Parisien,*
    cut into slices 1.2cm/½inch thick
50g/2oz raisins, soaked in 2
    tablespoons bourbon or whisky
    for at least 2 hours
2 large nectarines or peaches, stoned
    and sliced
300ml/10fl oz milk
150ml/5fl oz single cream
50g/2oz unsalted butter
2 eggs plus 1 egg yolk
125g/4oz caster sugar
1 teaspoon vanilla extract

¼ teaspoon almond extract
1 teaspoon cinnamon
¼ teaspoon grated nutmeg

For the sauce:
300ml/10fl oz single cream
100g/3½oz caster sugar
1 tablespoon cornflour
4 tablespoons bourbon
¼ teaspoon grated nutmeg
½ teaspoon vanilla extract
1 egg yolk

Arrange the bread in a single overlapping layer in a buttered gratin dish. Scatter the raisins over the bread and tuck the nectarines or peaches in amongst the slices. Heat the milk, cream and butter in a saucepan until just coming to the boil. Whisk together the eggs, yolk, sugar and flavourings, pour the hot milk on to the eggs, whisking all the time, then strain this custard over the bread. Set aside for 1–2 hours to allow the bread to soak up the liquid, pressing the bread down into the liquid from time to time.

Place the gratin dish in a water bath and bake at 150°C/300°F/Gas Mark 2 for 45–60 minutes or until the custard is firm in the centre and the tops of the bread slices browned.

Make the sauce shortly before serving the pudding. Heat the cream and sugar in a small saucepan until bubbling. Dissolve the cornflour in half the bourbon and stir briskly into the bubbling liquid, then bring back to the boil and simmer for 2 minutes or until thickened. Stir in the nutmeg and vanilla, then whisk in the egg yolk along with the rest of the bourbon. Heat through, but do not allow the sauce to boil.

Serve the pudding straight from the oven with the piping hot sauce.

CHOCOLATE CROISSANT PUDDING WITH WARM RASPBERRY SAUCE

You could use an enriched light bread instead of croissants for this undeniably rich yet irresistibly light pudding. Good, light brioche, bridge rolls or the less usual *panquemado* or *zopf* will all be fine. It's definitely at its best warm, and enticing enough without the sauce, though this adds a refreshingly sharp element.

125g/4oz stale croissants, sliced into rounds about 2.5cm/1 inch thick
100g/3½oz good-quality bitter chocolate
1–2 tablespoons rum (optional)
300ml/10fl oz milk
150ml/5fl oz double cream
1 vanilla pod or ½ teaspoon vanilla extract

2 eggs plus 2 egg yolks
50g/2oz light muscovado sugar
icing sugar, for dusting

For the raspberry sauce:
225g/8oz frozen raspberries
25g/1oz icing sugar
1–2 tablespoons framboise liqueur (optional)

Arrange the croissants loosely in a buttered ovenproof baking dish or soufflé dish. Melt the chocolate in a bowl set over a pan of hot water, or in the microwave, then stir in the rum, if using. Slowly bring to the boil the milk, cream and vanilla pod, if using, remove from the heat and leave to infuse if time allows. Whisk together the eggs, yolks and muscovado sugar until thick, pour in the milk and the vanilla extract, if using, then finally whisk in the melted chocolate. Strain the chocolate custard over the croissants and leave to soak for about 30 minutes, pressing the croissants below the surface of the liquid from time to time. Place the baking dish in a water bath and bake at 150°C/300°F/Gas Mark 2 for 45–60 minutes or until the pudding is set in the centre.

To make the sauce, stir the raspberries with the sugar and warm them gently (I find the microwave useful for this but a saucepan over the lowest possible flame will be fine) until the raspberries have just collapsed and the juices have started to run. Mash with a fork and press through a sieve into a clean saucepan or a microwave-proof serving jug. Stir in the liqueur, if using.

When the pudding is done, warm the sauce gently. Dust the pudding lightly with icing sugar and serve with the raspberry sauce, and cream for the figure-unconscious.

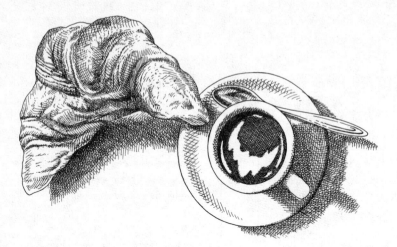

Austro-Hungarian Croissant Pudding

In memory of the Vienna/Budapest siege stories. At first glance the pudding seems a riot of flavours and textures, and dauntingly rich – but the result is light and billowy as a goosedown pillow, none too sweet, with a hint of spice and tart-edged fruit. Dried sour cherries are available from delicatessens and some large supermarkets.

100g/3½oz walnuts, grated or ground	600ml/1 pint milk
1 teaspoon cinnamon	3 large eggs, separated
4 tablespoons apricot conserve	100g/3½oz caster sugar
225g/8oz slightly stale croissants	½ teaspoon vanilla extract
75g/2½oz dried sour cherries, soaked in 3 tablespoons rum for at least 2 hours	150ml/5fl oz single cream
	pinch of salt

Mix together the nuts, cinnamon and 2 tablespoons of the apricot conserve, then slice open the croissants and spread this paste over them. Sandwich the croissants together again, slice them into 6 or 8 pieces and arrange them in a lightly buttered shallow baking dish just large enough to hold the croissants in a single layer. Press the soaked cherries between the slices, reserving any surplus rum.

Bring the milk to the boil and remove from the heat. Whisk together the egg yolks, sugar, vanilla and any reserved rum, then pour the hot milk into the egg mixture and whisk again. Strain this custard over the croissants and set aside for 30 minutes.

Shortly before baking, pour the cream over the pudding. Bake at 150°C/300°F/Gas Mark 2 for about 45 minutes, until the custard is almost set in the centre.

Gently heat the remaining apricot conserve and then strain it. Whisk the egg whites with the salt until fairly stiff, fold in the strained conserve and whisk again until stiff. Spoon this meringue over the pudding and return to the oven for a further 15–20 minutes, until just coloured. Serve shortly after removing from the oven.

DOUBLE CHOCOLATE PUDDINGS WITH BLUEBERRIES AND PECANS

These are very rich but far from overwhelming when served in individual pots. They are equally good hot or cold, and have the advantage of unmoulding easily once chilled, particularily if you use non-stick timbale moulds, which I find endlessly useful.

100g/3½oz chocolate bread, cut into small cubes
25g/1oz pecan nuts, broken
75g/2½oz fresh blueberries
100g/3½oz good–quality bitter chocolate, chopped into small chunks

300ml/10fl oz single cream
1 vanilla pod, split or ½ teaspoon vanilla extract
1 egg plus 2 egg yolks
100g/3½oz caster sugar

Divide the bread, nuts, blueberries and chocolate between 4 buttered ovenproof dishes, each about 200–250ml/7–8fl oz in capacity. Bring the cream slowly to the boil with the vanilla pod, if using, then remove from the heat and leave to infuse for a few minutes if time allows. Whisk together the eggs yolks and sugar until pale. Scrape some of the vanilla seeds into the cream and remove the pod, or add vanilla extract if using, and whisk the hot cream into the egg mixture. Strain the custard over the contents of the 4 dishes and set aside for 30 minutes, pressing the bread below the surface of the custard from time to time.

Put the dishes in a water bath and bake at 160°C/325°F/Gas Mark 3 for about 25 minutes, until the puddings are firm in the centre. Remove from the oven but leave in the water bath for 5 minutes. Serve hot, warm or chilled, perhaps with a little crème fraîche.

Variation

Substitute white or brown bread for the chocolate bread, and, instead of blueberries and pecans, use 75g/2½oz ready-to-eat dried apricots, soaked in 2 tablespoons rum for at least 2 hours.

MEXICAN SWEET AND SAVOURY BREAD PUDDING

Unlikely as this eggless bread pudding sounds, its constituent elements are little different from the currently fashionable cheese-and-dessert course of ripe pears, dolcelatte cheese and bread. You could substitute apples and apple juice for the pears, or (arguably closer to the original), omit fresh fruit altogether but use citrus juices to cut through the richness. This is simply my favourite version. For the pear juice, I use a concentrate I buy at wholefood stores and make up a fairly strong solution.

175g/6oz stale, light-textured white bread without crust, torn into small chunks
50g/2oz pine nuts
125g/4oz dark muscovado or molasses sugar
450ml/15fl oz pear juice (see above)
1 cinnamon stick
1 blade of mace

6 cloves
50g/2oz raisins
50g/2oz unsalted butter
150ml/5fl oz whipping or single cream
125g/4oz farmhouse Cheddar cheese, finely grated
350g/12oz pears, peeled, cored and cubed

Roast the bread in the oven at 200°C/400°F/Gas Mark 6 until golden brown – about 15 minutes. Toast the pine nuts at the same time for 5–7 minutes. Place the toasted bread and nuts in a mixing bowl.

Put the sugar and pear juice in a pan and heat gently until dissolved. For easy retrieval, tie the spices in a square of muslin, then add them to the pan along with the raisins and simmer for about 10 minutes. Remove from the heat and discard the spices.

Add the butter to the pan and stir until it has dissolved, then stir in the cream. Pour this mixture over the bread and nuts. Leave to stand for 10 minutes, then add most of the grated cheese and stir very gently.

Scatter the pear cubes into a well-buttered wide baking dish (earthenware or stoneware has the right look to it), transfer the bread mixture to the dish and sprinkle the surface with the remaining cheese. Bake, covered, at 190°C/375°F/Gas Mark 5 for 20 minutes, then remove the lid and bake for a further 15 minutes to allow the bread and cheese to crisp a little. Serve hot or warm, with cream or yoghurt. Leftovers can be refrigerated and served chilled if you wish, or microwaved briefly to warm.

BRIOCHE DIPLOMATE

The easiest tin to use for this pâtisserie classic is a non-stick charlotte mould with sloping sides; the most fun would be one of those turreted Edwardian constructions. Neither is particularly easy to find but you could use an ice-cream 'bombe' mould or a 900g/2lb non-stick loaf tin and decorate the turned-out Diplomate accordingly. The ideal capacity for the quantities below is 1.75 litres/3 pints.

225g/8oz slightly stale brioche without crust, cut into 1.2cm/½inch cubes
150g/5oz candied fruits and natural-dye glacé cherries, finely diced and soaked in 3 tablespoons dark rum for at least 2 hours
600ml/1 pint creamy milk
4 eggs plus 2 egg yolks
150g/5oz caster sugar
1 teaspoon vanilla extract

To glaze and decorate:
125g/4oz apricot conserve
1–2 tablespoons dark rum
25g/1oz candied fruits or pistachio nuts, finely chopped

Place a layer of the brioche cubes in the base of your chosen mould. Scatter some of the candied fruits over the brioche, reserving any unabsorbed rum, and cover with a second layer of brioche cubes. Repeat until the fruit and bread are used up.

Heat the milk to boiling point. Whisk together eggs, egg yolks, sugar, vanilla and any reserved rum. Pour the hot milk on to the egg mixture and whisk again, then strain this custard into the mould and set aside for 30 minutes, pressing down on the surface from time to time to encourage the bread to absorb the custard. Place the mould in a water bath (the water should reach at least halfway up the filled mould) and bake, uncovered, at 150°C/300°F/Gas Mark 2 for 45–60 minutes or until the pudding is just set – a skewer inserted in the centre should emerge clean. Remove from the oven, cool to room temperature, then chill before unmoulding and glazing.

To neaten and flatten the base, trim off any protruding bread if necessary. Run a knife around the sides of the mould and turn the Diplomate out on to a serving plate. Warm the apricot conserve and rum together in a saucepan, stirring. Strain it through a fine sieve and allow to cool a little, then brush it over the unmoulded Diplomate. Decorate with the candied fruit or pistachios and serve soon after glazing. (The unglazed pudding will keep in the fridge, still in its mould, for about 3 days.)

PANETTONE AND GLACÉ FRUIT PUDDING

A useful Christmas pudding, or perhaps even more welcome in February when leftover panettone has dried out and bargain candied fruits picked up at January sales still sit challengingly on the shelves. Fruits bottled in spirits are just as appropriate, and a good, brandied mincemeat will serve. With such intrinsic richness, this pudding will easily stretch to serve 6 or even 8.

150g/5oz panettone or pandoro
125–175g/4–6oz glacé fruits, liqueur
    fruits or mincemeat, soaked in 2
    tablespoons rum or brandy for at
    least 2 hours
150ml/5fl oz thick double cream or
    mascarpone cheese

300ml/10fl oz full cream milk
1 egg plus 2 egg yolks
50g/2oz caster sugar
½ teaspoon vanilla extract
extra rum or liqueur, for sprinkling
    (optional)
icing sugar, for dusting

Cut the panettone roughly into triangles – you could just use rough chunks if your leftover panettone is too bitty to slice. Dice the fruit as necessary. Butter a 1.2 litre (2 pint) baking dish and layer the panettone with spoonfuls of the fruit or mincemeat. Heat the cream or mascarpone and milk together until nearly boiling. Whisk together the egg, yolks, sugar and vanilla, pour on the hot milk mixture and whisk again. Strain the hot custard over the panettone and set aside for 1–2 hours, pressing the bread down gently from time to time to submerge it.

Place the dish in a water bath and bake in the centre of the oven at 150°C/300°F/Gas Mark 2 for about 40 minutes, until set in the centre. Sprinkle with rum or liqueur, if liked, and dust with a little icing sugar before serving hot, warm or cold.

CANARY AND CASTLE PUDDINGS

Serves 4–8
This is a sound, basic pudding mix you can adapt for all kinds of variations. Flour and breadcrumbs are used in equal proportions here for a rich but light result.

The name Canary probably refers to the use of Canary Islands wine (later Madeira) as a flavouring. Castle puddings use exactly the same sponge mixture but the puddings are steamed in individual dariole or timbale moulds.

125g/4oz softened unsalted butter

125g/4oz caster sugar or light
muscovado sugar

¼ teaspoon (or to taste) flavouring of
choice: vanilla, spice or lemon
zest

2 large eggs

50g/2oz self-raising flour

50g/2oz soft white breadcrumbs

pinch of salt (optional)

about 2 tablespoons Madeira or
sherry (or milk or water)

6 tablespoons red jam or jelly, or
marmalade

Butter a 1.2 litre/2 pint pudding basin, two 600 ml/1 pint basins or
6–8 individual ones. Cream the butter and sugar together until light
and fluffy. Stir in the flavouring and gradually beat in the eggs. Sift
the flour and mix it in gently, along with the breadcrumbs and salt
(omit this if the bread is salty). Stir in your chosen liquid to give a
soft dropping consistency (the mixture should drop readily from a
spoon).

Spoon the jam or marmalade into the pudding basins and spoon
the sponge mixture on top; the basins should be about two thirds full
to allow room for expansion. Either cover with a lid (for plastic
basins) or with a layer of greaseproof, folded over to give a 2.5cm/
1inch pleat and securely tied round the rim of the basin with string,
followed by a layer of foil pleated and tied in the same way.

Place the pudding or puddings on a rack or on a folded dish cloth
in a large pan of boiling water – the water should reach no more than
half way up the sides of the basin. Steam large puddings for 1½
hours – though up to an hour extra won't harm – and small
ones for about 40 minutes. Check the water level occasionally and, if
necessary, top up with hot water. Serve hot with custard, jam or fruit
sauce.

Variation: Glister Pudding

For this Dundee speciality, use a dark chunky orange marmalade to
cap the pudding, chopping up the peel a little. A small pinch of
ginger and a little grated orange zest should be added to the sponge
mixture.

VICTORIAN CHOCOLATE PUDDING

In its simplest form, this was made from a milk-soaked loaf with
grated chocolate and a little sweetening added – a good invalid's
pudding! This version is a little more indulgent but still very light
and fluffy, as long as it is made with a good, well-risen loaf.
Although it shrinks like a soufflé when cold, it tastes absolutely fine

and would make a good accompaniment to poached apricots, pears or pineapple.

75g/2½oz good-quality bitter chocolate
50g/2oz unsalted butter
175g/6oz slightly stale, white bread without crusts, broken into small chunks
450ml/15fl oz milk

50g/2oz light or dark muscovado sugar
1 vanilla pod or ½ teaspoon vanilla extract
2 eggs, separated
pinch of salt

Melt the chocolate and butter in a bowl over a pan of very hot water or in the microwave. Put the bread in a mixing bowl. Slowly bring the milk, sugar and vanilla pod, if using, almost to boiling point and strain it over the bread, adding the vanilla extract now, if using. Leave to stand for 10–15 minutes, then break up the bread with a fork. Beat in the egg yolks, followed by the melted chocolate mixture.

Whisk the egg whites with the salt until fairly stiff and fold gently into the pudding mixture. Tip into a buttered 1.2 litre/2 pint pudding basin and cover with a lid or with pleated greaseproof paper and foil. Steam in the usual way for 1½ hours (see Canary and Castle Puddings on page 290) and serve hot with pouring cream or with chocolate sauce (see page 293).

TRIPLE GINGER PUDDING

An old favourite in a new guise, strictly for ginger lovers. I feel wholewheat breadcrumbs match the assertiveness of the ginger better than white, and you could use wholewheat flour, too. This pudding suits a wide range of sauces, from low-fat fromage frais to crème fraîche, pouring cream, vanilla ice cream, orange-flavoured custard or an orange and whisky sauce.

100g/3½oz unsalted butter
100g/3½oz soft brown sugar
2 eggs
125g/4oz fresh wholewheat breadcrumbs
50g/2oz plain flour
1 teaspoon baking powder
small pinch of salt

1 teaspoon ground ginger
1 tablespoon grated fresh ginger root
50g/2oz preserved stem ginger
1 tablespoon syrup from the ginger jar
zest and juice of 1 orange
2 tablespoons whisky, brandy or orange liqueur

Cream together the butter and sugar until light and fluffy, then gradually beat in the eggs. Stir in the breadcrumbs and then sift in the flour with the baking powder, salt and ground ginger. Add the ginger root, stem ginger, syrup, orange zest and juice and alcohol, stirring well. If the pudding does not have a soft dropping consistency stir in a little water. Spoon into a buttered 1.2 litre/2 pint pudding basin, cover and steam for 1½–2 hours in the usual way (see Canary and Castle Puddings on page 290). Serve hot with one of the sauces suggested above. This could also be made in individual dariole moulds and steamed for 30 minutes.

VIENNESE COFFEE PUDDING WITH CHOCOLATE SAUCE

As light, sophisticated and elegant as a steamed pudding can be, this is definitely closer to Vienna coffee house than British nursery fare.

150ml/5fl oz freshly made strong black coffee

100g/3½oz slightly stale Vienna bread, milk bread, or fine white bread without crusts, cut into small cubes

100g/3½oz softened unsalted butter

100g/3½oz caster sugar

4 eggs, separated

75g/2½oz toasted hazelnuts, ground

pinch of salt

For the sauce:

175g/6oz dark bitter chocolate with a high cocoa content

300ml/10fl oz water

25–50g/1–2oz icing sugar

dash of rum

Pour the coffee over the bread, leave to stand for 10–15 minutes, then break up with a fork. Cream together the butter and sugar until pale and fluffy, then slowly beat in the egg yolks, alternately with the ground hazelnuts. Stir in the coffee-soaked bread. Whisk the egg whites with the pinch of salt until stiff and fold them into the mixture. Spoon into a buttered 1.2 litre/2 pint pudding basin and steam in the usual way for 45 minutes (see Canary and Castle Puddings on page 290).

To make the sauce, melt the chocolate with the water and icing sugar to taste in a bowl set over a pan of very hot water or in a microwave, stirring from time to time, until a smooth sauce is formed. Stir in a dash of rum and serve the hot pudding with the warm sauce and cold pouring cream.

FLOURLESS CHRISTMAS PUDDING

This is a light pudding, not one for suet-loving traditionalists. It has been a personal and family favourite for a number of years – all that varies is the nature of the fruit, which depends on the availability of semi-dried Agen prunes, dried sour cherries, or some other exotic import.

225g/8oz stoned muscatel raisins
225g/8oz vostizza currants
225g/8oz moist dried fruits, such as
    apricots, prunes or sour cherries,
    finely diced
125g/4oz candied citrus peel, finely
    diced
50g/2oz natural-dye glacé cherries,
    halved
50g/2oz pecans, finely chopped

50g/2oz dark muscovado sugar
1 teaspoon cinnamon
1 teaspoon mixed spice
175g/6oz fresh breadcrumbs
50g/2oz ground almonds or crushed
    ratafias
3 large or 4 small eggs
150ml/5fl oz port or sweet Marsala
5 tablespoons rum or brandy
1 eating apple, peeled and grated

Place all the dry ingredients in a large bowl and mix together thoroughly. Whisk together the eggs and alcohol and add to the dry ingredients along with the apple. Mix well and then leave to stand overnight. Butter a 1.75 litre/3 pint pudding basin (or three 600ml/ 1 pint basins or six 300ml/½ pint ones) and place a circle of baking parchment in the bottom. Press the pudding mixture into the basin(s) to within 2.5cm/1inch of the rim for large basins or 1.2cm/½inch for small basins. Cover and steam gently in the usual way (see Canary and Castle Puddings, page 290) for 5 hours, regardless of basin size.

Allow the puddings to cool completely, then discard the foil and greaseproof paper covering and feed with a little more alcohol if you like before covering with fresh layers of greaseproof and foil. The puddings are then ready to steam – 2 hours in the same manner – just before serving.

INVALID PLUM PUDDING

The digestion-challenging properties of the traditional British Christmas pudding have long been recognised and were of particular concern to the Victorians, who devised numerous alternatives for those of weak constitution. This positively delicious alternative is of a slightly later era: it was noted by Florence Irwin, an enterprising Irish cook who undertook a career as travelling domestic science instructor in County Down just after the turn of the century. The recipes she collected from country people were eventually compiled in book form and published in 1949 under the title *The Cookin' Woman*. This is something of an interpretation; instructions by Miss Irwin are in quotes.

25g/1oz granulated sugar	90g/3oz sultanas
300ml/10fl oz milk	grated zest of ½ lemon
150g/5oz slightly stale white or brown bread, finely diced	3 large eggs, beaten
90g/3oz caster sugar	3 tablespoons sherry
50g/2oz candied peel, finely diced	5 tablespoons double cream

In a small saucepan dissolve the sugar in 1 tablespoon of water and boil rapidly to form a caramel. The moment the syrup becomes dark and smells of toffee remove it from the heat and, standing back, pour in the milk. Whisk over a gentle heat until the caramel is completely dissolved. 'It should look like strong breakfast coffee.'

Put the bread in a mixing bowl with the sugar, candied peel, sultanas and lemon zest. Whisk together the caramel-milk, eggs and sherry and strain over the bread. Set aside for an hour to soak, then lightly whip the cream and fold it into the mixture. Spoon into a buttered 1.2 litre/2 pint pudding basin, cover and 'steam very slowly as you would a custard till firm – about 1 hour'. If you want a particularly delicate effect it would be better to bake the pudding in a water bath at 160°C/325°F/Gas Mark 3 for about an hour.

Miss Irwin suggests accompanying this with 'German sauce', which is a light sherry sabayon, but perhaps the Invalid might be permitted a little brandy butter at this stage; pouring cream would also be fine.

PAIN PERDU
(Poor Knights of Windsor, Eggy Bread)

Pain Perdu ('lost bread') is the name the French have always given to this favourite way of turning stale bread into a delicious treat. The earliest written record of 'Payn Pur-Dew' in Britain dates from 1420 and specifies 'fair yolks of eggs', 'fair bread' and 'fair butter that is clarified' – in other words, the best of everything. A number of writers attribute the recipe to Berkshire, and suggest that a joke at the expense of the local knights occasioned the English name. In Georgian times, according to Sara Paston-Williams, the dish was known as Spanish fritters, and the recipe she cites in *The National Trust Book of Traditional Puddings* includes sherry, as do a number of other versions. French toast is how the dish is known in the United

States but the British have been reluctant to concede Gallic influence and 'cream toast' or 'fried toast' have been our alternative names. I rather like the 'eggy bread' cited by Arabella Boxer in her *Book of English Food*.

Here is the basic formula. Sweet white wine or medium sweet sherry can replace part of the milk; and you can substitute 3 egg yolks for the whole eggs, if you prefer.

6 slices day-old white bread, crusts removed	50g/2oz clarified butter (see page 178)
2 eggs	*To serve:*
1 tablespoon caster sugar or vanilla sugar	caster sugar
	cinnamon
200ml/7fl oz milk, or milk and cream mixed	jam sauce (see below) or syrup
	whipped cream (optional)

Cut the bread into quarters or fingers. Beat together the eggs, sugar and milk and either pour this mixture over the bread or dip each slice into it. Melt half the butter in a large frying pan and fry half the bread until golden (but not brown) on both sides. Remove from the pan and repeat with the remaining butter and bread. Arrange the fried bread in a warm serving dish and sprinkle with sugar and cinnamon. Serve with jam sauce, syrup and/or whipped cream.

Jam Sauce

Put 225g/8oz apricot, blackberry or red fruit jam in a pan with 2–3 tablespoons water and 1 tablespoon lemon juice and heat gently, stirring well. Strain through a sieve if you like, then reheat and add 1 tablespoon rum or brandy. If it is very thick, dilute with a little more water.

Arabella Boxer's Raisin Sauce

A very rich, but very good sauce for plainer versions of 'eggy bread'. Put 4 tablespoons raisins, 2 tablespoons sugar and 15g/½oz butter in a small saucepan with 150ml/5fl oz water. Simmer gently for 10 minutes until the raisins are plump, then set aside until just before serving. Reheat the sauce, then stir in 1 tablespoon brandy and 2 tablespoons double cream. Serve in a sauceboat.

PAIN D'ÉPICES PERDU

This is based on a dessert I enjoyed immensely at a restaurant in Paris, called L'Oulette. It plays on the ever-popular conceit of serving an egg-based sauce in the emptied (and tidily trimmed) egg shell, as though you are dipping your food into soft-boiled egg yolk. If you can be bothered to wash and dry the shells and trim away any crumbled bits of shell, this is great fun – it seems to bring out childish delight in just about everyone.

225g/8oz (about 16 small slices) pain
  d'épices
2 eggs
150ml/5fl oz creamy milk
1 tablespoon caster sugar
½ teaspoon vanilla extract
50g/2oz clarified butter (see page 178)
cinnamon, for sprinkling

For the custard:
250ml/8fl oz creamy milk or single
  cream
½ vanilla pod
2–3 cardamom pods, lightly crushed
4 large egg yolks
50g/2oz caster sugar

To prepare the custard sauce, put the milk or cream in a pan with the vanilla and cardamom, heat slowly almost to boiling point and, if time allows, leave to infuse for 10 minutes. Whisk together the yolks and sugar and then strain the hot milk over them. Whisk again, then return the mixture to the rinsed-out pan and cook over a very low heat, stirring constantly, until the custard has thickened sufficiently to coat the back of a wooden spoon lightly. Strain into a jug.

Cut each slice of pain d'épices into 2 or 3 soldiers. Whisk together the eggs, milk, sugar and vanilla and dip the bread into the mixture, shaking off any surplus. Fry in the clarified butter in as many batches as necessary, until the bread is golden brown on both sides.

Place egg shells (see above) into egg cups, or rest them on napkin rings, and fill with the custard, then sprinkle cinnamon over each one. (If you prefer not to fiddle with the shells, use small glasses or ramekins rather than miss out the custard altogether.)

Place the filled shells in the centre of large, warmed dinner plates and surround with the pain d'épices soldiers, in a wheel-spoke arrangement.

SUMMER PUDDING

The great bread-based pudding of summer months, which really needs no recipe, just a basic guide to quantities. Somehow the simplest of dishes arouse the greatest controversy: opinions on the most authentic or simply the best summer pudding are heated. Elizabeth David insisted on raspberries and redcurrants only, and no water; Jane Grigson agreed with the notion of raspberries and redcurrants in the proportion of 4:1. Lizzie Boyd, charting British cookery for the British Tourist Authority, traced the pudding's origin to the eighteenth century, when it was served to spa patients forbidden pastry, and averred that any ripe berries could be used. The accommodating and original Jeremy Round admitted cherries and English plums, and also suggested a curiously pale version with white currants, dessert gooseberries and yellow raspberries.

The bread is, of course, supremely important. It need not be hand baked – some widely distributed, organic-flour, ready-sliced white loaves are actually perfect for the job – but it does need to be well made, and in no danger of turning into slime once damp. If the pudding contains a fair proportion of blackcurrants or blackberries, I feel it can happily cope with wholewheat bread (but not granary, multigrain or walnut, where the grain or nuts turn soggy and chewy).

It is a good idea to make a quick purée from frozen raspberries and a little sugar to pour over the unmoulded pudding if you are worried there might not be enough juice from the fruit.

about 750g/1½lb mixed soft fruit, with black or redcurrants playing a minor role
50–100g/2–3½oz caster sugar

6–10 fairly thick slices good white or wholewheat bread, crusts removed

Rinse and pick over the fruit. Place any blackcurrants in a heavy-based saucepan with the lesser amount of sugar and 1–2 tablespoons water. Cook gently for 5 minutes until the juices start to run, then add the remaining fruit and simmer for 5 minutes more. Taste for sugar and add more as needed, stirring gently until dissolved.

Line a 1.2 litre/2 pint pudding basin or soufflé dish with the bread. This should be cut to fit the base and sides exactly, which means that for a pudding basin you will need to cut triangular slices.

Use a slotted spoon to transfer the fruit to the pudding basin, adding enough juice to saturate the bread case (reserve the remaining juice). If you like, you can add a middle layer of bread (a useful idea if you find you have insufficient fruit to fill the basin); this makes the structure of the finished pudding a little more firm. When the basin is full, cover with more bread cut to fit and spoon over a little more juice. Cover the pudding with a plate that just fits, and place a heavy weight on the plate. Refrigerate overnight, preferably for 24 hours.

When ready to unmould the pudding, run the blade of a knife round the rim, place a deep dish or soup plate over the top, invert and shake gently to loosen. Spoon the reserved juice over the top of the pudding, making sure to cover any pale patches. If you have a good deal of leftover juice, you could thicken it with a little arrowroot and serve separately in a jug. Just about any style of cream can be served with the pudding, from thin pouring cream to thick clotted.

FILLED PANETTONE PUDDING

Serves 8–12

This is the perfect alternative to a traditional Christmas pudding – light, chilled, ready to serve at any stage, yet colourful and festive. Unlike that richest of steamed puddings it is also a suitable treat for any time of year, although you might reflect the season in your choice of fruit, using firm, fresh fruits and berries in the summer months.

As both panettone and pandoro are produced in a variety of sizes, you should be able to find a bread appropriate to the size of your party; the very smallest examples (around 100g/3½oz) can be used to make individual puddings for everyone. A rough guide that I use to estimate quantities of filling is equal weight of ricotta plus mascarpone to the original weight of the bread.

1 × 500g/1lb 2oz panettone or pandoro
250g/8½oz mascarpone cheese
250g/8½oz ricotta cheese
3 tablespoons sweetened chestnut purée
100g/3½oz caster sugar, or to taste
zest of 1 lemon
zest of 1 small orange
½ teaspoon cinnamon
½ teaspoon vanilla extract
1 tablespoon orange flower water

50g/2oz candied citrus peel, diced
50g/2oz natural-dye angelica, diced
50g/2oz natural-dye glacé cherries, diced
50g/2oz pistachio nuts, chopped
50g/2oz good-quality plain chocolate, chopped
2–3 tablespoons maraschino liqueur, kirsch or cointreau
icing sugar and cocoa powder, for dusting

Slice a 2.5cm/1inch lid off the bread and scoop out the centre to within 2.5cm/1inch of the edges (use this for Panettone and Glacé Fruit Pudding, page 290). Beat the mascarpone and ricotta until smooth, then beat in all the filling ingredients in the order given, tasting for sugar, citrus and alcohol balance and adjusting the flavours as needed. Pile the filling into the hollowed-out panettone and replace the lid. If you have excavated too enthusiastically and are left with a gap at the top you could pack back in some of the discarded centre, or top up with fresh fruit or a contrasting layer of mascarpone or ricotta, perhaps blended with coffee or chocolate. Chill for at least 2 hours and sift icing sugar and cocoa powder over the cake just before serving. If it's Christmas, top the filled panettone with a sprig of holly.

FRUIT-FILLED BRIOCHE BUNS

A French equivalent, perhaps, of strawberry shortcake, but these have a distinct advantage – they are easier to transport to a summer picnic. They also serve as a quick dessert. Frozen brioches defrost quite quickly, particularly if placed briefly in a warm oven or in the microwave on defrost setting, so it is worth having a small batch to hand in the freezer.

6 small (40g/1½oz) or 4 medium (75g/2½oz) 'top-knot' brioche buns

225g/8oz fresh raspberries

4 tablespoons soft-set strawberry jam strained, or raspberry or redcurrant jelly

1 heaped teaspoon per brioche of very thick or whipped Jersey cream

icing sugar, for dusting (optional)

raspberry sauce (see page 301)

Pull the top knots off each brioche and hollow them out slightly. Remove a good portion of crumb from the main part of the brioche but make sure that the sides are a good 6mm/¼inch thick. Gently stir together the raspberries and strained preserve or jelly and spoon them into the brioche shells – the level of the filling should fall just below the shoulder of each brioche. Spoon the cream into the centre of each one and press the hollowed top knots over the cream. Wrap for transporting to a picnic. If serving at dinner, dust the top of each brioche with a little icing sugar and serve with the raspberry sauce.

PEACH SOUFFLÉ

Unlike savoury soufflés, hot fruit soufflés are often made without any thickening, stabilising roux base. Although this ensures lightness and delicacy it also tends to make them rather fragile and prone to rapid collapse; adding bread to the mixture helps to stabilise the structure without weighing down the fruit. Although the bread is softened by soaking, it should be reasonably fresh, fine and flavourful in its own right.

150ml/5fl oz double cream
50g/2oz brioche crumbs or other enriched bread crumbs
100g/3½oz vanilla sugar
300ml/10fl oz rosé wine, white wine or water, or a mixture
4 ripe firm peaches, halved and stoned

1–2 tablespoons peach brandy, kirsch or other eau-de-vie
3 eggs, separated
2 tablespoons caster sugar
pinch of salt
1 tablespoon dried breadcrumbs
icing sugar, for dusting

Put the cream in a pan and heat it almost to boiling point, then remove from the heat, pour it over the crumbs and set aside. Put the vanilla sugar and wine or water in a pan and bring to the boil, stirring from time to time, then simmer, without stirring, for 3 minutes. Add the peaches and simmer very gently until just tender, then drain and leave to cool. Slip the skins off the peaches and purée the fruit in a blender, or simply sieve it.

Combine the crumb mixture and peach purée and add the alcohol. Whisk the egg yolks with half the caster sugar and stir them into the peach mixture. Whisk the whites with a pinch of salt until fairly stiff, then whisk in the remaining sugar. Stir a spoonful of the whites into the peach mixture, then gently fold in the remaining whites. Transfer the mixture to a buttered 1 litre/1¾ pint soufflé or baking dish that has been dusted with the dried breadcrumbs. Bake at 200°C/400°F/ Gas Mark 6 for 20–25 minutes until well risen and brown. Dust the surface with icing sugar and serve immediately.

Raspberry Sauce

The ideal accompaniment for this soufflé is a raspberry sauce or coulis: heat 225g/8oz fresh or frozen raspberries in 150ml/5fl oz of the peach poaching syrup, then purée and sieve. Serve warm or chilled.

FRIAR'S OMELETTE

This has little to do with monastic orders and rather a lot to do with fifteenth-century froise, fraise or frayse, which was a shallow-fried fritter made with fruit, bacon, meat and vegetables – a hash of leftovers, one suspects. Somewhere along the line – certainly by Edwardian times – the batter was lightened, with breadcrumbs replacing flour, the dish was baked like an oven soufflé omelette, and it became the exclusive province of apples.

500g/1lb 2oz baking apples, peeled, cored and sliced
a strip of lemon peel and a squeeze of juice
1 blade of mace
100g/3½oz soft brown sugar

100g/3½oz unsalted butter
3 eggs, beaten
100g/3½oz fresh white breadcrumbs
½ teaspoon cinnamon
demerara sugar, for sprinkling

Put the apples in a saucepan with the lemon peel and juice, mace and sugar and cook gently until soft and collapsed. Remove the peel and mace and continue to cook, stirring, until the purée is fairly dry. Beat in two thirds of the butter, then leave to cool.

Beat the eggs into the cooled purée. Butter a shallow ovenproof dish and sprinkle half the crumbs and cinnamon over the base and sides. Spoon in the apple mixture and cover with the remaining crumbs and cinnamon. Melt the remaining butter and drizzle it over the crumbs. Bake at 190°C/375°F/Gas Mark 5 for 30–40 minutes, until set. Sprinkle with demerara sugar and serve hot with pouring cream or cold with lightly sweetened whipped cream.

PANETTONE TRIFLE

Serves 8
I owe the recipe for this delectable dessert to my friend Eliska Turina, a fabric designer specialising in cashmere and with an abiding concern for quality and taste in all areas of life. Eliska makes this in party-size quantity with an entire full-size panettone; I have developed the following recipe to serve eight dessert lovers amply. All the ingredients are now blissfully easy to find in large supermarkets; failing your local supermarket, try an Italian deli or the food department of a large general store. You could use macaroons instead of amaretti biscuits but make sure they are not the kind that have flour added.

For the base:
300g/11oz fresh or stale panettone
  (about 250g/8½oz once crust is
  removed)
175g/6oz low-sugar apricot
  preserve
2–3 tablespoons Amaretto liqueur

For the custard:
300ml/10fl oz milk
150ml/5fl oz single cream
6 egg yolks
40g/1½oz caster sugar
1 level teaspoon cornflour
½ teaspoon vanilla extract

1 tablespoon Amaretto liqueur
50g/2oz amaretti biscuits, finely
  crushed

For the top layer:
100g/3½oz ready-to-eat dried
  apricots or peaches
2 tablespoons Amaretto liqueur
250g/8½oz mascarpone cheese
250g/8½oz low-fat fromage frais
1 tablespoon icing sugar
75g/2½oz amaretti biscuits, coarsely
  crushed
25g/1oz split, blanched almonds,
  toasted

Remove the brown crust from the panettone and slice the bread into 2cm/⅔inch rounds. Spread with the apricot preserve, which can be mixed with some of the Amaretto to lighten the texture. Break up the panettone into chunks and arrange it in a large glass bowl, jam-side up. Sprinkle with the remaining Amaretto.

To make the custard bring the milk and cream slowly to the boil. Whisk together the egg yolks, sugar and cornflour, then pour the hot milk into the egg mixture, stirring briskly. Return the mixture to the rinsed-out pan and heat very gently, stirring, until the custard is thick enough to coat the back of a spoon. Remove from the heat and strain into a jug. Stir in the vanilla, Amaretto and crushed biscuits and pour the custard over the panettone chunks. Leave to cool, then chill.

For the topping, soak the dried apricots or peaches in half the Amaretto for about an hour, then slice them. Whisk together the mascarpone and fromage frais and beat in the sugar, and the remaining Amaretto, plus any left over from soaking the apricots or peaches. Scatter the coarsely crushed amaretti over the custard, then cover with the topping. Decorate with the drained, sliced apricots or peaches and the toasted almonds and chill again until serving. This will keep in the fridge for a few days.

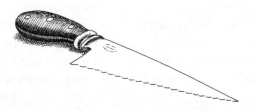

SALLY LUNN RASPBERRY TRIFLE

Serves 2 generously

This was inspired by the toasted Sally Lunn spread with a sweet raspberry purée that I enjoyed at Sally Lunn's Refreshment House in Bath. It is a very simple but really delicious combination. If you cannot find a Sally Lunn, substitute light milk bread.

75g/2½oz slice slightly stale Sally Lunn	2 teaspoons vanilla sugar
4–5 tablespoons Montilla wine or	150ml/5fl oz double Jersey cream
medium sweet cream sherry	naturally coloured angelica, to garnish
150g/5oz fresh raspberries	(optional)
3 tablespoons soft-set low-sugar	
raspberry preserve	

Place the slice of Sally Lunn in a bowl of the same width. Sprinkle with the sherry, which it will absorb rapidly. Crush about a third of the fresh raspberries into the preserve and spread this over the Sally Lunn, then arrange the remaining raspberries on top. If you are using a very thick or clotted cream that needs no whipping, sprinkle the vanilla sugar over the fruit. Otherwise whip the cream lightly with the sugar and then pile it on top of the fruit. Chill for at least 4 hours before serving, to allow some of the fruit juices to soak into the bun.

BLACKBERRIES AND BREAD

Blackberries have long been recognised as having an affinity with fine white bread and there are many simple recipes combining the two. This one started life as a sixteenth-century Venetian sauce for meat, was developed into a dessert by Elizabeth David and cited by Jane Grigson as 'A Mulberry and Almond Dish'. I have adapted it slightly to suit cultivated blackberries, reinstating the Venetian cinnamon and toasting the almonds.

450g/1lb blackberries	50g/2oz fine white breadcrumbs, as
125–175g/4–6oz caster sugar	fresh as possible
squeeze of lemon juice (optional)	pinch of cinnamon
50g/2oz ground almonds	

Very gently cook the blackberries with the smaller amount of sugar until the juice runs – taste and add more sugar and a little lemon juice as needed. Leave to cool.

    Toast the almonds in the oven at 180°C/350°F/Gas Mark 4 or under the grill, watching them very carefully and stirring from time to time. When they are lightly coloured and aromatic, remove from the heat, cool, and mix with the breadcrumbs and cinnamon. Fold in the cooked blackberries very gently – perhaps 3 or 4 movements of the spoon – then spoon the mixture into glass dishes and chill for 1–2 hours. Serve with single Jersey cream, pouring a little over each pudding before serving, if you wish.

Variation: Blackberries with Sally Lunn and Lemon Curd

Toast 4 slices Sally Lunn (or milk bread) and spread them with lemon curd (see page 210). Cook the blackberries with the sugar as above, then pour them over the toasted Sally Lunn and top each portion with a spoonful of thick Jersey cream.

BAKED PEAR ON BRIOCHE

Serves 1

Fruit baked on good bread can be as pleasing as any pie or tart and demands considerably less time and skill. Variations on this simple theme are as endless as those for bread-and-butter pudding. Here I have used apple and pear spread, a dark, sticky mixture resembling Marmite in consistency and the ultimate fruit juice concentrate in flavour. Look for it in wholefood shops but avoid the overly cloying ones sweetened with date syrup.

1 medium-thick slice brioche	1 ripe, juicy pear, preferably Comice
15g/½oz unsalted butter	or William, peeled, cored and cut
1 teaspoon apple and pear spread (see	into 6–8 wedges
above)	1 tablespoon caster sugar
	pinch of cinnamon (optional)

Preheat the oven and a baking sheet to 200°C/400°F/Gas Mark 6. Lightly butter one side of the brioche and place buttered-side down on a baking tray or a piece of foil, then place this directly on the hot baking sheet. Butter the top side, then coat with the fruit spread. Arrange the pear over the top and dot with the remaining butter. Finally sprinkle the fruit with the sugar, adding a pinch of cinnamon if you like. Bake for 10–15 minutes, until the bread is crisp and brown on the underside and the fruit is beginning to caramelise (if the pear staunchly refuses to caramelise you can either turn up the oven a notch or give the toast a quick, careful blast from a hot grill, perhaps adding a further dab of butter and sugar). Serve at once with very cold single cream or vanilla ice cream.

BOURBON-MAPLE CROUTES WITH
PEACHES AND PECANS

This Creole-style compilation takes moments to assemble and is packed with pleasing contrasts of texture and flavour. Use it as a basis for variations: light walnut bread, bottled pears, honey and calvados or brandy, for example. Ideally, the bread base should be light rather than dense, to encourage it to soufflé; this is a pudding for enjoying hot and light.

400g/14oz canned or bottled peaches
2 eggs, beaten
a few drops of vanilla extract
5 tablespoons single cream
125g/4oz slightly stale *Pain Parisien* or
    French stick, sliced 2cm/⅔inch
    thick

25g/1oz pecan halves
5 tablespoons maple syrup
2 tablespoons bourbon
grating of nutmeg

Drain the peaches, reserving the juice. If the peaches are in halves, slice each half into 4. Butter a wide baking dish or gratin dish generously. Whisk together the eggs, vanilla, cream and 5 tablespoons syrup from the peaches and dip each slice of bread into the mixture for 20–30 seconds. Pack the slices closely together in a single layer in the baking dish and cover with the peaches and pecans.

Warm the maple syrup until very runny then stir in the bourbon and drizzle the mixture slowly over the surface of the bread. Sprinkle a little nutmeg on top and bake at 180°C/350°F/Gas Mark 4 for 40 minutes, until the bread has swollen and the edges are brown and crisp. Serve plain or with a jug of single cream, stirring in the rest of the reserved peach syrup.

COOL AND CRISP MORELLO LAYER

Low-sugar preserves, or ones sweetened only with fruit juice, make ideal instant desserts, as the set is usually soft, almost runny. They blend particularly well with soft cheeses, cream and yoghurt. Add to that a sweet and crunchy element such as caramelised crumbs and you have an irresistible combination of flavours and textures.

200ml/7fl oz crème fraîche
200ml/7fl oz Greek yoghurt
225 g/8oz low-sugar morello cherry
    preserve

225g/8oz caramelised crumbs (see
    page 165), spiced with cinnamon
    and allspice

Use 4 syllabub glasses if possible. Mix together the crème fraîche and yoghurt, then make alternate layers of preserve, cream and crumbs, finishing with a layer of crumbs. Serve shortly after making.

Morello Compote

If you are unable to find a morello cherry preserve, make a quick compote from bottled morello cherries. You will need 225g/8oz drained weight of cherries, plus the syrup from a small jar. Mix 2 tablespoons of the syrup with 1 scant teaspoon arrowroot. Bring the rest of the syrup to the boil in a small saucepan, then whisk in the arrowroot mixture. Bring back to the boil and simmer for 1 minute only, then stir in the cherries and simmer for a further 30 seconds. Remove from the heat, cool and chill before using.

BLUEBERRY CARAMEL CHUNK

This versatile recipe also works well with ripe, firm banana slices, nectarines or perfectly ripe and flavourful apricots added to the blueberries. Poached or bottled fruit could be used, too.

50g/2oz unsalted butter
50g/2oz light muscovado sugar
125g/4oz slightly stale good-quality
white bread without crusts, cut
into 6mm/¼inch cubes

200ml/7floz Greek yoghurt
2 tablespoons Seville orange
marmalade, sieved
125g/4oz fresh blueberries

Melt the butter and sugar together gently in a frying pan, then add the bread cubes and stir to coat. Turn up the heat and cook, stirring constantly, for a few minutes, until caramelised. As soon as the mixture smells strongly of caramel, tip it out on to a sheet of greaseproof paper. The bread will crisp as it cools; break up any clumps as it does so.

When the bread is cold, stir two thirds of it into the yoghurt, together with the marmalade and a few of the blueberries, crushed with a fork. Cover and refrigerate overnight, or for at least 6 hours. Store the remaining bread cubes in a covered container until needed.

Just before serving, stir the chilled yoghurt mixture well (the bread should have softened and the caramel partly dissolved). Place the remaining blueberries in a serving bowl or individual glass dishes, spoon the yoghurt mixture over them and scatter with the remaining cubes of bread.

SHERRIED OSBORNE PUDDING

Evidently a popular Victorian pudding – Osborne was one of Queen Victoria's favourite residences. Occasionally brown bread-and-butter puddings were also termed Osborne; certainly a good brown bread, perhaps lightly malted, is the one to use here.

4 fairly thin slices good brown bread	450ml/15fl oz creamy milk
50g/2oz fine-cut orange marmalade	a few drops of vanilla extract
6 large or 8 small egg yolks	1–2 tablespoons medium sweet sherry
75g/2½oz caster sugar	150ml/5fl oz thick Jersey cream

Spread the bread with the marmalade, then cut off the crusts. Cut the bread into tiny pieces about 1.2cm/½inch square and place them in a mixing bowl. Beat the egg yolks with the sugar until pale and foamy. Warm the milk almost to boiling point and then pour it over the egg mixture, whisking gently. Return to the rinsed-out pan and cook very gently over a low heat until thickened (the custard should lightly coat the back of a wooden spoon – a finger drawn along the spoon will leave a trail). Strain the custard into a jug, add the vanilla and sherry and pour it over the bread. Stir gently, then cool, covered, to room temperature. Whip the cream lightly and fold it through the pudding. Transfer to a glass bowl and chill a little before serving.

BROWN BREAD CREAM

If you have a source of good wholewheat bread, it may be worth reviving this Victorian pudding, which is very good embellished with a little sherry or brandy, or perhaps an apricot compote (see next recipe). Make the pudding with crumbs that are no more than a day old and still noticeably aromatic.

300ml/10fl oz milk	75g/3oz caster sugar
150ml/5fl oz double cream	2–3 tablespoons rich sherry or brandy
1 vanilla pod, split, or vanilla extract	100g/3½oz fresh wholewheat
to taste	breadcrumbs
6 egg yolks	150ml/5fl oz whipping cream

Heat the milk and double cream with the vanilla pod, if using, until almost boiling; remove from the heat and leave to infuse for 10 minutes if time allows. Whisk together the egg yolks and sugar until pale, then strain in the hot milk mixture, add vanilla extract, if using, and whisk again. Return to the rinsed-out pan and cook very gently, stirring, until the custard is thick enough to coat the back of the spoon – do not allow it to approach boiling point. When thickened, cool rapidly by plunging the pan into cold water; stir occasionally as the custard cools. When it reaches room temperature stir in sherry or brandy to taste and the breadcrumbs. Chill, then fold in the lightly whipped cream. Serve soon after making.

CARAMELISED CRUMB CUSTARD MOULD

Both this recipe and the previous one are somewhat rich and indulgent and benefit from being cut by a fairly tart apricot compote; I would serve half the quantity of the dessert with an equal quantity of compote, which can be made from fresh apricots or dried. Cook fresh apricots with a minimal amount of water, plus sugar or honey to taste, until collapsed and thickened; soak dried apricots overnight in water to cover and cook in the soaking water until completely tender. You could add a squeeze of lemon juice and a little honey or sugar, but may not need to add either.

125g/4oz wholewheat breadcrumbs	25g/1oz caster sugar
50g/2oz demerara sugar	15g/½oz leaf or powdered gelatine
450ml/15fl oz creamy milk or single cream	3 tablespoons medium sweet sherry or Madeira
2 strips of lemon zest	150ml/5fl oz double cream
4 large or 5 small egg yolks	

Spread the crumbs and demerara sugar on a baking sheet and toast in the oven at 180°C/350°F/Gas Mark 4 for 20 minutes, stirring from time to time to prevent the edges darkening too much. Leave to cool.

Bring the milk or single cream and lemon zest slowly to the boil. Whisk together the egg yolks and caster sugar until pale, then strain in the milk and whisk again. Return the mixture to the rinsed-out pan and simmer very gently, stirring until the custard will coat the back of the spoon.

If using leaf gelatine, soften it in water for 20 minutes, then drain off the water; powdered gelatine does not need softening. Place the gelatine and sherry in a small mixing bowl, place this in a pan or bowl of hot water to warm until the gelatine dissolves (I do this in a microwave on a Low setting, stirring frequently). Whisk the gelatine mixture into the warm custard, then strain into a bowl and cool as rapidly as you can. When the custard is thickened but not set, stir in the caramelised crumbs, breaking up any clumps.

Whip the cream until it forms soft peaks and fold it into the custard. Spoon into a serving bowl and chill until lightly set.

BALKAN STRUDEL WITH WINE-SOAKED CRUMBS

Wine-soaked crumbs find their way into a number of Central European pastries. This one is a combination of favourite strudel fillings but if you are feeling adventurous you could make a strudel filled entirely with crumbs, doubling up the crumb filling ingredients below and adding 100g/3½oz of sugar to the buttered crumbs. It makes a very light, intriguing filling, excellent when hot but a little deflated once cold.

200g/7oz filo pastry
100g/3½oz clarified butter (see page
    178) or unsalted butter, melted
vanilla-flavoured icing sugar, for
    dusting

For the crumb filling:
50g/2oz unsalted butter
100g/3½oz fresh white breadcrumbs
6 tablespoons fortified dessert wine,
    such as Beaumes de Venise

For the cheese filling:
125g/4oz cream cheese
125g/4oz firm curd cheese
75g/3oz caster sugar
2 eggs, separated
½ teaspoon vanilla extract
pinch of salt

For the cherry filling:
100g/3½oz bottled morello cherries,
    well drained

Treat the pastry according to the instructions on the packet. Basically you need to bring it to room temperature before using and keep it in its wrapping, or covered with a slightly damp tea-towel, until needed. Sizes of filo sheet differ and this weight will produce 2 medium or 1 large strudel.

For the crumb filling, melt the butter in a frying pan until it foams. Add the breadcrumbs and stir over a fairly high heat until coated with butter and slightly brown. Remove the pan from the heat, stir in the wine and leave to cool.

For the cheese filling, beat together the cheeses and half the sugar by hand (don't use a food processor), then add the egg yolks and vanilla. Whisk the whites with a tiny pinch of salt until fairly stiff, add the remaining sugar and whisk again until stiff. Fold the egg whites into the cheese mixture.

Lay a sheet of filo pastry on a baking sheet or a tea-towel. Brush with melted butter and place a second sheet either directly on top of the first, or overlapping down one side to make a large rectangle. Continue layering and buttering the pastry until it is used up, then fold in 1.2cm/½inch down each edge. Cover the third of the pastry nearest you with crumbs, then the next third with cherries, then the bottom third with cheese. Roll up the pastry as lightly and loosely as possible and leave it seam-side down on the baking sheet (if using a tea-towel, roll the pastry gently on to a baking sheet). Brush with the remaining butter and bake at 160°C/325°F/Gas Mark 3 for about 25 minutes or until golden brown. Remove, cool slightly, then dust with icing sugar and serve warm or cool. No cream is necessary.

VENETIAN TORTE

Serves 6–8

This is basically a whisked sponge cake, with breadcrumbs and amaretti taking the place of flour. The texture is less smooth and close than that of a flour-based sponge but considerably moister and richer, and the cake keeps rather better, too. Moist wedges of this torte make an excellent accompaniment to strawberries in orange juice or segmented oranges in cointreau.

If you find the almond flavour too powerful, substitute more breadcrumbs for half the amaretti.

6 eggs, separated
125g/4oz caster sugar
1 teaspoon finely grated orange zest
75g/2½oz golden sultanas, soaked overnight in 3 tablespoons dark rum
25g/1oz candied orange peel in one piece, finely diced

100g/3½oz fresh crumbs from brioche, *pain de mie*, or good white bread
100g/3½oz amaretti biscuits, crushed to a powder
pinch of salt
vanilla-flavoured icing sugar, for dusting

Whisk together the egg yolks and three-quarters of the caster sugar until thick, pale and foamy. Stir in the orange zest, the sultanas with any unabsorbed rum, and the candied peel. Mix thoroughly, then stir in the crumbs and powdered amaretti.

Whisk the egg whites with a pinch of salt until almost stiff, then add the remaining sugar and whisk again until stiff. Fold one-third of the egg white thoroughly into the crumb base to lighten it, then carefully fold in the remaining white. Spoon the mixture into a buttered 25cm/10inch cake tin and gently smooth the surface. Bake in the centre of the oven at 180°C/350°F/Gas Mark 4 for about 40 minutes or until firm in the centre and shrinking away from the sides of the tin. Remove from the oven and leave in the tin for 5 minutes before turning out carefully on to a cake rack to cool.

Just before serving, sift icing sugar over the surface of the cake. Unlike flour-based fatless sponges, this torte can be made the day before you plan to serve it.

DUMPLINGS IN SCENTED MILK

Repapalos en leche, to give them their proper title, are as good to eat as they are unusual, and uniquely Hispanic in character, with a magical conjunction of aniseed, cinnamon and citrus. The level of sweetness is light even if, like me, you use *panquemado* or brioche rather than plain white bread. This makes the dish an ideal dessert for anyone with a barely sweet tooth – or perhaps as a mid-morning snack and, outrageous as it sounds, for breakfast.

3 large eggs
25g/1oz caster sugar
¼ teaspoon ground aniseed
125–150g/4–5oz fine fresh white
    breadcrumbs
olive oil for deep-frying
cinnamon, for dusting

For the scented milk:
1 litre/1¾ pints full cream milk
100ml/3½fl oz aniseed liqueur, such
    as *pastis*
100g/3½oz caster sugar
1 large cinnamon stick or 2 small
    ones
2 strips each orange and lemon zest

Lightly whisk together the eggs, sugar and aniseed and stir in enough breadcrumbs to make a soft dropping consistency. Chill for 30 minutes.

To make the scented milk, pour the milk into a heavy-based saucepan and add the liqueur, sugar, cinnamon and citrus zest. Bring slowly to the boil, then leave on the lowest possible simmer for 10–15 minutes.

Heat the oil until it is hot enough for a small cube of bread to start sizzling as soon as it is dropped in the pan. Test the consistency of the dumpling mixture by dropping a spoonful into the hot oil. If it breaks up you will need to add more crumbs; if it refuses to float and puff up you may need more egg to soften the mixture. Cook for 3 minutes, then cut open and check that it is cooked through. Time the rest of the dumplings accordingly.

Shape the dumplings by taking a dessertspoon of the mixture, moulding it slightly with another dessertspoon, then dropping it into the oil. Fry them in 2 or 3 batches, without crowding the pan, until golden brown, turning them over once or twice if necessary. Drain the dumplings on kitchen paper, then place them in a heatproof bowl and strain the simmering milk over them. Cover and set aside until cool, then refrigerate for 24 hours. Serve the dumplings floating in a little of the ice-cold milk, and sprinkle some cinnamon over the surface.

QUEEN OF PUDDINGS

This is perhaps my favourite childhood pudding and I daresay I'm not alone. I seem to recall the meringue layer being quite crunchy which, I now learn, means that it would have been baked for the same length of time as the crumb and yolk mixture and thus qualified as a Manchester pudding. The other difference between the Manchester pud and the Queen is that the former should always be served cold, whereas the Queen is served warm, with the meringue itself warm and puffy.

The bread should be reasonably light; my own favourite is a butter-enriched wholemeal, available at Marks & Spencer.

600ml/1 pint full-cream or 'breakfast' milk
25–50g/1–2oz butter (traditionally slightly salted)
zest of 1 lemon
125g/4oz day-old wholewheat breadcrumbs
150g/5oz caster sugar
pinch of freshly grated nutmeg (optional)
4 large eggs, separated
2 tablespoons apricot jam or red fruit jelly

Bring the milk, butter and lemon zest to the boil. Place the bread-crumbs and 25g/1oz of the sugar in a mixing bowl with the nutmeg, if using, and pour the milk over them. Leave to stand for about 15 minutes, then beat in the egg yolks. Pour this mixture into a buttered 1.5 litre/2½ pint pie dish and bake at 180°C/350°F/Gas Mark 4 for about 30 minutes until just set. A counsel of perfection would be to place the pudding dish in a water bath (a roasting pan half-filled with hot water) to keep the custard perfectly smooth throughout. Remove the pudding from the oven and reduce the temperature to 150°C/300°F/Gas Mark 2.

Melt the jam or jelly in a small saucepan or in the microwave and spoon it over the pudding. Whisk the egg whites until stiff, then fold in the remaining sugar, reserving a little to sprinkle over the top of the meringue. Pile the meringue over the jam, sprinkle with the reserved sugar and return the pudding to the oven for a further 20–30 minutes, until the meringue is lightly browned and slightly crisp on the outside. Serve warm; it's perfect as it is but you could gild the lily with cream.

MONMOUTH PUDDING

A bread and jam pudding but an extraordinarily light one, particularly prized as a 'hydropathic pudding', as served at Victorian hydros, or spas.

225g/8oz slightly stale white
    breadcrumbs
150ml/5fl oz milk (skimmed, if you
    wish)
25g/1oz unsalted butter
½ teaspoon vanilla extract

3 egg whites
small pinch of salt
75g/2½oz caster sugar
350g/12oz strawberry or raspberry
    jam

Place the breadcrumbs in a mixing bowl. Heat the milk and butter to boiling point, add the vanilla and pour this mixture over the crumbs. Leave to stand for 15–30 minutes, until the crumbs have absorbed the liquid. Whisk the egg whites with the salt until fairly stiff, then whisk in the sugar and whisk once more until stiff. Fold into the crumb mixture.

Spread half the jam in a buttered ovenproof dish and cover with half the pudding mixture. Spread the remaining jam on top of this and cover with the remaining mixture. Bake at 130°C/250°F/Gas Mark ½ for about 45 minutes or until set. Serve warm with single cream or custard.

BIJANE WITH STRAWBERRIES

The Touraine region of the Loire valley is particularly rich in concoctions of sweet or sweetened wine, fruit and brioche, known as *soupes*. These three elements represent the finest products of the area: the Vouvrays, Bourgueils and Chinons for which Touraine is famed worldwide, the strawberries and peaches produced by this market garden area of France, and the enriched bread which forms the foundation of a vast range of pastries and puddings.

The names of the pudding-soups are diverse, but each indicates a particular feature: *la panée* involves cooking the bread and liquid to form a porridge suitable for children; *la rotée* consists of toasted bread soaked in hot red wine sweetened with honey; *bijane* is made with red wine, and *chicolle* with white.

4 thick slices pain de campagne
1 bottle Chinon wine
100–150g/3½–5oz caster sugar, to taste

750g/1½lb strawberries, hulled, halved
    if large

Dry out the bread completely by baking it in the oven at 160°C/
325°F/Gas Mark 3, or use a microwave – it should not colour. Break
it up into small pieces and place in a glass bowl. Sweeten the wine
with the sugar, bearing in mind the sweetness or tartness of the
strawberries, then pour it over the bread. Add the strawberries to the
bread and wine, then chill for 6 hours or overnight before serving.

Variation: Chicolle with peaches

Substitute brioche or milk bread for the pain de campagne and 4
large peaches, peeled, stoned and halved, for the strawberries. Use
sweet Vouvray wine instead of the Chinon – you will probably need
a little less sugar.

BROWN BREAD ICE CREAM

This old favourite started life as the simplest of confections: just
caramelised crumbs and thick, whipped cream, lightly frozen. Inevitably, recipes grew richer and more adventurous, incorporating
custard, spice and spirits or liqueurs. This version is a personal
favourite simply on account of the speed and minimal effort required.
It is rich but you can cut the cream with Greek yoghurt or fromage frais.

125g/4oz fresh wholewheat
breadcrumbs
50g/2oz demerara sugar
3 tablespoons dark or tawny Seville
orange marmalade

1 tablespoon Irish whiskey (or whisky
or bourbon)
300ml/10fl oz Jersey double cream

Mix together the breadcrumbs and sugar and spread them out on a
baking sheet – if you line the sheet with tin foil you will save yourself
some soaking and scrubbing. Toast in the centre of the oven at
180°C/350°F/Gas Mark 4 for 25–30 minutes, stirring from the edge
to the centre every 5 minutes or so. At the end of this time the
crumbs should be dark, caramelised and crunchy.

Warm the marmalade gently with the whiskey, then press it
through a sieve to remove chunks of peel. Whip the cream softly
until it holds its shape but is not stiff, then stir in the marmalade and
the crumbs. Spoon into a plastic container, seal and freeze. You can,
if you like, turn the ice cream out while half frozen and beat it to
break down ice crystals but as the cream is so thick with crunchy
crumbs, crystals will not really be noticeable. Ideally, serve while still
only softly frozen. The flavour and texture are at their best shortly
after freezing but if you need to make the ice cream a day or two
ahead, soften in the fridge for an hour before serving.

APPLE CHARLOTTE

This is the classic baked cousin to summer pudding (see page 297), wonderful throughout the autumn and winter months. Two features have remained constant since the Charlotte's invention in the late eighteenth century: the apple filling should be good and thick to ensure the unmoulded pudding stands up proud, and the bread case should be firm, golden brown and crunchy.

For the apple purée:
50g/2oz unsalted butter
1kg/2lb 4oz fine eating apples with good acidity, peeled, cored and roughly chopped
125g/4oz caster sugar, or to taste
1 cinnamon stick, or powdered cinnamon to taste (optional)
squeeze of lemon juice (optional)

50g/2oz brioche crumbs, or 2 egg yolks, for extra thickening (optional)

For the bread case:
½ large loaf of slightly stale white or wholewheat bread, crusts removed
125g/4oz clarified butter, (see page 178) made from 175g/6oz butter, melted

Place the butter in a large, heavy-based saucepan and coat the base with a very thin layer of water. Add the apples, sugar, and cinnamon, if using; stir, then cover the pan and cook on a low heat until the juices run. Stir again, then half cover the pan and cook until the apples are tender, stirring from time to time. Now remove the lid, discard the cinnamon stick, if used, and stir the apple mass frequently, cooking over a fairly high heat to evaporate as much liquid as possible. Once a thick purée has formed, remove the pan from the heat and beat in the brioche crumbs or egg yolks as a 'thickener' if you wish. Finally check for sweetness and acidity, adding more sugar or a squeeze of lemon juice as needed. Set the purée aside to cool a little while you make the bread case.

Cut the bread into slices 1cm/⅓inch thick. Cut a large round, or several small ones, for the base, dip both sides briefly in the clarified butter and press on to the base of a 1 litre/1¾ pint Charlotte mould or soufflé dish, overlapping small slices, Reserve a slice or two for the top, then trim the remaining slices to the height of the mould and cut them into 4–5cm/1½–2inch widths. Once again, dip both sides of each piece into clarified butter, then line the sides of the mould with slightly overlapping slices.

Now spoon the apple purée into the mould and cover with a lid of butter-dipped bread. Bake in an oven preheated to 200°C/400°F/Gas

Mark 6 for 50–60 minutes, until the bread is deep golden brown all round – to check, press back the sides in one or two places with the blade of a knife or a slim spatula. Remove from the oven and leave the Charlotte for 10–15 minutes before unmoulding. Loosen the sides a little with a knife if necessary, then invert a plate over the mould, turn the pudding and plate the right way up and shake gently. If you find any bits of bread have stuck to the base or side of the mould, simply press them back on.

Variation

The nineteenth-century American Apple Pandowdy is a much simpler apple pudding. Quantities are governed by what you have to hand – basically you need enough bread to line a deep baking dish and enough apples to fill it. Slice and butter the bread and use butter-side out to line the base and sides of the dish. Fill the dish with layers of peeled, cored and roughly sliced apples interspersed with soft brown sugar, a good shake of cinnamon, nutmeg and cloves, and a drizzle of blackstrap molasses and maple syrup, if you have it. Cover with a bread lid, butter side up, and sprinkle this with sugar. Bake in a preheated oven at 150°C/300°F/Gas Mark 2 for 2 hours. If the top appears to be browning too quickly, cover with buttered greaseproof paper; if it still looks pale after 2 hours, turn up the temperature a couple of notches. Serve hot, with pouring cream.

· GLOSSARY ·

This lists a number of terms referring to the bread-baking process. It does not include types of flour or bread, which are covered by entries in the directory, or names of bread shapes, listed under British Bread Shapes in the directory.

Ascorbic acid Powdered Vitamin C, used as an 'improver' of dough, increasing its strength or tenacity for a good rise.

Bake-off Simply the process of oven-baking bread; most often used in relation to part-baked bread or imported, frozen ready-to-bake bread.

Baker's yeast Compressed fresh yeast of the genus *Saccharomyces cerevisiae* – 'the sugar fungus of beer' – packaged in blocks; can also refer to granular (dehydrated) yeast.

Bran The inert, protective envelope surrounding the wheatgerm and starchy endosperm of a grain berry. It comprises around 12–15 per cent of the weight of the grain.

Bread fat More often specified on a wrapper as 'vegetable fats' or 'hydrogenated vegetable oil'. A particularly necessary adjunct in the case of fast-fermented dough subjected to high-energy mechanical mixing, where it prevents dough collapse. Lard, butter and olive oil are usually classed and listed separately and are generally used to improve flavour and moistness as much as crumb quality.

Chorleywood Bread Process (CBP) A mechanical dough development process which uses a short period of fast, intense mechanical mixing in the presence of added fat and oxidising improvers to replicate traditional fermentation. The process is named after the centre of the Flour Milling and Baking Research Association in Britain, which collated information on the method into a set of rules published in 1961. Now used by virtually all large industrial bakeries, hot-bread shops and in store bakeries as well as a good number of independent, small bakeries. Variously regarded as the birth of consistency or the death of good bread.

Emulsifiers Chemical substances that increase the volume or keeping qualities of bread. There are two main types: Data esters, which bind with gluten-forming proteins to increase the strength of the gluten, are used most often in 'high-volume' breads and 'soft' flour breads to entrap more air and provide a fluffier texture. Monoglycerides bind with starch-proteins to slow down the rate of staling. Other substances can perform both functions. Most commonly indicated by their 'E' number.

Endosperm The starch and protein-containing portion of a grain berry, white in colour. White flour consists almost entirely of endosperm.

Extraction rate The percentage of whole grain left in the flour after milling: wholemeal flour has 100 per cent extraction, white flour around 75 per cent (almost all the bran and wheatgerm have been removed).

Fermentation The activity of bacteria or fungal micro-organisms in dough: after consuming sugars they release carbon dioxide which is then trapped within the dough and causes it to rise.

Gluten An elastic network of protein molecules developed by the kneading process, which surrounds and traps gas bubbles in the dough. High-gluten flours contain a high proportion of the protein types that can be enmeshed in this way.

Improvers Natural or chemical substances that 'improve' the generally accepted desirable qualities of a loaf: its volume, softness, crustiness, whiteness and so on. These include yeast nutrients, chemical oxidants, mould inhibitors, anti-caking agents (used in conjunction with emulsifiers) and caramel colouring.

Leaven Any form of yeast culture used to raise dough; most often used, however, in the sense of *levain*, the French (and subsequently American) term for a sourdough culture.

Organic flour and bread Flour certified as organic by the Soil Association (in the UK) and by similar bodies worldwide is milled from grain grown without the use of artificial fertilisers or pesticides. Organic bread is made from organic flour but not all the ingredients are necessarily of organic status: a number of breads labelled as organic contain a host of chemical emulsifiers in addition to suspect hardened (hydrogenated) fats.

Ovens Arguably the most important items of equipment in any bakery, these vary considerably in construction and mode of operation. A good number of 'craft' bakers would argue that the best ovens are brick built and internally heated, preferably woodfired. Most modern ovens have been designed with speed and volume of production in mind and are particularly suited to baking bread raised by the CBP (see page 318).

Oven sole At one time the floor or bottom of the oven, but may also consist of a drawplate or reversible band, or a specially constructed shelf made of brick, stone, or ceramic material in a multiple-deck oven. Essentially, a good deal of heat is conducted to the bottom crust of a baking loaf, with more gentle radiant heat applied on all sides – still considered the best way to achieve a superior 'free-form' bread in almost all categories.

Roller milling The process of milling grain between fluted or smooth circular steel rollers, rotating at different speeds in opposite directions, then sifting and 'purifying' the particles before remilling as necessary. Essentially, the grain is torn open and the bran and germ removed, then the endosperm (starch and protein) is ground fine by a gradual reduction process. Most flour is milled by some variant of this process.

Soft flour Technically, flour from wheat that mills easily and 'softly'. As soft flours tend also to be 'weak', i.e. with a low gluten (protein) content, the term is often used to indicate this quality. Soft flours tend to have the best flavour but need to be mixed with strong flours to ensure a good rise and crumb structure. Most European flours are classed as soft; French baguettes are most often made entirely from soft flour.

Sourdough Bread dough fermented by the action of wild yeasts (principally *Saccharomyces exiguus*) picked up from the environment; can also refer to dough fermented by the addition of a specific culture. The sour taste of the resultant bread comes from lactic and acetic acid produced by particular strains of bacteria feeding on the maltose in the flour starch.

Sponge A mixture of flour, water and yeast (generally baker's yeast) fermented for a variable number of hours before being added to the rest of the dough; use of the 'sponge and dough method' (French: *sur poolish*) usually indicates a slower, more painstaking and flavour-yielding approach than is now the norm.

Staling Technically, the recrystallisation of gelatinised starches and migration of moisture to the crust (and, if uncovered, the air) in baked bread. The process begins as soon as baked bread has cooled to below 55°C/131°F and is characterised by a noticeable increase in firmness, dryness and crumbliness of the crumb and leatheriness of the crust. Flavour and aroma are lost, and a dry, 'stale' taste develops. Eventually microbiological spoilage occurs and the bread moulds.

Rate of staling is greatest at a temperature of 0°C/32°F and is virtually arrested at − 10°C/14°F.

Starter A piece of dough fermented either by the sourdough process or with baker's yeast, added to a newly mixed dough to boost fermentation.

Stone grinding The process of milling grain between two large, flat, grooved, circular stones, one stationary and the other rotating. The grain is gradually pulverised by the edges of the grooves as it travels from centre to edge. The bran and germ are ground along with the endosperm (starch and protein) and are difficult to separate off from the resultant flour.

Strong flour Wheat flour with a high gluten (protein) content of good quality. The strongest flours come from wheat varieties grown in Canada, the USA and parts of Australia.

Wheatgerm The embryo (baby plant) and scutellum, which mobilises food stores from the endosperm to the growing embryo. Rich in vitamins, minerals, sugars and oils. Comprises around 3 per cent of the weight of the grain.

Yeast A microscopic, single cell organism classified with fungi. The name is derived from the Sanskrit *yaas*, meaning 'to seethe'. Yeast feeds on sugars in bread dough (both added sugars and starch-derived sugars) and produces carbon dioxide gas, causing dough to rise. It also contributes to the flavour of bread as complex chemical compounds are formed during the fermentation process.

There are two basic kinds of yeast: factory-produced, commercial yeast generally known as baker's yeast, and natural 'wild' yeast which exists in the air in many different forms and is selected and controlled by particular conditions. (Brewer's yeast is slightly different again, and is derived from the sediment left from brewing beer. Widely used in bread baking in the eighteenth century, its bitter taste and unreliable activity have made it redundant for this purpose.)

· UK BAKERS AND SUPPLIERS ·

The majority of breads described in the directory are available in supermarkets, bakery chains or delicatessens, though these outlets do not necessarily reveal the identity of the bakery. This is a short list of some of the smaller-scale bakeries I have mentioned in the text; if you would like to check whether a particular bread is available locally, I suggest you contact the bakery direct.

Abel Eastern Foods Ltd, Houston Industrial Estate, Grange Road, Livingston, Scotland EH54 5DD, Tel: 01506 112020

Bagatelle, 709 Tudor Estate, Abbey Road, London NW10 7UW. Tel: 0181 581 1551

Bakoven, Unit B, Coburg House, Coburg Road, London N22 6UB. Tel: 0181 889 7159

Barbakan Continental Bakery, 67/69 Manchester Road, Chorlton Cum Hardy, Manchester M21 1PW. Tel: 0161 881 7053

Everfresh Natural Foods (Sunnyvale breads), Gatehouse Close, Aylesbury, Buckinghamshire HP19 3DE. Tel: 01296 25333

Greenhalgh's Craft Bakery Ltd, Crescent Road, Lostock, Bolton, Lancashire BL6 4BU. Tel: 01204 696204

Innes, Highfields, Clifton Lane, Statfold, Staffordshire B79 0AQ. Tel: 01827 830097

Kolos Bakery, 128–132 Parkside Road, Bradford, W. Yorkshire BD5 8EH. Tel: 01274 729958

Kroustie European Bread, 622 Harrogate Road, Leeds LS17 8EN. Tel: 01132 697171

La Fornaia, 7–8 School Road, North Acton, London NW10 6TD. Tel: 0181 965 4477

The Loaves and Fishes Irish Brown Bread Company, Unit 3 Parmiter Industrial Centre, Parmiter Street, London E2 9HZ. Tel: 0181 983 0316

Maison Blanc, 5–6 Witan Park, Witney, Oxon OX8 6FH. Tel: 01993 778066

Natural Rise Foods, 21 Bernard Road, London NJ6 4PE. Tel: 0181 808 2007

The Village Bakery, Melmerby, Penrith, Cumbria CA10 1HE. Tel: 01768 881515

For Staffordshire oatcakes by mail:

High Lane Oatcakes, 599 High Lane, Burslem, Stoke-on-Trent ST6 7EP. Tel: 01782 810 180.

Sue & Glenn's Oatcakes, 62 Waterloo Street, Hanley, Stoke-on-Trent ST1 3PW. Tel: 01782 261 883.

· SELECT BIBLIOGRAPHY ·

Acton, Eliza: *Modern Cookery for Private Families* (Longmans Green 1845), Southover Press, 1993; *The English Bread Book* (Longmans Green, 1857), Southover Press, 1990

Andrews, Colman: *Catalan Cuisine*, Headline, 1989

Ayrton, Elizabeth: *The Cookery of England*, Penguin, 1974

Bailey, Adrian: *The Blessings of Bread*, Paddington Press, 1975

Bateman, Michael & Maisner, Heather: *The Sunday Times Book of Real Bread*, Rodale Press, 1982

Blanch, Lesley: *Around the World in Eighty Dishes*, John Murray, 1956

Boxer, Arabella: *Arabella Boxer's Book of English Food*, Penguin, 1993

Boyd, Lizzie (ed.): *British Cookery*, Christopher Helm for the British Tourist Authority, 1976

Collister, Linda & Blake, Anthony: *The Bread Book*, Conran Octopus, 1993

David, Elizabeth: *English Bread and Yeast Cookery* (Allen Lane, 1977), Penguin, 1987; *French Country Cooking*, Penguin, 1960, *Summer Cooking*, Penguin, 1965

Del Conte, Anna: *The Gastronomy of Italy*, Bantam Press, 1987

Duff, Gail: *The Complete Bread Book*, Pavilion, 1993

Fisher, M. F. K.: *The Art of Eating*, Collier Books, 1990

Galli, Franco: *The Il Fornaio Baking Book*, Chronicle Books, 1993

Garnier, André: *Pains et Viennoiseries*, Dormonval, 1992

Graham, Peter: *Classic Cheese Cookery*, Penguin, 1988

Green, Henrietta: *Food Lovers' Guide to Britain*, BBC Books, 1993

Grigson, Jane: *Good Things,* Penguin, 1981; *The Observer Guide to European Cookery*, Michael Joseph, 1983; *The Observer Guide to British Cookery*, Michael Joseph, 1984; *English Food* (revised edition), Penguin, 1992

Guillemard, Colette: *Les Mots de la Cuisine et de la Table*, Editions Belin, 1990

Hartley, Dorothy: *Food in England* (Macdonald, 1954), Futura, 1985

Goodwin, Gillian: *Manchet & Trencher* (*The Good Housewife Series*), The Gelofer Press, 1983

Irwin, Florence: *The Cookin' Woman* (1949), The Blackstaff Press, 1986

Lander, Nicholas: *Dinner for a Fiver*, Vermilion, 1994

Lebey, Claude (ed.): *L'Inventaire du Patrimoine Culinaire de la France*, Editions Albin Michel S. A., 1993

Master Bakers, National Association: *The Master Bakers' Book of Breadmaking*, Turret Press, 1982

Master Chefs of France: *Cuisine du Terroir*, Blenheim House, 1987

McGee, Harold: *On Food and Cooking*, Allen & Unwin, 1984

Norwak, Mary: *English Puddings*, B. T. Batsford, 1981

O'Neill, Molly: *New York Cookbook*, Workman Publishing, 1992

Ortiz, Joe: *The Village Baker*, Ten Speed Press, 1993

Poilâne, Lionel & Mathiot, Ginette: *Pain, Cuisine et Gourmandises*, Editions Albin Michel S. A., 1985

Roden, Claudia: *A New Book of Middle Eastern Food*, Penguin, 1985; *Claudia Roden's Picnic*, Penguin, 1981

Round, Jeremy: *The Independent Cook*, Barrie & Jenkins, 1988

Spry, Constance & Hume, Rosemary: *The Constance Spry Cookery Book*, Dent, 1978

Time-Life Books: *The Good Cook Series 'Breads'*, Time-Life Books, 1980

Toklas, Alice B.: *The Alice B. Toklas Cookbook*, Brilliance Books, 1983

Willan, Anne: *French Regional Cooking*, Hutchinson, 1981

Wilson, C. Anne: *Food and Drink in Britain* (Constable 1973), Penguin, 1976